NATIONAL ACADEMIES Sciences Engineering Medicine

School Active Shooter Drills

Mitigating Risks to Mental, Emotional, and Behavioral Health

Richard J. Bonnie and Rebekah Hutton,
Editors

Committee on the Impact of Active Shooter Drills on Student Health and Wellbeing

Board on Children, Youth, and Families

Committee on Law and Justice

Division of Behavioral and Social Sciences and Education

Consensus Study Report

NATIONAL ACADEMIES PRESS 500 Fifth Street, NW Washington, DC 20001

This activity was supported by a contract between the National Academy of Sciences and the Department of Education (91990023C0052). Any opinions, findings, conclusions, or recommendations expressed in this publication do not necessarily reflect the views of any organization or agency that provided support for the project.

International Standard Book Number-13: 978-0-309-99198-8
Digital Object Identifier: https://doi.org/10.17226/29105
Library of Congress Control Number: 2025946877

This publication is available from the National Academies Press, 500 Fifth Street, NW, Keck 360, Washington, DC 20001; (800) 624-6242; https://nap.nationalacademies.org.

The manufacturer's authorized representative in the European Union for product safety is Authorised Rep Compliance Ltd., Ground Floor, 71 Lower Baggot Street, Dublin D02 P593 Ireland; www.arccompliance.com.

Copyright 2025 by the National Academy of Sciences. National Academies of Sciences, Engineering, and Medicine and National Academies Press and the graphical logos for each are all trademarks of the National Academy of Sciences. All rights reserved.

Printed in the United States of America.

Suggested citation: National Academies of Sciences, Engineering, and Medicine. 2025. *School Active Shooter Drills: Mitigating Risks to Mental, Emotional, and Behavioral Health*. Washington, DC: National Academies Press. https://doi.org/10.17226/29105.

The **National Academy of Sciences** was established in 1863 by an Act of Congress, signed by President Lincoln, as a private, nongovernmental institution to advise the nation on issues related to science and technology. Members are elected by their peers for outstanding contributions to research. Dr. Marcia McNutt is president.

The **National Academy of Engineering** was established in 1964 under the charter of the National Academy of Sciences to bring the practices of engineering to advising the nation. Members are elected by their peers for extraordinary contributions to engineering. Dr. Tsu-Jae Liu is president.

The **National Academy of Medicine** (formerly the Institute of Medicine) was established in 1970 under the charter of the National Academy of Sciences to advise the nation on medical and health issues. Members are elected by their peers for distinguished contributions to medicine and health. Dr. Victor J. Dzau is president.

The three Academies work together as the **National Academies of Sciences, Engineering, and Medicine** to provide independent, objective analysis and advice to the nation and conduct other activities to solve complex problems and inform public policy decisions. The National Academies also encourage education and research, recognize outstanding contributions to knowledge, and increase public understanding in matters of science, engineering, and medicine.

Learn more about the National Academies of Sciences, Engineering, and Medicine at **www.nationalacademies.org**.

Consensus Study Reports published by the National Academies of Sciences, Engineering, and Medicine document the evidence-based consensus on the study's statement of task by an authoring committee of experts. Reports typically include findings, conclusions, and recommendations based on information gathered by the committee and the committee's deliberations. Each report has been subjected to a rigorous and independent peer-review process and it represents the position of the National Academies on the statement of task.

Proceedings published by the National Academies of Sciences, Engineering, and Medicine chronicle the presentations and discussions at a workshop, symposium, or other event convened by the National Academies. The statements and opinions contained in proceedings are those of the participants and are not endorsed by other participants, the planning committee, or the National Academies.

Rapid Expert Consultations published by the National Academies of Sciences, Engineering, and Medicine are authored by subject-matter experts on narrowly focused topics that can be supported by a body of evidence. The discussions contained in rapid expert consultations are considered those of the authors and do not contain policy recommendations. Rapid expert consultations are reviewed by the institution before release.

For information about other products and activities of the National Academies, please visit www.nationalacademies.org/about/whatwedo.

COMMITTEE ON THE IMPACT OF ACTIVE SHOOTER DRILLS ON STUDENT HEALTH AND WELLBEING

RICHARD J. BONNIE (*Chair*), Harrison Foundation Professor of Medicine and Law Emeritus; Director Emeritus of the Institute of Law, Psychiatry and Public Policy; University of Virginia

MELISSA J. BRYMER, Director of the Terrorism and Disaster Program, UCLA/Duke University National Center for Child Traumatic Stress, National Child Traumatic Stress Network

NATHANIEL G. HARNETT, Assistant Professor of Psychiatry, Harvard Medical School; Director, Neurobiology of Affective and Traumatic Experiences Laboratory, McLean Hospital

KRISTEN HARPER, Vice President for Public Policy and Engagement, Child Trends

JUSTIN HEINZE, Associate Professor, School of Public Health, University of Michigan

STEPHANIE M. JONES, Gerald S. Lesser Professor in Early Childhood Development, Harvard University (*until September 2024*)

SHERYL KATAOKA, Professor Emeritus, Department of Psychiatry, UCLA Semel Institute for Neuroscience and Human Behavior

CELESTE MALONE, Associate Professor of School Psychology, Howard University

ANTHONY PEGUERO, Foundation Professor of T. Denny Sanford School of Social and Family Dynamics & School of Criminology and Criminal Justice, Arizona State University

ANDREA PULSKAMP, Health and Safety Implementation Coordinator, Colorado Department of Education

SONALI RAJAN, Professor, Department of Health Studies & Applied Educational Psychology, Columbia University Teachers College

DAVID J. SCHONFELD, Founder/Director, National Center for School Crisis and Bereavement, Children's Hospital Los Angeles; Professor of Clinical Pediatrics, Keck School of Medicine

NATALIE SLOPEN, Assistant Professor, Department of Social and Behavioral Sciences, Harvard T.H. Chan School of Public Health

JEFF R. TEMPLE, Professor, Associate Dean for Clinical Research, Betty and Rose Pfefferbaum Chair in Child Mass Trauma and Resilience, School of Behavioral Health Sciences, University of Texas Health in Houston

Study Staff

REBEKAH HUTTON, Study Director
SUNIA YOUNG, Research Associate
TARA NAZARI, Senior Program Assistant
EMILY BACKES, Deputy Board Director

Consultant

LUCY GUARNERA, Assistant Professor, Institute of Law, Psychiatry and Public Policy, University of Virginia

BOARD ON CHILDREN, YOUTH, AND FAMILIES

JONATHAN TODRES (*Chair*), Georgia State University College of Law
DEBRA FURR-HOLDEN, New York University
TAMMY CHANG, University of Michigan
ANDREA GONZALEZ, McMaster University
NIA HEARD-GARRIS, Northwestern University Feinberg School of Medicine
NANCY E. HILL, Harvard University
CHARLES HOMER, Economic Mobility Pathways
MARGARET KUKLINSKI, University of Washington
MICHAEL C. LU, University of California, Berkeley School of Public Health
STEPHEN W. PATRICK, Vanderbilt University Medical Center
STEPHEN RUSSELL, The University of Texas at Austin
JENNY S. RADESKY, University of Michigan Medical School
JANE WALDFOGEL, Columbia University School of Social Work
JOANNA L. WILLIAMS, Search Institute

Staff

NATACHA BLAIN, Senior Board Director
EMILY P. BACKES, Deputy Board Director

COMMITTEE ON LAW AND JUSTICE

ROBERT D. CRUTCHFIELD (*Chair*), University of Washington
JOHN M. MACDONALD (*Vice Chair*), University of Pennsylvania
MONICA BELL, Yale University
ANTHONY BRAGA, University of Pennsylvania
ROD K. BRUNSON, University of Maryland, College Park
ELSA CHEN, Santa Clara University
JENS LUDWIG, The University of Chicago
SAMUEL L. MYERS JR., University of Minnesota
EMILY OWENS, University of California, Irvine
ALEXIS R. PIQUERO, University of Miami
JESENIA PIZARRO, Arizona State University
LAURIE O. ROBINSON, George Mason University
ADDIE ROLNICK, University of Nevada, Las Vegas
VINCENT SCHIRALDI, Maryland Department of Juvenile Services
CHRISTOPHER UGGEN, University of Minnesota
EMILY A. WANG, Yale University

Staff

NATACHA BLAIN, Senior Board Director
EMILY P. BACKES, Deputy Board Director

Reviewers

This Consensus Study Report was reviewed in draft form by individuals chosen for their diverse perspectives and technical expertise. The purpose of this independent review is to provide candid and critical comments that will assist the National Academies of Sciences, Engineering, and Medicine in making each published report as sound as possible and to ensure that it meets the institutional standards for quality, objectivity, evidence, and responsiveness to the study charge. The review comments and draft manuscript remain confidential to protect the integrity of the deliberative process.

We thank the following individuals for their review of this report:

MARGARITA ALEGRIA, Departments of Medicine and Psychiatry, Harvard Medical School and Massachusetts General Hospital
MO CANADY, Executive Director, National Association of School Resource Officers
G. MARIUS CLORE, Section of Molecular and Structural Biophysics, Laboratory of Chemical Physics, National Institutes of Health
ROBIN COGAN, School Nurse Specialty Program, Rutgers School of Nursing–Camden
JENNIFER L. FREEMAN, Special Education, Neag School of Education, University of Connecticut
EMILY HOTEZ, Division of General Internal Medicine & Health Services Research, Department of Medicine, University of California, Los Angeles

REVIEWERS

AARON KUPCHIK, Sociology and Criminal Justice, University of Delaware

JEFFREY LIEW, Educational Psychology, College of Education & Human Development, Texas A&M University

AMY LOWDER, School Psychologist, Cabarrus School District, NC

AMANDA B. NICKERSON, Alberti Center for Bullying Abuse Prevention, School Psychology, Graduate School of Education, University at Buffalo, SUNY

TARA C. RAINES, Deputy Director, Children's Advocacy Alliance, Las Vegas, NV

MELISSA A. REEVES, Past-President, National Association of School Psychologists and Senior Advisor, Safe and Sound Schools

Although the reviewers listed above provided many constructive comments and suggestions, they were not asked to endorse the conclusions or recommendations of this report, nor did they see the final draft before its release. The review of this report was overseen by **ALI ROWHANI-RAHBAR,** Study and Prevention of Violence, University of Washington, and **ELLEN CLAYTON,** Pediatrics, Law, and Health Policy, Vanderbilt University Medical Center. They were responsible for making certain that an independent examination of this report was carried out in accordance with the standards of the National Academies and that all review comments were carefully considered. Responsibility for the final content rests entirely with the authoring committee and the National Academies.

Acknowledgments

The committee thanks the U.S. Department of Education, which sponsored this study, for its support. We would also like to thank the following organizations and individuals for their support of the mission of the Board on Children, Youth, and Families: The Burke Foundation, the New Venture Fund, the Renaissance Charitable Foundation/RCF Giving Fund, the Robert Wood Johnson Foundation, David V. B. Britt, Tammy Chang, Greg J. Duncan, Sherry Glied, Andrea Gonzalez, Nia Heard-Garris, Nancy Hill, Charles J. Homer, Kay Johnson, Margaret Kuklinski, Michael Lu, Daniel Menelly, Linda A. Nelson, Stephen Patrick, Jenny Radesky, Stephen Russell, Nisha Sachdev, Jonathan Todres, Jane Waldfogel, Joanna Williams, and Barbara L. Wolfe.

This report would not have been possible without the contributions of many people. Special thanks go to the members of the committee, who dedicated extensive time, expertise, and energy to the drafting of the report, and the committee chair, Richard Bonnie, for his skilled leadership in guiding the committee throughout the study process. The committee also thanks the members of the staff of the National Academies of Sciences, Engineering, and Medicine for their significant contributions to the report: Rebekah Hutton for her expert direction of this study and contributions to the writing and editing of this report; Emily Backes for her many contributions to the conception, writing, and editing of the report throughout the study process; Sunia Young for her research, editing, and writing support and assistance with fact checking of the report; and Tara Nazari for providing essential administrative and logistical support to the committee's work.

ACKNOWLEDGMENTS

The committee is also grateful to Stacey Smit, Pamella Atayi, Javed Khan, Elise Mialou, Faye Hillman, and Lisa Alston for their administrative and financial assistance on this project. From the Office of Reports and Communication of the Division of Behavioral and Social Sciences and Education (DBASSE), Kirsten Sampson Snyder, Douglas Sprunger, and Kimberly Halperin shepherded the report through the review and production processes and assisted with its communication and dissemination. Dana Korsen and Solomon Self, of the Office of News and Public Information, and Sandra McDermin, of the Office of the Congressional and Government Affairs, were instrumental in the release and promotion of the report. The committee also thanks Clair Woolley of the National Academies Press and Bea Porter of DBASSE for their assistance with the production of the final report, and Anne Marie Hoppert, Christopher Lao-Scott, and Rebecca Morgan in the National Academies research library for their assistance with literature searches. We also extend our gratitude to Rona Briere and Allison Boman for their skilled editing of the report.

Throughout the project, Natacha Blain, director of the Board on Children, Youth, and Families, and Carlotta Arthur, Patti Simon (until December 2024), and Amy Stephens, executive director and associate executive directors of the Division of Behavioral and Social Sciences and Education, provided valuable oversight and guidance.

The committee extends its sincere thanks to Lucy Guarnera (University of Virginia) for her substantial contributions to the drafting of the report, her thoughtful feedback to the committee throughout the study process, and her valuable assistance with information-gathering to inform the committee's work. We also thank Kaelyn Sanders (Arizona State University) for her research and writing support.

Many individuals volunteered significant time and effort to address and educate the committee during our information-gathering sessions. Their willingness to share their perspectives, research, and personal experiences was essential to the committee's work. We thank Kevin Armstrong (National Association of Elementary School Principals),

ACKNOWLEDGMENTS

Sharnetta Boone-Ruffin (Parents Amplifying Voices in Education), Stephen E. Brock (California State University, Sacramento), Mo Canady (National Association of School Resource Officers), Michael T. Cappiello (New York City Department of Education), Robin Cogan (Rutger University), Christina Conolly-Chester (Montgomery County Public Schools, Maryland), Ayanna Cooper (Howard University), Matthew J. Cuellar (University of Alaska, Anchorage), Michael Dorn (Safe Havens International), Elizabeth M. Ducy (Sonoma State University), Verline M. Gaddis (School Social Workers Association of America), Keith Gambill (Indiana State Teachers Association), Brian J. Gerber (Arizona State University), Kristine D. Gile (Gallaudet University), Rose Emily Gonzalez (University of Virginia School of Medicine), Emily Goodman-Scott (Old Dominion University), Michele Gay (Safe and Sound Schools), Sunny G. Hallowell (Villanova University), Kassie Hameister (E-school Virtual Charter Academy), Anja Herrman (Student Researcher on Disability Rights, American University), Melissa A. Jackson (Hunter College), Cathy Kennedy-Paine (Springfield School District, Oregon), Joseph La Belle (Family Network on Disabilities), Gabriel I. Lomas (Gallaudet University), Heather Martin (Aurora Central High School), Isabel Mavrides-Calderon (White House Youth Policy Team), Donna J. Mazyck (National Association of School Nurses), Robert Murtfeld (former Community Education Council Member, New York City Public Schools), Zaria Naqvi (Maryland Association of Student Councils), George Roberts (Baltimore County Public Schools, Principal Recovery Network), Marissa (Apollo) Rodriguez (FEMA Youth Preparedness Council), Jennifer F. Samson (Hunter College), Jaclyn Schildkraut (Rockefeller Institute of Government), Laura Sharp (Lincoln Intermediate Unit, Pennsylvania), Andrea Warner Stidham (Kent State University), Laura M. Stough (Texas A&M University), Frank Straub (Safe and Sound Schools), Kenneth S. Trump (National School Safety and Security Services), Frederick Walton (Sandy Hook Promise Youth Advisory Board), La-Shanda West (Sandy Hook Promise School Advisory Committee, Cutler Bay Senior High School), and Lisa Wobbe-Viet (University of Southern California).

Contents

Preface	xxiii
Acronyms and Abbreviations	xxix
Summary	1
1 Introduction	19

    SCOPE OF THE STUDY, 20
        Interpreting the Study Charge, 22
        Study Process, 25
    FIREARM VIOLENCE AS A PUBLIC HEALTH ISSUE, 26
    SCHOOL SAFETY IN THE 21ST CENTURY, 27
        21st-Century School Shooting Events, 30
    DEFINITIONS AND TYPOLOGY, 35
        Pertinent Definitions, 36
        What are Active Shooter Events? 39
        What are School Active Shooter Drills? 40
    KEY CONCEPTS FROM CHILD AND ADOLESCENT DEVELOPMENT, 47
    CONCEPTUAL FRAMEWORK FOR THIS REPORT, 51
    ORGANIZATION OF THE REPORT, 54
    REFERENCES, 56

2 The Landscape of School Active Shooter Drills and Other School Security Measures   63

    CONTEXT OF SCHOOL SAFETY, 64
        The Importance of School Climate, 69

Social-Emotional Learning, 70
Restorative and Trauma-Informed Practices, 71
Access to Mental Health Services, 72
THE LANDSCAPE OF ACTIVE SHOOTER DRILLS, 74
State Mandates for School Active Shooter Drills, 75
Implementation of School Active Shooter Drills, 79
LANDSCAPE OF OTHER SCHOOL SECURITY MEASURES, 86
Physical Security Interventions, 90
Surveillance Interventions, 94
Personnel Interventions and Training, 103
EXPOSURE TO SCHOOL ACTIVE SHOOTER DRILLS AND SECURITY MEASURES, 112
CONCLUSION, 113
REFERENCES, 115

3 Mental, Emotional, and Behavioral Health Effects of School Active Shooter Drills   **129**

INCLUSION CRITERIA AND SEARCH STRATEGY, 130
OVERVIEW OF THE AVAILABLE RESEARCH BASE, 131
MENTAL, EMOTIONAL, AND BEHAVIORAL HEALTH OUTCOMES OF DRILLS, 133
Research Designs, 134
Review of Empirical Studies, 142
Insights from Qualitative Studies, 160
CONCLUSION, 168
REFERENCES, 170

4 Mental, Emotional, and Behavioral Health Effects of Selected School Security Measures   **175**

ADVANTAGES AND LIMITATIONS OF RESEARCH DESIGNS, 177
Quasi-Experimental Studies, 178

CONTENTS

           Cross-Sectional Studies, 178
           Longitudinal Studies, 179
           Systematic and Integrated Reviews, 180
           Qualitative Studies, 180
    CHARACTERISTICS AND LIMITATIONS OF THE EXISTING EVIDENCE BASE, 187
    REVIEW OF EVIDENCE ON PHYSICAL SECURITY INTERVENTIONS, 191
           Perceived Emergency Preparedness or Knowledge, 192
           Perception of Safety or Fear, 193
           Student Trauma and Mental Health Concerns, 194
           Student Perceptions of School Connectedness, 194
           Student Behavior, 194
    REVIEW OF EVIDENCE ON METAL DETECTORS, 194
           Perceived Emergency Preparedness or Knowledge, 196
           Perception of Safety or Fear, 196
           Student Trauma and Mental Health Concerns, 197
           Student Perceptions of School Connectedness, 198
           Student Behavior, 199
    EVIDENCE ON THE PRESENCE OF SCHOOL SECURITY PERSONNEL, 200
           Perceived Emergency Preparedness or Knowledge, 200
           Perception of Safety or Fear, 201
           Student Trauma and Mental Health Concerns, 203
           Student Perceptions of School Connectedness, 203
           Student Behavior, 204
    CONCLUSION, 206
    REFERENCES, 207

5 School Active Shooter Drills and Other School Security Measures: Developmental Contexts   213

CONSIDERATIONS FOR STUDENTS BY DEVELOPMENTAL STAGE, 214
  Early Childhood: Pre-K and Kindergarten (Ages 3–5), 215
  Elementary School: Grades 1–5 (Ages 6–10), 215
  Middle School: Grades 6–8 (Ages 10–13), 216
  High School: Grades 9–12 (Ages 14–18), 216
CONSIDERATIONS RELATED TO UNIQUE IDENTITIES OF STUDENTS, CAREGIVERS, TEACHERS, AND OTHER STAFF, 218
  Individuals with Prior Trauma Histories and Adverse Life Experiences, 222
  Racially/Ethnically Marginalized Students and Teachers, 226
  Cultural Influences as Protective Factors, 228
  The Role of Immigration and Migrant Status, 229
  Multilingual Learners, 231
  Individuals Who Use Communication Aids and Supports, 233
  Individuals with Emotional and Behavioral Support Needs, 233
  Individuals with Intellectual, Developmental, and Learning Disabilities, 235
  Individuals with Physical and Other Health Conditions, 236
  Children Involved with Other Formal Social Systems, 239
SUPPORTING RESILIENCE IN THE CONTEXT OF SCHOOL ACTIVE SHOOTER DRILLS, 240
  The Role of Teachers and School Support Staff, 241
  The Role of Caregivers and Families, 246
  Caregivers' Responses and Perceptions, 248
CONCLUSION, 252
REFERENCES, 253

6 Best Practices for Protecting the Mental, Emotional, and Behavioral Health of Students and Staff   269

STRATEGIES FOR MITIGATING MENTAL, EMOTIONAL, AND BEHAVIORAL HEALTH HARMS WHEN IMPLEMENTING SCHOOL ACTIVE SHOOTER DRILLS, 271

PRACTICES LEAST LIKELY TO CAUSE MENTAL, EMOTIONAL, AND BEHAVIORAL HEALTH HARMS, 274

    Best Practices When Planning for School Active Shooter Drills, 275
    Conducting School Active Shooter Drills, 295
    After School Active Shooter Drills Occur, 297
    Practices with High Likelihood of Mental, Emotional, and Behavioral Health Harm, 305
    Practices More Likely to Have Negative Than Positive Mental, Emotional, and Behavioral Health Impact, 311

IMPLEMENTATION CONSIDERATIONS, 314

    Guidance to Prioritize Health and Safety Across All School Settings, 315
    Training on School Safety Practices to Support Mental, Emotional, and Behavioral Health, 317
    Funding and Resources Needed to Implement Best Practices, 321
    Accommodations for Students and Staff with Disabilities and Functional and Access Needs, 324

CONCLUSION, 332
REFERENCES, 334

7 Future Research and Evaluation Needs   339

CURRENT RESEARCH LIMITATIONS, 339

    Challenges with Research Design and Funding, 340
    Data Needs, 341
    Limited Outcome Measures, 342

         Lack of Subgroup Analysis, 344
         Insufficient Focus on Individual Drill
           Components, 345
         Impacts on School Staff and Caregivers, 346
         Evidence on Impacts of School Security Measures
           on Mental, Emotional, and Behavioral Health
           Outcomes, 347
      RESEARCH PRIORITIES AND KEY QUESTIONS, 351
         Best Practices for Drill Implementation, 351
         Standardized Measures for Assessing the
           Effectiveness of Drills and Other Security
           Measures, 354
         Mental, Emotional, and Behavioral Health Effects
           on Students and Staff, 357
         Addressing Ethical Considerations, 359
         Funding and Cost of Implementation, 363
         Community and Population Context, 365
      IMPROVING DATA INFRASTRUCTURE, 367
      CONCLUSION, 373
      REFERENCES, 375

Appendix   Committee and Staff Biosketches   379

Boxes, Figures, and Tables

BOXES

S-1　　Summarized Statement of Task, 3

1-1　　Statement of Task, 21
1-2　　Key Components of the I Love U Guys Standard Response Protocol, 32
1-3　　Key Terminology, 36
1-4　　Overview of Options-Based Practices, 43

2-1　　School Resources Officers, 104

3-1　　A Reporter Investigates Students' Perceptions of School Active Shooter and Lockdown Drills, 164

5-1　　Students' Perspectives on Active Shooter Drills, 217
5-2　　Perceptions of Active Shooter Drills from School Staff, 220
5-3　　Providing Language Supports to Students During School Active Shooter Drills, 231
5-4　　Considerations for Students with Disabilities: Expert Perspectives, 237
5-5　　Teachers' Perspectives on Active Shooter Drills, 243
5-6　　Caregivers, Parents, and Families' Perspectives on Active Shooter Drills, 250

6-1　　General Emergency Preparedness Planning and Staff Training, 276

6-2   Perspectives from School Social Workers, School Psychologists, and School Nurses, 299

7-1   Schools Safety Resources, 367

FIGURES

1-1   Conceptual framework for this report, 52

2-1   States that require schools to carry out active shooter–related drills, as of February 4, 2024, 75
2-2   Trends in percentage of U.S. public K–12 schools with security staff and law enforcement personnel, school years 2005–2006 to 2021–2022, 106

TABLES

S-1   Strategies for Mitigating Mental, Emotional, and Behavioral (MEB) Health Harms When Implementing School Active Shooter Drills, 9

2-1   Preventive Strategies for Ensuring School Safety, 67
2-2   Frequency of School Active Shooter Drills Required by State Mandates, February 4, 2024, 77
2-3   Percentage of Public K–12 Schools That Drilled Students on the Use of Emergency Procedures, School Year 2021–2022, 81
2-4   Summary of K–12 School Security Measures, 88
2-5   Percentage of Public K–12 Schools with Controlled Access Security Measures, School Year 2021–2022, 92
2-6   Percentage of Public K–12 Schools with Various Surveillance Interventions, School Year 2021–2022, 95
2-7   Percentage of Public K–12 Schools with One or More Full- or Part-time Security Staff Present at Least Once a Week, School Year 2021–2022, 107

3-1	Overview of Studies About the Effects of Active Shooter Drills, 136
4-1	Studies About the Effects of School Security Measures (Other than Active Shooter Drills), 182
6-1	Strategies for Mitigating Mental, Emotional, and Behavioral (MEB) Health Harms When Implementing School Active Shooter Drills, 272
6-2	Selected Practices for Developmentally Appropriate Implementation of School Active Shooter Drills That Mitigate Adverse Mental, Emotional, and Behavioral Health Harms, 282
6-3	TEAMS Framework of School Safety and Emergency Planning Considerations for Individuals with Functional and Accessibility Needs, 284

Preface

Every parent sends their child to school to learn, to mature, and to enjoy interaction with others, and with a simple expectation—that their children will return home safely and happily every day. Unfortunately, however, efforts to ensure student safety have taken a prominent place in school life in recent years, including widespread implementation of school active shooter drills and security measures in the vast majority of K–12 schools in the United States. These practices are intended to prevent tragedy and to prepare students and staff to respond successfully should one occur. Yet in the process of preparing for rare but worrisome events, we must also ask: What is the impact of these heightened worries on the mental, emotional, and behavioral health of students and school staff?

This congressionally mandated study, conducted by the National Academies of Sciences, Engineering, and Medicine and supported by the U.S. Department of Education, examines the potential adverse effects of so-called active shooter drills and related security measures on students and staff. The committee was charged with evaluating the available evidence and recommending actions to mitigate potential harms, while ensuring healthy development and well-being in school environments.

In carrying out this important task, the committee faced a sobering reality: Although these protective practices have become ubiquitous in U.S. schools, there is remarkably little evidence to guide their design and implementation. While congressional enactment of the 1996 "Dickey Amendment" did not explicitly prohibit such research, it prohibited the Centers for Disease Control and Prevention from using funding appropriated for injury prevention and control to advocate for or promote gun control. The chilling effect of the

Dickey Amendment on the use of federal funding for research on gun violence more broadly also left critical questions unanswered and opportunities to learn from school practices unrealized. For more than 2 decades—spanning a period during which the number of school shootings markedly increased and these drills became routine—public health research on gun violence and related prevention strategies was significantly constrained.

As this report makes clear, continuing gaps in current evidence leave many unanswered questions about the potential risks associated with school active shooter drills, as well as their effectiveness. Needless to say, this uncertainty does not absolve us of the responsibility to take preventive action. We know a great deal about what children and youth need to thrive. We also know that some well-intentioned practices, when implemented without proper attention to developmental needs, can produce unintended and potentially harmful consequences for many of the children who are essentially treated as experimental subjects. A central purpose of this report is to avoid these unintended consequences. Instead, the recommendations offered in this report draw upon established developmental science, trauma-informed approaches to stressful events, and a growing body of knowledge about resilience. Our aim is to help school leaders make informed decisions to protect student and staff well-being.

This important assignment presents both a challenge and an opportunity. The committee's inquiry documented a broad and growing public interest in ensuring school safety. However, the nation lacks a unified research agenda, and few states or schools have the resources needed to undertake this work on their own. As a result, the work is fragmented and unsystematic: it is distributed across government agencies, state legislatures, professional associations, advocacy groups, researchers, and school districts. In the absence of a strong federal infrastructure designed to nurture child and adolescent development throughout the nation, state and regional collaboration will be essential so that evolving experience and knowledge is shared and emerging best practices are accessible to all. Key challenges include standardizing the collection of meaningful data,

PREFACE

evaluating policies already in use, and highlighting both successful and unsuccessful initiatives. By highlighting both innovation and failure, these jurisdictions are well positioned to lead the way in building the future knowledge base in a systematic and careful way. Indeed, without the development of a coordinated research enterprise, we risk losing yet another generation of opportunities to answer the questions that matter most: Which practices truly keep students and school staff safe, and which practices pose undue risks of harm?

The committee is hopeful that collaboration between state legislatures, universities, and other research organizations, supported by occasional national funding initiatives, will be able to nurture a long-term program of research and policy development. Our public sessions and interviews revealed an intense and growing commitment to act. The recommendations in this report aim to equip policymakers, educators, health professionals, and communities with the tools they need to make informed decisions that are grounded in evidence and that are appropriate for youth across the full range of development.

On behalf of the committee, we are pleased to offer this report to the nation as both a resource and a call to action. We are grateful to the U.S. Congress, the U.S. Department of Education, the staff of the National Academies, and the many individuals who contributed their expertise and insight over the course of our deliberations. Most of all, we are mindful of the students, families, educators, and school communities at the center of this work—those who are asking the right questions and who live with the consequences of these policies every day. Their experiences underscore the urgent need to act with care and clarity, ensuring that school safety measures support the well-being of the children and adults they are meant to protect.

Richard J. Bonnie, *Chair*
Committee on the Impact of Active Shooter Drills
on Student Health and Wellbeing
July 2025

Acronyms and Abbreviations

AAPI	Asian American and Pacific Islander
ADA	Americans with Disabilities Act
Add Health	National Longitudinal Study of Adolescent to Adult Health
ADHD	Attention Deficit Hyperactivity Disorder
ALERRT	Advanced Law Enforcement Rapid Response Training
ALICE	Alert, Lockdown, Inform, Counter, Evacuate
ASCA	American School Counselor Association
ASD	Autism Spectrum Disorder
CASEL	Collaborative for Academic, Social, and Emotional Learning
CDC	Centers for Disease Control and Prevention
CHDS	Center for Homeland Defense and Security
CISA	Cybersecurity and Infrastructure Security Agency
DEBH	Division of Emotional and Behavioral Health
DOJ	Department of Justice
ED	Department of Education
EOP	Emergency Operations Plan
FBI	Federal Bureau of Investigation
HB	House Bill
H.E.R.O	Hide Escape Run Overcome
HR	House of Representatives

ACRONYMS AND ABBREVIATIONS

IDEA	Individuals with Disabilities Education Act
IELP	Individual Emergency and Lockdown Plan
IEP	Individualized Education Plan
IOM	Institute of Medicine
K–12	Kindergarten to 12th Grade
MEB	Mental, Emotional, and Behavioral
NASP	National Association of School Psychologists
NASRO	National Association of School Resource Officers
NCES	National Center for Education Statistics
NCTSN	National Child Traumatic Stress Network
NICS	National Instant Criminal Background Check System
NIE	National Institute of Education
NRC	National Research Council
PBIS	Positive Behavioral Interventions and Supports
PFA-S	Psychological First Aid for Schools
PTSD	Post-Traumatic Stress Disorder
RCT	Randomized Controlled Trials
REMS	Readiness and Emergency Management for Schools
SB	Senate Bill
SCS	School Crime Supplement
SRO	School Resource Officer
SRM	Standard Reunification Method
SRP	Standard Response Protocol
SSOCS	School Survey on Crime and Safety
STAI	Spielberger State-Trait Anxiety Inventory
STOP	Student, Teachers, and Officers Preventing
SWAT	Special Weapons and Tactics
TA	Technical Assistance

ACRONYMS AND ABBREVIATIONS

U.S.C.	United States Code
WSCC	Whole School, Whole Community, Whole Child
YRBSS	Youth Risk Behavior Surveillance System

Summary[1]

"Active shooter drills" are a relatively recent addition to the variety of safety and emergency preparedness trainings offered for more than a century to students and teachers in U.S. schools. The term *active shooter drills* has been used to describe a range of practices including but not limited to lockdown drills, options-based drills, and full-scale simulation exercises. These terms—particularly *lockdown drills* and *active shooter drills*—are often conflated, though lockdowns represent only one practice on a broader spectrum of practices used in schools as part of active shooter drills.[2]

Following the 1999 school shooting at Columbine High School in Colorado, some schools began implementing active shooter drills as part of efforts to prepare for such incidents. These drills became more prevalent 13 years later following the Sandy Hook Elementary School shooting in Connecticut. Today, more than 25 years after Columbine, 95% of U.S. public schools conduct active shooter drills as part of emergency response training. Yet while these drills are now commonplace, evidence on their impact on the mental, emotional, and behavioral health of students and staff remains limited.

Increased public concern about school shooting incidents has coincided with increased implementation of safety and security measures, including active shooter drills and physical security

---

[1] This summary does not include references. Citations for the discussion presented in the Summary appear in the subsequent report chapters, as does a detailed discussion of the policies and evidence reviewed to support the committee's conclusions and recommendations.

[2] Where possible, the committee specifies the nature of the drills described in the evidence reviewed.

measures (e.g., metal detectors, armed personnel, police presence). As a result, many states now mandate active shooter drills; however, the ways in which those drills are defined, designed, and implemented and the frequency with which they are carried out vary significantly. Indeed, the conflation and imprecise use of terminology for the practices that are being used in school active shooter drills further contributes to confusion about what types of activities students and staff are experiencing.

STUDY OBJECTIVES AND STATEMENT OF TASK

As school active shooter drills and implementation of other physical security measures have increased, so too have concerns about their potential negative effects on the mental, emotional, and behavioral health of students and staff.

In this context, the 117th Congress requested a comprehensive study on the mental health effects of lockdown drills and active shooter drills in elementary and secondary schools in the United States. This legislation (Public Law 117-328)[3] directed the National Academies of Sciences, Engineering, and Medicine to undertake a study focused on the mental, emotional, and behavioral health outcomes of these drills. The goal was to better understand the potential risk of adverse psychological effects and to identify best practices for mitigating those effects, as well as to identify practices that can improve safety and security while minimizing harm. The National Academies convened an ad hoc committee of relevant experts to carry out this study (see Box S-1 for a summary of the committee's statement of task). The 14-member committee included experts in trauma-informed care, K–12 school administration and leadership, K–12 school security policy and programs, developmental-behavioral pediatrics, child and adolescent psychiatry and psychology, criminology, developmental neuroscience, developmental and

---

[3] The appropriation can be found in https://www.congress.gov/congressional-report/117th-congress/house-report/403.

family psychology, school psychology, public health, public policy, and program development.

**BOX S-1
Summarized Statement of Task**

- Identify the potential short- and long-term mental, emotional, and behavioral health effects of active shooter drills on students and school staff.
- Describe what is known about the potential effects of school active shooter drills on various populations of students including students with disabilities, Black and Latinx students, dual language learners, and students belonging to different age groups.
- Identify the components, criteria, features, best practices, and procedures for active shooter drills that can minimize negative mental, emotional, and behavioral health effects and that promote resilience in children, youth, and school staff.
- Determine the necessary supports, school programs, and staff experience needed to implement, monitor, and evaluate the identified best practices.

It is important to recognize that the statement of task did *not* ask the committee to evaluate the effectiveness of school active shooter drills or other school security measures. While the effectiveness of these practices is an important consideration—particularly if there are potential associated risks—the committee was tasked with assessing the known impacts of such drills and security practices on mental, emotional, and behavioral outcomes and to identify practices to mitigate adverse effects on students and staff. References to what is known about effectiveness of practices or interventions are included where relevant to contextualize the outcomes that may result from various policies, practices, and interventions. The question of whether school active shooter drills should be discontinued altogether was also outside of the scope of the committee's charge;

rather, the committee's report focuses on identifying best practices for mitigating risks to student and staff wellbeing when these practices are implemented.

In responding to its statement of task, the committee drew on the specific body of research related to the impact of school active shooter drills, and how these drills and other school safety and security measures fit within a broader framework of comprehensive emergency preparedness strategies that promote safe and supportive school environments. The committee paid particular attention to community, school, family, and individual factors that can inform best practices for the use of these measures as components of a broader school safety and security strategy. The committee also drew on complementary research literature in such related areas as child and adolescent development, trauma-informed and developmentally appropriate practices, school safety, emergency preparedness, and violence prevention. To further enrich this review, the committee also solicited expert testimony and input from constituent groups through public information-gathering and listening sessions.

Although active shooter events can take place in a variety of locations, the committee was tasked with focusing specifically on active shooter drills in schools to understand their potential impact on mental, emotional, and behavioral health. The committee views schools as fundamentally distinct from other types of settings where active shooter events may take place, such as movie theaters, hospitals, and other workplaces. Schools are institutions for child and adolescent development and learning, and children are legally mandated to attend them. The wide age range of students in K–12 schools also introduces developmental considerations that are essentially connected to school safety and that must be understood and accommodated in order to create safe and supportive learning environments.

EVIDENCE ON MENTAL, EMOTIONAL, AND BEHAVIORAL HEALTH OUTCOMES

The committee's review of the evidence informed the findings and conclusions that serve as a foundation for its guidance on best practices before, during, and after school active shooter drills. It also helped identify practices that should be avoided to prevent or mitigate the potential for adverse impacts on mental, emotional, and behavioral health. The committee's findings and conclusions served as the basis for policy recommendations to meet the needs of schools, students, staff, and communities in the implementation of school active shooter drills and other school safety and security measures.

In reviewing practices being implemented in elementary and secondary schools across the country, the committee noted the wide variety of practices referred to as "active shooter drills"—many of which were not designed for application in schools or to meet the unique needs of student populations. As previously noted, the committee also found that research on the mental, emotional, and behavioral health outcomes (e.g., fear, anxiety, perceptions of safety and preparedness, perception of school climate) resulting from school active shooter drills and school safety and security measures is limited. These two findings are not unrelated: the lack of standard guidance on implementing school active shooter drills and the limited evidence evaluating practices to identify areas for improvement have led to the wide variation in how drills are implemented.

The current evidence base on the effects of school active shooter drills on mental, emotional, and behavioral health is limited and mixed. While some studies show that drills may increase participants' sense of preparedness, others report increases in fear or distress—especially among students with existing vulnerabilities. Responses vary widely, and most studies reviewed by the committee relied on narrow outcome measures that may not fully capture more subtle or lasting effects. There is also a lack of long-term or causal data that could offer clearer guidance. Similarly, research on broader school safety and security practices offers mixed findings that make it difficult to differentiate the impacts of specific practices or how multiple security measures interact to influence mental, emotional, and behavioral health outcomes. For example, measures such as locked doors may be perceived as protective, while more intensive or visible security strategies—such as metal detectors or regular law enforcement personnel presence—can cause some students to perceive their school environment as less safe. As with school active shooter drills, the impact of these measures depends heavily on context, including the school environment, developmental needs of students, and how policies are implemented.

Given the limited research on mental, emotional, and behavioral health outcomes related to school active shooter drills and security measures, the committee regards systematic research on this specific topic as a high priority. Specifically, it envisions a robust research agenda aiming at better understanding the effectiveness of specific drill elements at preventing harm in the event of an actual emergency, the potential risk for adverse outcomes associated with practicing these elements, innovative preparedness strategies, and the varying impacts on diverse populations of students and staff in K–12 schools. The committee also found that existing guidance on best practices was developed by a variety of professional associations, researchers, state and federal policymakers, foundations, advocacy organizations, and other groups and is not always consistent. Thus, it identified opportunities to address and improve this fragmented nature of the evidence base.

Tailoring approaches to school active shooter drills to meet the needs of individual communities requires accounting for school and community contexts, which can complicate efforts to provide standardized guidance. However, schools can improve the effectiveness of their safety and security planning through collaboration among educators, families, community members, law enforcement and first responders, and mental and physical health professionals.

The literature points to confidence among students and staff in their preparedness and their development of skills in regulating emotional responses in emergency situations as factors that could improve their sense of safety. The committee identified opportunities to ensure that all students and staff are prepared, can develop emotion-regulation skills, have their needs considered, and can be included in emergency preparedness efforts. For example, students with disabilities or functional and access needs—including visual, hearing, communication-related, mobility-related, cognitive, attentional, and emotional—are sometimes not included in emergency management planning, which in turn may limit their opportunities for their full participation in emergency drills and preparedness for emergencies with potential consequences for mental, emotional, and behavioral health outcomes. Principles such as universal design[4] offer an approach that schools can use to develop usable and accessible practices to ensure that the needs of all students and staff are met.

BEST PRACTICES FOR PROTECTING MENTAL, EMOTIONAL, AND BEHAVIORAL HEALTH FOR STUDENTS AND STAFF

The committee's review of the available research and professional consensus on best practices for implementing school active shooter drills and on their impact—as well as the research literature on developmentally appropriate practices for fostering mental, emotional, and behavioral health—informed its formulation of strategies for mitigating potential risks to students and staff when implementing school active shooter drills.

While many schools conduct active shooter drills as part of their emergency response efforts, it is important for these drills to be grounded in the broader context of the school's comprehensive safety plan. When school active shooter drills are performed in isolation (as they often are), without taking adequate account of the children's emotional and psychological well-being, they can inadvertently arouse unnecessary anxiety or fear. When grounded in a positive school climate, these drills can foster a prepared, resilient,

---

[4] Universal design is "the design and composition of an environment so that it can be accessed, understood, and used to the greatest extent possible by all people regardless of their age, size, ability, or disability" (section508.gov).

and calm school community. Thus, rather than viewing drills as isolated events responding to a hypothesized immediate threat, schools can connect them to broader discussions about safety, school climate, and well-being.

> **Recommendation 1: Schools should adopt trauma-informed, developmentally appropriate approaches to school active shooter drills that balance preparedness with emotional and psychological safety. It is essential for the design and implementation of drills to prioritize student and staff well-being in order to prevent unnecessary mental, emotional, and behavioral health harms and ensure that drills foster environments conducive to the learning and skill-building they are intended to impart. State-level legislation mandating drills should require the implementation of trauma-informed, developmentally appropriate drills designed with input from experts in mental health and child development.**

The committee's review of the evidence also identified practices that are likely to cause mental, emotional, and behavioral health harms when implemented in the context of school active shooter drills: simulation exercises involving student participation; high-intensity, hyper-realistic, or high-sensorial components; and deception.

> **Recommendation 2: State legislatures and education agencies should enact policies prohibiting the use of high-intensity or high-sensorial simulations and exercises, as well as deception, as part of active shooter drills in K–12 schools. If statewide action is not taken, local school districts should prohibit the use of these practices as part of active shooter drills and should require that all drills be announced to students, staff, and parents before they begin.**

Table S-1 outlines practices that are least likely to cause MEB harms before, during, and after school active shooter drills (highlighted in green); practices that should be implemented with caution because they are more likely to have negative impact than positive impact on mental, emotional, and behavioral health (highlighted in yellow); and practices that professional consensus largely agrees should not be implemented due to their high potential to cause harm (highlighted in red). These practices are discussed in more detail in Chapter 6.

TABLE S-1 Strategies for Mitigating Mental, Emotional, and Behavioral (MEB) Health Harms When Implementing School Active Shooter Drills

Practices Least Likely to Cause MEB Health Harms
Before: <ul><li>Implement robust social-emotional programming to help students develop the skills needed to engage successfully in drills.</li><li>Design drills using discussion-based and standard response practices that foster skill-building, with clearly defined action steps.</li><li>Adapt drills for individuals with functional and access needs.</li><li>Consider the frequency and context of drills to minimize unnecessary stress and disruption.</li><li>Inform, engage, and collaborate with parents to ensure transparency and support.</li><li>Preplan drills with a multidisciplinary team, incorporating student and parent input in both planning and evaluation efforts.</li></ul> **During:** <ul><li>Use clear communication throughout the drill to ensure understanding and reduce anxiety.</li><li>Ensure that wellness supports are available for students and staff.</li></ul> **After:** <ul><li>Provide time for students and staff to debrief and process the experience.</li><li>Check in with vulnerable students and staff to assess and address emotional or psychological distress.</li></ul>

- Conduct an after-action assessment to evaluate results, identify gaps, document and demonstrate lessons learned, and highlight successes achieved.

Implement with Caution—More Likely to Have Negative Than Positive MEB Health Impacts:

- Implement options-based practices with caution as they may be more likely to have negative MEB health impacts. Guidance is needed on adapting options-based approaches for different groups and populations, as well as on the appropriateness of these practices for various developmental stages.

Do Not Implement—High Likelihood of MEB Health Harms:

- Do not conduct simulation exercises with students or require all school staff to participate. Simulation exercises often include high-intensity, hyper-realistic, or highly sensory components that can cause MEB health harms to both students and staff.
- Do not include high-intensity, hyper-realistic, or high-sensorial components in any school active shooter drill.
- Do not use deception or mislead students and staff to believe a real active shooter event is occurring.

Overall, the committee concluded that a positive school climate[5] is foundational to the effective implementation of school active shooter drills, and that school safety preparedness plans can be integrated into a broad framework that addresses prevention, mental health supports, and school climate. Currently, however, access to

---

[5] *School climate* refers to the overall quality and character of school life, shaped by the shared experiences of students, families, and educators. It encompasses the school's norms, values, relationships, teaching practices, and organizational structures. A positive school climate promotes safety, respect within the school community, collaboration, and engagement, supporting both learning and healthy development (schoolclimate.org).

the resources required to implement best practices effectively—not only funding, but also staff capacity and time—varies across schools. In addition to these resource constraints, schools may face context-specific challenges such as urbanicity and distance from first responders. The resulting variations in timing, methods, and decision-makers involved in implementing practices that are less likely to cause MEB harms can significantly shape the experiences of both students and staff. Thus, there is a need for strategies to ensure that schools have access to the necessary resources.

IMPLEMENTATION CONSIDERATIONS

Considerable autonomy exists at the state, district, and school levels to select programs and strategies that address local needs. Decision-makers balance policies, feedback from key constituencies, appropriateness and context fit, perceived effectiveness, implementation capacity, and cost—among other factors—when deciding which policies and practices to adopt.

The committee formulated recommendations, summarized in this section, aimed at fostering consistent implementation and a unified understanding of best practices in school active shooter drills, ending the use of practices likely to cause mental, emotional, and behavioral health harms, addressing disparities in access to resources critical for a safe and supportive school environment, improving accessibility to ensure that all students and staff are considered in emergency planning, and promoting training for law enforcement personnel working in schools.

Responsibility for developing guidance on active shooter drills has been spread across multiple entities, including professional associations, researchers, state and federal agencies, foundations, and advocacy organizations. While these groups have offered valuable recommendations, including best practices and policies, a cohesive, coordinated approach is necessary to ensure that schools have the resources, training, and support needed to implement strategies that are safe for all students. The committee's recommendations outline actionable strategies tailored to each level of potential influence, ranging from national policy initiatives to school-based implementation efforts. Additionally, the committee highlights opportunities for philanthropic organizations and interested researchers to support schools in identifying, refining, and evaluating best practices. By fostering multilevel collaboration, schools can strengthen their emergency preparedness strategies while ensuring that the well-being of students and staff remains at the center of these efforts.

> **Recommendation 3: Federal agencies, including the Department of Education, the Department of Health and Human Services, the Federal Emergency Management Agency, and the Centers for Disease Control and Prevention, should issue national best-practice guidelines aligned with the committee's guidance to follow trauma-informed and developmentally appropriate principles.**
>
> **Recommendation 4: Research funders, including philanthropic organizations and research institutions, should fund independent studies on the effects of school active shooter drills on mental, emotional, and behavioral health, and support the adoption of trauma-informed safety practices to ensure that school safety practices are evidence based and centered on the health of students and school staff.**
>
> **Recommendation 5: School districts should ensure that school nurses, school counselors, school psychologists, school social workers, and other school-based health professionals are engaged in proactively monitoring students for signs of anxiety or distress during and following school active shooter drills. School districts should provide educators and school staff with training that equips them to recognize and monitor signs of psychological distress in students when school active shooter drills are implemented. School districts, informed by mental health professionals, should ensure that appropriate mental, emotional, and behavioral**

health support services for students are available when drills are conducted.

Recommendation 6: Any sworn law enforcement officer assigned to work in elementary or secondary schools should be properly trained to work with students in an educational environment and properly prepared to respond in a developmentally appropriate manner to the mental, emotional, and behavioral health needs of school-aged children and adolescents.

- **State legislatures should require that all law enforcement officers assigned to schools—including full-time school resource officers and other sworn law enforcement officers stationed temporarily in schools—complete specialized training in supporting student well-being and contributing to safe, developmentally appropriate emergency responses that mitigate adverse mental, emotional, and behavioral health outcomes for students and school staff.**
- **Law enforcement officers assigned to work in elementary or secondary schools should be trained in the specific drills and security measures used in the schools they serve to ensure coordinated and effective responses.**
- **School districts and law enforcement agencies should verify that all officers working in schools have completed the required training prior to any school assignment.**
- **Researchers, education policy organizations, law enforcement training institutes, and law enforcement professional organizations should conduct research on the effectiveness of school resource officer training for all law enforcement officers assigned to schools, with a particular focus on their role in school active**

shooter drills and develop standardized training curricula for use nationwide.

Recommendation 7: To ensure that all schools have sufficient resources to implement best practices in school safety, federal, state, and local governments should ensure that adequate funding is provided and sustained to promote a positive school climate; to foster safe and healthy learning environments; and to design, monitor, and evaluate school safety measures and policies, especially as they relate to reducing potential negative mental, emotional, and behavioral health impacts.

- Congress should fund the provisions of the Bipartisan Safer Communities Act pertaining to school safety initiatives, violence prevention efforts, and programs that promote a positive school climate.
- In the absence of federal action, state legislatures and education agencies should establish school safety grant programs to provide targeted funding for safety initiatives, student mental health, and program evaluation.
- Local school boards and municipal governments should allocate discretionary education funds to support school safety programs if federal or state funding is unavailable or inadequate.
- Foundations, corporate sponsors, and community organizations should be engaged to provide supplemental funding for developmentally appropriate school safety initiatives, particularly in underfunded districts.

Recommendation 8: Students with disabilities should have equal access to emergency preparedness activities—including school active shooter drills—to ensure their safety during emergencies. Policies at the federal, state, and local levels should ensure that emergency preparedness measures address the individual needs of students, and schools should provide accommodations that allow students with disabilities to participate effectively in active shooter drills without compromising their well-being.

- Federal agencies, including the U.S. Department of Education, the Department of Justice, and the Federal Emergency Management Agency, should issue formal guidance clarifying how schools should apply the Americans with Disabilities Act, the Individuals with Disabilities Education Act, and Section 504 of the Rehabilitation Act of 1973 to school active shooter drills.
- If federal action is delayed, state education agencies, legislatures, and emergency management agencies should take the lead in ensuring that students with disabilities are fully included in emergency drills with necessary accommodations. State laws and policies should mandate that schools plan proactively for accessibility in preparedness efforts.
- School districts, local education agencies, and municipal governments should take immediate steps to ensure that active shooter drills are accessible to students with disabilities by integrating clear accessibility measures into their planning and implementation.
- Disability advocacy organizations, educational foundations, and private- sector partners should collaborate to develop training materials and best-practice toolkits that support schools in implementing accessible active shooter drills.
- Researchers, universities, and disability advocacy organizations should collaborate to study the effectiveness of accessible active shooter drills, particularly their impact on students with disabilities.

Recommendation 9: Schools should establish clear standards to ensure that active shooter drills are accessible to all students and staff and accommodate functional and access needs to ensure full participation and safety during emergencies. To address this obligation, specific requirements should be established to guide the planning and implementation of school active shooter drills that prioritize safety for all students and staff.

- The U.S. Department of Education, the Federal Emergency Management Agency, and the Department of Justice should issue guidance for ensuring that functional and access needs are addressed in school emergency preparedness efforts.
- State legislatures and education agencies should implement policies requiring schools to proactively identify and support students and staff with functional and access needs in emergency preparedness activities.
- School districts should develop clear protocols for meeting functional and access needs during school active shooter drills.
- Philanthropic organizations and private-sector partners should support the development of training materials and guidance for school staff and safety teams, as well as pilot programs that help schools implement inclusive emergency preparedness practices.
- Universities, research institutions, and advocacy groups should collaborate to study the effectiveness of accessible emergency preparedness measures, particularly their impact on students with functional and access needs.

THE CHALLENGE AHEAD: BUILDING THE EVIDENCE BASE

Although an important goal of school active shooter drills is to enhance feelings of safety and preparedness, research exploring the actual effects of these drills on the mental, emotional, and behavioral health and well-being of those required to participate in them is sparse. The committee's review of the available research on this topic and on the impacts of other commonly used security measures, identified limitations in the areas of research design and funding, data and outcome measures, subgroup analysis, attention to individual drill components and adult/staff populations, and guidance on the roles of school resource officers and community engagement strategies. The committee noted opportunities to fill these gaps by focusing on the following research priorities:

- Identifying and refining best practices in the implementation of school active shooter drills
- Identifying suitable variations in varied community and population contexts
- Developing standardized measures for assessing the effectiveness of school active shooter drills
- Ascertaining the effects of school active shooter drills on individual mental, emotional, and behavioral health outcomes
- Identifying and exploring ethical considerations bearing on research on the effectiveness and impact of school active shooter drills
- Quantifying and managing costs while assuring best practices

The committee also identified opportunities to improve the current data infrastructure and support future research by strengthening current data collection efforts to ensure more comprehensive tracking of safety and security policies and practices across schools—for example, by adding questions to existing surveys to capture more information about the mental, emotional, and behavioral health outcomes associated with those measures. Leveraging existing data sources as a starting point has the potential to advance the evidence base more rapidly than would otherwise be possible.

1
Introduction

Fully 95% of U.S. public schools conduct active shooter drills. However, the lack of consistent standards informing these practices has led to significant variations in their implementation, raising questions about both efficacy and possible negative impact on students and staff (Executive Office of the President, 2024). These drills may increase preparedness, but they may also induce feelings of anxiety and fear among students, their families and school staff. Limited research on the long- and short-term effects of school active shooter drills on the mental, emotional, and behavioral health of students and staff has left many of these questions without definitive answers. Accordingly, Congress directed the National Academies of Sciences, Engineering, and Medicine to study the mental, emotional, and behavioral health outcomes resulting from the implementation of school active shooter drills and the use of school-based security to ascertain what is known about the impact of these interventions on outcomes among K–12 students and staff. The appropriation can be found in House Report 117-403 (U.S. House of Representatives, 2022).

In 2003, a National Research Council report on the history of school violence (*Deadly Lessons: Understanding Lethal School Violence*) found that, while school violence is statistically rare, it can have lasting psychological effects on students and staff. However, recent studies indicate that school active shooter drills—designed to prepare students for such incidents—may also exacerbate anxiety, fear, and stress. Two National Academies reports—*The Promise of Adolescence* (2019b) and *Vibrant and Healthy Kids* (2019c)—emphasize the importance of addressing the unique needs of children and youth and the potential negative effects of stress on their development. These reports explain that failing to do so can lead to academic struggles, adverse mental health effects, and other long-term health consequences.

Some students and staff may be particularly vulnerable to negative effects of school active shooter drills (NASEM, 2019b,c). For example, individuals with anxiety disorders, histories of past trauma, or disabilities may experience heightened distress and require individualized accommodations to enable them to participate in drills. Similarly, some students may need individualized emergency preparations to process information quickly or maintain silence during drills. Others may need language supports to understand and follow instructions or mobility supports to accommodate physical limitations. Unfortunately, little research or guidance is currently available to help staff understand and to address the needs of all students.

Schools face a complex challenge: balancing preparedness with the need to safeguard student well-being. A trauma-informed approach to school safety, grounded in evidence-based practices, is essential to ensure that drills are effective and do not cause harm. The aim of this report is to ascertain what is currently known about the impacts of school active shooter drills on the mental, emotional, and behavioral health of students and school staff and to provide guidance that can inform policy and practice on how to prepare for active shooter drills in K–12 schools, while also exploring some of the broader complexities of school safety. The report identifies a variety of school safety and security practices that are likely to be effective while minimizing unintended harms.

SCOPE OF THE STUDY

In 2023, the 117th Congress requested a comprehensive study on the mental health effects of lockdown drills and active shooter drills[6] in elementary and secondary schools in the United States. This legislation, the Consolidated Appropriations Act of 2023, directed the National Academies to undertake a study focused on the mental, emotional, and behavioral health outcomes of these drills. The goal of this legislation is to gain a better understanding the potential risk of adverse psychological effects and to identify best practices for mitigating those effects, as well as to identify practices that can improve safety and security while minimizing harm. The legislation forms the basis for the committee's statement of task (Box 1-1).

In response to this congressional direction, the National Academies Board on Children, Youth, and Families convened an expert committee in 2024 to carry out the requested study and develop this report. The 14-member committee includes experts in trauma-informed care, K–12 school administration and leadership, K–12 school security policy and program, developmental-behavioral pediatrics, child and adolescent psychiatry and psychology, criminology, developmental neuroscience, developmental and family psychology, school psychology, public health, public policy, and program development.

BOX 1-1
Statement of Task

The National Academies of Sciences, Engineering and Medicine (the National Academies) will convene an ad hoc Committee of experts to conduct a consensus study on the impact of active shooter drills and other school security

---

[6] The term *active shooter drills* encompasses a range of practices, including but not limited to lockdown drills, options-based drills, and full-scale simulation exercises. These terms—particularly *lockdown drills* and *active shooter drills*—are often used interchangeably, though lockdowns represent only one component of a broader spectrum of practices used in schools. Where possible, the committee specifies the nature of the drills described in the evidence reviewed. Additional key terminology is defined later in the chapter.

measures on student mental, emotional, and behavioral health and wellbeing. The committee will consider potential effects on children and youth in grades K–12, as well as those with disabilities. The report will include recommendations on policy and practice that take children's diversities into consideration and minimize potential adverse effects for students and school staff. The committee's report will address questions including, but not limited to, the following:

- What is known about the possible mental, emotional, and behavioral health effects (either long- or short-term) on students and school staff resulting from active shooter/lockdown drills and related school security measures (e.g., metal detectors, police presence)?
- What is known about potential effects on students with disabilities, Black and Latinx children, dual language learners, children with special needs, as well as those belonging to different age groups?
- What are the components, criteria, and/or features of active shooter/lockdown drills, as well as best practices and procedures both leading up to and following the drills that can promote resiliency and minimize adverse mental, emotional, and behavioral health effects on children, youth, and school staff?
- What supports, school programs, and staff expertise are needed in order to implement, monitor and evaluate the best practices identified?

Interpreting the Study Charge

The committee's statement of task was focused narrowly on understanding the short- and long-term impacts of school active shooter drills and related school security measures on the mental, emotional, and behavioral health of students and staff. Importantly, the committee was not charged with determining whether school-based active shooter drills or related security measures are effective in preventing school violence—although questions of effectiveness are important, especially in light of potential psychological risks. Where relevant, the report references existing evidence on effectiveness to help frame the outcomes associated with different approaches. However, the committee recognizes that school leaders, policymakers, families, and other decision-makers face complex decisions and contend with difficult trade-offs in the face of uncertainty when balancing the imperative to protect the physical safety of students and school staff with the need to protect their mental, emotional, and behavioral health. Accordingly, the committee does not offer conclusions regarding the effectiveness of specific strategies in protecting students and school staff from active shooters; instead, the report focuses on the available evidence related to mental, emotional, and behavioral health outcomes and best practices that can mitigate potential harms. The committee did not consider whether such drills should be eliminated entirely, as its charge was to identify strategies that can reduce potential harm and support the well-being of those affected when these practices are used.

The committee interpreted the statement of task to refer specifically to drills designed to prepare for firearm-related threats. As noted, the term *lockdown*, which is mentioned in the statement of task, is one of many practices that are sometimes used as part of school active shooter drills; however, lockdowns are also used for other types of threats or emergencies. Although some organizations have adopted broader terminology, such as *armed assailant drills*, that does not specify the type of weapon, the committee uses the term *school active shooter drills* to focus on drills related to the threat of active shooters as specified in its charge.

The statement of task also specifies both metal detectors and police presence as security measures of interest, guiding the committee's judgment that Congress intended the study to include in-depth examination of these other security measures in addition to school active shooter drills. Recognizing that some schools may not have sworn law enforcement personnel on site, the committee also inferred that Congress intended consideration of police presence to include other types of school safety personnel. In addition, the committee identified *locked doors* as a security measure related to the implementation of school active shooter drills with the potential to impact mental, emotional, and behavioral health outcomes for students and staff. Although a wide range of school security measures are available to K–12 schools, the committee prioritized consideration of metal detectors, police presence, and locked doors, because they are widely implemented among schools in the United States.

Although active shooter events take place in a many other settings, including movie theaters and workplaces, the statement of task focused clearly on school active shooter drills—specifically in K–12 (elementary and secondary) school settings and in pre-K settings as applicable, given that some elementary schools may also serve pre-K students. The committee views schools as fundamentally distinct from other settings because all states require children to attend schools, and because schools are generally intended and understood to serve as a distinct environment for development and learning. Accordingly, the committee did not investigate youth-oriented settings other than schools or companion facilities that are designed with the developmental needs of students in mind.

Research highlights the need to consider students' developmental stages when assessing school safety plans, strategies, and training. Ensuring safe and secure environments supports students' physical, emotional, social, and cognitive growth. Accommodating these developmental changes is essential for fostering a safe and supportive learning environment (Berk, 2022; Kingston et al., 2018; Sprague & Walker, 2021).

Unfortunately, the existing research evidence bearing directly on the impact of school active shooter drills is quite thin. To address this challenge, the committee also drew on complementary research related to child and adolescent development, trauma-informed and developmentally appropriate practices, school safety, emergency preparedness, and violence prevention to supplement the evidence directly related to the impact of school active shooter drills. Also, although it was not asked to address strategies for preventing active shooter events, the committee recognizes that school active shooter drills are an emergency preparedness strategy implemented in response to firearm violence, and that the threat of active shooter events itself may also have adverse impacts on the mental, emotional, and behavioral health of students and staff. In addition, recognizing that school environments and school climate shape how interventions are implemented, and that drills do not occur in isolation from these factors, the committee considered school active shooter drills and other school security measures within a broader context of comprehensive emergency preparedness strategies that promote safe and supportive school environments.

As directed by the statement of task, the committee also paid particular attention to the specific groups of students identified in the statement of task, including students with disabilities, students with special needs, Black and Latinx children, multilingual learners, and children in different age groups. Giving specific consideration to these groups enabled the committee to provide comprehensive guidance on best practices for the implementation of drills and security measures focused on prevention, intervention, and responsiveness as components of a broader safety strategy for minimizing harm. Consideration of these groups also informed the committee's identification of supports, programs, and expertise needed to implement, monitor, and evaluate recommended best practices.

Study Process

The committee met five times over a 1-year period in 2024–2025. To inform its deliberations, the committee adopted a broad approach to evidence-gathering, drawing on a wide range of methodologies, evidence types, and scientific perspectives. Thus, the committee reviewed literature relevant to the statement of task, including peer-reviewed articles, policy papers and reports, book chapters, government documents, existing legislation, editorials, and relevant National Academies reports.

In addition, the committee conducted two public information-gathering sessions and eight listening sessions. The listening sessions included several panels and provided perspectives from students, teachers, parents, school nurses, school psychologists, school counselors, school social workers, experts on students with disabilities, and experts on students who require language supports. While these sessions were not designed to be representative of all perspectives, practices, or lived experiences within these groups, they highlighted key issues included in the statement of task and offered valuable context for understanding the real-world implementation of drills and for identifying areas of potential concern regarding adverse outcomes. These discussions also provided important background information that enriched the committee's review of the empirical literature, served as an important input to the committee's deliberations, and helped contextualize—though not determine—its conclusions, recommendations, and the future research agenda described in Chapter 7.

FIREARM VIOLENCE AS A PUBLIC HEALTH ISSUE

It is important to understand the social environment in which school active shooter drills are being implemented. According to the Centers for Disease Control and Prevention (2022), firearm violence persists as a "significant and growing" public health issue in the United States. Indeed, the U.S. surgeon general issued an advisory report on firearm violence in 2024, underscoring the urgency of this challenge. Each year, more than 100,000 individuals in the United States, including more than 17,000 children, are shot directly with firearms. Indeed, firearms are now the leading cause of death among children and teens in the United States (Villarreal et al., 2024). Recent studies have found that exposure to gun violence has a profound impact on surviving communities, families, and schools, and has particular impacts on children (Holloway et al., 2023; Leibbrand et al., 2020; Mitchell et al., 2019). The long-term consequences associated with these exposures are substantial, including poor mental and physical health, recidivism for injury and crime, and a threatened sense of safety and well-being (Rajan, 2024).

Over the past several years, firearm violence in K–12 schools has increased. The *Washington Post* reported that nearly 400,000 students have been exposed to gun violence (specifically in K–12 schools) since the Columbine mass shooting that took place in Littleton, Colorado, in 1999 (Cox et al., 2025). Notable upticks in school-based firearm violence have been documented since 2015. In this context, K–12 schools across the United States have begun implementing numerous safety and security policies and practices in an effort to secure their buildings and prepare their communities for the possibility of gunfire on school grounds. These security measures include metal detectors, armed guards, and zero-tolerance policies, and school active shooter drills have become one of the most commonly implemented safety practices.

These policies and practices have significantly changed daily school experience over a relatively short time frame (Rajan et al., 2022; Turanovic et al., 2022). In 1999, before Columbine, fewer than 20% of schools had security cameras; now more than 80% do. Similarly, as of 2019, 98% of K–12 schools were conducting lockdown drills[7]; far fewer had implemented such procedures prior to the Sandy Hook school shooting of 2012 (National Center on Safe Supportive Learning Environments, 2022). As described in detail in this report, evidence related to the effects of these widespread practices is limited, and their implementation therefore warrants careful study and guidance.

SCHOOL SAFETY IN THE 21ST CENTURY

The Safe School Study (National Institute of Education, 1978) was the first comprehensive national assessment of school safety. It demonstrated that students' increased exposure to violent behavior and criminal activity in the communities where they lived was associated with aggression, misbehavior, victimization, and disorder within their schools, as well as declines in academic progress and

---

[7] *Lockdown* refers to a protocol that is used when there is a credible threat inside or near a school and typically includes procedures such as locking all doors of a school, turning off lights, covering windows or moving out of sight of windows, and remaining silent until an all-clear signal is given.

success. This landmark study highlighted the intrinsic relationship between communities and schools and recommended further investigation to deepen and expand understanding of these relationships and how they affect safe and healthy learning for students (Gottfredson, 2001; Mayer & Furlong, 2010; Peguero & Bondy, 2021). In the wake of the Safe Schools Study, many social science studies have explored how to establish barriers or safeguards to attenuate the corrosive impact of community violence on school safety.

Shortly after the Safe School Study was issued, however, the crack-cocaine epidemic of the mid-1980s ushered in a rapid and unprecedented increase in rates of urban crime and violence across the nation, with firearm-related homicides more than doubling from 1985 to 1990 (Astor & Benbenishty, 2018; Cornell, 2017; Gottfredson, 2001). In response, Congress enacted the Gun-Free School Zones Act (1990), prohibiting the possession or discharge of a firearm in a public school zone; this bill also declared it to be unlawful for an individual to discharge or attempt to discharge a firearm in a public-school zone—defined as a distance of less than 1,000 feet from the property of a public school (Astor & Benbenishty, 2018; Cornell, 2017; Gottfredson, 2001). However, the Supreme Court declared this law to be unconstitutional in *United States v. Lopez,* and its policies were never enacted.

In 1993, the Gun-Free Schools Act conditioned continued access to federal funding under the Elementary and Secondary Education Act (1965) on the willingness of public schools to expel for at least a year any student bringing a gun, knife, or other weapon to school. The act also required schools to report such incidents to the local criminal or juvenile legal system. The act included funding for schools to buy security equipment and train security personnel (Astor & Benbenishty, 2018; Cornell, 2017; Gottfredson, 2001). Recent research has indicated that an unintended consequence of the "zero-tolerance" safety policies included in the Gun Free Schools Act was the so called "hardening" of conceptual and physical barriers between communities and schools (Cornell et al., 2020; Morris, 2016; Noguera & Syeed, 2020; Skiba & Peterson, 2000).

A number of other school safety policies and approaches have also deepened and strengthened barriers between communities and schools. In accordance with the notion of "target hardening" (making a building more secure so that it is more difficult to attack), schools have increased their use of multiple perimeters of fencing, conducted "identification checks" for entry; deployed metal detectors and security cameras; controlled access to school buildings and yards; and used biometric scanners, bullet-resistant glass, fortified school entrances, and increased law enforcement presence to oversee entry to the school (Ebsary, 2018; Kupchik, 2010, 2016; Tanner-Smith et al., 2018). Additionally, research suggests that there has been a significant decrease in family engagement with schools because of reductions in school-related extracurricular activities that often welcomed and included community partners, especially within under-resourced and underserved communities and schools (Bradshaw et al., 2021; Kupchik, 2010, 2016; Noguera & Syeed, 2020). Some research indicates further that families and community partners have encountered increased complexities, barriers, and restrictions inhibiting engagement and communication with school faculty, administration, and personnel (Astor & Benbenishty, 2018; Morris, 2016; Rios, 2011, 2020).

School safety encompasses more than just security policies or the implementation of measures designed to "harden" campuses against external threats. While such strategies are designed to prevent violent incidents, they often overlook a critical dimension of safety: students' psychological well-being (Cornell et al., 2020; Nickerson et al., 2021). Research on school safety underscores the importance of fostering psychological safety as an additional area of harm prevention. This broader perspective widens the focus of school safety to include cultivating positive school climates and implementing multitiered systems of support that encourage prosocial behavior, emotional development, and a sense of belonging (Cornell et al., 2020). These approaches align with growing consensus that safe schools are not merely those free from violence—but also those that nurture connection, respect, and structure.

By contrast, punitive measures such as zero-tolerance policies and aggressive security protocols have shown limited effectiveness and, in some cases, may contribute to negative academic and behavioral outcomes (Cornell et al., 2020). Yet, despite this evolving understanding, definitions of what it means for a school to be "safe" still vary widely among educators, researchers, policymakers, and the public. Bridging these perspectives highlights the need for a balanced approach that integrates physical and psychological safety, grounded in the specific context and climate of each school community.

21st-Century School Shooting Events

A series of school shooting events at the turn of the 21st century is widely understood to have shaped the social and cultural understanding of school violence in the United States as well as the policies or practices that it evoked. These events also highlight some of the contextual variations that have made it difficult to address and prevent violence at schools.

The shooting at Columbine High School occurred on April 20, 1999. At the time, it was the deadliest mass shooting at a K–12 school in U.S. history. This tragic event remains one of the most infamous school shootings in the United States and is often mentioned when a new school shooting occurs. Although school shootings did not start at Columbine, some observers contend that this tragic event signified the emergence of a distinctive era of mass shootings (King & Bracy, 2019; Muschert et al., 2013; Schildkraut & Elsass, 2016). Associated with this belief is the frequent reference to the *Columbine Effect*, the idea that school shootings have changed, socially and culturally, how U.S. society thinks about school violence, shootings, and security (King & Bracy, 2019; Muschert et al., 2013). The term first appeared as the title of a December 6, 1999, article in *Time* magazine in which the author discussed the post-Columbine movement toward tightened security measures in schools (King & Bracy, 2019; Muschert et al., 2013). After the Columbine shooting, the now-common term *active shooter*, once used mainly by law enforcement, became mainstream in the nation's school safety discourse (Fortin, 2022; Martaindale & Blair, 2019; Muschert et al., 2013).

In 2002, the Advanced Law Enforcement Rapid Response Training (ALERRT) Center at Texas State University was established through a partnership among the San Marcos Police Department, the Hays County Sherriff's Office, and Texas State University. The ALERRT program was created in response to the need for new tactics to respond to active shooter events and uses a "Special Weapons and Tactics" (SWAT) approach focused on conducting active shooter training for professionals and agencies with responsibility for responding to these incidents. The purpose of this training is to prepare first responders to isolate, distract, and neutralize an active shooter; to improve coordination and integration of law enforcement, fire, telecommunications, and emergency medical services; and to educate and certify local and state law enforcement officers in teaching strategies for surviving active shooter events. In 2003, ALERRT received federal funding and began to train officers across the country. Since that time, it has trained more than 1,500,000 law enforcement officers from more than 9,000 law enforcement agencies across the nation. Officers in approximately half of U.S. law enforcement agencies have received the training (Blair et al., 2013; Doss & Shepherd, 2015; Martaindale & Blair, 2019).

In 2002, the U.S. Secret Service and the U.S. Department of Education released a report titled *The Final Report and Findings of the Safe School Initiative: Implications for the Prevention of School Attacks in the United States.* This report was the culmination of the 1999 Safe School Initiative, a study undertaken through a partnership between the Secret Service and the Department of Education following the Columbine event that examined the thinking, planning, and other preattack behaviors of individuals who carried out school shootings. The 2009 report describes the prevalence of school violence in American schools, defines "targeted" school violence, describes some common—but not predictive—characteristics observed among perpetrators or school violence, and lays a foundation for systematic "threat assessment" and "targeted" school violence prevention. As a result of this report, many schools and districts have incorporated threat assessments into their school safety planning (Borum et al., 2010; Vossekuil et al., 2002).

Following the 2006 Platte Canyon shooting in Bailey, Colorado, in which seven female students were taken hostage and one was killed, the parents of the slain student created the "I Love U Guys" Foundation. The foundation's Standard Response Protocol was introduced to districts, departments, and agencies in 2009 (The "I Love U Guys" Foundation, 2022; see Box 1-2). Since then, thousands of U.S. schools, districts, departments, agencies, and organizations have adopted this protocol, and some states have adapted it for their respective law enforcement agencies (see Box 1-2 for an overview).

BOX 1-2
Key Components of the I Love U Guys Standard Response Protocol

The "I Love U Guys" Standard Response Protocol has three overarching goals: (1) to provide a simple, easy-to-remember framework that can be used across a range of potential crisis events and practiced as part of school emergency preparedness activities including school active shooter drills; (2) to enhance coordination between schools, students, staff, parents, and first responders; and (3) to improve overall safety and reduce response times during emergencies. Five standard responses in the Standard Response Protocol can be performed by participants—including students, staff, teachers, and first responders—to respond to various emergencies.[a] Which actions are used depends on the circumstances or nature of the situation:

- The first action is **hold** in location, such as "in your room or area"; this action is used to clear a specific area and hallways in order to manage a situation.

Staff close and lock the door and continue with regular activities.

- Second is **secure,** which means "get inside, lock outside doors"; it is used to safeguard students and staff within the building. Once students and staff are inside and doors are locked, regular activities proceed as usual. This is used for threats that can be mitigated by bringing everyone inside.

- Third is **lockdown,** which indicates "locks, lights, and out of sight"; it is used to secure individual rooms and keep students quiet and in place. Students and staff maintain silence and do not open doors. A lockdown is called when there is an active threat—such as an active shooter—inside or very close to the building that requires immediate protective action.

- Fourth is **evacuate,** used to move students and staff from one location to a different location in or out of the building.

- Fifth is **shelter**, which is used for hazards such as tornados, earthquakes, or hazardous materials spills. When the shelter directive is given, the hazard and the appropriate safety strategy are named (e.g., "Shelter! Earthquake. Drop, cover and hold.").

For each of the standard responses, there are specific student and staff actions. The Standard Response Protocol emphasizes shared vocabulary and clear communication to reduce confusion and includes plans for notifying parents. Training and drills are emphasized to reinforce familiarity with the protocol and may involve law enforcement and other first responders. The protocol is designed to integrate with broader emergency response systems and can be adapted to meet the specific needs of a school or district, allowing for local adjustments while maintaining a consistent core structure.

> ^a The "I Love U Guys" Foundation also has a curriculum on Standard Reunification Method, which outlines a process for school staff to reunite students with their parents/caregivers after each of these standard response actions and provides guidance to school staff for practicing reunification exercises with school and district personnel, emergency responders, and community partners.
>
> SOURCE: Committee generated, based on "I Love U Guys" Foundation (2022).

On December 14, 2012, the deadliest school shooting at an elementary school in U.S. history occurred at Sandy Hook Elementary School. As a result of this event, elementary schools in school districts across the United States reviewed safety protocols, added school resource officers to their staffs, and instituted additional hardening measures. This shooting prompted renewed debate about ensuring school safety and spurred eventual congressional action. The federal Safe Communities, Safe Schools Act (2013) amended the National Instant Criminal Background Check System (NICS) Improvement Amendments Act (2007), the Brady Handgun Violence Prevention Act (1993), the Omnibus Crime Control and Safe Streets Act (1968), and various provisions of the federal criminal code. The amendments required background checks for all firearm sales, prohibited straw purchases of firearms, and expanded the school safety grant program. In 2013, the Federal Bureau of Investigation (FBI) certified the ALERRT program and officially designated it as the national standard for active shooter training (Flannery et al., 2021; Malloy, 2015; Martaindale & Blair, 2019; Rygg, 2015).

On February 14, 2018, a shooting at Marjory Stoneman Douglas High School in Parkland, Florida, resulted in 17 deaths—the deadliest school shooting at a high school to date. Following this shooting, the federal Student, Teachers, and Officers Preventing (STOP) School Violence Program was signed into law on March 23, 2018, as part of the Consolidated Appropriations Act (2018), increasing funding for metal detectors, security training, and similar safety and security measures. STOP's purpose is to give students and teachers the tools they need to recognize, respond quickly to, and prevent school shootings and other acts of violence (Flannery et al., 2021; Schildkraut & Nickerson, 2022).

On May 24, 2022, a shooting at Robb Elementary School in Uvalde, Texas, resulted in the deaths of 19 students and two teachers. Some commentators suggested that language barriers and proximity to the U.S.–Mexico border may have led to less timely responses to the shooting, as well as miscommunication, confusion, and delays in getting critical information to families during and after the shooting (U.S. Department of Justice [DOJ], 2024). On May 18, 2023, Texas State Bill HB3 enacted measures to enhance public school safety, including the developing, implementing, and funding public school safety and security requirements and providing safety-related resources. Additionally, a federal action report by DOJ in January 2024 recommended initiatives to bolster school safety, including enhanced training for law enforcement and school staff; upgraded security infrastructure for school doors and locks; mental health screenings for victims; and better communication among law enforcement, school officials, and the community (DOJ, 2024; Lopez, 2024).

DEFINITIONS AND TYPOLOGY

Lack of consensus on the definition of an *active shooter drill*, its components, and its implementation has resulted in wide variation in school practices. This lack of uniformity not only creates challenges in understanding how specific practices are linked to outcomes for students and staff but also creates a patchwork approach to school safety in the United States. This section describes the key concepts and terminology related to school active shooter drills and provides key definitions that are used throughout this report.

Pertinent Definitions

Box 1-3 defines terms used throughout this report. Less frequently used terms not defined in this box are defined as necessary in the chapters where they appear.

**BOX 1-3
Key Terminology**

School active shooter drill
A procedure in which a school practices an emergency protocol designed to protect students and school staff against assault by an armed assailant with a firearm. This term is often used to refer to a broad spectrum of practices used in schools, including but not limited to, lockdown drills, options-based drills, and full-scale simulation exercises.

Active shooter simulation
Exercises that mimic active shooter events and can include (but are not limited to) the following components:

- The activation of emergency alarms.
- The presence of an individual pretending to be an active shooter or law enforcement officer, or both, inside a school.
- The firing of a gun with blanks.
- Recordings of the sound of a gun being fired.
- Simulated injury or violence.
- An attempt by an intruder to breach classroom doors inside a school.
- The expectation that individuals inside the school will role play fighting an intruder.

Elementary school
"A non-profit institutional day or residential school, including a public elementary charter school, that provides elementary education, as determined under state law" (Elementary

---

and Secondary Education Act of 1965 [20 U.S.C. § 7801(19)]); typically includes grades K–5. As some elementary school settings may also include pre-K classrooms, the committee includes pre-K populations where relevant.

Lockdown
A protocol used when there is a credible threat inside or near a school; typically includes procedures such as locking all doors of a school, turning off lights, covering windows or moving out of sight of windows, and remaining silent until an all-clear signal is given.

Mental, emotional, and behavioral health
The interconnected aspects of a child's psychological well-being, emotional regulation, and social functioning; encompasses their ability to manage emotions, form relationships, and engage in adaptive behaviors that support healthy development and lifelong well-being.

Mental health services provider
A state-licensed or state-certified school counselor, school psychologist, or school social worker, or a mental health professional qualified under state law to provide mental health services to children and adolescents.

Options-based practices
Practices that provide students and school staff with a range of strategies that can be used in the event of a threat (e.g., locking/barricading doors or evacuating the school building) and are intended to allow participants to consider the nature of the threat as well as contextual factors, such as their immediate physical setting and the broader school environment, to determine the appropriate response.

Secondary school
"A nonprofit institutional day or residential school, including a public secondary charter school, that provides secondary education, as determined under State law, except that the

term does not include any education beyond grade 12" and typically includes both middle and high school (Elementary and Secondary Education Act of 1965 [20 U.S.C. § 7801(45)]).

Secured-perimeter lockout
A protocol in response to a safety threat outside of the school or campus. It involves moving all students and staff are moved from outside to inside the school building and then locking the outside doors of a school building. Entry to and exit from the school are prohibited, but instruction can continue.

School resource officer
A law enforcement officer with sworn authority who has specific training in school-based law enforcement and crisis response and who is assigned by a law enforcement agency to work collaboratively with one or more schools using community-oriented policing concepts (National Association of School Resource Officers, n.d.).

Standard response practices
Individual, predefined actions or procedures designed to guide students and staff in responding to different types of emergency situations, including school active shooter events. For each response practice, staff and students are taught specific steps to take to complete the response. The intent is to teach the specific actions that can be used to respond to most emergencies—rather than emphasizing the specific dangers—and emphasize procedural repetition, with the aim of helping students and staff respond quickly and efficiently in an emergency.

Standard Response Protocol
An action-based safety framework developed by the "I Love U Guys" Foundation that integrates multiple standard response practices into a structured and unified system. The protocol includes five standard response practices that can

> be used for schools to respond to emergencies (Hold, Secure, Lockdown, Evacuate, Shelter). It provides a common language and set of directives that guide students, staff, and first responders in effectively managing threats and crises. It emphasizes clear, consistent communication and coordinated actions to enhance safety and emergency preparedness.
>
> **Walkthrough**
> An activity designed to familiarize students, school staff, and first responders with their roles and responsibilities in the event of an emergency. These exercises are conducted at a pace that allows participants to go through emergency procedures step by step with opportunities to ask questions, clarify roles, and have discussion.

What Are Active Shooter Events?

U.S. federal agencies define an *active shooter* as "an individual actively engaged in killing or attempting to kill people in a confined and populated area" with a firearm (Federal Emergency Management Agency, 2020). The FBI (n.d.) expands this definition to include more than one individual in an incident and omits the word "confined" because the term excludes incidents that occur outside buildings. Active shooter events can take place in many different locations, including schools, movie theaters, and workplaces. U.S. federal agencies also limit the definition of active shooter events to those that involve deadly force (i.e., the attack is in progress and involves deadly force), unrestricted access (i.e., the attacker[s] has unrestricted access to multiple victims), immediate action (i.e., direct and immediate law enforcement action is necessary and likely to save lives), and dynamic pace (situation is exigent, dynamic, and rapidly evolving). The FBI and Department of Homeland Security stress that these additional factors are needed to define active shooter events because such events warrant a coordinated response by multiagency law enforcement and other first responders to save lives. The FBI (n.d.) has established the ALERRT framework as the standard law enforcement response to active shooter events in schools (see also Federal Emergency Management Agency, 2020). It is also important to define the official response in a way that includes distinct federal, state, and local agencies.

A variety of terminology has been used to refer to active shooter events, including *active shooter attack, armed assailant incident, active attack, mass casualty attack*, and the like. In this report, the term *active shooter event* is used consistently to refer to these incidents (Blair et al., 2013; Doss & Shepherd, 2015; Martaindale & Blair, 2019).

The definition of an active shooter event in a school setting is closely tied to the terminology used for *active shooter drills*, as the way drills are framed may shape perceptions, policies, and response strategies for real incidents. Although individual states, cities, counties, districts, and localities may establish distinct definitional parameters for what constitutes an active shooter event at school, this report focuses on cases involving a firearm. In addition, the definitions used by some states, cities, counties, districts, and localities may include events outside of school; however, this report focuses specifically on active shooter events occurring within the physical parameters of a school campus (Blair et al., 2013; Doss & Shepherd, 2015; Martaindale & Blair, 2019).

What Are School Active Shooter Drills?

Before discussing the specific features of school active shooter drills, it is worth noting that some experts consider these drills to fall within a broader general category of school emergency drills. All-purpose school emergency drills have been conducted over many years to prepare students and faculty members for fires and extreme weather events where geographically appropriate (Blair et al., 2013; Cornell et al., 2020; Schildkraut & Nickerson, 2022; U.S. Department of Education [ED], 2013). The committee decided, however, that school active shooter drills need to be analyzed on their own terms rather than as illustrative of school emergency drills precisely because school active shooter events are dynamically different from all other emergency threats. Specifically, a school active shooter drill involves children of all ages and is likely to have mental, emotional, and behavioral health effects that are distinctly different from those associated with other safety drills.

In reviewing the types of active shooter drills and programs commonly used in schools, the committee identified three primary categories of practices that are associated with school active shooter drills: discussion-based practices, standard response practices, and options-based practices. These practices, used to prepare students and staff for potential threats, are conceptually distinct with different learning goals and objectives; however, they may share common activities that are implemented differently depending on the approach. This section of the report describes each category and discusses practice terminology shared across categories and exercises or activities designed to prepare for complex emergency responses to active shooter events. The committee notes that none of these practices is applied across schools universally (Blair et al., 2013; National Association of School Psychologists [NASP] et al., 2021; Rygg, 2015; Schildkraut & Nickerson, 2022).

Discussion-Based Practices

Discussion-based practices introduce students to the purpose and procedures of school active shooter drills; familiarize them with the role of emergency responders; and orient them to basic safety protocols, such as identifying the nearest exits and entry points. These practices do not require students to physically practice emergency actions. Instead, they focus on foundational knowledge through activities such as staff-led discussions, social stories or storybook readings, coloring books, and student–teacher tabletop exercises that use games or child-friendly activities to teach emergency procedures.

Walkthroughs are a discussion-based practice that focus on familiarizing students and staff with roles and responsibilities in a school active shooter drill. School leaders, staff, and—in some cases—students conduct a joint walkthrough to understand each other's roles. First responders may sometimes also be included. Walkthroughs are meant to be a thoughtful, slow-motion drill that allows for questions and discussion along the way (Blair et al., 2013; NASP et al., 2021; Rygg, 2015).

Standard Response Practices

Standard response practices are designed to provide structured, predefined actions that students and staff can take for different emergency situations, including school active shooter events, rather than relying on situational decision-making. For each response practice, staff and students are taught specific steps for completing the response. The intent is to emphasize the specific actions required during an emergency—rather than the specific nature of the threat—and to develop mastery of skills through repeated exposure, with the aim of helping students and staff respond quickly and efficiently in an emergency.

Lockdowns and secured-perimeter lockouts are two examples of practices that can be taught as standard response practices. The actions practiced in a lockdown during a standard response drill typically involve locking doors to secure the space, turning off lights, moving students out of sight, and requiring students to remain quiet. While performing these steps, students and staff are nonresponsive to anyone at the door, and ignore all bells and alarms unless instructed otherwise. At the end of the lockdown, an all-clear signal may be given, followed by an announcement over the school public address system.

Secured-perimeter lockouts, often simply referred to as lockouts (the Secure action in the I Love U Guys Standard Response Protocol), involve bringing all students and staff inside the school before locking exterior doors and windows. Once students and staff are inside, entry to and exit from the school building are prohibited. Whereas in a lockdown, an active shooter is believed to be inside the school building, in a secured-perimeter lockout, the imminent threat of danger is outside the school building (e.g., an unauthorized person on school grounds, a potential threat in the neighborhood such as a robbery with a suspect at large; Blair et al., 2013; Schildkraut & Nickerson, 2022; Schildkraut et al., 2020).

As described above, the "I Love U Guys" Foundation's Standard Response Protocol (see Box 1-2) includes standard response practices. This program has been adopted widely in school settings across the United States and adapted by state school safety centers and individual schools to tailor protocols to meet specific state requirements.[8]

Options-Based Practices

Options-based practices emphasize in-the-moment action and adaptive decision-making in situations where standard response strategies may not be feasible, such as in response to an immediate threat (e.g., an active shooter enters a classroom or hallway). These practices emphasize situational awareness and response strategies based on the type of threat and available options (Donovan, 2023; Miotto & Cogan, 2023; Schonfeld et al., 2020; Simonetti, 2020). Box 1-4 discusses examples of some common options-based practices.

BOX 1-4
Overview of Options-Based Practices

A range of options-based protocols has been developed to offer strategies for responding to immediate active shooter threats within schools. These protocols typically promote a framework in which staff and students are trained to assess their surroundings and choose among different protective actions. Common elements include the ability to evacuate when possible, secure classrooms or hide from danger when necessary, and disrupt or defend against an assailant as a last resort (Blair et al., 2013; Coleman, 2018, 2020; Martaindale & Blair, 2019; O'Regan, 2019).

---

[8] See, e.g., https://txssc.txstate.edu/tools/srp-toolkit.

Each program uses distinct language and instructional methods, and varies in its degree of adaptation for K–12 audiences:

- **ALICE** stands for Alert (be aware of danger); Lockdown (barricade the room and prepare to evacuate or counter if needed); Inform (communicate about the shooter); Counter (create noise, distraction, movement, and distance to reduce shooter's ability to cause harm); and Evacuate (when safe to do so). In early grades, such as preschool and kindergarten, the focus is on basic skills like listening to adults and recognizing alarm sounds, sometimes taught through games and songs. For early elementary students, the emphasis shifts to understanding different types of emergencies and practicing following adult instructions to stay safe in a variety of situations and to evacuate safely. Late elementary students are introduced to response options such as identifying exits and creating basic barriers. Middle school students learn more involved techniques, including more structured barricading and distraction methods. In high school, students are taught how to assess evacuation options in more complex scenarios—such as using windows—and how to create distractions to protect themselves, while reinforcing that direct confrontation is not expected or encouraged (Navigate360, 2023).

- **Avoid-Deny-Defend**, developed by the Advanced Law Enforcement Rapid Response Training (ALERRT Center), is a civilian-oriented model focused on escaping the area, hiding, creating barriers, and defending oneself only when necessary. To address the unique needs of school settings, ALERRT collaborated with Safe and Sound Schools to create the *Staying Safe: Student Safety Preparedness Curriculum*, which includes tailored strategies for younger and older students. For pre-K and

INTRODUCTION

> elementary grades, the framework uses terms such as "Getting Out," "Keeping Out," and "Hiding Out." For middle and high school students, the language shifts to "Deny, Defend, and Disrupt," with "Disrupt" offering a broad range of actions—such as shouting or creating distractions—rather than physical resistance.
>
> - The **H.E.R.O.** program is designed specifically for schools and uses developmentally varied instructions and approaches. H.E.R.O. stands for Hide; Escape; Run; and Overcome (for preschoolers, O = Obey). Younger students, including preschoolers, are taught to follow adult direction through use of stories and classroom lessons before physical enactment of drill procedures are practiced. Older students receive instruction on independent decision-making through discussions and classroom activities before practicing drill procedures (Safe Kids Inc., n.d.).

Common Activities Across Practice Categories

In preparing this report, the committee found many inconsistencies in how terms are used, the goals of different drills, and the action steps taken in the drills. While defining the goals of each practice brings some clarity, it is important to note that some terms used to describe actions that may be part of school active shooter drills are shared across categories of drill practices. They may, however, be used in varied ways depending on the purpose, context, or approach of the drill. For example, in the context of a standard response practice, the term *lockdown* refers to a specific, predefined set of actions that students and staff are expected to follow (i.e., locking doors, turning off lights, remaining quiet, and moving out of sight). The purpose of these drills is to reinforce consistent, repeatable responses. In contrast, in options-based drills, a lockdown is one possible strategy that can be used to respond to the specific circumstances of an emergency. Because options-based practices emphasize in-the-moment decision-making, the specific actions taken during a lockdown may vary depending on the nature of the threat and the safest available option. The specific actions may also go beyond those typically practiced in a standard response practice (e.g., barricading entry and exit points).

Activities or Exercises Designed to Prepare for Complex Emergency Responses to School-Based Active Shooter Events

Some school safety activities and exercises are designed to bring together school leaders, staff, law enforcement, first responders, members of the school safety team, and other community partners to review or rehearse emergency response protocols. These practices involve collaborative planning for complex emergency scenarios and provide an opportunity to clarify roles, procedures, and coordination strategies among participants.

Tabletop activities can be guided discussions related to emergency management techniques to increase preparedness. They are designed to occur in a safe and controlled environment where school safety partners focus on problem-solving rather than performing the specific actions they might use in an emergency. Their purpose differs from discussion-based practices mentioned earlier (where a school staff member orients students to an emergency response protocol). In tabletop activities, a facilitator guides participants—law enforcement personnel, members of the school crisis team, school leaders, faculty, staff, and other partners—in discussing a hypothetical active shooter event at school. The participants discuss such an event verbally and imagine what they would do to respond. The facilitator introduces complicating variables, inviting the group to think critically about their plans as they become more comfortable with critical and adaptive thinking and responsive behaviors. Tabletop exercises are designed to invite discussion and interactive engagement focused on understanding and preparing for a school-based active shooter event (Gerlinger & Schleifer, 2021; NASP et al., 2021).

Full-scale active shooter simulations or exercises are often used as part of training for emergency responders and law enforcement personnel; they may also involve members of the school safety team, school leaders, school staff, and other members of the community who are involved in implementing a response to an imminent threat. The purposes of a full-scale active shooter simulation or exercise are to equip first responders and school leaders with the skills and confidence needed to lead a response to school active shooter event, and to test their protocols and identify potential weaknesses (Blair et al., 2013; Martaindale & Blair, 2019; NASP et al., 2021; Rygg, 2015). Full-scale simulations or exercises vary considerably. At one end of the spectrum, they are unannounced and may incorporate such components as real or simulated gunshot sounds, guns with blank ammunition, pellet guns, fake text messages, theatrical makeup with fake blood, informed actor volunteers, and individuals pretending to be an active shooter roaming the halls and attempting to open classroom doors; such simulations have sometimes been carried out with students (Schonfeld et al., 2020). At the other end of the spectrum, simulations or exercises are conducted without student involvement during nonschool hours, and the school and broader community are informed well in advance when emergency responders and law enforcement will be participating (Blair et al., 2013; Martaindale & Blair, 2020; NASP et al., 2021; Rygg, 2015).

KEY CONCEPTS FROM CHILD AND ADOLESCENT DEVELOPMENT

The mental, emotional, and behavioral health of students and staff are key components of well-being, success, and safety within the school setting. Paying careful attention and responding to potential adverse outcomes associated with school safety and security practices is critical, as they can impact a student's ability to learn and the educator's ability to teach effectively and support healthy development (Harding et al., 2019; Lee & Schute, 2010; McLean et al., 2018; NASEM, 2019a; Ruzek et al., 2016). Healthy development in these core areas is generally associated with greater success and general health both early and later in life. In contrast, decrements to broad mental, emotional, and behavioral well-being are associated with the development of disorders (e.g., anxiety, depression, externalizing aggression, violence, antisocial behavior), as well as worsened performance and long-term health outcome (NASEM, 2019a,b; National Research Council [NRC] & Institute of Medicine [IOM], 2009).

In its statement of task, the committee was asked to summarize the current state of the evidence on the effects of school active shooter drills and other security measures on mental, emotional, and behavioral health and well-being in the context of what we have learned, more broadly, about child and adolescent development over the last several decades. To help contextualize the outcomes examined in this report, this section provides a brief overview of what is meant by "mental, emotional, and behavioral health and well-being." Understanding this concept is essential to interpreting the committee's findings and assessing the potential impacts of school safety and security practices on students and staff. This section also summarizes key insights from child and adolescent development literature that can inform the implementation of developmentally appropriate practices.

The Institute of Medicine (now the Health and Medicine Division) released its first report on mental, emotional, and behavioral well-being in 1994, with a specific focus on risks associated with "mental disorders" (IOM, 1994). Subsequent reports by the National Academies in 2009 and 2019 broadened this focus, shifting from a disorder-specific lens to a more comprehensive view of developmental health and well-being across the lifespan (NASEM, 2019a; NRC & IOM, 2009). *Fostering Healthy Mental, Emotional, and Behavioral Development in Children and Youth* (NASEM, 2019a), conceptualizes *well-being* as including healthy development in the face of risk and protective factors that contribute to optimal cognitive development, psychological and behavioral health, and social and emotional competence. *Cognitive development* refers to the expected trajectories of executive functioning abilities, such as impulse control and reasoning, given the individual's age, which are associated broadly with outcomes such as academic performance and general success. *Psychological and behavioral health* refers to both the ability to understand and regulate internal states (e.g., emotion regulation) and engage in productive and appropriate ways with the outside world. Finally, *social and emotional competence* refer to the individual's ability to form relationships and engage with other individuals and groups and to understand the perspectives of others, which is key to forming healthy relationships (NASEM, 2019a).

In the present report, the committee discusses and operationalizes several indicators of mental, emotional, and behavioral health and well-being. These include negative indicators such as symptoms of anxiety, depression, posttraumatic stress disorder, aggression, and violence, as well as positive indicators such as feelings of safety and security, creativity, curiosity, and determination. Chapters 3 and 4 include responses to school safety and security practices, including perceptions of fear in relation to school active shooter drills or other school security measures and perceptions of the school and wider environment, such as feelings of school connectedness. While the committee's primary focus is on mental, emotional, and behavioral health and well-being, the committee also examines students' feelings of preparedness to respond to an emergency recognizing that these perceptions are potentially tied to students' overall well-being.

When determining which practices to incorporate and when to schedule active shooter drills, the National Association of School Psychologists, National Association of School Resource Officers, and Safe and Sound Schools recommend that schools take into account students' developmental and ability levels, as well as the overall mental and emotional well-being of the school community (NASP et al., 2021). It is important to recognize, however, that K–12[9] schools serve children and adolescents with a broad range of developmental levels, strengths, and needs. Child development

---

[9] As noted earlier in this chapter, some elementary school campuses may have pre-K classrooms with children under the age of 5. The committee notes their developmental needs given the potential for their inclusion in school active shooter.

scholars emphasize the importance of age-appropriate school safety strategies.

Young children (pre-K–Grade 2) require clear, simple instructions, visual cues, and close adult supervision. From a developmental perspective, these young children are less likely than older children to anticipate consequences and tend to rely heavily on adults for guidance and emotional regulation (Berk, 2022; Dickson & Vargo, 2017; Kingston et al., 2018; Sprague & Walker, 2021). Older elementary school students (Grades 3–5) have the cognitive ability to begin to understand the notion of cause and effect and to engage in decision-making (Berk, 2022; Kingston et al., 2018; Sprague & Walker, 2021). In other words, school safety education and training can begin to focus on problem-solving and on recognizing unsafe situations. Instead of having an emotional vocabulary to express how they feel, both younger and older elementary school children may instead express feeling upset through behaviors such as tantrums, fights, and regressed skills such as toileting. Middle and high school students (Grades 6–12) are becoming more independent, as well as experiencing more peer pressure, risk-taking behaviors, and emotional challenges (Berk, 2022; Kingston et al., 2018; Sprague & Walker, 2021). In turn, school safety can focus on building resilience among these older students, fostering critical thinking, and addressing mental health more directly.

It is important, therefore, to tailor school active shooter drills to the developmental levels and diverse learning needs and preferences of all students and teachers on campus when implementing school active shooter drills. Chapter 5 provides a more in-depth discussion of contextual and population considerations entailed in planning school active shooter drills, including those associated with students with functional and access needs, multilingual learners, students being served by special education supports, and students with past histories of trauma and loss. The needs of all individuals on a school campus can be incorporated in school active shooter drills in ways that minimize potential negative effects to mental, emotional, and behavioral health and well-being. Additionally, the broader

INTRODUCTION 51

environment and preventive resources on a school campus can be instrumental in supporting safety preparedness (see Chapter 6).

These developmental principles provide a foundation for understanding how students may experience and respond to school active shooter drills and other school safety practices. The committee's conceptual framework, described in the next section, builds on this foundation and situates school active shooter drills within an ecological systems model.

CONCEPTUAL FRAMEWORK FOR THIS REPORT

The committee takes a public health perspective that considers individual, family, school, community, and broader policy factors in discussing how school active shooter drills can be implemented in ways that minimize adverse mental, emotional, and behavioral health effects. Ecological theories of child development, which position children within families, families within schools, schools within communities, communities within municipalities, and beyond, provide an essential framework for understanding proximal and distal influences on child development and for achieving emergency preparedness that considers mental, emotional, and behavioral health and well-being. Accordingly, this report uses an ecological framework that conceptualizes school active shooter drills in the broader contexts within which these drills are implemented (Figure 1-1).

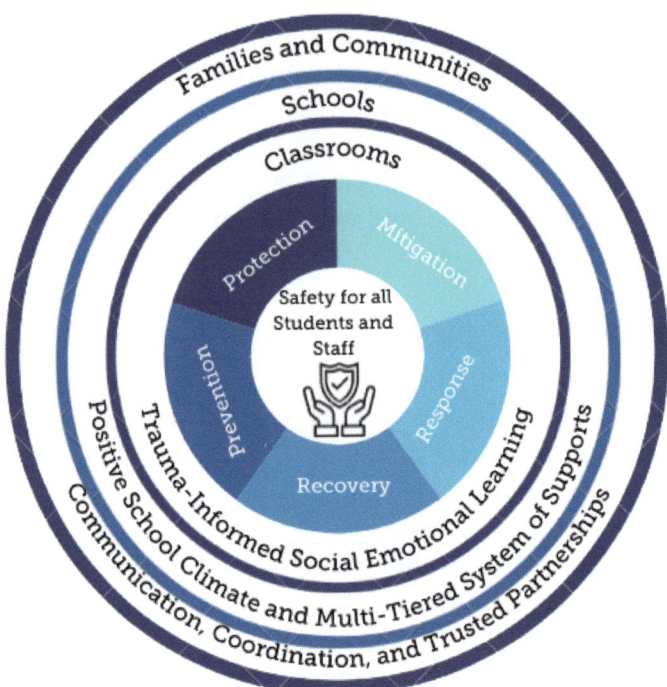

FIGURE 1-1 Conceptual framework for this report.

The committee's framework centers the safety of all students and staff; it is supported by the essential components of emergency preparedness and school safety: prevention, protection, mitigation, response, and recovery. The framework uses a comprehensive approach that aims to balance preparedness for immediate threats with ongoing strategies for preventing violence. A narrow focus on school active shooter drills alone risks overlooking opportunities for prevention. By considering the mental, emotional, and behavioral health needs of students and staff as well as the specific needs and context of a school community, schools can adopt practices that create an environment that both responds to potential threats and aims to reduce their likelihood. The committee views trauma-informed, developmentally appropriate approaches as essential to integrating school active shooter drills into a broader vision of school safety that supports mental, emotional, and behavioral well-being. When these drills are embedded within clear communication, supportive relationships, and a safe and supportive school environment, they can reinforce a sense of safety and agency rather than provoke fear or distress. In this way, preparedness becomes part of a psychologically safe environment, strengthening both emergency readiness and everyday well-being for students and staff.

As described by the Readiness and Emergency Management for Schools technical assistance center, emergency planning in schools starts with *prevention*—the efforts schools take to address safety and security as well as promote a positive school climate (ED, 2013). *Protection* can include school safety policies and trainings, including training staff on school active shooter drills. *Mitigation* efforts minimize loss of life by lessening the impact of an emergency through practicing emergency response and drills. *Response* occurs to stabilize an emergency once it happens and to reestablish a safe school environment. Finally, *recovery* restores the school environment by supporting the academic, social, mental, emotional, and physical well-being of everyone in the school community.

School classrooms provide an important context for students to learn and thrive. Ideally, students receive support from both classroom peers and teachers; healthy classrooms are embedded within schools and school systems that can boost mental, emotional, and behavioral well-being, such as self-efficacy and coping skills (Fenwick-Smith et al., 2018). Connectedness to peers and healthy relationships with other students are associated with beneficial mental, emotional, and behavioral health outcomes (Foster et al., 2017; Oldfield et al., 2016; Widnall et al., 2022). Furthermore, healthy schools exist in relationship with students' families and within wider communities. Caregivers' support is vital for development and promotes children's resilience to adverse health outcomes (Gee & Cohodes, 2023; Ungar, 2004; World Health Organization, 2004).

Ecological models of child development (see, e.g., Figure 1-1) encourage consideration of the balance of risk and protective factors that can impact children's responses to school active shooter drills.

At the individual level, children's experiences with school active shooter drills will be affected by personal characteristics such as age, cognitive and socioemotional development, physical and mental health, and history of traumatic stress. Furthermore, children's responses to school active shooter drills are shaped by relationships with peers, teachers, and families, as well as their parents' and teachers' experiences with drills. Classroom and school contexts—including overall organizational structures and systems, and relationships with peers, teachers, and administrators—play a fundamental role. As will be discussed in Chapter 2, healthy schools offer a stable, nurturing, and trustworthy setting in which to learn how to engage in safety procedures.

Children's responses to drills can also be affected by their broader social context beyond the school setting. For example, children in communities that have experienced high levels of trauma may respond differently from those who reside in safer communities. Positive school and neighborhood climates can be important sources of resilience for students and staff in relation to school active shooter drills and other school security measures.

ORGANIZATION OF THE REPORT

This report is organized in three parts:

Part I (Chapters 1 and 2) provides background and context for understanding the purpose and impact of active shooter drills and other school safety and security measures. Chapter 2 describes variations in implementation of school active shooter drills, state-level requirements for these drills, personnel who participate, and procedures leading up to and following a drill.

Part II (Chapters 3 and 4) focuses on the design and effects of school active shooter drills and other school safety and security measures on mental, emotional, and behavioral health outcomes. These chapters summarize available research on the impacts of these measures on students and staff, and also consider differential impacts that may exist based on such factors as age, race/ethnicity, home language, and disability status. Chapter 3 focuses specifically on mental, emotional, and behavioral health outcomes for students and staff attributable to active shooter drills. Chapter 4 presents a discussion of these outcomes as they relate to other school safety and security measures in K–12 settings. The committee highlights the strengths and limitations of the available evidence, areas of consensus and uncertainty, and opportunities for future research.

Part III (Chapters 5–7) focuses on the challenges of mitigating the mental, emotional, and behavioral health impacts of school active shooter drills and other school safety and security measures; it also sets forth an agenda for much-needed research. Specifically, Chapters 5 and 6 apply the findings described in Parts I and II to the design and implementation of developmentally appropriate and trauma-informed school active shooter drills and to school safety and preparedness planning more broadly. Chapter 5 reviews current research on developmental science and trauma and on the relationship between the environment and the individual; it also describes the risk and protective factors that might be considered in implementing protective measures, including active shooter drills. Chapter 6 describes the supports, programs, and expertise needed to implement, monitor, and evaluate best practices in protecting children from harmful events or exposures. It includes a discussion of components and features of active shooter drills and other school security measures that can minimize potential adverse effects on the mental, emotional, and behavioral health of students and staff. Chapter 6 also identifies best practices that can be implemented before, during, and after drills; the implications for school climate and culture; and the importance of implementation context in building resiliency and achieving effective implementation. Finally, Chapter 7 outlines a future research agenda by identifying existing research gaps, summarizing methodological considerations for future research, and describing important data needs.

REFERENCES

Astor, R. A., & Benbenishty, R. (2018). *Bullying, school violence, and climate in evolving contexts: Culture, organization, and time.* Oxford University Press. https://doi.org/10.1093/oso/780190663049.001.0001

Berk, L. E. (2022). *Development through the lifespan.* Sage Publications. https://books.google.com/books?id=pj4uzwEACAAJ

Blair, J. P., Nichols, T., Burns, D., & Curnutt, J. R. (2013). *Active shooter events and response.* CRC Press.

Borum, R., Cornell, D. G., Modzeleski, W., & Jimerson, S. R. (2010). What can be done about school shootings? A review of the evidence. *Educational Researcher, 39*(1), 27–37.

Bradshaw, C. P., Cohen, J., Espelage, D. L., & Nation, M. (2021). Addressing school safety through comprehensive school climate approaches. *School Psychology Review, 50*(2–3), 221–236. https://doi.org/10.1080/2372966X.2021.1926321

Centers for Disease Control and Prevention. (2022). *Firearm deaths grow, disparities widen.* U.S. Department of Health and Human Services. https://www.cdc.gov/vitalsigns/firearm-deaths/index.html

Coleman, S. (2018). Safe Kids Inc.: H.E.R.O. Curriculum: Grades K–8—Efficacy findings in prominent afterschool program, public school district, and private school—Pilot study report. https://static1squarespace.com/static/6570f71970ad2a50a4b8df60/t/65f1c82ba46c35510367d8af/1710344246172/Pilot+Study+White+Paper+K-8.pdf

———. (2020). Safe Kids Inc.: H.E.R.O. Curriculum: Grades 9–12—Efficacy findings in public school district and charter high school—Pilot study report. https://safekidsinc.ai/wp-content/uploads/2021/02/High-School-Pilot-Study.pdf

Cornell, D. G. (2017). *School violence: Fears versus facts.* Routledge.

Cornell, D. G., Mayer, M. J., & Sulkowski, M. L. (2020). History and future of school safety research. *School Psychology Review, 50*(2-3), 143–157. https://doi.org/10.1080/2372966X.2020.1857212

Cox, J. W., Rich, S., Trevory, L., Muyskens, J., & Ulmanu, M. (2025). *School shootings database.* https://www.washingtonpost.com/education/interactive/school-shootings-database/

Dickson, M. J., & Vargo, K. K. (2017). Training kindergarten students lockdown drill procedures using behavioral skills training. *Journal of Applied Behavior Analysis, 50*(2), 407–412. https://doi.org/10.1002/jaba.369

Donovan, D. J. (2023). Active shooter drills in schools: Are we helping or hurting our kids? *Clinical Pediatrics, 63*(4), 441–443. https://doi.org/10.1177/00099228231180707

Doss, K., & Shepherd, C. (2015). *Active shooter: Preparing for and responding to a growing threat.* Butterworth-Heinemann.

Ebsary, N. J. (2018). Biometric monitoring using facial recognition, data collection, and storage: Safety and privacy perceptions of high school students. *Journal of Computer Science & Systems Biology, 11*(6), 313–318. http://doi.org/10.4172/jcsb.1000291

Executive Office of the President. (2024). Combating emerging firearms threats and improving school-based active-shooter drills (Executive order 14127). *Federal Register 89*(191). https://www.federalregister.gov/documents/2024/10/02/2024-22938/combating-emerging-firearms-threats-and-improving-school-based-active-shooter-drills

Federal Bureau of Investigation (FBI). (n.d.). *FBI active shooter safety resources.* https://www.fbi.gov/how-we-can-help-you/active-shooter-safety-resources.

Federal Emergency Management Agency. (2020, March). Active shooter attacks: Security awareness for soft targets and crowded places [PDF]. FEMA. https://www.fema.gov/sites/default/files/2020-03/fema_faith-communities_active shooter.pdf

Fenwick-Smith, A., Dahlberg, E. E., & Thompson, S. C. (2018). Systematic review of resilience-enhancing, universal, primary school-based mental health promotion programs. *BMC Psychology, 6*(1), 30. https://doi.org/10.1186/s40359-018-0242-3

Flannery, D. J., Fox, J. A., Wallace, L., Mulvey, E., & Modzeleski, W. (2021). Guns, school shooters, and school safety: What we know and directions for change. *School Psychology Review, 50*(2–3), 237–253. https://doi.org/10.1080/2372966X.2020.1846458

Fortin, J. (2022, May 25). What does "active shooter" mean? *The New York Times.* https://www.nytimes.com/article/active-shooter-what-is-it.html

Foster, C., Horwitz, A., Thomas, A., Opperman, K., Gipson, P., Burnside, A., Stone, D., & King, C. (2017). Connectedness to family, school, peers, and community in socially vulnerable adolescents. *Children and Youth Services Review, 81*, 321-331.https://doi.org/10.1016/j.childyouth.2017.08.011

Gee, D. G., & Cohodes, E. M. (2023). Leveraging the developmental neuroscience of caregiving to promote resilience among youth exposed to adversity. *Development and Psychopathology, 35*(5), 2168–2185. https://doi.org/10.1017/s0954579423001128

Gerlinger, J., & Schleifer, C. (2021). School characteristics associated with active shooter drill implementation. *Analyses of Social Issues and Public Policy, 21*(1), 917–940. https://doi.org/10.1111/asap.12251

Gottfredson, D. C. (2001). *Schools and delinquency.* Cambridge University Press.

Harding, S., Morris, R., Gunnell, D., Ford, T., Hollingworth, W., Tilling, K. Evans, R., Bell, S., Grey, J., Brockman, R., Campbell, R., Araya, R., Murphy, S., & Kidger, J. (2019). Is teachers' mental health and wellbeing associated with students' mental health and wellbeing? *Journal of Affective Disorders, 242*, 180–187. https://doi.org/10.1016/j.jad.2018.08.080

Holloway, K., Cahill, G., Tieu, T., & Njoroge, W. (2023). Reviewing the literature on the impact of gun violence on early childhood development. *Current Psychiatry Reports*, 1– 9. https://doi.org/10.1007/s11920-023-01428-6

The "I Love U Guys" Foundation. (n.d.). *Home.* https://iloveuguys.org

———. (2022). *The Standard Response Protocol.* https://iloveuguys.org/The-Standard-Response-Protocol.html

Institute of Medicine (IOM). (1994). Reducing risks for mental disorders: Frontiers for preventive intervention research. National Academy Press.

King, S., & Bracy, N. L. (2019). School security in the post-Columbine era: Trends, consequences, and future directions. *Journal of Contemporary Criminal Justice, 35*(3), 274–295.https://doi.org/10.1177/1043986219840188

Kingston, B., Mattson, S. A., Dymnicki, A., Spier, E., Fitzgerald, M., Shipman, K., Goodrum, S., Woodward, W., Witt, J., Hill, K. G., & Elliott, D. (2018). Building schools' readiness to implement a comprehensive approach to school safety. *Clinical Child and Family Psychology Review, 21*(4), 433–449. https://doi.org/10.1007/s10567-018-0264-7

Kupchik, A. (2010). Homeroom security: School discipline in an age of fear (Vol. 6). NYU Press.

———. (2016). The real school safety problem: The long-term consequences of harsh school punishment. University of California Press.

Lee, J., & Schute, V. (2010). Personal and social-contextual factors in K–12 academic performance: An integrative perspective on student learning. *Educational Psychologist, 45*(3), 185–202. https://doi.org/10.1080/00461520.2010.493471

Leibbrand, C., Hill, H., Rowhani-Rahbar, A., & Rivara, F. (2020). Invisible wounds: Community exposure to gun homicides and adolescents' mental health and behavioral outcomes. *SSM—Population Health, 12.* https://doi.org/10.1016/j.ssmph.2020.100689

Lopez, B. (2024, January 19). Texas' new school safety law mostly addresses the Justice Department's advice. But funding fixes is still an issue. *The Texas Tribune.* https://www.texastribune.org/2024/01/19/texas-school-safety-uvalde-doj-report/

Malloy, G. D. P. (2015). *Final report of the Sandy Hook advisory commission.* Sandy Hook Advisory Commission.

Martaindale, M. H., & Blair, J. P. (2019). The evolution of active shooter response training protocols since Columbine: Lessons from the Advanced Law Enforcement Rapid Response Training Center. *Journal of Contemporary Criminal Justice, 35*(3), 342–356. https://doi.org/10.1177/1043986219840237

Mayer, M. J., & Furlong, M. J. (2010). How safe are our schools? *Educational Researcher, 39*(1), 16–26. http://www.jstor.org/stable/27764550

McLean, L., Abry, T., Taylor, M., & Connor, C. M. (2018). Associations among teachers' depressive symptoms and students' classroom instructional experiences in third grade. *Journal of School Psychology, 69*, 154–168. https://doi.org/10.1016/j.jsp.2018.05.002

Miotto, M. B., & Cogan, R. (2023). Empowered or traumatized? A call for evidence-informed armed-assailant drills in U.S. schools. *The New England Journal of Medicine, 389*(1), 6–8. https://doi.org/10.1056/NEJMp2301804

Mitchell, K., Jones, L., Turner, H., Beseler, C., Hamby, S., & Wade, R. (2019). Understanding the impact of seeing gun violence and hearing gunshots in public places: Findings from the youth firearm risk and safety study. *Journal of Interpersonal Violence, 36*, 8835–8851. https://doi.org/10.1177/0886260519853393

Morris, M. (2016). *Pushout: The criminalization of Black girls in schools*. The New Press.

Muschert, G., Henry, S., & Bracy, N. L. (Eds.). (2013). *Responding to school violence: Confronting the Columbine effect*. Lynne Rienner Publishers.

National Academies of Sciences, Engineering, and Medicine (NASEM). (2019a). *Fostering healthy mental, emotional, and behavioral development in children and youth: A national agenda*. The National Academies Press. https://doi.org/10.17226/25201

———. (2019b). *The promise of adolescence: Realizing opportunity for all youth*. The National Academies Press. https://doi.org/10.17226/25388

———. (2019c). *Vibrant and healthy kids: Aligning science, practice, and policy to advance health equity*. The National Academies Press. https://doi.org/10.17226/25466

National Association of School Psychologists (NASP), National Association of School Resource Officers (NASRO), & Safe and Sound Schools. (2021). *Best practice considerations for armed assailant drills in schools*. https://www.nasponline.org/assets/Documents/Research%20and%20Policy/Advocacy%20Resources/Armed-Assailant-Guide-Revised-SEPT-2021.pdf

National Association of School Resource Officers (NASRO). (n.d.). *Frequently asked questions*. https://www.nasro.org/faq/

National Center on Safe Supportive Learning Environments. (2022). *State report on the implementation of the Gun-Free Schools Act: U.S. states and other jurisdictions 2019–20 school year*. U.S. Department of Education. https://safesupportivelearning.ed.gov/sites/default/files/StateRtImplGFSA-2019-20-508_2022.03.07.pdf

National Institute of Education (NIE). (1978). *Violent schools-safe schools: the safe school study report to the Congress: Executive summary* (Vol. 1). https://www.ojp.gov/pdffiles1/Digitization/45988NCJRS.pdf

National Research Council (NRC). (2003). *Deadly lessons: Understanding lethal school violence*. National Academies Press. https://doi.org/10.17226/10370

National Research Council (NRC) and Institute of Medicine (IOM). (2009). *Preventing mental, emotional, and behavioral disorders among young people: Progress and possibilities.* The National Academies Press. https://doi.org/10.17226/12480

Navigate360 (Age Appropriate Guidelines for ALICE Training® at Any Age). (2023, April 7). Age appropriate guidelines for ALICE training at any age [PDF]. Navigate360. https://info.navigate360.com/hubfs/ALICE%20Content%20PDFs/Guides/ALICE-K12-EB-040723-Age%20Appropriate%20Guidelines.pdf

Nickerson, A., Randa, R., Jimerson, S., & Guerra, N. (2021). Safe places to learn: Advances in school safety research and practice. *School Psychology Review, 50,* 158–171. https://doi.org/10.1080/2372966X.2021.1871948

Noguera, P. A., & Syeed, E. (2020). City schools and the American dream 2: The enduring promise of public education (2nd Ed.). Multicultural Education.

Oldfield, J., Humphrey, N., & Hebron, J. (2016). The role of parental and peer attachment relationships and school connectedness in predicting adolescent mental health outcomes. *Child and Adolescent Mental Health, 21*(1), 21–29. https://doi.org/10.1111/CAMH.12108

O'Regan, S. V. (2019, December 13). The company behind America's scariest school shooter drills. *The Trace.* https://www.thetrace.org/2019/12/alice-active-shooter-training-school-safety/

Peguero, A. A., & Bondy, J. M. (2021). *Immigration and school safety.* Routledge.

Rajan, S. (2024). The impacts of firearm violence exposure on youth in the US: Building the evidence and the solutions. *Youth & Society, 56*(8), 1391–1395. https://doi.org/10.1177/0044118X241285222

Rajan, S., Reeping, P. M., Ladhani, Z., Vasudevan, L. M., & Branas, C. C. (2022). Gun violence in K-12 schools in the United States: Moving towards a preventive (versus reactive) framework. *Preventive Medicine, 165,* 107280. https://doi.org/10.1016/j.ypmed.2022.107280

Rios, V. M. (2011). *Punished: Policing the lives of Black and Latino boys.* NYU Press.

———. (2020). Human targets: Schools, police, and the criminalization of Latino youth. University of Chicago Press.

Ruzek, E. A., Hafen, C. A., Allen, J. P., Gregory, A., Mikami, A. Y., & Pianta, R. C. (2016). How teacher emotional support motivates students: The mediating roles of perceived peer relatedness, autonomy support, and competence. *Learning and Instruction, 42,* 95–103. https://doi.org/10.1016/j.learninstruc.2016.01.004

Rygg, L. (2015). School shooting simulations: At what point does preparation become more harmful than helpful. *Children's Legal Rights Journal, 35*(3), 215.

Safe Kids Inc. (n.d.). The H.E.R.O. Program: Empower PreK 12 Kids [Program overview]. Safe Kids Inc. https://www.safekidsinc.com/hero-program-overview

Schildkraut, J., & Elsass, H. J. (2016). *Mass shootings: Media, myths, and realities.* Bloomsbury Publishing.

Schildkraut, J., & Nickerson, A. B. (2022). *Lockdown drills: Connecting research and best practices for school administrators, teachers, and parents.* MIT Press.

Schildkraut, J., Nickerson, A. B., & Ristoff, T. (2020). Locks, lights, out of sight: Assessing students' perceptions of emergency preparedness across multiple lockdown drills. *Journal of School Violence, 19*(1), 93–106. https://doi.org/10.1080/15388220.2019.1703720

Schonfeld, D. J., Melzer-Lange, M., Hashikawa, A. N., Gorski, P. A., & Council on Children and Disasters, Council on Injury, Violence, and Poison Prevention, Council on School Health (2020). Participation of children and adolescents in live crisis drills and exercises. *Pediatrics, 146*(3), e2020015503. https://doi.org/10.1542/peds.2020-015503

Simonetti J. A. (2020). Active shooter safety drills and US students—Should we take a step back? *JAMA Pediatrics, 174*(11), 1021–1022. https://doi.org/10.1001/jamapediatrics.2020.2592

Skiba, R. J., & Peterson, R. L. (2000). School discipline at a crossroads: From zero tolerance to early response. *Exceptional Children, 66*(3), 335–346. http://doi.org/10.1177/001440290006600305

Sprague, J. R., & Walker, H. M. (2021). *Safe and healthy schools: Practical prevention strategies.* Guilford Publications.

Tanner-Smith, E. E., Fisher, B. W., Addington, L. A., & Gardella, J. H. (2018). Adding security, but subtracting safety? Exploring schools' use of multiple visible security measures. *American Journal of Criminal Justice, 43*(1), 102–119. https://doi.org/10.1007/s12103-017-9409-3

Turanovic, J. J., Pratt, T. C., Kulig, T. C., & Cullen, F. T. (2022). *Confronting school violence: A synthesis of six decades of research.* Cambridge University Press.

Ungar, M. (2004). The importance of parents and other caregivers to the resilience of high-risk adolescents. *Family Process, 43*(1), 23–41. https://doi.org/10.1111/j.1545-5300.2004.04301004.x

United States Department of Justice (DOJ). (2024). *Critical incident review—Active shooter at Robb Elementary School.* https://portal.cops.usdoj.gov/resourcecenter/content.ashx/cops-r1141-pub.pdf

U.S. Department of Education (ED). (2013). Guide for developing high-quality school emergency operations plans. https://rems.ed.gov/docs/School_Guide_508C.pdf

U.S. House of Representatives. (2022). House report 117-403. https://www.congress.gov/congressional-report/117th-congress/house-report/403

Villarreal, S., Kim, R., Wagner, E., Somayaji, N., Davis, A., & Crifasi, C. (2024). Gun violence in the United States 2022: Examining the burden among children & teens. Johns Hopkins Center for Gun Violence Solutions. United States of America. https://coilink.org/20.500.12592/2qldvc9

Vossekuil, B., Fein, R. A., Reddy, M., Borum, R., & Modzeleski, W. (2002). *The final report and findings of the Safe School Initiative*. U.S. Secret Service and ED.

Widnall, E., Winstone, L., Plackett, R., Adams, E., Haworth, C., Mars, B., & Kidger, J. (2022). Impact of school and peer connectedness on adolescent mental health and well-being outcomes during the COVID-19 pandemic: A longitudinal panel survey. *International Journal of Environmental Research and Public Health, 19*. https://doi.org/10.3390/ijerph19116768

World Health Organization. (2004). *The importance of caregiver-child interactions for the survival and health development of young children: A review*. https://iris.who.int/bitstream/handle/10665/42878/924159134X.pdf

2

The Landscape of School Active Shooter Drills and Other School Security Measures

School safety and security measures generally encompass a wide range of tools, interventions, practices, and policies that work in tandem to ensure that schools, students, teachers, and staff are safe. They also equip school communities with reasonable emergency preparedness and response tools in anticipation of a wide variety of potential health and security concerns. These policies and practices range from firearm violence prevention and fire safety to preparation for weather-related emergencies and deterrence of bullying.

Schools across the United States implement tactics and policies specific to firearm violence prevention and preparedness, including active shooter drills. This report focuses primarily on mitigating the potential adverse mental, emotional, and behavioral health outcomes resulting from implementing school active shooter drills. In accordance with its statement of task (Box 1-1 in Chapter 1), however, the committee also reviewed other commonly used security interventions and policies being implemented in K–12 schools that might influence or shape existing procedures for school active shooter drills—including the use of metal detectors and the presence of school resource officers and other school security personnel.

Building on the foundational terminology, key concepts, and conceptual framing introduced in Chapter 1, this chapter provides an overview of active shooter drills and other school security measures currently used in K–12 schools in the United States. The chapter begins by situating school active shooter drills and other school security measures in the broader context of a comprehensive approach to school safety. Such an approach encompasses not only drills and other security measures but also interventions that support students' mental, emotional, and behavioral health; these include promoting positive school climate, social-emotional learning, restorative and trauma-informed practices, and access to school-based health professionals. The chapter then describes the current landscape of school active shooter drills, including the federal and state mandates that guide them. Finally, the chapter reviews the implementation of other school security measures in K–12 schools in the United States, highlighting their variations. This examination of these practices informs the committee's assessment of evidence regarding potential adverse outcomes in these domains and serves as the foundation for the committee's recommendations for school leaders, legislators, and decision-makers in Chapter 6 and the future research agenda set forth in Chapter 7.

CONTEXT OF SCHOOL SAFETY

School active shooter drills and other school security measures are best understood as components of a comprehensive school safety approach. The U.S. Department of Justice defines *comprehensive school safety* as a holistic approach to creating a secure, inclusive, and supportive learning environment that protects students, staff, and visitors from various threats, hazards, and risks; this approach integrates multiple aspects of safety, including physical, emotional, social, and environmental well-being, and is guided by policies, practices, and programs that foster a positive school climate and positive student behavior (U.S. National Institute of Justice, 2020). A comprehensive school safety framework typically includes the following elements:

- **Prevention and preparedness**—implementing proactive measures such as school policies, emergency planning, bullying prevention, and mental health support to reduce risks before they occur. Prevention activities include all efforts to promote a positive and trauma-informed school climate,

including teaching and modeling social-emotional skills, applying a trauma-informed lens, setting behavioral expectations, supporting student mental health, and addressing bullying.
- **Protection and security**—policies and practices that secure or safeguard students, staff, visitors, and property from threats or hazards. These measures include conducting suicide risk and threat assessments; creating safety plans for individual students; conducting drills; ensuring visible signage and emergency exits; ensuring the physical security of school facilities through controlled access, surveillance, and door lock policies; and collaborating with law enforcement.
- **Health and well-being**—supporting the mental and physical health of students and staff through counseling, social-emotional learning, and wellness programs.
- **Mitigation**—minimizing the impacts of threats or hazards and reducing the likelihood that threats and hazards will occur. Mitigation efforts include preplanning about what to do in case of an emergency, including determining and practicing the protocols for each type of response (i.e., lockdown, shelter in place, and evacuation). Additionally, mitigation activities include establishing partnerships with emergency services and conducting assessments that identify vulnerabilities in the built environment, as well as emergency response activities. Assessment results may identify appropriate actions to take such as securing access points, using metal detectors or video cameras, and employing other physical safety measures.
- **Response and crisis management**—encompasses the immediate actions taken during an emergency to stabilize the situation and save lives and property. Response activities include activating the emergency response plan, including specifying the type of emergency response required, contacting and coordinating with emergency responders, and communicating with families and the broader community, as is possible.

- **Recovery and resilience**—providing resources and support to help students, staff, and the school community recover from crises, trauma, or disasters and restore the learning environment to normalcy by attending to the physical environment, academic routines, and the emotional well-being of students and staff. Recovery activities include providing crisis and mental health support, ensuring open and transparent communication about the event, debriefing the event, and engaging in activities that foster connection and support.
- **Supportive environment**—promoting well-being and a sense of belonging to ensure that all students feel safe and valued.

A comprehensive school safety strategy is typically based on the Whole School, Whole Community, Whole Child approach, aligning national and local education policies, emergency management guidelines, and public health initiatives into an operational framework that schools can apply to address the safety, security, and well-being of their students (Centers for Disease Control and Prevention, 2021).

In the context of comprehensive school safety, some efforts are geared more specifically toward preventing a potential threat, whereas others are in place specifically to react/respond to an active threat (Mayer et al., 2021). Generally, *preventive measures* are taken to avoid incidents before they occur (e.g., physical barriers, security training for staff, behavioral threat assessment processes). *Reactionary measures* are responses implemented during or after an incident.

A public health framework conceptualizes different types of prevention and their role in keeping schools safe (Mayer et al., 2021; Rajan et al., 2022). However, the available evidence bearing on the effectiveness of many of these safety policies and tactics varies and ought to be considered in that light (Rajan et al., 2022). *Primary prevention* entails strategies aimed at preventing the occurrence of firearm-related incidents before they emerge as credible threats to a school community. *Secondary prevention* comprises measures for addressing and managing incidents when they occur (e.g., door locks). *Tertiary prevention* encompasses interventions aimed at minimizing the harms and impacts of incidents after they occur (e.g., grief counseling services). In this framing, preventive and reactionary safety measures overlap, and an assessment bearing on when use active shooter drills requires understanding their specific role as an emergency preparedness (secondary prevention) tool.

In the committee's view, a comprehensive approach to school safety requires a balance between preparedness for immediate threats and long-term prevention strategies that address the root causes of violence. Schools that focus too narrowly on active shooter drills may miss opportunities to prevent violence before it occurs. By focusing not only on physical safety but also on positive school climate through social-emotional learning and trauma-informed practices, schools can create an environment that both responds to threats and works actively to prevent them. These interventions are crucial for promoting prosocial behaviors, modeling conflict resolution, and fostering positive student relationships. Among many other benefits, they play an essential role in reducing instances of violence and aggression and anchoring a comprehensive school safety plan.

The next sections briefly describe these concepts and summarize findings from available research related to prevention strategies typically implemented in K–12 schools across the country; Table 2-1 summarizes these points briefly. Program implementation varies significantly, and individual schools and school districts vary considerably in their ability to build this kind of programming into their curricula, based on financial and staff resources and student needs.

TABLE 2-1 Preventive Strategies for Ensuring School Safety

	Safety Tactics and Policies	**Findings from Research Literature**
Social Interventions	1. Social-emotional learning programs 2. School climate promotion programs and restorative practices	An extensive body of rigorous research confirms that social interventions are crucial for promoting prosocial behaviors, modeling conflict resolution, and

	3. Dating violence prevention programs 4. Trauma-informed practices 5. Positive behavioral interventions and support	fostering positive relationships among students among many other benefits (Acosta et al., 2019; Cipriano et al., 2023; Durlak et al., 2022; Taylor et al., 2017). Their role—whether direct or indirect—in reducing instances of violence and aggression are critical to a comprehensive school safety plan. For example, several studies have demonstrated that positive behavioral interventions and support can lead to reductions in disciplinary incidents and overall improvements in school climate (Bradshaw, 2013; Bradshaw et al., 2009; Gage et al., 2018; Grasley-Boy et al., 2019; McIntosh et al., 2021).
Mental Health and Materials Needs Services	1. Mental health first aid training programs 2. Presence of and ready access to school-based mental health personnel (school social workers, school psychologists, and/or school counselors).	Mental health first aid[a] training programs can complement behavioral threat assessment and management[b]; they are designed to help individuals identify and assist those experiencing mental health issues (National Council for Mental Wellbeing, n.d.). Mental health first aid training can improve school staff's ability to support students and respond to mental health crises

(Gryglewicz et al., 2018; Jorm et al., 2010; Sanchez et al., 2020).

Access to school counselors, social workers, school psychologists, and other trained mental health professionals can significantly improve the mental health and well-being of both students and staff (Hoover & Bostic, 2020; O'Connor et al., 2018; Taras, 2004; Zabek et al., 2022). These services play an important role in reducing the likelihood of aggression and violence in schools and in fostering the healthy development of youth (Lazarus et al., 2021; Morgan-Lopez et al., 2020; Sanchez et al., 2017).

[a] *Mental health first aid* includes identifying, understanding, and providing initial support to individuals who may be developing mental health issues or who may be experiencing a mental health crisis (mentalhealthfirstaid.org).

[b] *Behavioral threat assessment and management* is the systematic process of investigating and assessing concerning behaviors. Its primary goal is to evaluate the difference between making a threat and posing a threat to a school community and then to build a management plan that supports the safety of the entire community (U.S. Department of Homeland Security, 2025).

The Importance of School Climate

In its simplest form, *school climate* refers to "the quality and character of school life" (National School Climate Center, 2007). The U.S. Department of Education (ED) expands on that definition and observes that a "positive school climate includes policies and practices that foster school safety for all; promote a supportive academic, disciplinary, and physical environment, and encourage and maintain respectful, trusting, and caring relationships throughout the school community" (Office of Planning, Evaluation, and Policy Development, 2023, p. 7). A positive school climate helps to promote and maintain the physical and psychological safety of both students and staff, thereby contributing to an environment that supports desired student behaviors (e.g., respectful communication), while reducing problematic behaviors (e.g., bullying, threats of violence). Research has shown that a positive school climate and positive student behaviors are essential to school safety and violence prevention (see, e.g., Center on Positive Behavioral Interventions and Supports, n.d.; Ice et al., 2015). Students who feel connected to their school are less likely to engage in violent behavior (Dow-Fleisner et al., 2023), experience bullying (Dow-Fleisner et al., 2023; Smalley et al., 2017), or suffer from emotional distress (Lester & Cross, 2015). Additionally, desired student behaviors, such as respect for teachers and peers and compliance with school rules, lead to safer school environments (Cornell & Mayer, 2010).

Social-Emotional Learning

Strategies such as social-emotional learning can be employed to create a positive school climate by nurturing students' emotional intelligence, social skills, and self-regulation. Extensive research shows that these programs can reduce behavioral problems and improve social-emotional skills and indicators of well-being (e.g., academic success, prosocial behaviors), contributing to overall school safety (Durlak et al., 2011; Taylor et al., 2017).

Social-emotional learning refers specifically to the process through which all young people and adults acquire and apply the knowledge, skills, and attitudes to develop healthy identities, manage emotions, achieve personal and collective goals, feel and show empathy for others, establish and maintain supportive relationships, and make responsible and caring decisions (Collaborative for Academic, Social and Emotional Learning [CASEL], n.d.). As specified in the CASEL framework, these skills include five essential capacities: self-awareness, self-management, healthy relationships, social awareness, and responsible decision-making. Broadly speaking, these skills encompass the ability to recognize and regulate emotions, advocate for oneself, develop empathy, resolve conflicts peacefully, and consider others' perspectives. For example, bullying and victimization prevention programs that are grounded in principles of social-emotional learning aim to build students' skills in emotion regulation, prosocial behavior, and capacity for empathy as strategies for reducing aggression and fostering a supportive school environment (Espelage et al., 2015; Farrington et al., 2019; NASEM, 2016).

Positive behavioral interventions and supports is another well-established and evidence-informed framework for improving student behavior through a tiered system of support, focusing on proactive measures and data-driven decision-making. Several studies have demonstrated that implementing this framework can help reduce disciplinary incidents and improve school climate overall (Bradshaw et al., 2012).

Problematic student behavior is often the result of a skill deficit(s) in social-emotional competencies. Therefore, to increase desired behaviors among students and build a positive school climate, schools need to ensure that these skills are consistently taught and modeled by staff and administrators.

Restorative and Trauma-Informed Practices

In addition to a lack of or a deficit in social-emotional skills, behavior can also be anteceded by previous traumatic experiences. Individuals who have experienced trauma, such as abuse, neglect, or witnessing a violent event, often have difficulty regulating their emotions and behavior (Maynard et al., 2019) and may engage in behaviors that can be viewed as unpredictable, volatile, or extreme (National Child Traumatic Stress Network [NCTSN], n.d., 2022; see also Chapter 5). These behavioral responses are tied to the limbic system's physiological responses of "fight," "flight," or "freeze" when faced with a perceived threat. To support students who have experienced trauma and to ensure that all students are in an emotionally regulated state for learning, some schools are implementing restorative and trauma-informed practices.

Restorative practices emphasize repairing harm and building community. Studies suggest that restorative practices can reduce suspensions and improve school climate, which may indirectly enhance security (Gregory et al., 2016). Additionally, dating violence prevention programs are designed to prevent and address dating violence among students, providing education on healthy relationships and intervention strategies. Evidence suggests that these programs can reduce incidents of violence generally and improve students' understanding of healthy relationships (Foshee et al., 2004).

Trauma-informed practices are not explicitly a type of program; they are best understood as a set of practices that allow school staff, teachers, and leadership to recognize and respond to the effects of trauma on students' behavior and learning, aiming to create a supportive and empathetic school environment (NCTSN, 2018). Extensive research supports the ability of trauma-informed approaches to improve behavioral outcomes and academic performance for students who have experienced trauma (Cohen & Mannarino, 2015). Incorporating trauma-informed practices into the school and classroom settings allows educators to better understand trauma and its impact and to respond appropriately when both they and their students are exhibiting signs of dysregulation (Avery et al., 2021; Cafaro et al., 2023). And integrating trauma-informed practices has been documented in research literature as part of an evidence-informed school safety strategy (Asmussen et al., 2019; Brueck, 2016; Rajan et al., 2022; Rones & Hoagwood, 2000; Weist & Evans, 2005).

Access to Mental Health Services

Extensive research shows that access to school counselors, school social workers, school psychologists, and other trained mental health professionals can improve the mental health and well-being of both students and staff and plays a critical role in reducing the likelihood of aggression and violence in schools and fostering the healthy development of children and youth (Hoover & Mayworm, 2017; Rossen & Cowan, 2014; Tomé et al., 2021). However, many K–12 schools lack the staff and resources needed to support these services. Indeed, there is a national shortage of school-based health and mental health professionals, which limits the capacity of schools to support students' health and well-being (Gratz et al., 2023; Nwabuzor, 2007; Willgerodt et al., 2024a,b).

A 2023 national survey on school safety found that 60% of K–12 school leaders identified student mental health challenges as the greatest threat to school safety, and more than half of respondents reported feeling unprepared to address this challenge (Raptor Technologies & National Association of School Resource Officers [NASRO], 2023). Staffing guidelines from both the American School Counselor Association (ASCA) and the National Association of School Psychologists (NASP) further underscore the scope of this shortage. The ASCA (2024) recommends one school counselor for every 250 students; however, the national average in 2023–2024 was one for every 376. Similarly, the NASP (2023) recommends a ratio of one school psychologist for every 500 students, but the national average is approximately one school psychologist for every 1,127 students.

These shortages impact service delivery in K–12 schools. Data from the National Center for Education Statistics (NCES, 2024) reveal that, during the 2023–2024 school year, only 48% of public schools reported being able to meet the mental health needs of all students who needed support—a nearly 10% decline from 2021 to 2022. Insufficient staffing (55%), inadequate funding (54%), and limited access to licensed mental health professionals (49%) were cited as barriers to providing mental health services. In addition, fewer schools reported drawing on federal funding sources to support these services (NCES, 2024b).

Workforce and staffing shortages extend beyond traditional mental health. National data show that only about two-thirds (65.7%) of schools have access to a full-time school nurse, with access significantly lower in rural (56.2%) compared with urban (70.3%) areas (Willgerodt et al., 2024a). These disparities can limit the broader range of student supports that school health professionals often facilitate.

School-based health professionals are integral not only to physical and mental health services but also to broader student support systems. These professionals frequently serve as connectors—helping to identify unmet material needs and guiding students and families to additional services. Whether through coordinating with other staff, initiating referrals, or managing programs that supply basic necessities, these professionals help reduce barriers to care and supports that promote health and positive educational outcomes (Kjolhede et al., 2021; NASP, 2021b).

THE LANDSCAPE OF ACTIVE SHOOTER DRILLS

As described in Chapter 1, the implementation of active shooter drills in schools has become increasingly common in the United States, driven by the rising number of school shooting incidents and growing public concern about school safety. State-mandated school active shooter drills are intended to prepare students, staff, and communities for potential incidents by outlining specific protocols and practices. However, these requirements vary significantly in scope and detail, highlighting differences in state resources, legislative priorities, and local approaches. Some states and localities prioritize the frequency of drills and the role of external stakeholders such as law enforcement, while others provide detailed guidance on drill procedures and rely more heavily on training for school staff.

Differences in drill frequency, type, and participant accommodations underscore the need for thoughtful implementation that achieves preparedness while protecting the well-being of participants. Many schools face disparities in resources and infrastructure that affect their ability to implement effective safety strategies, including active shooter drills. The complex landscape of school active shooter drills includes state mandates; logistical considerations; and the mental, emotional, and behavioral impacts on students and staff. Each of these topics is discussed in detail in the sections that follow.

State Mandates for School Active Shooter Drills

The number of school active shooter events has been increasing since the early 2000s. While these events remain statistically rare, they have a profound impact on communities and school systems. A number of state legislatures have responded by mandating the implementation of active shooter drills in schools to prepare for the possibility of an active shooter event (Blair et al., 2013; Martaindale & Blair, 2019; Rygg, 2015). According to reporting from ProPublica, as of early 2024, at least 37 states required K–12 schools to conduct school active shooter–related drills, typically on an annual basis (Churchill & Kriel, 2024b) (see Figure 2-1). Although 13 states do not have mandates for such drills, school districts in these states may conduct them voluntarily.

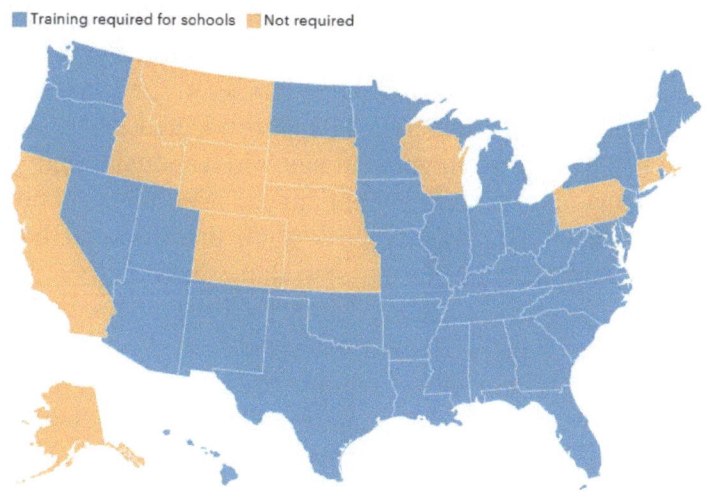

FIGURE 2-1 States that require schools to carry out active shooter–related drills, as of February 4, 2024.
SOURCE: Churchill & Kriel, 2024.

Most statutes focus on the logistics of a drill, such as whom they should include (e.g., local law enforcement officials and personnel at each school) (Blair et al., 2013; Martaindale & Blair, 2019; Rygg, 2015). For instance, Illinois legislation mandates that all schools (i.e., public, private, and charter) perform school active shooter drills with local law enforcement. In addition, some states prescribe who should be involved in the development and planning of active shooter drills. In Texas, for example, legislation passed in 2021 (Tex. S.B. 168, 2021) requires schools to plan drills with input from first responders, mental and behavioral health professionals, students, families, and school staff.

Some states require specific types of school active shooter drills or have promulgated guidelines on how the drills should be implemented. Missouri, for example, enacted the "Active Shooter and Intruder Response Training for Schools Act" in 2013, which requires all school personnel (i) to participate in simulated active shooter and intruder response drills that are led by certified law enforcement professionals and (ii) to conduct annual training for teachers and school personnel on responding to students who report threatening situations and addressing scenarios involving dangerous or armed intruders (Mo. S.B. 75, 2013). In 2025, Missouri updated its legislation with House Bill 416, which mandated that initial annual training sessions last 8 hours and that subsequent annual sessions last 4 hours.

Most state mandates specify how often drills should be performed. For example, Nevada requires that school active shooter drills take place five to six times every school year, Minnesota five times every school year, and Oklahoma and New York four times every school year. Other states require drills only once or twice every school year or do not designate frequency in their mandates. Table 2-2 shows the variation in frequency of school active shooter drills required by state mandates.

Comprehensive explanations from state or local agencies regarding active shooter drills and training policies remain limited. However, recent reporting sheds light on the decentralized and often fragmented nature of these practices. Many states leave decisions about training requirements for school-based law enforcement to local districts, resulting in inconsistent implementation across jurisdictions (Churchill & Kriel, 2024b). Reports from *The Texas Tribune* and ProPublica suggest that financial and logistical barriers, particularly in rural or under-resourced areas, may underlie the lack of statewide mandates (Churchill & Kriel, 2024a,b). However, these factors are not always explicitly acknowledged. At the same time, concerns over student mental health have begun to influence policy decisions. For example, New York recently introduced a bill to reduce the number of required annual active shooter drills from four to two, citing both the psychological toll such drills can take on students and the lack of compelling evidence that they enhance school safety (Colon, 2024). Collectively, these developments highlight how a combination of resource limitations, policy decentralization, and ethical concerns continues to shape a complex and evolving landscape for school active shooter preparedness.

TABLE 2-2 Frequency of School Active Shooter Drills Required by State Mandates, February 4, 2024

State	Frequency of Drill Requirements in Schools
Alabama	2 every school year
Alaska	None
Arizona	3 every school year
Arkansas	1 every school year
California	None
Colorado	None
Connecticut	Optional: state requires annual safety drills but allows schools to select which type of drill to conduct
Delaware	2 every school year
Florida	1–4 every school year
Georgia	1 every school year
Hawaii	1 every school year
Idaho	None
Illinois	1 every school year
Indiana	1 every school year
Iowa	1 every school year

Kansas	Optional: state requires annual safety drills but allows schools to select which type of drill to conduct
Kentucky	2 every school year
Louisiana	1 every school year
Maine	1 every school year
Maryland	1 every school year
Massachusetts	None
Michigan	1 every school year
Minnesota	5 every school year
Mississippi	2 every school year
Missouri	Law requires active shooter drills but does not specify how often
Montana	Optional: state requires annual safety drills but allows schools to select which type of drill to conduct
Nebraska	None
Nevada	5–6 every school year
New Hampshire	1 every school year
New Jersey	4 every school year
New Mexico	1 every school year
New York	4 every school year
North Carolina	1 every school year
North Dakota	Law requires active shooter drills but does not specify how often
Ohio	1 every school year
Oklahoma	4 every school year
Oregon	1 every school year
Pennsylvania	Optional: state requires annual safety drills but allows schools to select which type of drill to conduct
Rhode Island	2 every school year
South Carolina	2 every school year
South Dakota	Optional: state requires safety drills but allows schools to select which type of drill to conduct and how often
Tennessee	1 every school year
Texas	2 every school year

Utah	Law requires active shooter drills but does not specify how often
Vermont	2 every school year
Virginia	2 every school year
Washington	1 every school year
West Virginia	1 every school year
Wisconsin	Optional: state requires annual safety drills but allows schools to select which type of drill to conduct
Wyoming	None

SOURCE: Churchill & Kriel, 2024b.

Implementation of School Active Shooter Drills

Although state mandates for school active shooter drills vary, schools often have discretion to specify how the drills are defined, implemented, and practiced. Information on how frequently different types of drills are used in practice is limited. Even when statutory requirements exist, how requirements are interpreted and carried out at the school level varies widely, including differences in planning procedures, participation, and notification practices. Variations in how school active shooter drills are implemented may be influenced by differences in resources (e.g., finances, faculty and staff turnover), community contexts, and the developmental needs of students (Lindstrom Johnson, 2009; Sprague & Walker, 2021).

Organization and Planning

States and localities vary as to who organizes and implements these drills. In some localities, school administrators employ private companies to facilitate active shooter response training. In other cases, local law enforcement or school resource officers organize and implement the drills. In still other jurisdictions, drills are organized and implemented by the school leaders or school safety teams (Blair et al., 2013; Martaindale & Blair, 2019; Tex. S.B. 168, 2021).

Participation

In some states, a student or group of students may be permitted to opt out of a planned active shooter drill. Conversely, some cities, counties, districts, and localities do not provide opportunities to opt out, requiring all students, faculty, and staff to participate (Doss & Shepherd, 2015; NASP et al., 2021). The ED (2025) encourages schools to evaluate individual needs and offer accommodations or alternative activities (e.g., discussion-based practices) for students unable to participate in some standard drills, stressing that schools need to collaborate with families and multidisciplinary teams to identify and implement these accommodations.

Schools also vary in the degree to which educators and school staff participate in school active shooter drills. For instance, some schools engage school mental health professionals in these drills. As discussed in detail later in this report, evidence suggests that integrating mental health professionals and services in these drills could be beneficial and mitigate potential harm or trauma that students, faculty, staff, families, and community stakeholders may experience during these drills (Dickson & Vargo, 2017; NASP et al., 2021). Of course, as previously noted, the availability of additional school staff or community partners to participate in school active shooter drills varies based on a school's or community's resources and geography. In rural schools, for instance, access to emergency first responders or proximity to law enforcement, health care providers, and other community resources may be limited and restricted because of geographic isolation (Nickerson & Schildkraut, 2024; Schildkraut & Nickerson, 2022). Under-resourced schools may also lack school mental health providers or school nurses to engage in the planning, implementation, and follow-up for school active shooter drills (Gratz et al., 2023; Lee et al., 2009; Ramos et al., 2014).

Notifications/Announcements

Active shooter drills at a school may be publicly preannounced or may occur without being announced to staff, families, students, and community stakeholders. Notifications and announcements may be communicated in various ways, such as in the classroom; in a school assembly; or by email, texts, or social media.

Drill Type

As described in Chapter 1, school active shooter drills can take a variety of forms. For example, walkthrough active shooter practices are aimed at helping participants with emergency roles through untimed exercises and discussions. Staff, leaders, first responders, and occasionally students participate to improve coordination (Blair et al., 2013; NASP et al., 2021; Rygg, 2015). Tabletop exercises include guided discussions aimed at enhancing preparedness, allowing school crisis teams, law enforcement, and—in some cases—students to examine plans and adapt to complex scenarios. These sessions are intended to promote critical thinking and readiness, while allowing participants to engage at their own comfort level (Gerlinger & Schleifer, 2021; NASP et al., 2021).

By contrast, lockdown drills secure classrooms with locked doors, darkened rooms, and silence, addressing internal threats, while secured-perimeter lockouts protect against external risks. According to the School Survey on Crime and Safety (SSOCS), in school year 2021–2022, 95.5% of all public K–12 schools had conducted a lockdown drill with students that year (NCES, 2022; see Table 2-3).

TABLE 2-3 Percentage of Public K–12 Schools That Drilled Students on the Use of Emergency Procedures, School Year 2021–2022

	Drilled Students on the Use of Emergency Procedures (%)	
School Characteristic	Lockdown[a]	Shelter-in-place[b]
All public schools	**95.5**	**93.5**
School type		
Traditional public school	96.1	93.6

Charter school	89.4	91.7
Level[c]		
Elementary	95.8	93.9
Middle	95.6	93.1
High/secondary	94.9	93.0
Combined/other	93.0	87.8
Enrollment size		
Fewer than 300 students	91.7	89.0
300–499 students	95.1	94.6
500–999 students	97.3	94.7
1,000 or more students	98.9	95.8
Locale		
City	97.0	94.8
Suburb	96.8	95.8
Town	94.6	92.7
Rural	92.8	89.6
Region		
Northeast	95.8	92.4
Midwest	95.3	94.1
South	97.9	95.0
West	92.0	91.4
Percent students of color[d]		
Less than 5%	92.0	90.0
5% to less than 20%	93.6	91.3
20% to less than 50%	97.7	95.7
50% or more	95.5	93.5
Percent of students eligible for free or reduced-price lunch		
0% to 25%	92.5	92.4
More than 25% to 50%	95.1	93.1
More than 50% to 75%	96.7	94.3
More than 75%	96.6	93.7

^{a} *Lockdown* was defined for respondents as a procedure that involves securing school buildings and grounds during incidents that pose an immediate threat of violence in or around the school.

^{b} *Shelter-in-place* was defined for respondents as a procedure that requires all students and staff to remain indoors because it is safer inside the building or a room than outside. Depending on the threat or hazard, students and staff may be required to move to rooms that can be sealed (such as in the event of a chemical or biological hazard) or have no windows, or to a weather shelter (such as in the event of a tornado).

^{c} *Elementary schools* are defined as schools that enroll more students in grades K–4 than in higher grades. *Middle schools* are defined as schools that enroll more students in grades 5–8 than in higher or lower grades. *High/secondary schools* are defined as schools that enroll more students in grades 9–12 than in lower grades. *Combined/other schools* include all other combinations of grades, including K–12 schools.

^{d} The term *students of color* is being used synonymously with *minority students*. Students of color include those who are Black, non-Hispanic; Hispanic, regardless of race; Asian, non-Hispanic; Pacific Islander, non-Hispanic; American Indian/Alaska Native, non-Hispanic; and students of two or more races, non-Hispanic.

NOTE: Responses were provided by the principal or the person most knowledgeable about school crime and policies for providing a safe environment.
SOURCE: NCES, 2024a.

Full-scale simulation exercises at school are intended to equip first responders and school leaders with the skills and confidence needed to lead a response to an active shooter event at school, and to test their protocols and identify potential weaknesses, although their implementation varies widely (Blair et al., 2013; Martaindale & Blair, 2020; NASP et al., 2021; Rygg, 2015). Some are unannounced and include high-sensorial elements (e.g., sounds of gunfire, use of fake blood, simulated violence), while others are organized and announced in advance (Blair et al., 2013; Martaindale & Blair, 2019; NASP et al., 2021; Rygg, 2015).

There has been a push for schools to use options-based practices, which originated in law enforcement agencies and focus on independent, in-the-moment decision-making (Donovan, 2023; Miotto & Cogan, 2023; NASP et al., 2021; Schonfeld et al., 2020; Simonetti, 2020). Some schools use options-based strategies that have been subsequently adopted for school systems; however, in some cases, practices that were originally developed for adults are used without adaptation in school active shooter drills and do not account for whether they are appropriate for the developmental level of student participants (NASP et al., 2021). For example, guidance from NASP, NASRO, and Safe and Sound Schools emphasizes that students should not be instructed that they are expected to engage (i.e., fight or counter) with assailants in a life-threatening emergency.

Research has produced little empirical evidence regarding the mental, emotional, and behavioral health effects of these practices, leaving questions regarding the appropriateness of options-based practices for all students and staff. In addition, there are some indications that these practices may not be suitable for certain age groups, for individuals with severe functional and access needs, or for those with trauma histories (NASP et al., 2021; Safe and Sound Schools, 2016). Despite these concerns, options-based practices are included in current federal guidance to schools on responding to an active shooter event, which in some cases includes considerations for developmentally appropriate adaptations (ED & REMS TA Center, n.d.; ED et al., 2013; Federal Bureau of Investigation, 2024).

Other schools have implemented the use of standard response practices[10] (described in Chapter 1). For each standard response, there are specific student and staff actions. In drills using standard response practices, students and staff physically rehearse consistent, predefined actions needed to respond to an emergency, such as a school active shooter event. The response to practice a lockdown (used to respond to an immediate threat inside of the school), for example, includes the actions of locking the door, turning off the lights, moving out of sight, and remaining quiet. These practices emphasize procedural repetition to reinforce emergency responses ("I Love U Guys" Foundation, 2023). A number of states and local school districts have adapted the "I Love U Guys" Foundation's Standard Response Protocol, a framework that includes five core

---

[10] For the purposes of this report, the committee uses the term *standard response practices* to refer to individual, predefined actions or procedures designed to guide students and staff in responding to different types of emergency situations, including school active shooter events.

standard response practices for implementation in schools, or have incorporated it into guidance for schools in response to input from state and national practitioners, including those in New York (New York State Education Department, n.d.), Maryland (Maryland Center for School Safety, 2024), and Texas (Texas School Safety Center, n.d.a).

Frequency

School active shooter drills can occur monthly, quarterly, annually, and/or randomly. Some statutes requiring school active shooter drills indicate that frequent drills aim to establish "muscle memory" or "motor learning," so that students' safety responses and behavior to an active shooter event at school becomes almost instinctive or reflexive (Gerlinger & Schleifer, 2021; Schildkraut & Nickerson, 2022). As reported previously in Table 2-1, there is a great deal of variation across states and schools in how frequently drills take place. However, there is limited information on how frequently different types of drills are carried out in practice.

Debrief and Evaluation

In some instances, an informational debrief and evaluation is conducted after each active shooter drill at a school; again, the content of such debriefs and evaluations varies greatly across schools. For some schools, debrief and evaluation provides school leaders an opportunity to communicate the successes or failures that occurred during the drill to the school community. For other schools, a debrief and evaluation can be more extensive. For example, students might receive mental health counseling and be provided an optional quiet space to calm down; school leaders might ask participants what went well and what did not. Families might be informed about the occurrence of the drill and be provided with calming strategies and potential resources for mental health care. School administrators might be asked to prepare an after-action review for the school community, evaluating results, identifying gaps, and documenting lessons learned and successes achieved (NASP et al., 2021).

LANDSCAPE OF OTHER SCHOOL SECURITY MEASURES

In addition to school active shooter drills, the committee was charged with examining "other school security measures" (see the statement of task, Box 1-1 in Chapter 1). Security measures comprise strategies and tools implemented to ensure the safety and security of students, teachers, and staff in a K–12 school. They typically aim to prevent or mitigate threats ranging from firearm violence to unauthorized building access. This section organizes school security measures into three categories: surveillance interventions, personnel interventions and training, and physical security interventions. The committee broadens its examination of school security measures beyond metal detectors, door locks, and school security personnel to encompass a wider range of practices and interventions currently used in U.S. schools, in order to provide a more comprehensive view of the existing landscape.

Researchers have described such security measures as part of a phenomenon known as "hardening" of schools (Chambers, 2022; Kim et al., 2021; Lindstrom Johnson et al., 2018; Thompson, 2023). The past 2 decades have seen an uptick in *school-hardening efforts*, defined as physical and procedural modifications for reducing vulnerabilities within a school and preventing or minimizing damage from an attack (Barroso, 2022; Burr et al., 2024; Warnick & Kapa, 2019). They typically involve enhancing the resilience of buildings and systems against external threats and often also involve physical changes to improve security (e.g., locks, barriers).

Along with school active shooter drills, these other security measures are part of a comprehensive school safety and security strategy, which encompasses a range of interventions (including those aimed at improving school climate and student). In their comprehensive review of literature on factors that contribute to school safety, Nickerson et al. (2021) highlight the importance of considering both physical and behavioral aspects of school security and emphasize the importance of school context and climate.

Recent literature has become more specific in how it addresses school environment. Stilwell et al. (2024), in particular, build on the existing evidence base on school safety and violence by proposing a multidisciplinary, comprehensive framework designed to guide research and practice. This framework advocates for the creation of school environments that promote attentiveness and vigilance among school personnel and students as key strategies for preventing violence and improving safety. Table 2-4 briefly describes the various categories of school security interventions and the tactics and policies within each category; it also summarizes findings from the existing research literature.

The following subsections describe what is known about how K–12 schools are implementing physical security interventions, surveillance interventions, and personnel interventions and training. Comprehensive, national data on the frequency with which these interventions are being used in schools are limited. However, the School Survey on Crime and Safety (SSOCS), a nationally representative survey conducted by the National Center for Education Statistics (NCES), provides some insights from its recent 2021–2022 school year data collection. These findings, where available, are summarized in the subsections that follow; however, additional data and research are needed to fully understand the scope and use of various security measures in K–12 schools in the United States (see Chapter 7).

TABLE 2-4 Summary of K–12 School Security Measures

Category	Tactics and Policies	Findings from Research Literature
Physical security interventions	Door locks/access controls (indoor and outdoor) External barriers (e.g., perimeter fencing, reinforced windows) Buffer zones[a] Establishment of "hard corners"[b]	For many of these physical interventions, the evidence describing or documenting their effectiveness in preventing violence, and firearm violence in particular, is very mixed (e.g., Cornell et al., 2020; Perumean-Chaney et al., 2013; Tanner-Smith et al., 2018). Nonetheless, many of these interventions are widely implemented and certain aspects (e.g., door locks and use of hard corners) have been built into school active shooter drill procedures (Moore et al., 2021). While the research is limited, taken together, these efforts may serve as ways to reduce the likelihood of unauthorized access to a school building, and especially during the school day or at other times when the school is open (Moore et al., 2021).

Surveillance interventions	Metal detectors
Security cameras (indoor and outdoor)
Anonymous reporting systems
Clear backpack/no backpack policies
Locker/person searches/screenings
Behavioral threat assessment processes	The effectiveness of several of these surveillance measures is understudied. Available evidence suggests that visible security measures, such as metal detectors and security cameras, do not improve school safety or academic achievement, and may increase student anxiety and stress (Lindstrom Johnson et al., 2018; Mowen & Parker, 2017; Schildkraut & Grogan, 2019; Schildkraut & Muschert, 2019). These surveillance interventions may also exacerbate disparities in school discipline outcomes (Johnson & Jabbari, 2021). Anonymous reporting systems allow students and staff to report safety concerns and research suggests that these systems can be an effective way to share information about concerning student behaviors (Hsieh et al., 2022).
Research suggests that behavioral threat assessment models can be used to help identify and mitigate potential threats to school safety (Cornell, 2021).

Personnel interventions and training	Law enforcement officers (school resource officers and others) Non–law enforcement security staff Policies that allow teachers or other school staff to be armed with firearms	Existing research and studies on law enforcement officers in schools provide limited and mixed evidence on their effectiveness in deterring firearm violence (Crichlow-Ball et al., 2022; Flannery et al., 2021; Sorensen et al., 2023). Non–law enforcement security personnel (e.g., school safety officers or school security officers) may enhance safety by providing a less intimidating presence than that of law enforcement officers while effectively managing security concerns. Their efficacy in deterring firearm violence in unknown (Vernon & Curran, 2023). There is currently no evidence that arming teachers is effective in deterring firearm violence or reducing the lethality of a shooting should one occur (Smart et al., 2024).

[a] *Buffer zones* are areas intended to create separation between the school and a potential threat; they include other security elements, such as fencing, gates, or controlled access points.

[b] A *hard corner* is a designated safe area in a classroom where occupants can seek refuge away from doors and windows in the event of an emergency.

Physical Security Interventions

Physical security measures implemented in K–12 schools—such as door locks and access controls (indoor and outdoor), perimeter fencing, reinforced windows, buffer zones,[11] and hard corners[12]—encompass tactics and policies designed to protect schools from unauthorized access, violence, or other physical threats (Moore et al., 2021). These measures, when implemented as part of a broader systems approach are intended to help schools detect, delay, and respond to potential threats. A 2021 synthesis of literature on physical security planning in K–12 schools found that a layered school security model—addressing the potential for threats at the campus perimeter, on school grounds, at the building perimeter, and in interior spaces—is generally regarded as the most effective, particularly when these approaches are aligned with clearly defined policies, staff roles, and training (Moore et al., 2021). Evidence from national surveys and implementation studies suggests that such measures are adopted widely, especially in response to concerns about school shootings and other acts of targeted violence (NCES, 2024a; Schwartz et al., 2016). Some studies have also explored integrating these physical features with staff training and emergency planning, particularly in the context of drills and lockdown procedures (Schildkraut et al., 2020).

Door locks and access controls restrict building access to authorized individuals and enhance lockdown capabilities. According to the SSOCS for school year 2021–2022, approximately 97% of public schools reported controlling access to school buildings during school hours, such as through locked or monitored doors, and about 61% of schools reported controlling access to school grounds during school hours, using measures such as locked or monitored gates (NCES, 2024a; see Table 2-5). And according to the 2021–2022 data collection, 76.1% of U.S. public K–12 schools reported equipping classrooms with locks so that doors can be locked from the inside. Among schools where at least three-quarters of students

---

[11] *Buffer zones* are areas intended to create separation between the school and a potential threat; they may include other security elements such as fencing, gates, or controlled access points.

[12] A *hard corner* is a designated safe area in a classroom where occupants can seek refuge away from doors and windows in the event of an emergency.

qualify for free or reduced-price school lunch, 74.4% had locking doors in their classrooms in the 2021–2022 school year, compared with 78.4% at schools where a quarter or fewer students qualify for free or reduced-price lunch (NCES, 2024a). Charter schools were more likely than traditional public schools to have doors that locked from the inside in the 2021–2022 school year (80.0% vs. 75.7%) (NCES, 2024a).

TABLE 2-5 Percentage of Public K–12 Schools with Controlled Access Security Measures, School Year 2021–2022

School Characteristic	Controlled Access (%)		
	School Buildings[a]	School Grounds[b]	Classrooms That Can Be Locked from the Inside
All public schools	**97.1**	**61.1**	**76.1**
School type			
Traditional public school	97.5	60.7	75.7
Charter school	92.7	65.8	80.0
Level[c]			
Elementary	98.1	65.6	76.2
Middle	97.0	53.6	76.0
High/secondary	94.2	54.6	75.2
Combined/other	96.1	58.4	80.0
Enrollment size			
Fewer than 300 students	96.2	50.8	76.8
300–499 students	96.5	60.1	77.2
500–999 students	98.5	65.7	74.9
1,000 or more students	96.4	71.3	75.3
Locale			
City	96.9	70.0	74.7
Suburb	97.1	68.1	76.2
Town	97.5	51.4	74.8
Rural	97.1	48.0	77.9

Region			
Northeast	99.2	56.2	75.6
Midwest	99.3	47.4	76.5
South	97.8	63.1	74.2
West	92.6	74.8	78.7
Percent students of color[d]			
Less than 5%	93.7	42.7	73.8
5% to less than 20%	98.5	47.2	74.9
20% to less than 50%	97.9	58.0	81.5
50% or more	96.3	71.6	73.6
Percent of students eligible for free or reduced-price lunch			
0%–25%	96.8	57.4	78.4
More than 25% to 50%	96.9	52.4	76.9
More than 50% to 75%	96.9	57.1	75.9
More than 75%	97.5	71.1	74.4

[a] Examples of controlled access to school buildings provided to respondents were locked or monitored doors and loading docks.

[b] Examples of controlled access to school grounds provided to respondents were locked or monitored gates.

[c] *Elementary schools* are defined as schools that enroll students in more of grades K–4 than in higher grades. *Middle schools* are defined as schools that enroll students in more of grades 5–8 than in higher or lower grades. *High/secondary schools* are defined as schools that enroll students in more of grades 9–12 than in lower grades. *Combined/other schools* include all other combinations of grades, including K–12 schools.

[d] The term *students of color* is being used synonymously with *minority students*. Students of color include those who are Black, non-Hispanic; Hispanic, regardless of race; Asian, non-Hispanic; Pacific Islander, non-Hispanic; American Indian/Alaska Native, non-Hispanic; and students of two or more races, non-Hispanic.

NOTE: Responses were provided by the principal or the person most knowledgeable about school crime and policies designed to provide a safe environment.
SOURCE: NCES, 2024a.

While the primary goals of physical security measures relate to restricting access and emergency response, research has also examined their potential influence on school climate. For instance, research suggests that highly visible or restrictive security measures may contribute to increased perceptions of surveillance and reduced perceptions of trust or belonging among students (Bachman et al., 2011; Tanner-Smith et al., 2018). These findings are particularly relevant in discussions of school active shooter preparedness, where physical design features such as door locks or hard corners are often deployed as part of school active shooter drills. Taken together, existing literature points to a complex interplay among physical security infrastructure, emergency preparedness practices, and students' perceptions of safety and emotional security within school settings.

Surveillance Interventions

Specific tactics and policies in the category of surveillance interventions include metal detectors, security cameras (indoor and outdoor), anonymous reporting systems, clear backpack or no backpack policies, locker and person searches and screenings, and behavioral threat assessment processes. According to the SSOCS for school year 2021–2022, approximately 93% of schools used security cameras to monitor the school, 23% implemented random sweeps for contraband, and about two-thirds of schools (65%) reported having a threat assessment team in place (NCES, 2024). Only 6% of schools used random metal detector checks on students, 2.4% used daily metal detector checks on students, and 3.7% of schools required backpacks to be clear or banned them outright (NCES, 2024; see Table 2-6).

TABLE 2-6 Percentage of Public K–12 Schools with Various Surveillance Interventions, School Year 2021–2022

School Characteristic	Metal Detectors and Sweeps				Communication Systems and Technology					
	Backpacks must be clear or are banned	Random metal detector checks	Daily metal detector checks	Sweeps for contraband[a]	Panic button(s) or silent alarm(s)[b]	Electronic notification system[c]	Structured anonymous threat-reporting system[d]	Security cameras to monitor the school	Non-academic cellphone use prohibited	Threat assessment team[e]
All public schools	3.7	6.2	2.4	23.1	43.0	69.4	62.4	92.6	76.1	65.0
School type										
Traditional public school	3.5	6.2	2.4	23.4	44.7	69.1	63.9	93.5	75.5	65.0
Charter school	5.5!	6.5	‡	20.3	24.7	71.8	47.1	84.0	82.2	64.4
Level[f]										
Elementary	2.2	2.3	0.5!	7.7	45.2	69.5	56.1	90.7	87.0	61.8
Middle	6.4	10.4	4.2	38.9	43.0	68.1	72.7	95.9	77.0	71.3
High/secondary	5.3	14.2	6.2	54.2	38.3	70.7	73.3	96.7	43.0	70.3
Combined/other	5.4!	8.3!	4.7!	33.4	24.8	62.7	55.4	82.5	70.4	52.7

96

Enrollment size										
Fewer than 300 students	4.1!	5.6	2.6	26.6	31.4	67.2	50.5	91.9	75.7	49.5
300–499 students	3.4	3.9	1.4	15.1	45.3	69.2	59.1	92.1	82.3	64.6
500–999 students	3.0	6.6	3.0	21.3	46.1	70.0	67.7	92.7	79.1	70.4
1,000 or more students	5.4	12.9	2.6	44.7	51.0	72.2	80.5	95.4	48.5	81.5
Locale										
City	4.2	8.5	4.8	16.9	40.2	69.1	62.0	87.9	77.0	71.0
Suburb	2.3	5.3	1.5	15.8	53.3	71.8	67.7	93.5	76.9	69.5
Town	3.5!	5.1	1.5!	29.9	33.6	67.7	61.6	96.9	77.1	64.1
Rural	4.8	5.5	1.4	35.2	37.7	67.4	56.9	94.5	73.7	53.7
Region										
Northeast	2.9!	8.8	4.2	12.9	51.8	72.0	51.1	96.4	72.0	56.6
Midwest	2.8	3.6	2.3	28.8	45.8	71.2	63.0	94.5	73.8	59.7
South	6.7	10.3	3.1	31.0	46.7	69.1	69.6	97.8	79.4	72.0
West	0.7!	1.3!	‡	13.2	28.9	66.2	59.4	81.0	76.4	65.7

Percent students of color[g]										
Less than 5%	‡	‡	8.2!	2.3!	43.3	38.0	60.9	57.8	90.4	71.1	58.9
5% to less than 20%	2.0	2.9	‡	30.0	45.9	70.9	61.9	97.5	73.1	56.1	
20% to less than 50%	2.2	3.4	0.6!	18.2	52.7	69.4	70.3	93.9	76.8	68.1	
50% or more	5.2	9.4	4.5	20.7	36.2	69.4	58.4	89.7	77.6	68.0	
Percent of students eligible for free or reduced-price lunch											
0%–25%	‡	1.0!	‡	16.1	55.5	75.0	64.6	93.1	73.0	61.2	
More than 25% to 50%	2.9!	4.3	0.7!	25.5	41.7	66.3	61.1	93.4	71.4	59.6	
More than 50% to 75%	2.1	5.8	0.9!	29.1	38.5	63.9	64.7	93.0	76.7	64.4	
More than 75%	6.4	10.5	5.7	21.6	39.8	71.6	60.8	91.6	80.4	70.9	

! Interpret data with caution. The coefficient of variation (CV) for this estimate is 30%–50%.
‡ Reporting standards not met. Either there are too few cases for a reliable estimate, or the standard error represents more than 50% of the estimate.

a Examples of random sweeps provided to respondents were locker checks and dog sniffs. Examples of contraband provided to respondents were drugs and weapons. *Weapon* was defined for respondents as any instrument or object used with the intent to threaten, injure, or kill, including lookalikes if used to threaten others.
b Refers to buttons or alarms that directly connect to law enforcement in the event of an incident.
c Refers to systems that automatically notify parents in the event of a schoolwide emergency.
d Examples of structured anonymous threat-reporting systems provided to respondents were online submissions, telephone hotlines, and written submission via drop box.
e Threat assessment was defined for respondents as a formalized process of identifying, assessing, and managing students who may pose a threat of targeted violence in schools.
f Elementary schools are defined as schools that enroll students more in grades K–4 than in higher grades. *Middle schools* are defined as schools that enroll students more in grades 5–8 than in higher or lower grades. *High/secondary schools* are defined as schools that enroll students more in grades 9–12 than in lower grades. *Combined/other schools* include all other combinations of grades, including K–12 schools.
g The term *students of color* is being used synonymously with *minority students*. Students of color include those who are Black, non-Hispanic; Hispanic, regardless of race; Asian, non-Hispanic; Pacific Islander, non-Hispanic; American Indian/Alaska Native, non-Hispanic; and students of two or more races, non-Hispanic.

NOTE: Responses were provided by the principal or the person most knowledgeable about school crime and policies designed to provide a safe environment.
SOURCE: NCES, 2024a.

The share of schools with surveillance interventions has increased over the last decade. For example, the proportion of schools with an anonymous threat-reporting system has nearly doubled, from 36% in the 2009–2010 school year to 62.4% in 2021–2022. There has been a 30-point increase in the use of security cameras to monitor schools, from 61% in 2009–2010 to 92.6% in 2021–2022 (NCES, 2011, 2024a). Adoption of these systems differs somewhat based on the school's characteristics and the region of the country where it is located. In the 2021–2022 school year, middle and high schools were more likely than elementary schools to have anonymous threat-reporting systems (72.7% of middle schools and 73.3% of high schools, vs. 56.1% of elementary schools) and security cameras (95.9% of middle schools and 96.7% of high schools, vs. 90.7% of elementary schools). Regionally, about three-quarters of schools in the West (81%) reported using security cameras in 2021–2022, compared with other regions, where more than 90% of schools reported using security cameras (Northeast, 96.4%; Midwest, 94.5%; and South, 97.8%). Schools with higher enrollment are more likely than smaller ones to have implemented these surveillance interventions (NCES, 2024a). Of the 65% of schools implementing threat assessment teams, schools in cities (71%) and suburbs (69.5%) more often had such a team compared with those in rural areas (53.7%). Threat assessment teams were also more common at the middle and high school levels, at schools with higher enrollment numbers, and at schools with a larger proportion of racial or ethnic minority students (NCES, 2024a).

The role of surveillance measures in contributing to school safety has a mixed evidence base. Evidence suggests that such interventions may disproportionately affect Black and Hispanic students without reducing the likelihood of exposure to violence (Lindstrom Johnson et al., 2018; Mowen & Parker, 2017). For example, Mowen and Parker (2017), using data from the Education Longitudinal Study, found that the presence of both Black and Hispanic students was associated with a greater overall number of school security measures. In addition, the authors found that secondary schools with higher percentages of Black students were more likely to implement such measures as metal detectors, security personnel, surveillance cameras, designated check-in points, and perimeter fencing, although they did not examine student perspectives on how these measures were experienced. Given that the types and nature of surveillance options have evolved in recent years, this section reviews the current options typically available to and implemented by K–12 schools in the United States.

Metal Detectors

Schools use metal detectors to identify and deter weapons at entry points. Their use in schools became more common in the 1980s, and by the mid-1990s, approximately one in ten U.S schools had a metal detector. Although slight increases were observed following the school shootings at Columbine High School and Sandy Hook Elementary, their prevalence has remained largely unchanged since the 1990s (Schildkraut & Grogan, 2019). Yet while metal detectors may detect prohibited items, research has not consistently shown that their use leads to a meaningful reduction in serious school violence. Additionally, questions have been raised about the psychological and equity-related impacts of metal detector screening, including the possibility that these measures may contribute to negative perceptions of school climate or be used disproportionately in schools with higher proportions of students of color (Nance, 2017; Schildkraut & Grogan, 2019; Schildkraut & Muschert, 2019).

Security Cameras

Security cameras are typically used to monitor school premises and deter potential threats. However, research does not conclusively support their effectiveness in deterring school-based violence. An analysis of national data by Fisher et al. (2021) found that use of security cameras was not associated with reductions in school crime, social disturbances, or exclusionary discipline. A qualitative analysis by Lindstrom Johnson et al. (2018), using data from 54,350 middle and high school students in Maryland, examined perceptions of school safety in relation to the use of security cameras. The study found that indoor security cameras were associated with lower perceptions of safety, support, and equity. In contrast, moderate use of outdoor cameras was linked to higher perceptions of safety among all students. Black compared with White students reported feeling safer and more supported when outdoor cameras were present; they felt less safe than their White peers in schools with a high number of indoor cameras (Lindstrom Johnson et al., 2018). Across all racial and ethnic groups, as well as among female and younger students, high levels of camera surveillance were associated with a decreased sense of equity in the school environment.

Anonymous Threat-Reporting Systems

Anonymous threat-reporting systems, including tip lines and mobile apps, have received increased attention as a proactive tool for threat detection. NCES data for 2021–2022 indicate that 62.4 percent of K–12 schools reported using a formal anonymous threat-reporting system (e.g., online submissions, telephone hotlines, and written submission via drop box; NCES, 2022). A 2022 randomized controlled trial of more than 700 middle school students in Miami found that schools using an anonymous threat-reporting system experienced fewer violent incidents, particularly when tips were acted upon promptly and effectively (Hsieh et al., 2022). Students were also surveyed on their perceptions of safety, feelings of school connectedness, and feelings of trust in their classmates. Use of a reporting system appeared to prevent declines in these measures that were observed in the schools not using such a system (Hsieh et al., 2022).

Other Measures

Other measures, such as policies requiring clear backpacks or permitting locker searches, are intended to limit the concealment of weapons or contraband. NCES data for 2021–2022 show that 3.7% of K–12 schools required the use of clear backpacks, and 23.1% conducted contraband sweeps (NCES, 2022). While such practices are sometimes implemented in response to specific threats or incidents, the empirical support for their effectiveness is limited. Some experts have noted negative student perceptions of these practices, as well as concerns about the potential for these measures to stigmatize students or violate their civil liberties (Addington, 2009; Brown, 2005; Lesneskie & Block, 2017; Moore et al., 2021).

Behavioral Threat Assessment

Some surveillance methods are put in place not to monitor general student behaviors or actions per se, but to serve as tools for evaluating specific individual threats or risks should they arise. *Behavioral threat assessment* is a structured approach to identifying, assessing, and managing potential threats by evaluating individuals' behavior and risk factors. Behavioral threat assessment practices are currently implemented in an estimated 85% of public schools across the United States (NASEM, 2024), and like many safety and security measures, their implementation varies widely across schools and states. Some states use tiered or multidisciplinary models (Kim et al., 2021), while others provide standardized toolkits, and still others provide only general guidelines for implementation. This inconsistency in implementation often results from a variety of factors, including differences in local laws, school and district-level resources, and individual school and student needs, leading to uneven application of threat assessment procedures. However, behavioral threat assessment in its various forms is a tool that, when implemented as intended, has a strong evidence base for its effectiveness and as part of a broader school safety framework (Rajan et al., 2022).

The use of evidence-based behavioral threat assessment practices is critical if this tool is to be effective in preventing violence and managing potential threats (Cornell & Maeng, 2018), and for making sure that interventions are fair and do not cause breakdowns in trust within the school system, and to ensure that students are well supported even in—one might argue especially in—moments of crisis.

Examples of well-established behavioral threat assessment processes include the Comprehensive School Threat Assessment Guidelines, which have been shown to improve safety outcomes and reduce bias (Cornell, 2018). In addition, and to better support school systems, several organizations and agencies offer resources to guide schools in implementing the process. For example, NASP (2021a) has synthesized the existing literature to provide a detailed framework for K–12 schools, including how to establish a multidisciplinary team, how to implement a structured referral process, best practices for communication, and even ongoing professional development resources. Similarly, several states (e.g., school safety efforts in North Carolina and Texas) have provided tailored guidelines for schools that are driven by the existing evidence and readily accessible. Resources such as these are examples of resources that can help K–12 schools align their practices with proven methods, increasing both efficacy and equity in managing potential threats.

Mental Health First Aid

Mental health first aid training programs can complement behavioral threat assessment by helping individuals identify and assist those experiencing mental health issues. Research indicates that such training can improve the ability of school staff to support students and respond to mental health crises (Gryglewicz et al., 2018; Jorm et al., 2010; Sanchez et al., 2020).

Personnel Interventions and Training

In general, there are three broad categories of school security personnel (Fisher et al., 2023; James & McCallion, 2013; NASRO, n.d.). First are *school resource officers* (SROs)—sworn law enforcement officers who have received training and are certified specifically for working within a school. Second, some school districts may use non-SRO law enforcement officers. These officers are sworn law enforcement but have not received SRO training. Box 2-2 describes school resources officers in more detail. Third, non–law enforcement school security personnel have not received training or special certification to work within schools. In the face of recent reported shortages of SROs and other law enforcement officers who can be assigned to schools (Fisher et al., 2023; Turanovic et al.,

2022; Woulfin & Sadler, 2023), however, some schools have come to rely solely on non–law enforcement security personnel.

BOX 2-1
School Resource Officers

School resource officers are sworn law enforcement officers assigned to work in schools who engage in community-oriented policing in partnership with school districts, using community-oriented policing practices. Their responsibilities may include collaborating with school administrators, ensuring safety, preventing crime, developing community justice initiatives, training students in conflict resolution and restorative practices, and addressing disorder in and around the school. School resource officers may also help identify changes to the school's physical environment that could reduce crime and may assist in shaping school policies related to safety and crime prevention (National Association of School Resource Officers [NASRO], n.d.; U.S. Department of Justice, 2019).

NASRO focuses on training and certifying school-based police, school administrators, and school security and/or safety professionals who work as partners to protect schools and their students, faculty, and staff members. NASRO emphasizes a triad model that establishes three main roles of a school resource officer: (1) law enforcement officer, (2) public safety educator, and (3) informal counselor/mentor. The NASRO triad model trains school resource officers to establish trust with students, staff, parents, and the school community, with the goals of contributing to the creation of safe learning environments; providing support and resources to school staff; fostering positive relationships with students, teachers, and parents; and developing strategies for resolving problems and protect students. NASRO training also includes implementing active shooter drills at school (James & McCallion, 2013; NASRO, n.d.; Raymond, 2010).

According to the SSOCS, 60.6% of public K–12 schools had one or more security staff member[13] present at the school at least once a week in 2021–2022, up from 43% in 2013–2014 (NCES, 2024a). In about half of schools (44.8%) in the 2021–2022 school year, the security staff included at least one sworn law enforcement officer who routinely carried a firearm. In the 2009–2010 school year, 28% of public schools reported having any security staff member[14] who routinely carried a firearm (NCES, 2011; see Figure 2-2 shows these trends).

The presence of security staff varies somewhat based on certain school characteristics. For instance, security staff are more common at larger schools: schools with 1,000 or more students reported having one or more school resource officer (74.4%), other sworn law enforcement personnel (12.1%), or security officers or security personnel (54.9%) in 2021–2022, compared with schools with fewer than 300 students, which reported having school resource officers (31.5%), other sworn law enforcement personnel (11.6%), or security officers or security personnel (15.7%) (NCES, 2024a). More than 60% of middle (62%) and high (62.4%) schools had school resource officers present at least once a week during the 2021–2022 school year, compared with 33% of elementary schools (NCES, 2024a; see Table 2-7).

---

[13] *Security staff* include security guards/officers, security personnel, school resource officers, and sworn law enforcement officers who are not school resource officers. *Security guards/officers* and *security personnel* do not include law enforcement personnel. *School resource officers* include all career law enforcement officers with arrest authority who have specialized training and are assigned to work in collaboration with school organizations.

[14] Prior to 2015–2016, the SSOCS questionnaire asked respondents whether any of the security guards, security personnel, or sworn law enforcement officers at their school routinely carried a firearm. In 2015–2016 and later years, the SSOCS questionnaire asked respondents only whether any of the sworn law enforcement officers (including school resource officers) at their school routinely carried a firearm. While data across years are not directly comparable because of these changes in categorization, they illustrate a broader trend of growth in the proportion of schools with security staff who routinely carry a firearm.

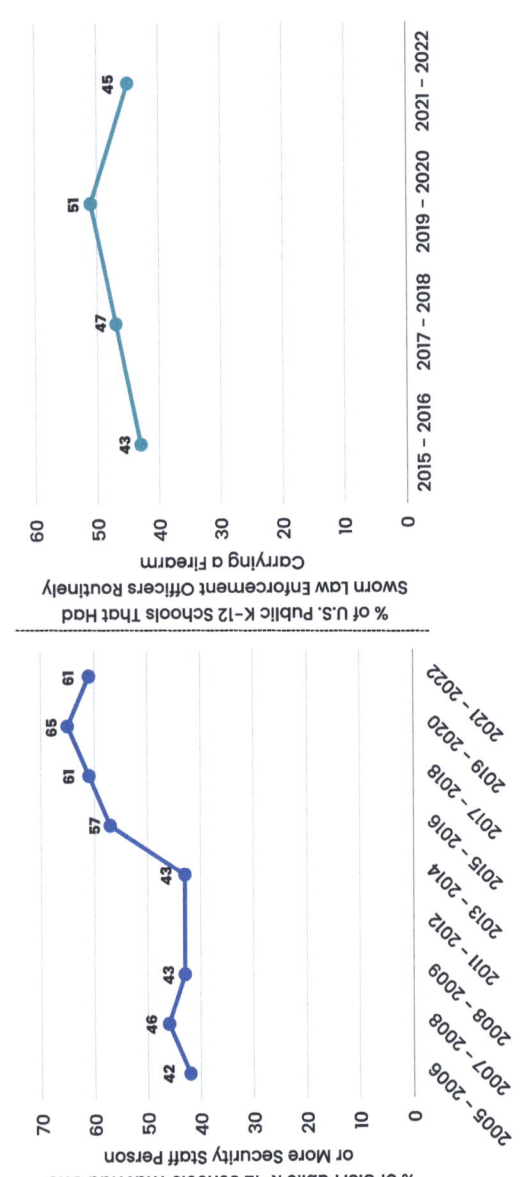

FIGURE 2-2 Trends in percentage of U.S. public K–12 schools with security staff and law enforcement personnel, school years 2005–2006 to 2021–2022.
NOTE: Security staff include security guards/officers, security personnel, school resource officers, and sworn law enforcement officers who are not school resource officers.
SOURCE: Data from NCES, 2023.

TABLE 2-7 Percentage of Public K–12 Schools with One or More Full- or Part-time Security Staff Present at Least Once a Week, School Year 2021–2022

School Characteristic	School Resource Officers[a]			Other Sworn Law Enforcement Personnel[b]			Security Officers or Security Personnel		
	Total	Full-time	Part-time	Total	Full-time	Part-time	Total	Full-time	Part-time
All public schools	**43.7**	**29.2**	**16.0**	**10.5**	**5.1**	**5.7**	**25.5**	**18.6**	**9.7**
School type									
Traditional public school	46.2	30.8	17.0	10.8	5.2	5.9	24.6	17.7	9.4
Charter school	17.6	12.5	5.6!	7.3!	‡	3.5!	35.3	28.6	12.3
Level[c]									
Elementary	33.0	17.6	16.2	8.4	3.2	5.2	18.6	11.1	8.9
Middle	62.0	45.0	19.1	11.7	6.5	5.6	30.0	25.3	8.4
High/secondary	62.4	51.8	13.2	15.8	9.6	7.3	43.3	36.1	13.3
Combined/other	22.3	13.2	9.8!	10.5!	‡	6.3!	18.7	12.6	7.5!
Enrollment size									
Fewer than 300 students	31.5	18.0	14.7	11.6	4.8	7.2	15.7	10.8	5.9
300–499 students	35.6	20.0	16.4	9.5	4.4	5.2	19.6	10.7	11.3

500–999 students	49.6	33.5	17.8	10.2	4.8	5.5	28.4	21.4	9.5
1,000 or more students	74.4	65.9	11.7	12.1	8.6	4.5	54.9	49.5	13.5
Locale									
City	32.1	24.0	9.6	8.9	4.8	4.2	34.0	26.9	10.7
Suburb	44.3	28.3	16.9	9.5	5.6	4.0	32.6	24.5	12.2
Town	55.6	32.4	24.7	11.2	4.1	7.4	16.3	10.3	7.2
Rural	49.5	34.1	17.4	13.1	5.1	8.4	12.6	6.9	6.6
Region									
Northeast	45.0	26.0	20.7	11.8	6.4	5.6	37.4	30.1	10.8
Midwest	39.0	22.0	17.8	9.3	3.9	5.9	13.7	9.3	5.7
South	58.7	47.3	13.7	14.7	7.2	7.7	28.3	19.2	11.5
West	26.1	12.4	14.2	4.9	2.2!	2.7	25.0	19.0	10.1
Percent students of color[a]									
Less than 5%	45.2	28.9	17.5!	14.3!	2.9!	12.3!	12.0!	3.1!	8.9!
5% to less than 20%	52.4	33.3	20.4	11.7	4.6	7.4	13.0	6.6	7.0
20% to less than 50%	47.1	31.5	16.9	10.6	5.0	5.7	22.8	16.5	8.0
50% or more	37.3	25.8	13.1	9.5	5.6	4.2	34.6	27.4	12.0

Percent of students eligible for free or reduced-price lunches									
0%–25%	41.7	25.8	16.8	9.5	4.2!	5.4	20.4	13.5	9.3
More than 25% to 50%	44.1	26.7	18.4	11.9	4.9	7.5	19.1	12.8	7.4
More than 50% to 75%	52.4	39.1	16.0	7.8	3.8	4.2	26.8	19.8	10.6
More than 75%	39.4	26.7	13.9	11.7	6.5	5.5	31.7	24.5	10.8

! Interpret data with caution. The coefficient of variation (CV) for this estimate is 30%–50%.
‡ Reporting standards not met. Either there are too few cases for a reliable estimate, or the standard error represents more than 50% of the estimate.

[a] *School resource officers* were defined for respondents as sworn law enforcement officers with arrest authority who have specialized training and are assigned to work in collaboration with school organizations.

[b] Includes all sworn law enforcement officers who are not school resource officers.

[c] *Elementary schools* are defined as schools that enroll students more in grades K–4 than in higher grades. *Middle schools* are defined as schools that enroll students more in grades 5–8 than in higher or lower grades. *High/secondary schools* are defined as schools that enroll students more in grades 9–12 than in lower grades. *Combined/other schools* include all other combinations of grades, including K–12 schools.

[d] The term *students of color* is being used synonymously with *minority students*. Students of color include those who are Black, non-Hispanic; Hispanic, regardless of race; Asian, non-Hispanic; Pacific Islander, non-Hispanic; American Indian/Alaska Native, non-Hispanic; and students of two or more races, non-Hispanic.

NOTE: "At school" was defined for respondents to include activities happening in school buildings, on school grounds, on school buses, and at places that hold school-sponsored events or activities. If school security staff worked full-time across various schools in the district, respondents were instructed to count these staff as "part-time" for their school. Some schools

reported more than one type of school security staff at their school; these schools are counted in more than one category. Responses were provided by the principal or the person most knowledgeable about school crime and policies designed to provide a safe environment.
SOURCE: NCES, 2024a.

School resource officers and/or law enforcement personnel may be assigned to schools specifically to provide security and build relationships with students. Existing research focusing on their effects on students, staff, and school climate is limited and has yielded mixed results (e.g., Crichlow-Ball et al., 2022; Flannery et al., 2021; Sorensen et al., 2023). The presence of school security staff (both law enforcement and non–law enforcement) may affect various groups of students differently. For example, school resource officers may enhance feelings of safety for some students (Theriot & Orme, 2014), but they may also be associated with higher rates of exclusionary discipline, which impacts students of color disproportionately (Fisher & Hennessy, 2016).

School districts sometimes use non–law enforcement security personnel who are trained to handle security issues in schools to contribute to increased safety and greater opportunities for surveillance, interventions in the moment, and relationship building. These personnel have been associated with lower rates of student arrest and exclusionary discipline, although their efficacy at deterring firearm violence in particular is not known (Vernon & Curran, 2023).[15]

Finally, it bears noting that policies at the school district level and in more than 30 states allow teacher to carry firearms as a means of defending against threats. There is currently no evidence that arming teachers is effective at deterring firearm violence nor reducing the lethality of a shooting should one occur (Smart et al., 2024).[16] A synthesis of existing research on gun policies in the United States found no qualifying studies showing a benefit from arming teachers as a way of reducing firearm violence in schools;

---

[15] Vernon and Curran (2023)'s epidemiological analysis using representative data from the Civil Rights Data Collection found that use of non-sworn security personnel may minimize the student arrests and use of exclusionary discipline.

[16] Smart and colleagues (2024) conducted a systematic review of scientific evidence on laws related to allowing for K–12 staff to carry a firearm or associated outcomes. No studies met the authors' inclusion criteria related to the impact of such laws on outcomes such as mass shootings, violent, crimes, or unintended injury. The authors also note that there exists no comprehensive accounting of the extent to which school districts allow teachers or other school personnel to carry a firearm.

the authors noted concerns among school safety experts related to the potential risks of introducing more firearms into school environments (Smart et al., 2024).

EXPOSURE TO SCHOOL ACTIVE SHOOTER DRILLS AND SECURITY MEASURES

Previous sections of this chapter highlight potential differences in how students and school staff are exposed to school active shooter drills, hardening and surveillance measures, and the presence of law enforcement officers and other security personnel.

Certain school security measures have higher visibility than others. Although literature on *crime prevention through environmental design*—an approach for reducing crime though strategic management of the physical environment—emphasizes designing for both safety and positive social interaction, some school security measures, such as visible security cameras, fences, and the presence of armed personnel can signal safety concerns or heighten the sense of surveillance (Lamoreaux & Sulkowski, 2019; Lindstrom Johnson et al., 2018). Current data highlight differential exposures to school security measures, particularly along racial and ethnic lines (Cuellar & Coyle, 2020; Mowen & Parker, 2017; Payne & Welch, 2023).

By contrast, data are more limited on variations in exposure of students' and staff exposure to school active shooter drills—particularly regarding the specific practices and approaches that are encompassed by this broad category. Given that active shooter drills are widely implemented in U.S. schools, it is more likely that students will differ in the types of drills they experience than in whether they experience them at all.

Geographical differences also matter, as urban, suburban, and rural residence, along with state or regional requirements, can influence the types and frequency of safety measures implemented. For example, variation in state requirements for active shooter drills—as noted in Table 2-1—range from zero to four or more mandated drills per year, resulting over time in large differences in student exposure to drills. To date, there has been little research on the cumulative effects of exposure to multiple school active shooter drills and other school security measures, despite the potential for various safety measures to act collectively to shape student perceptions and behaviors, either positively or negatively (Lindstrom Johnson et al., 2018; Mowen & Freng, 2018; Perumean-Chaney & Sutton, 2013). As researchers and practitioners gain a deeper understanding of individual approaches, they need to consider the interaction among different strategies and whether exposure to multiple strategies could amplify adverse effects. For example, school active shooter drills led by law enforcement personnel might be more concerning for students relative to those facilitated by school staff or mental health professionals.

The fact that school safety and security strategies vary and may be implemented in combination (discussed further in Chapter 4) raises questions about whether specific strategies interact positively or negatively, and about how individual strategies may affect mental, emotional, and behavioral health outcomes. When research designs examine more than one school safety strategy simultaneously, the results are typically conflated, making it difficult to determine the effects of each on school safety and school climate overall. Such a research approach leads to a situation in which either all strategies are deemed to work, or none. Thus, more studies are needed to investigate whether individual strategies complement each other, affect the well-being of students and staff positively or negatively, improve school safety, or potentially counteract one another. It is also crucial to determine whether certain groups of strategies are more effective than others. Chapter 7 provides the committee's detailed agenda for future research on these and related topics.

CONCLUSION

The landscape of school safety in the United States is shaped by a broad array of strategies, including school active shooter drills, other security measures, and broader efforts to foster a positive school climate. These components, while often implemented together, vary considerably across states, communities, and individual schools, reflecting differences in available resources, regional policies, and local priorities. A comprehensive approach to school safety integrates practices that support the mental, emotional, and behavioral health of students and staff with emergency preparedness practices and security measures.

Despite the widespread adoption of school active shooter drills and other security measures, the evidence base on their effectiveness remains fragmented. Existing research often combines individual measures without examining their interactive effects, limiting understanding of whether specific strategies complement or counteract one another. This gap in the literature underscores the need for more rigorous, holistic research that evaluates school safety strategies not only in isolation but also in combination, particularly in how they shape student and staff perceptions of safety, preparedness, and well-being.

Furthermore, gaps in resources and access to supportive interventions pose critical challenges, particularly for under-resourced schools. Schools with limited funding, for example, are less likely to have access to essential health professionals, such as school counselors, school psychologists, school social workers, and school nurses, despite evidence indicating that these supports play an important role in promoting student resilience, social-emotional skills, and prosocial behavior. Trauma-informed practices, which recognize and respond to the effects of trauma on student behavior and learning, represent another important component of a holistic school safety strategy. Without access to these supports, schools may be left with a reactive rather than a preventive approach, focusing narrowly on security measures instead of addressing the root causes of violence and behavioral challenges.

As the committee has emphasized, the available evidence shows that a balanced and evidence-informed school safety strategy needs to extend beyond immediate crisis preparedness to encompass long-term efforts that cultivate a secure, inclusive, and supportive learning environment, one that fosters resilience and well-being. The cumulative effects of exposure to various school security measures and school active shooter drills, the role of trauma-informed and developmentally appropriate interventions, and the intersection of these approaches with students' perceptions of safety and well-being warrant deeper investigation. Chapters 3 and 4 explore the empirical evidence on how school active shooter drills and other security measures influence key mental, emotional, and behavioral outcomes—including sense of preparedness, feelings of belonging, and perceived safety, as well as potential adverse effects on experiences of trauma and student behavior—further advancing the discussion on the complex and multifaceted nature of school safety.

REFERENCES

Acosta, J., Chinman, M., Ebener, P., Malone, P., Phillips, A., & Wilks, A. (2019). Evaluation of a whole-school change intervention: Findings from a two-year cluster-randomized trial of the Restorative Practices Intervention. *Journal of Youth and Adolescence, 48*, 876–890. https://doi.org/10.1007/s10964-019-01013-2

Addington, L. A. (2009). Cops and cameras: Public school security as a policy response to Columbine. *American Behavioral Scientist, 52*(10), 1426–1446. https://doi.org/10.1177/0002764209332556

American School Counselor Association (ASCA). (2024). *Student-to-school-counselor ratio 2023–2024.* https://www.schoolcounselor.org/getmedia/f2a319d5-db73-4ca1-a515-2ad2c73ec746/Ratios-2023-24-Alpha.pdf

Asmussen, K., McBride, T., & Waddell, S. (2019). The potential of early intervention for preventing and reducing ACE-related trauma. *Social Policy and Society, 18*(3), 425–434. http://doi.org/10.1017/S1474746419000071

Avery, J. C., Morris, H., Galvin, E., Misso, M., Savaglio, M., & Skouteris, H. (2021). Systematic review of school-wide trauma-informed approaches. *Journal of Child & Adolescent Trauma, 14*(3), 38–397.

Bachman, R., Randolph, A., & Brown, B. L. (2011). Predicting perceptions of fear at school and going to and from school for African American and White students: The effects of school security measures. *Youth & Society, 43*(2), 705–726. https://doi.org/10.1177/0044118X10366674

Barroso, A. (2022, July 27). U.S. school security procedures have become more widespread in recent years, but are still unevenly adopted. *Pew Research Center.* https://www.pewresearch.org/short-reads/2022/07/27/u-s-school-security-procedures-have-become-more-widespread-in-recent-years-but-are-still-unevenly-adopted/

Blair, J. P., Nichols, T., Burns, D., & Curnutt, J. R. (2013). *Active shooter events and response*. CRC Press.

Bradshaw, C. P. (2013). Preventing bullying through Positive Behavioral Interventions and Supports (PBIS): A multitiered approach to prevention and integration. *Theory Into Practice, 52*, 288–295. https://doi.org/10.1080/00405841.2013.829732

Bradshaw, C. P., Koth, C., Thornton, L., & Leaf, P. (2009). Altering school climate through school-wide positive behavioral interventions and supports: Findings from a group-randomized effectiveness trial. *Prevention Science, 10*, 100–115. https://doi.org/10.1007/s11121-008-0114-9

Bradshaw, C. P., Waasdorp, T. E., & Leaf, P. J. (2012). Effects of school-wide positive behavioral interventions and supports on child behavior problems. *Pediatrics, 130*(5), e1136–e1145. https://doi.org/10.1542/peds.2012-0243

Brown, B. (2005). Controlling crime and delinquency in the schools. *Journal of School Violence, 4*, 105–125. https://doi.org/10.1300/J202V04N04_07.

Brueck, M. (2016). Promoting access to school-based services for children's mental health. *AMA Journal of Ethics, 18*(12), 1218–1224. https://doi.org/10.1001/journalofethics.2016.18.12.pfor1-1612

Burr, R., Kemp, J., & Wang, K. (2024). *Crime, violence, discipline, and safety in U.S. public schools: Findings from the School Survey on Crime and Safety: 2021–22* (NCES 2024-043). U.S. Department of Education. National Center for Education Statistics. https://nces.ed.gov/pubsearch/pubsinfo.asp?pubid=2024043

Cafaro, C., Molina, E., Patton, E., McMahon, S., & Brown, M. (2023). Meta-analyses of teacher-delivered trauma-based and trauma-informed care interventions. *Psychological Trauma: Theory, Research, Practice and Policy, 15*(7) 1177–1187. https://doi.org/10.1037/tra0001515

Center on Positive Behavioral Interventions and Supports. (n.d.). What is PBIS? https://www.pbis.org/pbis/what-is-pbis

Centers for Disease Control and Prevention (CDC). (2021). Whole School, Whole Community, Whole Child (WSCC). U.S. Department of Health and Human Services. https://www.cdc.gov/whole-school-community-child/about/?CDC_AAref_Val=https://www.cdc.gov/healthyschools/wscc/index.htm

Chambers, D. (2022). How school security measures harm schools and their students. Educational *Theory, 72*(2), 123–153. https://doi.org/10.1111/edth.12523

Churchill, L., & Kriel, L. (2024a, February 8). Active shooter training: State-specific requirements for schools and law enforcement. *The Texas Tribune*. https://www.texastribune.org/2024/02/08/active-shooter-training-schools-law-enforcement/

———. (2024b, February 8). Check your state: Here are the active shooter training requirements for schools and law enforcement. *ProPublica.* https://www.propublica.org/article/state-active-shooter-training-schools-law-enforcement?taid=65c8c4dee58ebf0001b9e683

Cipriano, C., Strambler, M., Naples, L., Ha, C., Kirk, M., Wood, M., Sehgal, K., Zieher, A., Eveleigh, A., McCarthy, M., Funaro, M., Ponnock, A., Chow, J., & Durlak, J. (2023). The state of evidence for social and emotional learning: A contemporary meta-analysis of universal school-based SEL interventions. *Child Development, 94*(5), 1181–1204. https://doi.org/10.1111/cdev.13968

Cohen, J. A., & Mannarino, A. P. (2015). Trauma-focused cognitive behavioral therapy for traumatized children and families. *Child and Adolescent Psychiatric Clinics of North America, 24*(3), 557.

Collaborative for Academic, Social, and Emotional Learning (CASEL). (n.d.). What is the CASEL framework? https://casel.org/fundamentals-of-sel/

Colon, S. (2024, July 24). New York bans realistic active shooter drills in schools. *The New York Times.* https://www.nytimes.com/2024/07/24/nyregion/school-lockdown-drills.html

Cornell, D. (2021). Reflections on school safety from a threat assessment perspective. *International Journal of Applied Psychoanalytic Studies, 18*(3), 277–284. https://doi.org/10.1002/aps.1720

Cornell, D. G. (2018). *Comprehensive school threat assessment guidelines.* School Threat Assessment Consultants LLC.

Cornell, D., & Maeng, J. (2018). Statewide implementation of threat assessment in Virginia K-12 schools. *Contemporary School Psychology, 22,* 116–124. https://doi.org/10.1007/s40688-017-0146-x

Cornell, D. G., & Mayer, M. J. (2010). Why do school order and safety matter? *Educational Researcher, 39*(1), 7–15. http://doi.org/10.3102/0013189X09357616

Cornell, D., Mayer, M., & Sulkowski, M. (2020). History and future of school safety research. *School Psychology Review, 50,* 143–157. https://doi.org/10.1080/2372966X.2020.1857212

Crichlow-Ball, C., Cornell, D., & Huang, F. (2022). Student perceptions of school resource officers and threat reporting. *Journal of School Violence, 21,* 222–236. https://doi.org/10.1080/15388220.2022.2054423

Cuellar, M., & Coyle, S. (2020). Assessing disparities in school safety: Implications for promoting equality in current efforts to keep kids safe. *Security Journal, 34,* 658–684. https://doi.org/10.1057/s41284-020-00254-2

Dickson, M. J., & Vargo, K. K. (2017). Training kindergarten students lockdown drill procedures using behavioral skills training. *Journal of Applied Behavior Analysis, 50*(2), 407–412. https://doi.org/10.1002/jaba.369

Donovan, D. J. (2023). Active shooter drills in schools: Are we helping or hurting our kids? *Clinical Pediatrics, 63*(4), 441–443. https://doi.org/10.1177/00099228231180707

Doss, K., & Shepherd, C. (2015). *Active shooter: Preparing for and responding to a growing threat.* Butterworth-Heinemann.

Dow-Fleisner, S., Leong, A. D., & Lee, H. (2023). The interaction between peer bullying and school connectedness on youth health and wellbeing. *Children and Youth Services Review, 155,* 107147. https://doi.org/10.1016/j.childyouth.2023.107147

Durlak, J., Mahoney, J., & Boyle, A. (2022). What we know, and what we need to find out about universal, school-based social and emotional learning programs for children and adolescents: A review of meta-analyses and directions for future research. *Psychological Bulletin, 148*(11–12). https://doi.org/10.1037/bul0000383

Durlak, J. A., Weissberg, R. P., Dymnicki, A. B., Taylor, R. D., & Schellinger, K. B. (2011). The impact of enhancing students' social and emotional learning: A meta-analysis of school-based universal interventions. *Child Development, 82*(1), 405–432. https://doi.org/10.1111/j.1467-8624.2010.01564.x

Espelage, D., Rose, C., & Polanin, J. (2015). Social-emotional learning program to reduce bullying, fighting, and victimization among middle school students with disabilities. *Remedial and Special Education, 36,* 299–311. https://doi.org/10.1177/0741932514564564

Farrington, D., Ttofi, M., & Zych, I. (2019). Protective factors against bullying and cyberbullying: A systematic review of meta-analyses. *Aggression and Violent Behavior, 45,* 4–19. https://doi.org/10.1016/j.avb.2018.06.008

Federal Bureau of Investigation. (2024, February 8). Run. Hide. Fight. [Video]. https://www.fbi.gov/video-repository/run-hide-fight-020824.mp4/view

Fisher, B., & Hennessy, E. (2016). School resource officers and exclusionary discipline in U.S. high schools: A systematic review and meta-analysis. *Adolescent Research Review, 1,* 217–233. https://doi.org/10.1007/S40894-015-0006-8

Fisher, B. W., Higgins, E. M., & Homer, E. M. (2021). School crime and punishment and the implementation of security cameras: Findings from a national longitudinal study. *Justice Quarterly, 38*(1), 22–46. https://doi.org/10.1080/07418825.2018.1518476

Fisher, B. W., Petrosino, A., Sutherland, H., Guckenburg, S., Fronius, T., Benitez, I., & Earl, K. (2023). School-based law enforcement strategies to reduce crime, increase perceptions of safety, and improve learning outcomes in primary and secondary schools: A systematic review. *Campbell Systematic Reviews, 19*(4), e1360. https://doi.org/10.1002/cl2.1360

Flannery, D., Fox, J., Wallace, L., Mulvey, E., & Modzeleski, W. (2021). Guns, school shooters, and school safety: What we know and directions for change. *School Psychology Review, 50*, 237–253. https://doi.org/10.1080/2372966X.2020.1846458

Foshee, V. A., Bauman, K. E., Ennett, S. T., Linder, G. F., Benefield, T., & Suchindran, C. (2004). Assessing the long-term effects of the Safe Dates program and a booster in preventing and reducing adolescent dating violence victimization and perpetration. *American Journal of Public Health, 94*(4), 619–624.

Gage, N. A., Lee, A., Grasley-Boy, N., & Peshak George, H. (2018). The impact of school-wide positive behavior interventions and supports on school suspensions: A statewide quasi-experimental analysis. *Journal of Positive Behavior Interventions, 20*(4), 217–226. https://doi.org/10.1177/1098300718768204

Gerlinger, J., & Schleifer, C. (2021). School characteristics associated with active shooter drill implementation. *Analyses of Social Issues and Public Policy, 21*(1), 917–940. https://doi.org/10.1111/asap.12251

Grasley-Boy, N. M., Gage, N. A., & Lombardo, M. (2019). Effect of SWPBIS on disciplinary exclusions for students with and without disabilities. *Exceptional Children, 86*(1), 25–39. https://doi.org/10.1177/0014402919854196

Gratz, T., Goldhaber, D., Willgerodt, M., & Brown, N. (2023). The frontline health care workers in schools: Health equity, the distribution of school nurses, and student access. *The Journal of School Nursing, 39*(5), 357–367. https://doi.org/10.1177/10598405211024277

Gregory, A., Clawson, K., Davis, A., & Gerewitz, J. (2016). The promise of restorative practices to transform teacher-student relationships and achieve equity in school discipline. *Journal of Educational and Psychological Consultation, 26*(4), 325–353. https://doi.org/10.1080/10474412.2014.929950

Gryglewicz, K., Childs, K., & Soderstrom, M. (2018). An evaluation of youth mental health first aid training in school settings. *School Mental Health, 10*, 48–60. https://doi.org/10.1007/s12310-018-9246-7.

Hoover, S., & Bostic, J. (2020). Schools as a vital component of the child and adolescent mental health system. *Psychiatric Services, 72*(1). https://doi.org/10.1176/appi.ps.201900575

Hoover, S. A., & Mayworm, A. M. (2017). The benefits of school mental health. In *Handbook of rural school mental health* (pp. 3-16). Cham: Springer International Publishing.

Hsieh, H. F., Lee, D. B., Zimmerman, M. A., Pomerantz, N., Cunningham, M. C., Messman, E., Stoddard, S. A., Grodzinski, A. R., & Heinze, J. E. (2022). The effectiveness of the Say-Something anonymous reporting system in preventing school violence: A cluster randomized control trial in 19 middle schools. *Journal of School Violence*, *21*(4), 413–428. http://doi.org/10.1080/15388220.2022.2105858

Ice, M., Thapa, A., & Cohen, J. (2015). Recognizing community voice and a youth-led school-community partnership in the school climate improvement process. *School Community Journal*, *25*(1), 9–28.

I Love U Guys Foundation. (2023). The Standard Response Protocol (SRP) K-12. https://iloveuguys.org/The-Standard-Response-Protocol.html

James, N., & McCallion, G. (2013). *School resource officers: Law enforcement officers in schools (R43126)*. Congressional Research Service.

Johnson Jr., O., & Jabbari, J. (2021). Suspended while Black in majority White schools: Implications for math efficacy and equity. *The Educational Forum*, *86*(1), 26–50. Routledge. http://doi.org/10.1080/00131725.2022.1997312

Jorm, A., Kitchener, B., Sawyer, M., Scales, H., & Cvetkovski, S. (2010). Mental health first aid training for high school teachers: A cluster randomized trial. *BMC Psychiatry*, *10*, 51. https://doi.org/10.1186/1471-244X-10-51

Kim, H., Carlson, J. S., & Nelson, S. R. (2021). Towards a three-dimensional hardening of schools to promote effective school safety practices in the United States: A systematic review. *Advances in Social Sciences Research Journal*, *8*(8), 147–162. https://doi.org/10.14738/assrj.88.10614

Kjolhede, C., Lee, A. C., Duncan De Pinto, C., O'Leary, S. C., Baum, M., Savio Beers, N., Moran Bode, S., Gibson, E. J., Gorski, P., Jacob, V., Larkin, M., Padrez, R. C., & Schumacher, H. (2021). School-based health centers and pediatric practice. *Pediatrics*, *148*(4). https://doi.org/10.1542/peds.2021-053758

Lamoreaux, D., & Sulkowski, M. (2019). An alternative to fortified schools: Using crime prevention through environmental design (CPTED) to balance student safety and psychological well-being. *Psychology in the Schools*. https://doi.org/10.1002/pits.22301

Lazarus, P. J., Suldo, S., Suldo, S. M., & Doll, B. (Eds.). (2021). *Fostering the emotional well-being of our youth: A school-based approach*. Oxford University Press.

Lee, S. W., Lohmeier, J. H., Niileksela, C., & Oeth, J. (2009). Rural schools' mental health needs: Educators' perceptions of mental health needs and services in rural schools. *Journal of Rural Mental Health*, *33*(1), 26.

Lesneskie, E., & Block, S. (2017). School violence: The role of parental and community involvement. *Journal of School Violence*, *16*(4), 426–444. https://doi.org/10.1080/15388220.2016.1168744

Lester, L., & Cross, D. (2015). The relationship between school climate and mental and emotional wellbeing over the transition from primary to secondary school. *Psychology of Wellbeing, 5*, 1–15. https://doi.org/10.1186/s13612-015-0037-8

Lindstrom Johnson, S. (2009). Improving the school environment to reduce school violence: A review of the literature. *Journal of School Health, 79*(10), 451–465. https://doi.org/10.1111/j.1746-1561.2009.00435.x

Lindstrom Johnson, S., Bottiani, J., Waasdorp, T., & Bradshaw, C. (2018). Surveillance or safekeeping? How school security officer and camera presence influence students' perceptions of safety, equity, and support. *The Journal of Adolescent Health, 63*(6), 732–738. https://doi.org/10.1016/j.jadohealth.2018.06.008

Martaindale, M. H., & Blair, J. P. (2019). The evolution of active shooter response training protocols since Columbine: Lessons from the Advanced Law Enforcement Rapid Response Training Center. *Journal of Contemporary Criminal Justice, 35*(3), 342–356. https://doi.org/10.1177/1043986219840237

Maryland Center for School Safety. (2024). *Active assailant drill guidelines for schools.* https://schoolsafety.maryland.gov/Documents/Reports-Docs/Guidelines/MCSS-AA-Drill-Guidelines-2024.pdf

Mayer, M. J., Nickerson, A. B., & Jimerson, S. R. (2021). Preventing school violence and promoting school safety: Contemporary scholarship advancing science, practice, and policy. *School Psychology Review, 50*(2-3), 131–142. https://doi.org/10.1080/2372966X.2021.1949933

Maynard, B. R., Farina, A., Dell, N. A., & Kelly, M. S. (2019). Effects of trauma-informed approaches in schools: A systematic review. *Campbell Systematic Reviews, 15*(1–2). https://doi.org/10.1002/cl2.1018

McIntosh, K., Girvan, E., Falcon, S., McDaniel, S., Smolkowski, K., Bastable, E., Santiago-Rosario, M., Izzard, S., Austin, S., Nese, R., & Baldy, T. (2021). Equity-focused PBIS approach reduces racial inequities in school discipline: A randomized controlled trial. *School Psychology, 36*(6), 433–444. https://doi.org/10.1037/spq0000466

Miotto, M. B., & Cogan, R. (2023). Empowered or traumatized? A call for evidence-informed armed-assailant drills in U.S. schools. *The New England Journal of Medicine, 389*(1), 6–8. https://doi.org/10.1056/NEJMp2301804

Moore, P., Jackson, B. A., Augustine, C. H., Steiner, E. D., & Phillips, A. (2021). *A systems approach to physical security in K–12 schools (RR-A1077-1).* RAND Corporation. https://www.rand.org/pubs/research_reports/RRA1077-1.html

Morgan-Lopez, A., Saavedra, L., Yaros, A., Trudeau, J., & Buben, A. (2020). The effects of practitioner-delivered school-based mental health on aggression and violence victimization in middle schoolers. *School Mental Health, 12*, 417–427. https://doi.org/10.1007/s12310-020-09361-2

Mowen, T., & Freng, A. (2018). Is more necessarily better? School security and perceptions of safety among students and parents in the United States. *American Journal of Criminal Justice, 44,* 376–394. https://doi.org/10.1007/s12103-018-9461-7

Mowen, T., & Parker, K. (2017). Minority threat and school security: Assessing the impact of Black and Hispanic student representation on school security measures. *Security Journal, 30,* 504–522. https://doi.org/10.1057/SJ.2014.42

Nance, J. P. (2017). Student surveillance, racial inequalities, and implicit racial bias. *Emory Law Journal, 66*(4), 765–837.

National Academies of Sciences, Engineering, and Medicine (NASEM). (2016). *Preventing bullying through science, policy, and practice.* The National Academies Press. https://doi.org/10.17226/23482.

———. (2024). *K-12 behavioral threat assessment efficacy and implementation evaluation research: Proceedings of a workshop—in brief.* The National Academies Press. https://doi.org/10.17226/27980

National Association of School Psychologists (NASP). (2021a). Behavioral threat assessment and management (BTAM): Best practice considerations for K–12 schools. https://www.nasponline.org/resources-and-publications/resources-and-podcasts/school-safety-and-crisis/systems-level-prevention/threat-assessment-at-school/behavior-threat-assessment-and-management-(btam)-best-practice-considerations-for-k–12-schools

———. (2021b). Comprehensive school-based mental and behavioral health services and school psychologists. https://www.nasponline.org/resources-and-publications/resources-and-podcasts/mental-and-behavioral-health/additional-resources/comprehensive-school-based-mental-and-behavioral-health-services-and-school-psychologists

———. (2023). Student-to-school psychologist ratios by state, 2021–2022. https://www.nasponline.org/Documents/Research%20and%20Policy/Research%20Center/Ratio_by_state_21-22.pdf

National Association of School Psychologists (NASP), National Association of School Resource Officers (NASRO), & Safe and Sound Schools. (2021). Best practice considerations for schools in active shooter and other armed assailant drills. https://www.nasponline.org/resources-and-publications/resources-and-podcasts/school-safety-and-crisis/systems-level-prevention/best-practice-considerations-for-armed-assailant-drills-in-schools

National Association of School Resource Officers (NASRO). (n.d.). Frequently asked questions. https://www.nasro.org/faq/

National Center for Education Statistics (NCES). (2022). *Crime, violence, discipline, and safety in U.S. public schools: Findings from the School Survey on Crime and Safety: 2019–20 (NCES 2022-029).* U.S. Department of Education. https://nces.ed.gov/pubs2022/2022029.pdf

———. (2011). *Crime, violence, discipline, and safety in U.S. public schools: Findings from the school survey on crime and safety: 2009-10.* U.S. Department of Education. https://nces.ed.gov/pubs2011/2011320.pdf

———. (2023). Table 233.70. Percentage of public schools with various safety and security measures: Selected years, 1999–2000 through 2021–22. U.S. Department of Education and Institute of Education Sciences. https://nces.ed.gov/programs/digest/d23/tables/dt23_233.70.asp

———. (2024a). *Crime, violence, discipline, and safety in U.S. public schools: findings from the school survey on crime and safety: 2021–22.* U.S. Department of Education. https://nces.ed.gov/pubs2024/2024043.pdf

———. (2024b). *School pulse panel: Mental health services in public schools.* U.S. Department of Education and Institute of Education Sciences. https://nces.ed.gov/surveys/spp/results.asp

National Child Traumatic Stress Network (NCTSN). (n.d.). Effects. https://www.nctsn.org/what-is-child-trauma/trauma-types/complex-trauma/effects

———. (2018). Trauma-informed schools for children in K-12: A system framework. https://www.nctsn.org/sites/default/files/resources/fact-sheet/trauma_informed_schools_for_children_in_k12_a_systems_framework.pdf

———. (2022). Supporting trauma-informed schools to keep students in the classroom. https://www.nctsn.org/sites/default/files/resources/brief/supporting-trauma-informed-schools-to-keep-students-in-the-classroom-brief-1.pdf

National Council for Mental Wellbeing. (n.d.). What is mental health first aid? *Mental Health First Aid USA.* https://www.mentalhealthfirstaid.org/about/

National School Climate Council. (2007). What is school climate? *National School Climate Center.* https://schoolclimate.org/about/our-approach/what-is-school-climate/

New York State Education Department. (n.d.). Standard response protocol and standard reunification method. https://www.nysed.gov/student-support-services/standard-response-protocol-and-standard-reunification-method

Nickerson, A. B., Randa, R., Jimerson, S., & Guerra, N. G. (2021). Safe places to learn: Advances in school safety research and practice. *School Psychology Review, 50*(2-3), 158–171.

Nickerson, A. B., & Schildkraut, J. (2024). State anxiety prior to and after participating in lockdown drills among students in a rural high school. School Psychology Review, 53(6), 1–13. https://doi.org/10.1080/2372966X.2021.1875790

Nwabuzor, O. M. (2007). Legislative: Shortage of nurses: The school nursing experience. *Online Journal of Issues in Nursing, 12*(2). https://doi.org/10.3912/OJIN.Vol12No02LegCol01

O'Connor, C., Dyson, J., Cowdell, F., & Watson, R. (2018). Do universal school-based mental health promotion programmes improve the mental health and emotional wellbeing of young people? A literature review. *Journal of Clinical Nursing, 27*, e412–e426. https://doi.org/10.1111/jocn.14078

Office of Planning, Evaluation and Policy Development. (2023). *Guiding principles for creating safe, inclusive, supportive, and fair school climates.* U.S. Department of Education. https://www.ed.gov/sites/ed/files/policy/gen/guid/school-discipline/guiding-principles.pdf

Payne, A., & Welch, K. (2023). Minority threat in schools and differential security manifestations: Examining unequal control, surveillance, and protection. *Crime & Delinquency, 71*(6–7). https://doi.org/10.1177/00111287231194718

Perumean-Chaney, S., & Sutton, L. (2013). Students and perceived school safety: The impact of school security measures. *American Journal of Criminal Justice, 38*, 570–588. https://doi.org/10.1007/S12103-012-9182-2

Rajan, S., Reeping, P. M., Ladhani, Z., Vasudevan, L. M., & Branas, C. C. (2022). Gun violence in K-12 schools in the United States: Moving towards a preventive (versus reactive) framework. *Preventive Medicine, 165*, 107280. https://doi.org/10.1016/j.ypmed.2022.107280

Ramos, M. M., Fullerton, L., Sapien, R., Greenberg, C., & Bauer-Creegan, J. (2014). Rural-urban disparities in school nursing: Implications for continuing education and rural school health. *The Journal of Rural Health, 30*(3), 265-274.

Raptor Technologies & National Association of School Resource Officers (NASRO). (2023). Navigating school safety: Insights from Raptor's NASRO survey. https://raptortech.com/resources/blog/navigating-school-safety-insights-from-raptors-nasro-survey/

Raymond, B. (2010). *Assigning police officers to schools* (Vol. 10). U.S. Department of Justice and Office of Community Oriented Policing Services.

Rones, M., & Hoagwood, K. (2000). School-based mental health services: A research review. *Clinical Child and Family Psychology Review, 3*, 223–241. https://doi.org/10.1023/a:1026425104386

Rossen, E., & Cowan, K. C. (2014). Improving mental health in schools. *Phi Delta Kappan, 96*(4), 8–13.

Rygg, L. (2015). School shooting simulations: At what point does preparation become more harmful than helpful. *Children's Legal Rights Journal, 35*, 215.

Safe and Sound Schools. (2016). *Toolkit two: ACT—Stay safe choices.* https://d12b1c87-439e-47fd-8767-5821f38c7b68.usrfiles.com/ugd/d12b1c_96bfaf285abc4ddc85bf77aaadeb78d2.pdf

Sanchez, A., Cornacchio, D., Poznanski, B., Golik, A., Chou, T., & Comer, J. (2017). The effectiveness of school-based mental health services for elementary-aged children: A meta-analysis. *Journal of the American Academy of Child and Adolescent Psychiatry, 57*(3), 153–165. https://doi.org/10.1016/j.jaac.2017.11.022

Sanchez, A., Latimer, J., Scarimbolo, K., Von Der Embse, N., Suldo, S., & Salvatore, C. (2020). Youth Mental Health First Aid (Y-MHFA) trainings for educators: A systematic review. *School Mental Health, 13*, 1–12. https://doi.org/10.1007/s12310-020-09393-8

Schildkraut, J., & Grogan, K. (2019). *Are metal detectors effective at making schools safer?* WestEd. https://wested2024.s3.us-west-1.amazonaws.com/wp-content/uploads/2024/07/11165928/resource-are-metal-detectors-effective-at-making-schools-safer.pdf

Schildkraut, J., & Muschert, G. W. (2019). *Columbine, 20 years later and beyond: Lessons from tragedy.* Praeger.

Schildkraut, J., & Nickerson, A. B. (2022). *Lockdown drills: Connecting research and best practices for school administrators, teachers, and parents.* MIT Press.

Schildkraut, J., Nickerson, A. B., & Ristoff, T. (2020). Locks, lights, out of sight: Assessing students' perceptions of emergency preparedness across multiple lockdown drills. *Journal of School Violence, 19*(1), 93–106. https://doi.org/10.1080/15388220.2019.1703720

Schonfeld, D. J., Melzer-Lange, M., Hashikawa, A. N., Gorski, P. A., & Council on Children and Disasters, Council on Injury, Violence, and Poison Prevention, Council on School Health (2020). Participation of children and adolescents in live crisis drills and exercises. *Pediatrics, 146*(3), e2020015503. https://doi.org/10.1542/peds.2020-015503

Schwartz, H. L., Ramchand, R., Barnes-Proby, D., Grant, S., Jackson, B. A., Leuschner, K., Matsuda, M. and Saunders, J. M. (2016). *The role of technology in improving K-12 school safety.* Rand Corporation. https://www.rand.org/content/dam/rand/pubs/research_reports/RR1400/RR1488/RAND_RR1488.pdf

Simonetti, J. A. (2020). Active shooter safety drills and U.S. students—Should we take a step back? *JAMA Pediatrics, 174*(11), 1021–1022. https://doi.org/10.1001/jamapediatrics.2020.2592

Smalley, K. B., Warren, J. C., & Barefoot, K. N. (2017). Connection between experiences of bullying and risky behaviors in middle and high school students. *School Mental Health, 9*, 87–96. https://doi.org/10.1007/s12310-016-9194-z

Smart, R., Morral, A. R., Murphy, J. P., Jose, R., Charbonneau, A., & Smucker, S. (2024). The science of gun policy: A critical synthesis of research evidence on the effects of gun policies in the United States. *Rand Health Quarterly, 12*(1), 3.

Sorensen, L., Avila-Acosta, M., Engberg, J., & Bushway, S. (2023). The thin blue line in schools: New evidence on school-based policing across the U.S. *Journal of Policy Analysis and Management, 42*(4). https://doi.org/10.1002/pam.22498.

Sprague, J. R., & Walker, H. M. (2021). *Safe and healthy schools: Practical prevention strategies*. Guilford Publications.

Stilwell, S. M., Heinze, J. E., Hsieh, H. F., Torres, E., Grodzinski, A., & Zimmerman, M. (2024). Positive youth development approach to school safety: a comprehensive conceptual framework. *Journal of School Health, 94*(9), 848–857. https://doi.org/10.1111/josh.13485

Tanner-Smith, E. E., Fisher, B. W., Addington, L. A., & Gardella, J. H. (2018). Adding security, but subtracting safety? Exploring schools' use of multiple visible security measures. *American Journal of Criminal Justice, 43*(1), 102–119. https://doi.org/10.1007/s12103-017-9409-3

Taras, H. (2004). School-based mental health services. *Pediatrics, 113*(6), 1839–1845. https://doi.org/10.1542/PEDS.113.6.1839.

Taylor, R., Oberle, E., Durlak, J., & Weissberg, R. (2017). Promoting positive youth development through school-based social and emotional learning interventions: A meta-analysis of follow-up effects. *Child Development, 88*(4), 1156–1171. https://doi.org/10.1111/cdev.12864.

Texas School Safety Center. (n.d.a). K-12 standard response protocol toolkit. Texas State University. https://txssc.txstate.edu/tools/srp-toolkit

———. (n.d.b). School behavioral threat assessment toolkit. https://txssc.txstate.edu/tools/sbta-toolkit/

Theriot, M. T., & Orme, J. G. (2014). School resource officers and students' feelings of safety at school. *Youth Violence and Juvenile Justice, 14*(2), 130-146.

Thompson, M. D. (2023). The role of school district superintendent in school violence and prevention: Softening schools while hardening buildings. In T. W. Miller (Ed.), *School violence and primary prevention* (pp. 347–358). Springer International Publishing.

Tomé, G., Almeida, A., Ramiro, L., Gaspar, T., & de Matos, M. G. (2021). Intervention in Schools promoting mental health and well-being: A systematic review. *Global Journal of Community Psychology Practice, 12*(1).

Turanovic, J. J., Pratt, T. C., Kulig, T. C., & Cullen, F. T. (2022). *Confronting school violence: A synthesis of six decades of research*. Cambridge University Press.

U.S. Department of Justice (DOJ). (2019). School resource officers: School-based law enforcement. https://cops.usdoj.gov/pdf/SRO_School_Policing_Fact sheet.pdf

U.S. Department of Education (ED). (2025). Considerations for education leaders in preparing for active shooter drills in schools. https://www.ed.gov/media/document/considerations-education-leaders-preparing-active-shooter-drills-schools

U.S. Department of Education (ED), Department of Health and Human Services (HHS), Department of Homeland Security (DHS), Department of Justice (DOJ), Federal Bureau of Investigation, & Federal Emergency Management Agency (FEMA). (2013). *Guide for developing high-quality school emergency operations plans.* https://rems.ed.gov/docs/School_Guide_508C.pdf

U.S. Department of Education (ED) & Readiness and Emergency Management for Schools Technical Assistance (REMS TA) Center. (n.d.). K-12 response to an active shooter. https://rems.ed.gov/k12respondtoactiveshooter.aspx

U.S. Department of Homeland Security. (2025). Behavioral threat assessment and management (BTAM). https://www.schoolsafety.gov/resource/behavioral-threat-assessment-and-management-btam

U.S. National Institute of Justice. (2020). *A comprehensive school safety framework: Report to the committees on appropriations.* https://www.ojp.gov/pdffiles1/nij/255078.pdf

Vernon, K., & Curran, F. (2023). On guard but not sworn: The relationship between school security guards, school resource officers, and student behavior, discipline, and arrests. *Criminology & Public Policy, 23*(2), 327–360. https://doi.org/10.1111/1745-9133.12653

Warnick, B. R., & Kapa, R. (2019). Rethinking school safety: Why education is the best defense against school shootings. *Education Next, 19*(2), 44–50. https://www.educationnext.org/wp-content/uploads/2022/01/ednext_XIX_2_warnick_kapa.pdf

Weist, M. D., & Evans, S. W. (2005). Expanded school mental health: Challenges and opportunities in an emerging field. *Journal of Youth and Adolescence, 34*, 3–6. https://doi.org/10.1007/s10964-005-1330-2

Willgerodt, M. A., Choi, S., Iovan, S., & Magnuson, A. (2024a). National workforce data on school nurse availability and distribution. *The Journal of School Nursing, 40*(5). https://doi.org/10.1177/10598405241253565

Willgerodt, M. A., Tanner, A., McCabe, E., Jameson, B., & Brock, D. (2024b). Public school nurses in the United States: National school nurse workforce study 2.0. *The Journal of School Nursing, 40*(5), 468–481. https://doi.org/10.1177/10598405241253565

Woulfin, S., & Sadler, J. (2023). A is for Apple, B is for Bulletproof: The racialized fortification of schools. *Berkeley Review of Education, 12*(2). https://doi.org/10.5070/B812260100

Zabek, F., Lyons, M., Alwani, N., Taylor, J., Brown-Meredith, E., Cruz, M., & Southall, V. (2022). Roles and functions of school mental health professionals within comprehensive school mental health systems. *School Mental Health, 15*, 1–18. https://doi.org/10.1007/s12310-022-09535-0

3

Mental, Emotional, and Behavioral Health Effects of School Active Shooter Drills

The committee was tasked with examining the potential short- and long-term mental, emotional, and behavioral health effects of school active shooter and lockdown drills, as well as other school security measures (e.g., metal detectors, police presence, locked doors/controlled access) on students and school staff. Given that both the nature and volume of empirical evidence on school active shooter drills differ significantly from what is available for other school security measures, this chapter focuses only on literature related to school active shooter drills. Specifically, the literature reviewed in this chapter includes all empirical studies identified by the committee that examine the responses of K–12 students and school staff to these drills.

The chapter begins by outlining the committee's inclusion criteria for the literature reviewed. It then presents an overview of the available evidence, including the methodological challenges that have contributed to gaps in the research base. The chapter next examines the mental, emotional, and behavioral health outcomes associated with school active shooter drills, detailing the research designs of the identified studies and reviewing the empirical findings on key outcomes of interest as identified by the committee. These include perceptions of emergency preparedness, perceptions of safety or fear, negative mental health symptoms (including traumatic stress), and student behavior. Additionally, the committee highlights insights from qualitative studies, which offer critical perspectives on student and staff reactions to school active shooter drills, complementing the findings from quantitative research.

In Chapter 4, the committee continues with a review of evidence regarding the mental, emotional, and behavioral health effects of other school security measures—specifically, metal detectors, law enforcement presence, and locked doors.

INCLUSION CRITERIA AND SEARCH STRATEGY

This chapter consists of a narrative literature review and assessment of the available research base regarding the health impacts of school active shooter drills. Studies included in this review met the following criteria: they contained empirical data; assessed the mental, emotional, or behavioral health impacts of drills; examined health impacts among K–12 students or school staff; and were published in English and accessible by the conclusion of the search period (January 15, 2025). The committee used standard academic search procedures to identify relevant studies, including keyword searches of research databases, consultation of key summative texts (e.g., Schildkraut et al., 2024b; Walsh et al., 2023), reverse-citation lookups within included studies, and input from experts in the field. Additionally, the committee reviewed an annotated bibliography created by the U.S. Department of Health and Human Services (2025) in January 2025 and confirmed that all studies referenced in that document had already been identified in the committee's search.

The committee also acknowledges several adjacent categories of studies that were *not* included in this review. Dissertations, master's theses, and other unpublished student work were excluded. Also excluded were studies conducted in school contexts outside of K–12 settings (e.g., college campuses), those focused on groups other than students and school staff (e.g., parents), and those examining types of drills not specified in the statement of task (e.g., fire drills). Studies on active shooter drills in nonschool contexts (e.g., hospitals) were excluded as well given the distinct developmental and contextual considerations pertinent to K–12 schools. Finally, the review excluded studies assessing the effectiveness of drills from a security standpoint, specifically those evaluating whether drills reduce morbidity and mortality during a simulated or actual school shooting event.

The committee identified some studies aimed at investigating the effectiveness of drills using computer simulations or after-action analyses of real-world active shooter events. Such research is difficult to carry out with precision given the statistical rarity of school shootings and the many uncontrolled variables involved in such an event. Moreover, the committee emphasizes that (a) the security effectiveness and (b) the mental, emotional, and behavioral health outcomes are two distinctly different dimensions of drills that may be related or entirely unrelated; they must therefore be considered separately. The committee's review does not take up the question of "security effectiveness" here; rather, the focus is limited to mental, emotional, and behavioral health outcomes for students and staff. School policymakers must balance information about potential harms of drills such as that presented in this report against the potential benefits of drills in light of their individual context and circumstances.

OVERVIEW OF THE AVAILABLE RESEARCH BASE

As noted in Chapter 1, empirical research on the mental, emotional, and behavioral health effects of active shooter drills is limited. Only a small number of empirical studies—fewer than two dozen in total—have investigated how drills affect K–12 students or school staff. In many ways, this limited research base is surprising—millions of students and school staff across the country participate in an intervention whose the health effects are largely unknown. On the other hand, the lack of robust research in this area is perhaps to be expected. Active shooter drills in schools appear not to have been a priority for federal research funding, as none of the papers included in the committee's review list a federal funding source. This may be related to the 1996 Dickey Amendment, which banned federal funding for research related to gun control from 1996—prior to the widespread implementation of active shooter drills in K–12 schools—until 2018. While the Dickey Amendment did not specifically ban research on gun violence or school active shooter drills, its interpretation resulted in significant restrictions on research addressing firearm-related injuries and deaths (Rostron, 2018). In 2019, Congress allocated $25 million to the Centers for Disease Control and Prevention and the National Institutes of Health to study firearm violence as a public health issue, which marked the first federal funding for such research in 2 decades. Furthermore, most research on school active shooter drills necessitates partnerships with a school or school district, and all research partnerships with schools entail practical, financial, and political considerations. Given these complexities, researchers may face barriers to engaging schools, as participation in such research can require significant time, energy, and resources and may raise concerns about undermining their current safety policies.

Within the small group of included studies, the mental, emotional, and behavioral health outcomes assessed vary and are limited, ranging from knowledge of drill procedures to perceptions of school safety, to feelings of fear and anxiety, to self-reported behavioral changes such as days of school missed. Many studies do not specify the precise nature of the drills assessed, making it difficult to distinguish whether different types or features of emergency preparedness procedures (e.g., didactic instruction vs. controlled rehearsal vs. realistic simulation) might have different health outcomes. Available studies used a range of methodologies, but virtually none employed the most rigorous research designs (e.g., random assignment to experimental vs. control groups), which would allow for the most confident conclusions about causation. Most studies had significant limitations—including small sample sizes, ad hoc outcome measures, and unmatched pre–post groups—that reduced the strength of conclusions that can be drawn.

Another striking characteristic of this body of research on active shooter drills is that more than one-third of all the empirical studies were produced by a single research team that assessed an anonymized school district (or districts) in central New York using the same training and lockdown drill paradigm. Thus, when considering the strength of the entire research base on mental, emotional, and behavioral health outcomes of active shooter drills, it is important to highlight that many findings are drawn from the same geographic region, possibly from the same school district. This is a limitation of the research base, as these findings may not generalize to or be representative of the varied contexts of school systems across the country.

Unsurprisingly, given the small total number of empirical studies, there are many important issues regarding active shooter drills for which no studies exist. As one key example, aside from a single qualitative study of teachers' perceptions, no peer-reviewed studies have assessed how students with functional or access needs (e.g., students with disabilities, students with sensory sensitivities, multilingual learners) react to drills.

Thus, while the following section presents a careful discussion of the available empirical research related to the committee's statement of task (see Box 1-1 in Chapter 1), the committee emphasizes that the gaps in knowledge about the mental, emotional, and behavioral health effects of school active shooter drills overwhelm the limited research base. Considering that millions of students and school staff participate in these drills each year, more high-quality research in this area is urgently needed.

MENTAL, EMOTIONAL, AND BEHAVIORAL HEALTH OUTCOMES OF DRILLS

Many sources (e.g., National Association of School Psychologists et al., 2021; Schonfeld et al., 2020) have expressed concerns that active shooter drills could increase fear and anxiety and decrease perceptions of school safety among students and staff. These sources hypothesize that the experience of the drills themselves—especially realistic or high-intensity drills that convincingly simulate a real active shooter event—may be distressing. Even low-intensity drills may cause participants to perceive a genuine active shooter event as more likely, increasing fear or decreasing perceptions of school safety. Conversely, some have argued that active shooter drills may increase perceptions of school safety for some students and staff by making them feel more prepared in the event of an actual active shooter event (Cunningham, 2020; Moore-Petinak et al., 2020).

To shed light on these important questions, the committee reviewed the limited empirical research base, identifying around two dozen studies that assessed some aspect of the personal reactions of K–12 students or school staff to active shooter drills (e.g., emotions, perceptions, self-reported behaviors).[17] Most of these studies assessed student reactions, with just a few assessing staff reactions. Most involved direct quantitative surveying of students or staff. One study involved analyzing a very large sample of social media posts to assess changes in language (e.g., words associated with anxiety, stress, or depression) from before and after a drill. The remaining handful of studies involved collecting qualitative responses via individual interviews, focus groups, or written responses to a text message poll. Studies differed in the constructs they measured (e.g., stress, anxiety, well-being, avoidance), as well as in the instruments they used to assess these constructs (e.g., unvalidated, ad hoc instruments created by the research team vs. more standardized, "brand name" instruments assessing well-studied constructs such as state anxiety).

Research Designs

One factor hampering the already limited research base on the mental, emotional, and behavioral outcomes of active shooter/lockdown drills is the relative weakness of many of the research designs. In general, the research design sets a ceiling for a study's ability to make causal attributions between drills and any ensuing participant

---

[17] This total count is approximate because some studies are described in two different manuscripts, and some manuscripts contain two separate studies (e.g., a qualitative and a quantitative study).

reactions. To be clear, ethical and practical constraints may make it challenging—or even impossible—to implement the most rigorous research designs (e.g., randomized controlled trials). But even if the limitations of the existing research base are understandable in light of these barriers, it does not change the fact that the committee's confidence in the meaningfulness, precision, and generalizability of the findings of existing studies are limited as a result. Existing studies fall into four major categories of research design, which are described briefly in this section in rough descending order of rigor with respect to causal attribution (see Table 3-1).

TABLE 3-1 Overview of Studies About the Effects of Active Shooter Drills

Study	Study Design				Outcome Measures					Population	
	Control group	Pre–post	Cross-sectional	Qualitative	Implementation	Emergency preparedness or knowledge	Perception of safety or fear	Trauma or mental health	Student behavior	Students	Staff
Zhe & Nickerson, 2007	X				X	X	X	X		X	
Dickson & Vargo, 2017		X			X					X	
Schildkraut et al., 2020		X				X	X			X	X
Schildkraut & Nickerson, 2020		X			X	X				X	X
Schildkraut & Nickerson, 2022		X				X	X				X
Schildkraut et al., 2022		X				X	X		X	X	X
Schildkraut et al., 2023		X			X					X	X

Study	C1	C2	C3	C4	C5	C6	C7	C8	C9	C10	C11	C12
Schildkraut et al., 2024c		X									X	
Schildkraut et al., 2024a		X			X		X	X			X	
Nickerson & Schildkraut, 2024		X				X					X	
Everytown for Gun Safety, 2020		X			X	X					X	X
Moore et al., 2024				X	X	X	X				X	X
Huskey & Connell, 2021				X			X				X	
Riggs et al., 2023				X		X		X			X	
Rauk et al., 2023				X			X				X	
Jonson et al., 2020				X	X	X	X				X	
Stevens et al., 2019				X		X						X
Laguardia et al., 2024				X	X	X					X	
Moore-Petinak et al., 2020			X									
ElSherief et al., 2021			X		X	X	X				X	X
Bonanno et al., 2021			X		X	X	X				X	

Goodman-Scott & Eckhoff, 2020; Eckhoff & Goodman-Scott, 2023	X		X	X	X		X
Jackson & Golini, 2024	X		X	X	X	X	X

Control Group Designs

Control group designs have the greatest potential to enable causal attributions as to any effects drills may have on participants' emotions or perceptions. Random assignment to an experimental group versus a control group means that any observed differences between the groups are likely attributable to the drill rather than to unrelated events, unmeasured differences between the groups, or other confounding factors.

There are certainly challenges to conducting effective control group studies assessing reactions to active shooter drills. For example, states or school districts may have rules stipulating that all students must complete drills, drills may initiate a full-school response that must involve all students in the school, and most students will already have completed dozens of active shooter drills of some sort by the time researchers begin studying their reactions. However, these challenges can be overcome to some extent with thoughtful research designs (e.g., a modified waitlist-control procedure, in which schools within a district implement their drills on different schedules to facilitate comparisons).

Perhaps because of ethical and practical barriers, only one study (Zhe & Nickerson, 2007) employed a control group design. And that study had a notably small sample size of only 74 students.

Pre–Post Designs

Pre–post designs assess the same set of participants both before and after participation in a drill. Pre–post studies do not allow for the degree of causal attribution enabled by control group studies. For example, participants in a pre–post study may be aware of the intended outcome of the drill and respond in a manner intended to fulfill the researchers' expectations. Nonetheless, pre–post designs successfully eliminate many potential sources of error by comparing participants against themselves. As a result, at least some potential confounding factors (e.g., students' demographics, early life experiences, personality traits, and mental health conditions) are eliminated. This advantage dissipates, however, when the pre- and post-drill groups are otherwise not identical (e.g., when participants drop out or new participants are added between the pre- and post-drill measurements).

Ten studies used pre–post designs to assess student or staff responses to active shooter drills. The studies tended to use very large samples (thousands of students and/or staff) across the school district; unfortunately, responses were anonymous because of school privacy requirements and so could not be linked pre- and post-drill. Furthermore, there were often large differences between the pre- and post-drill groups, across which all responses were aggregated. In many studies of student reactions, for example, the pre-drill surveys were placed in teacher mailboxes to administer to students and only a fraction of students completed them; similarly, only a fraction (presumably a different fraction) of students completed the post-drill surveys. As a result, statistical analyses had to treat the pre- and post-drill groups as completely separate (i.e., cross-sectional), significantly limiting confidence that any post-drill changes must be attributable to the drill rather than to changes in the composition of the groups being surveyed or unrelated events occurring in students' lives when the baseline measures were administered approximately a week prior to the drill.

Cross-Sectional Designs

Cross-sectional designs collect data from participants at a single point in time. This design allows researchers to calculate statistical *correlations* between theorized predictors and outcomes of interest. However, given the maxim that "correlation does not imply causation," cross-sectional designs cannot establish that a theorized predictor *caused* an outcome even if a statistical correlation is found. Causation may run in the opposite direction, or an unmeasured third variable may be driving both the theorized predictor and the outcome of interest. Therefore, cross-sectional designs are lower on the hierarchy of methodological rigor when it comes to establishing causal links between active shooter drills and mental, emotional, and behavioral health outcomes. Correlational designs can be strengthened using statistical methods to control for other variables that may be driving an association between the theorized predictor and outcome.

Seven cross-sectional studies assessed student or staff perceptions and emotional reactions following active shooter drills. However, most of these cross-sectional studies did relatively little to control for potential confounds between groups, and thus the ability to draw a causal inference is particularly suspect. For example, Huskey and Connell (2021) surveyed 379 undergraduate college students and found that those who reported participating in at least one active shooter drill in high school also reported increased fear, increased perceptions of risk, and decreased perceptions of school safety compared with undergraduates who did not report participating in a drill. However, given the lack of statistical controls for confounds, it is possible that undergraduate students who were already more fearful or had greater concerns about school shootings were simply more likely to *recall* participating in active shooter drills (i.e., "reverse causation").

Qualitative Designs

Qualitative research designs allow participants to provide open-ended responses about a subject of interest (e.g., via interviews, focus groups, or writing prompts). These kinds of open-ended responses cannot establish causation or statistically significant associations between variables. Indeed, qualitative research is not designed to furnish representative data on how frequently negative reactions to drills occur or how often they are related to other variables of interest. Instead, qualitative designs can yield rich, nuanced information about a problem, highlight individual stories that would be lost in aggregated quantitative data, and elicit ideas about solutions to problems. Commonly, qualitative research is used to help researchers gather preliminary information about understudied topics, generate new hypotheses about potential causal mechanisms, or elicit "raw material" that can be converted into quantitative survey content. Five qualitative studies assessed student or staff reactions to active shooter drills, using individual interviews, focus groups, or open-ended text message polls.

Committee's Observations

Overall, the methodological rigor of the studies identified by the committee was low. Only one study (Zhe & Nickerson, 2007) used a control group design, and only two studies (Nickerson & Schildkraut, 2024; Zhe & Nickerson, 2007) used well-validated outcomes measures as opposed to ad hoc instruments with unknown reliability and validity. While the committee recognizes researchers' efforts to undertake *any* empirical investigation on this important yet understudied topic, the small number of studies and relative weakness of the research designs limit the ability to draw strong causal inferences about the effects of drills. Additionally, many studies had additional methodological weaknesses beyond their research design, such as short follow-up periods, ad hoc outcome measures, unmatched pre–post groups, and lack of precision about what was considered a drill.

Review of Empirical Studies

With the above caveats about the quantity and strength of the research base in mind, the results of the available empirical studies differed depending on the study design, sample, type of drill, and outcome measures. Some studies showed positive reactions to drills (e.g., feelings of increased confidence about responding to emergencies); some showed no changes in emotions or perceptions; and some showed negative reactions to drills (e.g., increased depression or anxiety; however, only two studies assessed anxiety and depression using standardized measures with students in conjunction with actual drill participation [Nickerson & Schildkraut, 2024; Zhe & Nickerson, 2007]). In the discussion that follows, studies with quantitative measures are organized according to the type of outcomes assessed: (1) emergency preparedness; (2) perceptions of safety or fear; (3) mental health symptoms, including traumatic stress; and (4) self-reported behavior. Some studies assessed multiple types of outcomes falling into more than one of these categories and were therefore discussed more than once. Qualitative studies are discussed separately, given that participants providing open-ended reflections on drills gave responses touching on many types of outcomes.

Drills and Emergency Preparedness

Implementation Correct implementation of drill procedures is not in itself a health effect. However, basic data on how well a drill taught the intended knowledge and skills could be crucial backdrop for understanding the drill's health effects. For example, *if* drills have harmful effects, conducting them at the minimum frequency required to teach the correct procedures adequately might mitigate those effects. But this kind of fine-tuned adjustment requires knowing how quickly students learn the correct procedures and how frequently drills must be repeated to maintain the desired level of skill.

Four studies assessed implementation issues regarding active shooter drills. Zhe and Nickerson (2007) randomly assigned 74 students in grades 4–6 in an upstate New York suburban school district to one of two groups: (1) students receiving a brief training on emergency procedures and participated in one "intruder crisis drill" (30 minutes total) or (2) a control group. This study found that students who received the training and participated in the drill demonstrated greater knowledge of correct drill procedures on a five-question multiple-choice questionnaire compared with students in the control group. Observation of the group that received the training showed that, during the drill, all students successfully moved their desks to a safe location in the room in under 2 minutes (the first compliance criterion), but no classroom remained entirely silent for 7 minutes during the drill (the second compliance criterion). These results suggest that a single brief training on drill procedures imparts some knowledge and skills but is insufficient to achieve the desired level of skill acquisition.

The remaining three studies on implementation issues used pre–post designs. Researchers assessed participants' implementation skills at baseline (i.e., before receiving any training), provided didactic training on correct drill procedures, and conducted a series of monitored drills to assess whether drill implementation skills improved following training and practice.

Dickson and Vargo (2017) used this pre–post design to assess drill implementation among 32 kindergartners at a single Texas elementary school in a low-income area. The full research protocol involved a series of 13–25 observed drills conducted at a frequency of two to three per week. Results indicated that prior to any training, the kindergarteners could complete zero correct lockdown steps and remained noisy during drills. The kindergarteners required five to seven training sessions to attain adequate skill acquisition (around 80% of correct lockdown steps). They were able to maintain this level of implementation fidelity for three additional drills conducted over the course of approximately 1 week, with no refresher trainings. This result demonstrates short-term retention of skills for even the youngest students, although long-term retention was not assessed.

Schildkraut and Nickerson (2020) and Schildkraut et al. (2023) conducted two studies on implementation issues. Both took place within a large urban school district in central New York that was transitioning to a standardized, district-wide emergency response program (SRP-X). Because these studies assessed compliance with correct drill procedures classroom by classroom, they can be considered an assessment of both student and staff skill acquisition. Both studies involved averaging large sample sizes (thousands of students and staff) at each timepoint.

The first of these implementation studies (Schildkraut & Nickerson, 2020) demonstrated that a single training session significantly increased correct implementation of lockdown procedures but was insufficient to reach full compliance. Classrooms demonstrating perfect compliance increased from 27.7% pre-training to slightly more than half (54.4%) post-training. After a single training session, each classroom demonstrated approximately 85% compliance for three of the four required behaviors (lock door, lights off, no responses to door knock) and somewhat lower compliance (around

70%) for staying out of sight. Although the researchers did not conduct statistical analyses comparing compliance across grade levels, it appears that dedicated middle schools (grades 6–8) had the lowest average compliance compared with elementary schools, pre-K[18]–8 schools, and high schools (Schildkraut & Nickerson, 2020).

The second of these implementation studies (Schildkraut et al., 2023) yielded similar results, although this study improved upon the first by observing nine drills spread across 4 years, rather than just a single post-training drill. While the other three implementation studies were conducted across just a few months, this was the only study assessing long-term retention of skills across years. As in the prior study, classroom compliance rose quickly to high levels (approximately 85% or higher) after just one training, for all steps aside from staying out of sight (71.3%), which apparently is the most difficult step for classrooms to complete successfully. Encouragingly, correct implementation of skills was maintained or even increased across subsequent drills conducted over the next 3 years, even without additional trainings. Classrooms with perfect compliance increased from 54.4% after the first post-training drill (year 1) to 81.1% after the fourth post-training drill (year 3). Perfect compliance then remained steady, hovering around the 80% mark, for the remaining five post-training drills through year 4 (Schildkraut et al., 2023).

Schildkraut et al. (2023) demonstrated that relatively high levels of implementation compliance can be achieved and maintained over a duration of years even without repeated training, perhaps because teachers and students provide informal instruction and feedback to each other following drills. However, although 80% of classrooms demonstrating perfect compliance is an encouraging result, it means that one of five classrooms (20%) were still failing to complete all four required lockdown steps after 4 years of practice.

---

[18] The committee included pre-K students only when these students attended a school that also contained K–12 students. Some elementary school campuses include pre-K classrooms whose students may participate in school active shooter drills.

In sum, the four existing studies on implementation of drills show that even a single training can quickly improve compliance with the required drill procedures. However, repeated training or drills (around four to seven implementations) are necessary to reach adequate—though not perfect—compliance. Some elements of lockdown procedures appear to be more difficult than others for classrooms to perform correctly in practice. Keeping out of sight and staying quiet appear to be most difficult for K–12 students and kindergartners, respectively.

Perceptions of Emergency Preparedness While just four studies measured participants' implementation of correct emergency procedures during actual drills, other studies assessed *perceptions* of emergency preparedness.[19] Six pre–post studies by Schildkraut and colleagues captured brief, ad hoc measures of student or staff perceptions of emergency preparedness (Schildkraut & Nickerson, 2020, 2022; Schildkraut et al., 2020, 2022, 2024a,c). Participants rated agreement with the statement "I know what to do" in response to each of the SRP-X training program's scenarios: (1) lockout (now called secure), (2) lockdown, (3) evacuate, (4) shelter, and (5) hold.

Across these six studies, the researchers generally found that perceptions of emergency preparedness ("I know what to do" in different emergency scenarios) increased among both students and staff following training and participation in a drill (Schildkraut & Nickerson, 2020, 2022; Schildkraut et al., 2020, 2022, 2024a,c). In the subset of studies that reassessed perceptions following a second drill (Schildkraut & Nickerson, 2020; Schildkraut et al., 2020, 2022, 2024c), findings showed that student and staff perceptions of emergency preparedness continued to improve after the second drill. In other words, perception of students and staff that they "know what to do" did not always reach their zenith following just a single

---

[19] These different research questions were at times contained within the same published article. For example, Schildkraut & Nickerson (2020) contains data *both* about classrooms' implementation of emergency procedures during actual drills (i.e., how many classrooms closed their doors) *and* about student and staff's perceptions that they "know what to do" in response to various emergency scenarios.

training or drill, and generally continued to rise following a second drill. This result again suggests that a single training or drill is insufficient.

Furthermore, Schildkraut et al. (2024c) demonstrated that perceptions of emergency preparedness did not change significantly following a single "drill as usual," but did increase following a formal training on a Standard Response Protocol and then an additional drill. This result suggests that providing *training* on how to respond to emergency scenarios such as active shooter events—rather than just the act of completing a drill itself—may be important to improving feelings of emergency preparedness.

Moore et al. (2024) collected a much broader dataset to assess teachers' perceptions of their own and their students' emergency preparedness. They surveyed a randomly selected cross-sectional sample of 1,020 K–12 teachers and then weighted this sample to make it representative of the national population of K–12 public school teachers. Among the 90% of teachers who reported participating in at least one active shooter drill during the 2022–2023 school year, responses on emergency preparedness were divided: About half (47%) indicated that drills made them feel *more* prepared to respond to an active shooter incident, while the other half (50%) indicated that drills made them feel *neither more nor less* prepared. Rural teachers were more likely than their urban counterparts to indicate that drills made them feel more prepared to respond to an active shooter incident (Moore et al., 2024). The survey also asked teachers to comment on their perceptions of how drills affected students' sense of emergency preparedness, although of course teachers' perceptions of their students feelings may be inaccurate. About half (54%) of teachers indicated that they perceived that drills helped students feel *more* prepared, while one-third (32%) thought drills had *no impact* on students' feelings of emergency preparedness. Furthermore, 11% of teachers said they did not know how drills affected students' feelings of preparedness. Almost no teachers indicated that drills they made themselves or their students feel *less* prepared (Moore et al., 2024).

Taken together, the results of the Schildkraut et al. and Moore et al. studies suggest that on average, drills increase student and staff perceptions of emergency preparedness to some extent. However, averaging perceptions across all participants may mask the apparent finding that large portions of participants (e.g., fully half of all teachers in Moore et al., 2024) felt that drills had no impact on their perceptions of emergency preparedness. While these seven studies shed some light on the issue of perceptions of emergency preparedness, considerable uncertainty remains. For example, participants agreeing that they "know what to do" in the scenarios aligning with the SRP-X training may simply indicate that they effectively learned the responses they were taught, not that they perceive those prescribed responses will protect them in a real active shooter event. More detailed research is needed on student and staff perceptions of emergency preparedness and the specific practices that contribute to perceptions of preparedness.

Drills and Perceptions of Safety, Fear, or Risk

Some have argued that active shooter drills may make students feel more fearful or perceive their schools as less safe (Huskey & Connell, 2021; Moore-Petinak et al., 2020). Drills may cause students to imagine themselves in a life-threatening school shooting event or may create an impression that an active shooter event is likely to occur. Multiple studies with a variety of research designs assessed these kinds of outcome measures.

Just one previously discussed study in K–12 schools (Zhe & Nickerson, 2007) used a control group design to assess student reactions to active shooter drills. As a reminder, the researchers randomly assigned a small group of 74 of students in grades 4–6 to one of two groups: (1) a group in which students received a brief training on the correct procedure for an "intruder crisis drill" and participated in one drill (30 minutes total) or (2) a control group. The researchers assessed students' perceptions of school safety (including anxiety about school violence) via a 10-item, ad hoc adaptation of two existing measures (the School Violence Anxiety Scale [Reynolds, 2003] and the School Crime Supplement to the National Crime

Victimization Survey [National Center for Education Statistics & Bureau of Justice Statistics, 2001]). The researchers also assessed students' state anxiety, which is covered in the following section assessing mental health outcomes. Students in the drill group completed the questionnaires immediately after completing the training and drill.

Researchers found no statistically significant differences between the two groups regarding perceptions of school safety, which suggests that a carefully conducted active shooter drill did not make 4th through 6th graders more concerned about school violence when using a control group design. However, the small sample size of 74 would have precluded detection of anything smaller than medium-to-large effects (Cohen's $d = 0.66$ at 80% power and alpha = 0.05 two-tailed), even though such large differences are relatively rare in research on educational interventions (Hill et al., 2008).

Six pre–post studies (also discussed above) assessed perceptions of school safety, fear, or perceived risk (Schildkraut & Nickerson, 2020, 2022; Schildkraut et al., 2020, 2022, 2024a,c). Perceptions of school safety were assessed in all six of these studies via a series of brief, ad hoc items. Students or staff rated agreement with the statement "I feel safe" for four different locations: (1) "at my school," (2) "in my classroom," (3) "in the hallway," and (4) "outside on school grounds." In three of the four studies assessing student samples, the researchers showed that students' perceptions of school safety *decreased* following participation in a series of two lockdown drills (i.e., lower ratings of "I feel safe" in various school locations) (Schildkraut & Nickerson, 2022; Schildkraut et al., 2020, 2024c). In contrast, the fourth of these studies (Schildkraut et al., 2022) showed that student perceptions of school safety *did not change* following participation in one active shooter drill. Thus, although students reported feeling more prepared following participation in drills in these studies, they generally also reported feeling less safe (or at least not *more* safe). The only study directly assessing school staff's perceptions of school safety found that these perceptions *did not change* following a series of two lockdown drills (Schildkraut et al., 2022).

Schildkraut et al. (2024c) merits noting because this study sought to determine how a key student variable—*prior exposure to violence*—may influence the relationship between perceptions of school safety and participation in repeated drills. The researchers found that, across their entire pooled sample of three cross-sections comprising 8,627 students in grades 6–12, higher exposure to violence was associated with lower perceptions of school safety. The researchers also found that this relationship weakened over time (i.e., after students participated in two drills and one training on a Standard Response Protocol). The researchers speculated that the effect of prior exposure to violence on perceptions of school safety may matter less once students have been trained and rehearsed on lockdown procedures (Schildkraut et al., 2024c).

Two of additional pre–post studies by Schildkraut and colleagues measured students' feelings of *fear* and *perceived risk of victimization*, although in slightly different ways. These fear and risk variables are distinct from the items inquiring about a more generalized sense of school safety (i.e., "I feel safe" in various school locations) described above, and they returned contradictory results. First, for about 10,000 students in grades 6–12, Schildkraut and Nickerson (2022) assessed their (1) fear that they would be harmed at school or traveling to/from school and (2) perceived risk that "I think a school shooting could happen at my school." This study found that both fear and perceived risk decreased significantly after students participated in a series of two lockdown drills (Schildkraut et al., 2022). Second, Schildkraut et al. (2024a) assessed approximately 300 high schoolers' perceptions in 2022, including (1) fear of a school shooting happening at their school during that year and (2) perceived fear of being a victim of a school shooting. In contrast to the study by Schildkraut and Nickerson (2022), which found reduced fear and perceived risk post-drill, this study showed that students' perceived risk of victimization increased significantly after participating in one drill, although fear did not change post-drill (Schildkraut et al., 2024a).

In sum, evidence from the control group and pre–post studies is mixed and limited regarding the commonly raised concern that participating in active shooter drills may make students feel more afraid or perceive a school shooting as more likely. Some studies showed post-drill perceptions of fear and/or risk increasing, some decreasing, and some remaining unchanged. Given that many of these studies used similar student populations within the same central New York area, it is unclear why students reacted differently to drills in different studies.

Several cross-sectional studies also assessed outcome measures related to perceptions of school safety, fear, or perceived risk. Again, the committee emphasizes the limited ability of cross-sectional studies to establish causality, as well as typically limited or missing information about what constituted a "drill" across these large, in some cases national, cross-sectional surveys. In other words, students and teachers may be responding to meaningfully different drill procedures (e.g., high-sensorial vs. not) when responding to survey items. For example, Moore et al. (2024) surveyed about 1,000 K–12 teachers and *did* inquire about realistic, sensorial elements in drills. Findings indicated that few teachers reported high-sensorial elements during the 2022–2023 school year: 6% reported that drills included sounds of real gunfire; 5% reported police or security officers firing blanks; 4% reported prop or toy firearms; 1% reported the sounds of explosions; and 1% reported the use of fake blood. Most teachers (55%) reported no realistic elements during drills, which included no presence of police or other uniformed security personnel inside the school (the most common "realistic" element reported, at 44%). Unfortunately, Moore et al. (2024) did not analyze teachers' perceptions of emergency preparedness or school safety according to the number or type of sensorial elements, so we cannot know the effect of these realistic drill components on teachers. With these caveats, we describe the results of cross-sectional studies about school safety, fear, or perceived risk:

- Moore et al. (2024) surveyed about 1,000 youth12 teachers (as previously discussed) to inquire about sense of school safety. A majority of teachers (69%) indicated that drills had *no impact* on their sense of school safety. Of the remainder, 20% of teachers indicated that drills made them feel *safer* at school, while 12% indicated that drills made them feel *less safe* at school. Rural teachers were more likely than their urban counterparts to report that drills made them feel *safer* at school. The split was roughly similar when teachers were asked about their perceptions of how drills affected their students' sense of safety, although of course teachers' perceptions of student responses may be inaccurate: 38% of teachers thought drills had *no impact* on students' sense of safety; 24% thought drills made students feel *safer*, and 20% thought drills made students feel *less safe*. The remainder of teachers said they did not know how drills affected students' sense of safety.

- Huskey and Connell (2021) surveyed 379 undergraduate students and found that those who reported participating in at least one active shooter drill in high school also reported increased fear, increased perceptions of risk, and decreased perceptions of school safety compared with undergraduates who did not report participating in a drill.
- Rauk et al. (2023) used nationally representative data collected from more than 2,000 adolescents to investigate how students' race (students of color compared with White students) influenced associations between reported school safety policies and perceptions of school safety. They found that students of color who reported a greater number of total safety policies (including active shooter drills) at their school also reported lower perceptions of school safety, but White students showed no association between these variables. When only active shooter drills were considered, however, there was no moderating effect of students' race on perceptions of school safety.
- Jonson et al. (2020) surveyed approximately 1,250 students in grades 4–12 from a single Midwestern school district following the implementation of discussion-based exercises used to teach the ALICE multi-option protocol (see Chapter 1 for a description of the ALICE protocol). Using two surveys—one for elementary school (grades 4–5) and one for

junior high and high school students (grades 6–12)—the researchers found that 10% of students reported increased negative emotions post-drill, including fear, worry, and confusion after teacher-led discussions of ways they may respond to a dangerous person entering the school using the ALICE protocol. In comparison, 85% of students reported either no emotional changes or increased positive emotions, including feelings of safety, confidence, and emergency preparedness after discussions about the ALICE protocol.[20]

Overall, these cross-sectional studies yielded mixed results regarding student and staff perceptions of school safety, fear, or perceived risk following active shooter drills. In very rough terms, it appears that the most common outcome is *no change* to perceptions of safety, fear, or risk due to drills.

Drills and Mental Health Symptoms, Including Traumatic Stress

Few studies have investigated whether drills contributed to more significant or long-lasting mental health symptoms such as anxiety, depression, or traumatic stress. Virtually all used brief, but previously published and well-validated self-report questionnaires about anxiety, depression, traumatic stress, or well-being.

The single control group study was Zhe and Nickerson (2007) (discussed previously), assessing 74 students grades 4–6. The researchers assessed changes in students' anxiety post-drill via the 20-item A-State Scale from the well-validated State-Trait Anxiety Inventory for Children (Spielberger, 1973). They found no statistically significant differences between the group who participated in a brief training and drill and the control group. The use of a control group design and a well-validated measure of state anxiety are significant and unusual strengths for this study, which suggests that a carefully

---

[20] For questions related to fear, respondents could choose between "less scared," "no change," or "more scared." Similarly, for questions about school safety, respondents indicated whether training made them feel "less safe," whether there was "no change," or whether they felt "more safe." Responses were collapsed into two categories: 0 = no harm (i.e., no change, more safe, less fear) and 1 = harm (less safe, more fear).

conducted active shooter drill did not make 4th- through 6th-graders more anxious in the moment (Zhe & Nickerson, 2007). Aside from the small sample size of 74, which precludes detection of anything less than medium-to-large effect sizes, we also note that this study was conducted almost 20 years ago. It is possible that the greater number and cultural salience of school shootings since 2007 may have changed students' perceptions of drills in recent years.

Just one of the pre–post studies by Schildkraut and colleagues included mental health variables (Nickerson & Schildkraut, 2024). After participating in an active shooter drill, 763 out of 925 students in a rural high school completed a brief measure of state anxiety (although only 610 students completed the pre-drill questionnaire, and there was no analytical linkage of individual students pre- and post-drill). State anxiety was measured with the 6-item short-form adaptation of the well-validated Spielberger State-Trait Anxiety Inventory (Marteau & Bekker, 1992). The researchers used exploratory factor analysis to divide the six items into two factors of three items each, which they labeled anxiety-present ("I am tense," "I am worried," "I feel upset") and anxiety-absent ("I feel calm," "I am relaxed," "I feel content"). Post-drill, students showed small decreases in state anxiety (anxiety-present items) and small increases in well-being (anxiety-absent items), although students tended to show low anxiety and moderate well-being at both time points (Nickerson & Schildkraut, 2024). These results appear to be at odds with the consistent findings across Schildkraut and colleagues' studies that students felt less safe following participation in active shooter drills. Idiosyncrasies in the changing samples, contexts, and metrics may explain this apparent contradiction.

Just three cross-sectional studies assessed student mental health variables. Riggs et al. (2023) surveyed 108 youth–caregiver pairs presenting to a single emergency department in a large, Midwestern metropolitan area. They found that approximately one-third of the youths reported increased depression and anxiety symptoms post-drill. The questions used for the assessment appear to have been drawn from the well-validated National Institutes of Health's Patient-Reported Outcomes Measurement Information System measures (HealthMeasures, 2023). Interestingly, the caregivers consistently perceived the youths' post-drill anxiety and depression as less severe than was reported by the youths themselves (Riggs et al., 2023). This result suggests that parents may not always be able to detect when their children are bothered by drills. It should be noted, however, that this study was conducted during the COVID-19 pandemic when schools were closed, and survey participants were asked to reflect on their experiences with drills over the prior 2 years.

Moore et al. (2024) (described previously) asked teachers to comment on how they believe active shooter drills affected students' mental health. In a national survey of around 1,000 K–12 teachers, about one-third of respondents (29%) indicated that "they were aware of students at their schools who experienced trauma or heightened anxiety and stress following their participation in a drill designed to prepare them for school shootings" (p. 21). Perceptions of student trauma, anxiety, or stress were higher among elementary and middle school teachers compared with high school teachers; higher among teachers who reported multiple drills in a school year compared with just one drill; and higher among teachers who reported more realistic elements during drills (although the use of any realistic elements beyond police presence was quite rare). However, just 1 out of 10 teachers reported that their school provided mental health supports to students after the completion of drills. Furthermore, only a minority of teachers reported that drills were designed to meet the needs of diverse students. Only 12%–26% of teachers believed that drills were designed to meet the needs of students with physical disabilities, developmental disabilities, emotional challenges, or prior traumatic experiences, although a somewhat greater percentage (40%) believed that drills were designed to address the needs of students in different age groups (Moore et al., 2024).

A smaller survey of preservice teachers (N = 97), most of whom were interning in schools at the time, also asked about their perceptions of the impact of active shooter drills on students' mental health (Laguardia et al., 2024). Almost all the preservice teachers (89.7%) believed that drills can have an impact on students' psychological well-being, while a lesser percentage (58.8%) believed that drills can have an impact on students' academic performance. The survey results indicate that preservice teachers "generally felt underprepared to address the psychological and emotional needs of students related to active shooter response training" and desired better training in this area (Laguardia et al., 2024, p. 194).

Another cross-sectional study assessed trauma symptoms among teachers. Stevens et al. (2019) surveyed approximately 300 teachers (preschool through high school) regarding associations between exposure to drills and secondary traumatic stress. The researchers prompted teachers to describe the elements of the drills in which they had participated (e.g., shelter-in-place vs. simulation components) and then created a sum score in which a higher score indicated a greater number of different drill components. There was no significant relationship between the number of different drill components reported by teachers and their reported degree of secondary traumatic stress (Stevens et al., 2019).

Finally, ElSherief et al. (2021) assessed post-drill mental health using a very different methodology (see also Everytown for Gun Safety, 2020). Rather than asking participants to complete questionnaires about mental health variables, this study used a complex web-scraping scheme to assess how the language used in social media posts changed following school active shooter drills. According to the researchers, collecting voluntarily shared, publicly available social media data has many benefits over traditional survey methods. Researchers explain that this method "constitutes a promising opportunity to study psychological states unobtrusively and passively" when existing survey methods have shown little ability to capture rich, real-world data about mental health changes following crises (ElSherief et al., 2021, p. 3). The researchers also argue that this method can establish causation between an intervention and outcomes of interest, particularly when randomized control group designs may be "infeasible or unethical" (ElSherief et al., 2021, p. 3). This social media study is a clear outlier within the limited research base on school safety drills in terms of approach, sample size, and statistical attempts to control for confounds.

In their report, research team explains the complex methodology at length. Briefly, they first surveyed stakeholders involved in a gun violence advocacy group to identify the precise dates when recent active shooter drills had occurred in their children's schools (114 schools spanning 33 states; ElSherief et al., 2021). They then used web-scraping procedures to compile more than 27 million Twitter posts and 1,400 Reddit posts that could be tied to one of the identified schools (e.g., via geography or following the school's official Twitter account). These social media posts could be authored by school staff, parents, students, or community members and spanned 90 days pre-drill and 90 days post-drill. This is the only research the committee found that attempted to measure longer-term post-drill reactions. Finally, the researchers used lexical models to analyze changes in the language of social media posts pre- to post-drill (e.g., changes in the frequency of words statistically associated with stress, anxiety, depression, and concerns about death). The researchers used a variety of statistical comparison techniques to approximate causal inference, asserting that observed changes in social media posts are best attributed to the drills themselves, rather than unrelated seasonal or temporal changes.

Results indicated that active shooter drills are followed by social media posts showing a 39% increase in words associated with depression, a 42% increase in words associated with stress and anxiety, and a 23% increase in words associated with physiological health problems (e.g., *blood, pain, clinics,* and *pills*). Likewise, words associated with concerns about death increased 22% following active shooter drills. Other post-drill trends included increases in expressions of social and personal concerns, fewer positive statements, more requests for help, and increased profanity. These trends were sustained throughout the 90-day post-drill period, suggesting that the negative impacts of active shooter drills are not fleeting but last at least 3 months. Although all school levels (elementary, middle, and high school) demonstrated negative post-drill effects, social media posts associated with high schools showed the largest changes. The researchers theorized that, because most school shootings occur at high schools, the perceived impact of drills may be greater within those schools (ElSherief et al., 2021).

In sum, ElSherief et al. (2021) purport to demonstrate consistent, pervasive negative emotional effects of drills on students, parents, and school staff via changes in social media posts. These findings are more consistently and strongly negative regarding the results of drills than the more mixed pre–post survey results generated by Schildkraut and colleagues. Numerous differences between the social media and survey methodologies may explain these differences (e.g., many states vs. a single school or school district; social media data vs. brief self-report measures; a 3-month follow-up period vs. immediate post-drill measurement). While ElSherief et al. (2021) argue that their methodology produces a more accurate, nuanced understanding of reactions to drills compared with traditional surveying, others may question the indirect way in which the researchers culled social media posts and associated the words in those posts with emotional outcomes. The results may have been skewed by selecting only schools identified by gun violence advocates, since these schools could have had exaggerated negative post-drill social media activity compared with the average American school. Furthermore, because the methodology captured all social media posts associated with a specific school, the researchers could not distinguish among posts by students, teachers, parents, activists, community members, or others. In other words, the social media analysis does not necessarily reflect the responses (or *only* the responses) of students and school staff who were exposed to drills. In addition, the wide variation in drill practices and protocols across K–12 schools, along with the inconsistent use of terminology to describe these activities, means the types of drills that occurred in the sampled schools are unknown. The researchers did ask the initial respondents who identified dates of local drills about high-sensorial elements (i.e., "Did the drill involve simulations that mimic an actual active shooter incident?", see Table S-1 in the Summary). However, researchers did not gather any further details about what was meant by "simulations," nor did they publish analyses that statistically associated changes in social media posts at a particular school with the presence versus absence of simulation elements at that school. Finally, since the data collection period encompassed multiple mass violence events and heightened activism following the 2018 school shooting at Marjory Stoneman Douglas High School in Parkland, Florida, the results need to be replicated during other time periods to rule out period effects.

Drills and Student Behavior

Within the limited research base on the mental, emotional, and behavioral health outcomes of active shooter drills, studies have almost exclusively assessed internalizing variables (e.g., emotions, perceptions) rather than behaviors. Only three studies (Riggs et al., 2023; Schildkraut & Nickerson, 2022; Schildkraut et al., 2024a) assessed any kind of behavioral outcome. All three employed self-report questionnaires about participants' recollections and perceptions of their own behavior rather than any direct metric of behavior (e.g., disciplinary incidents or absences as documented in school records). Of course, students' recollections of their own past behaviors may be inaccurate for any number of reasons (e.g., tending to reflect personality traits or present emotional state).

Two of the pre–post studies by Schildkraut and colleagues queried students about their self-reported avoidance behaviors. First, Schildkraut & Nickerson (2022) found that, while students in grades 6–12 reported less fear and perceived risk following a series of two lockdown drills, they also reported more avoidance behaviors (i.e., staying home or avoiding class because of fears about victimization) after the two drills. Second, Schildkraut et al. (2024a) found that high schoolers reported more total self-protective behaviors following training on a Standard Response Protocol and participation in a single lockdown drill. The researched used a self-protective behaviors scale consisting of subscales for avoidant and proactive behaviors. In contrast to Schildkraut & Nickerson (2022), which found an increase in self-reported behaviors post-drill, Schildkraut et al. (2024a) did not find a change in avoidant behaviors post-drill. This study did find a significant post-drill increase in both the proactive behaviors subscale and the broader self-protective behaviors scale.

However, these findings of increased proactive and general self-protective behaviors may be experimental artifacts, since both measures involved items assessing "attended trainings on emergency plans" and "participated in a lockdown drill." Endorsement of both items would be expected to increase after students were required to participate in a training and drill as part of the study, so these increased scale scores may not reflect students' volitional self-protective behavior changes post-drill.

The third and final study to assess self-reported behavior changes following school active shooter drills was authored by Riggs et al. (2023). As previously discussed, the researchers surveyed 108 youth–caregiver pairs presenting to a single emergency department and found that approximately one-third of the youth reported increased depression and anxiety symptoms post-drill, when asked to reflect on any active shooter drills experienced over the past 2 years. Furthermore, youth that reported feeling anxious about drills were more likely to report being bullied, skipping school because of concerns about victimization, and participating in an unannounced drill (i.e., a drill they did not know was a drill at the time; Riggs et al., 2023). This study provides some support for the idea that anxiety about drills may contribute to absenteeism and lost learning time, at least for some proportion of students, although all the limitations about cross-sectional research designs continue to apply here.

Insights from Qualitative Studies

The committee identified five qualitative studies assessing participants' reactions to active shooter drills. Two involved only students, two involved only staff, and one involved both students and staff. As discussed, qualitative studies are not intended to be representative and cannot establish causality. Instead, these qualitative studies furnish rich, nuanced examples of the kinds of responses that some participants experience to drills. Because participants' responses are open-ended, the wide-ranging information they shared spans many of the outcome categories discussed earlier in this chapter. These five qualitative studies varied in the data collection method and population assessed. They tended to suggest mixed responses to drills, but with negative responses outweighing positive or neutral ones. Of course, negative responses to drills may be more memorable or salient than positive or neutral responses, and participants who experienced or observed negative responses to drills may have been particularly motivated to share these perceptions in a voluntary qualitative study. Box 3-1 presents additional qualitative information about student responses to school active shooter drills, as documented in the popular media by an investigative reporter, rather than in a peer-reviewed scientific article.

Student Participants Only

- Moore-Petinak et al. (2020) collected written responses to five open-ended probes from 815 youth (aged 14–24) who responded to a national text message poll. About 50% of youth reported that drills made them feel unsafe or scared (e.g., "scared because we thought they were real"). Another 15% of the youth reported other negative emotions such as sadness, helplessness, or frustration. In contrast, 20% of the youth reported feeling more prepared (e.g., "safer to know what to do in an active threat"). Approximately one-quarter of youth felt that drills had no emotional effect on them or failed to prepare them effectively for a real shooter (e.g., because drills also informed potential school shooters about emergency response procedures). We note that this age range (14–24) certainly includes students who are no longer in high school, who may have been recollecting their reactions to secondary school drills from many years ago.
- Bonanno et al. (2021) conducted individual, semi-structured interviews with 11 White students aged 8–11 living in a New York City suburb. Most of the students described feeling fearful of drills (e.g., "I worry if something bad is happening, if the lockdown drill is real, and this is a real emergency"; "It just freaks me out; I don't like it at all"). Many described the need to engage in coping strategies to help them address

their fear or anxiety (e.g., reminding themselves that they are safe, talking to adults). A couple of students described the drills as fun or exciting, but most described them as frustrating and disruptive to the school day. The students expressed general sentiments about the need for emergency preparedness, but many were unclear about precisely what kind of threats the drills were meant to guard against.

Student and Staff Participants

ElSherief et al. (2021), who conducted the social media web-scraping study previously discussed, also conducted a series of six virtual focus groups with a total of 34 participants (students, parents, teachers) from across the country who had participated in at least one drill or had a child who had done so. Many of the focus group participants described negative emotional reactions to drills, such as students "texting their parents, praying, crying" because they "thought they were going to die"; students becoming hypersensitive to signs of potential danger at school (e.g., a door handle jiggling); or teachers "break[ing] down at recess" because of stress following a drill. Other participants reported that students were desensitized to active shooter drills and unbothered by them.

Staff Participants Only

Goodman-Scott and Eckhoff conducted a series of four focus groups with a total of 26 school counselors from the southeastern United States (Eckhoff & Goodman-Scott, 2023; Goodman-Scott & Eckhoff, 2020). Numerous school counselors mentioned unintentional emotional fallout from participation in drills, including students' fear and anxiety; parents' worry and protectiveness; and school counselors' fear, anxiety, and uncertainty. For example, one school counselor shared, "[Even when you tell the students], 'This is just practice,' it still gets them upset. They end up having a mini meltdown." Others described simulation aspects of drills (e.g., a school staff member jiggling the door handle to check if it is locked) as "traumatic," noting that students with past traumas are particularly sensitive (e.g., "I had a student with a past trauma. . . . When there was a lockdown drill, his anxiety kicked in. . . . He would relive it [the trauma] during the lockdown drills"). School counselors also described the drills as stressful and anxiety provoking for themselves, not just the students (e.g., "It's a lot of wear and tear mentally, going through the drills"; "Your anxiety's up, your fear is heightened, and you do go into a fight-or-flight response"). Some school counselors mentioned how drills evoke troubling uncertainty about what would really happen in the case of a genuine school shooting, including fears about their own safety and perceptions of the weight of responsibility to protect students (e.g., "We're responsible for all those babies and I don't want one of them to get hurt. . . . It's a huge responsibility").

Jackson & Golini (2024) interviewed 10 teachers or paraprofessionals who were employed in a classroom with at least one 4- to 8-year-old child with autism spectrum disorder (ASD) during the 2018–2019 school year. Staff described numerous difficulties when attempting to teach and practice drills with students with ASD. For example, because children with ASD tend to thrive on routine, the abruptness of drills created particular disruption for these students. Furthermore, drills often involved atypical sensory experiences that could be markedly stressful for children with ASD (e.g., being crowded in close proximity to other students within a small space). Staff also reported that the challenging behaviors of children with ASD (e.g., tantrums, aggression, elopement) made it difficult for those students to learn and perform the drills correctly. Regarding mental, emotional, and behavioral responses to drills, participants described the drills as sometimes "traumatizing" for both students and staff, particularly if the drills involved realistic simulations (e.g., actors shooting blanks). One participant described the perspective of a student with ASD as follows: "Why would I want to gather with all of you in a small space in the dark? Like what is happening? Why are you telling me to be quiet? It's just overwhelming . . . definitely fight or flight." Another participant emphasized that even the staff could become "dysregulated" during drills because of sensory overload. Many participants reported feeling stressed by the weight of their responsibility for protecting students with ASD or other special needs. For example, one participant described physically carrying a student with ASD to safety when a drill occurred while the student was on the playground: "I had to yell, 'Grab him!' because he was breaking down. . . . He didn't know why he had to leave recess. So I just scooped him up and ran inside." In general, participants stated that they wished there were more resources for teaching students with ASD about drills.

Committee Observations

Overall, the qualitative research demonstrates that some proportion of students and school staff feel afraid, uncertain, or overwhelmed by active shooter drills, while others feel desensitized and unbothered. A consistent theme was that students and staff participating in drills often feel unsure whether a drill is a simulation or a real emergency, which increases feelings of anxiety and uncertainty. Furthermore, school staff reported feeling burdened by the weight of physically protecting students from harm, which is a role they do not normally enact. However, in the largest qualitative study (Moore-Petinak et al., 2020), a sizeable minority of students reported feeling more prepared or experiencing no emotional changes post-drill.

BOX 3-1
A Reporter Investigates Students' Perceptions of School Active Shooter and Lockdown Drills

Qualitative research on children's perceptions of active shooter drills is limited, though some qualitative and anecdotal media reports shed light on students' perceptions of active shooter drills. Through partnership with The Trace and Slate, Van Brocklin (2019) interviewed over 24 K–12 students across the United States in 2019 to learn about what they see, hear, and feel during lockdown drills. Using a podcast-style format, Van Brocklin (2019) found that some students interviewed felt worried during the lockdown drills, especially those experiencing drills that incorporated school staff acting as fake intruders. Students perceived drills as worrisome if they were unable to tell whether a drill was occurring or an active threat was underway, when they were not informed of the drills beforehand. Students also reported experiencing confusion about what to do if they are stuck in an area like the bathroom during the drill, as well as concerns about other students' behavior (e.g., being loud) during the drill, as this could increase their risk of harm during a real incident. Experiencing anxiety or fear during drills was commonplace for students, whether it was a personal experience or watching other students express these feelings. One student even mentioned that they witnessed another student experiencing a panic attack during a drill, even though that student knew it was a drill. Below are some specific quotes highlighted in the article:

- "They say it's a drill on the loudspeaker, most of the time, but they might be lying just to make sure you're not going to panic: 'I repeat, this is a code red lockdown drill.' I was so scared. I stood on top of the toilet, but then I remembered my teacher told me this year to sit on the toilet and put my feet up. And then last year, my teacher told me to stand on the toilet. So I was like, wait, what do I do? I was panicking. Then I heard footsteps outside. I was like, oh my gosh, is someone coming? I tried to stay as quiet as I could be. . . . I just hear footsteps, click-clack, click-clack . . . and then I heard the shifting of the doorknob, and I was like oh my gosh, what's going to happen? I was just hoping . . . hoping that it was the principal coming, not anybody that was going to kill me." —Phoebe, Grade 5
- "You're supposed to feel safe at school, you have your teachers . . . you're in your community. But it's really stressful to think about a random person doing that. And really just sad. If something

happened, the first thing I'd do is really get worried and maybe start to cry, and then I would hide, but I feel it's important that someone needs to fight back. Maybe not me, because I'm very scared. I would tell everyone to push all the tables to the doors and just start hiding, and if someone breaks in, do something crazy, pull something elaborate off. But I'd probably just start crying." —Ava, Grade 9

- "One kid, he was kind of worried and thought it was real. So he had a panic attack. He started breathing heavily and crying, and everyone was really worried about him. So then we had waited for a few minutes and then everyone started to calm him down. Like, 'It's OK, it's OK, it's just fake, we're just practicing.' One kid, he's really funny, he said, 'It's OK, man, it's OK, cool your beans!' Everyone started laughing and giggling—it was really funny." —Kennedi, Grade 5

- "I was in gym. . . . I think it was 7th grade. . . . To preface, I have ADHD. We heard it over the loudspeaker, we were sitting in our squads. We heard it, 'We will be entering a lockdown drill, please prepare.' So we go in the locker room, and I'm standing there. I start playing with my fingers because I'm incredibly bored. . . . And the gym teacher, who I don't particularly like, decided to put me up to the front because he did not like me playing with my fingers because he thought it was distracting to other children. I was not making a sound. . . . And then I sneezed. And everybody thought I was dabbing. Dabbing is sort of a dance move from a few years ago. . . So then he gave me detention because he thought I was trying to get everybody to laugh."—Colin, Grade 10

- "Why would we do the lockdown drill? Because if a wild animal or a robber or something came barging in. We first did a lockdown drill, and we only did it about two times last year, in kindergarten. So, how

the teacher explained it, she was thinking, like, if a wild animal came, and we hid in the bathroom—if it were a mouse or something, we probably wouldn't have to do that. But if it were a zebra or lion or something." —Foster, Grade 1
- "Last week there was a real stranger in the building, and we saw it on the security cameras. And I was very frightened, and I got a feeling stuck in my head about . . . I was thinking if we were going to be OK because the stranger was literally just outside the door of our classroom. And it was actually just our principal dressed in stranger clothes. I saw her wearing like a boy wig with her hair up in a bun. She had, like, a white shirt, a green tank top, and some, like, greyish blueish pants. I thought it was kind of scary because I didn't know who her true self was. So, we hid in the backroom or the closet. And it was very crowded, and we were very quiet." —Leah, Kindergarten
- "I remember it being a very weird shift from thinking about calculus to how I would escape if someone had a gun in my school." —Margot, Grade 12
- "I think lots of us are faced with this and we go: I know what I'd do. And we go: I'd totally be able to this, that, and the other. But I think practically, knowing myself, I would be in abject terror, and would almost be hard to get myself to do anything, much less heft a heavy object at someone trying to get in. If I had to rank on all this, of things I would be worried about in school, I think it would be: No. 1, getting a bad grade. No. 2, school shooter." —Shawn, Grade 10
- "I've always been worried about this. Like, every time I have a lockdown drill, I always am really scared by people talking and playing chopsticks or whatever. Because I always do the thing—not in like a, 'Oh, I always do the right thing'—but it's because I don't want to die. And I thought there was a

> significant possibility that I could. So I was, like, why is everyone playing games, what's going on here? Maybe this is a super common feeling or maybe nobody feels this way. It's hard to tell, because people don't talk about it much. That drill made me get mad at the school and everything. . . It really made me angry and sad and feel kind of trapped, because what am I supposed to do?" —Macie, Grade 8
>
> - "My first thought was, 'What should I do?' My second thought, 'Oh my gosh, we're all gonna die if they don't shut up.' The substitute closed the blinds, and she turned off the lights. We locked the doors, made sure every window was locked and every blind is closed on each window. We hide and sit. Everybody was acting all goofy and playing. I was about to cry because I didn't know if it was real or not, and everybody was just freaking out and acting like fools, like they didn't know what to do. They knew what they were doing, but instead of just going straight to where they were supposed to go, they were playing. I was behind my teacher's desk, by the wall, scared, crunched up, with my head in my legs, about to cry." —Kareena, Grade 5
>
> SOURCE: Committee generated, based on Van Brocklin, 2019.

CONCLUSION

The available research base on the mental, emotional, and behavioral health outcomes of active shooter drills in K–12 schools is mixed and limited. Overall, the published literature tends to suggest that these practices increase perceptions of emergency preparedness post-drill, coupled with increases in negative responses such as fear, anxiety, and avoidance. However, these are only inferences grounded in average trends; multiple studies suggest that students and staff have varied responses to drills. Studies indicate that somewhere between 10% and 65% of students demonstrated negative emotional reactions post-drill, reactions that may be more common among students with preexisting vulnerabilities (e.g., self-reported bullying victimization). Nonetheless, the results still indicate that the proportion of students reporting no changes or positive changes (e.g., greater confidence in their ability to respond to an emergency) post-drill ranges from a substantial minority to a majority of students. Studies that allowed richer, more nuanced observations of post-drill responses (i.e., the social media webscraping study and qualitative studies) tended to document more negative reactions compared with studies that surveyed participants directly using discrete, limited outcome measurements (i.e., circling responses on Likert scales). This observation suggests that researchers need to give more attention to *how* they are assessing potential negative reactions, as brief or unvalidated outcome measures may not be effective at capturing subtle mental or emotional changes post-drill, particularly if those changes affect only a minority of students and may be washed out by calculating only average trends across a large sample (see Chapter 7 for an in-depth discussion of future research needs).

In sum, the limited available research on student and staff responses to active shooter drills in K–12 schools raises concerns that these drills may be associated with negative mental, emotional, and behavioral health outcomes for many (though not all, or maybe even not most) people exposed to them. These potential risks must be weighed against the potential benefits accompanying any emergency preparedness procedure. However, existing data paint with a broad brush because of the lack of high-quality research investigating so many important dimensions of drills—most notably the effects of different drill components, the importance of drill frequency, the effects on staff, the occurrence of changes in behaviors of interest, and the needs of students from vulnerable groups. This lack of relevant research using rigorous research designs is striking given that active shooter drills are an intervention that has been applied to millions of students and staff across the country for many years. One might reasonably ask whether the existing scientific evidence base is sufficient to guide those making decisions about active shooter drills, or to settle on default procedures. But because drills are already happening in some fashion, and will continue to happen, waiting for more data is not an option. Schools and state legislatures will need to continue to draw on the limited existing research on drills; perceived security considerations; basic scientific knowledge on stress, learning, and child development; applicable laws and regulations; and their personal understanding of their own students and school contexts. While we wait for more high-quality and detailed scientific research, decision-makers will need to take all these considerations into account and make a reasoned choice about whether, how, and under what circumstances to implement school active shooter drills.

REFERENCES

Bonanno, R., McConnaughey, S., & Mincin, J. (2021). Children's experiences with school lockdown drills: A pilot study. *Children and Schools, 43*(3), 175–185. https://doi.org/10.1093/cs/cdab012

Cunningham, M. (2020). 183 student perceptions of lockdown drills. *Injury Prevention, 26.* https://doi.org/10.1136/injuryprev-2020-savir.129

Dickson, M. J., & Vargo, K. K. (2017). Training kindergarten students lockdown drill procedures using behavioral skills training. *Journal of Applied Behavior Analysis, 50*(2), 407–412. https://doi.org/10.1002/jaba.369

Eckhoff, A., & Goodman-Scott, E. (2023). School counselors' perceptions and understandings of lockdown drills: Navigating the paradox of safety and fear. *Educational Policy, 37*(2), 523–553. https://doi.org/10.1177/08959048211032667

ElSherief, M., Saha, K., Gupta, P., Mishra, S., Seybolt, J., Xie, J., O'Toole, M., Burd-Sharps, S., & De Choudhury, M. (2021). Impacts of school shooter drills on the psychological wellbeing of American K-12 school communities: A social media study. *Humanities and Social Sciences Communications, 8*(1), 315. https://doi.org/10.1057/s41599-021-00993-6

Everytown for Gun Safety. (2020). The impact of active shooter drills in schools. https://everytownresearch.org/report/the-impact-of-active-shooter-drills-in-schools/

Goodman-Scott, E., & Eckhoff, A. (2020). School counselors' experiences with lockdown drills: A phenomenological investigation. *Journal of Counseling and Development, 98*(4), 435–445. https://doi.org/10.1002/jcad.12345

HealthMeasures. (2023). Why use PROMIS? Northwestern University. https://www.healthmeasures.net/explore-measurement-systems/promis

Hill, C. J., Bloom, H. S., Black, A. R., & Lipsey, M. W. (2008). Empirical benchmarks for interpreting effect sizes in research. *Child Development Perspectives*, *2*(3), 172–177. https://doi.org/10.1111/j.1750-8606.2008.00061.x

Huskey, M. G., & Connell, N. M. (2021). Preparation or provocation? Student perceptions of active shooter drills. *Criminal Justice Policy Review*, *32*(1), 3–26. https://doi.org/10.1177/0887403419900316

Jackson, M. A., & Golini, E. J. (2024). Lockdown drills and young children with autism spectrum disorder: Practitioner confidence, experiences, and perceptions. *Journal of Autism and Developmental Disorders*, *55*. https://doi.org/10.1007/s10803-023-06201-5

Jonson, C. L., Moon, M. M., & Gialopsos B. M. (2020). Are students scared or prepared? Psychological impacts of a multi-option active assailant protocol compared to other crisis/emergency preparedness practices. *Victims and Offenders*, *15*(5), 639–662. https://doi.org/10.1080/15564886.2020.1753871

Laguardia, E. D., Campbell, L. O., Kelchner, V. P., Hilaire, B., Frawley, C., & Howard, C. (2024). Pre-service teachers' preparedness and perceptions: Active shooter response training. *Educational Research: Theory and Practice*, *35*(1), 186–198.

Marteau, T. M., & Bekker, H. (1992). The development of a six-item short-form of the state scale of the Spielberger State-Trait Anxiety Inventory (STAI). *The British Journal of Clinical Psychology*, *31*(3), 301–306. https://doi.org/10.1111/j.20448260.1992.tb00997.x

Moore, P., Diliberti, M. K., & Jackson, B. A. (2024). *Teachers' experiences with school violence and lockdown drills: Findings from a 2023 American Teacher Panel Survey*. RAND Corporation.

Moore-Petinak, N., Waselewski, M., Patterson, B. A., & Chang, T. (2020). Active shooter drills in the United States: A national study of youth experiences and perceptions. *Journal of Adolescent Health*, *67*(4), 509–513. https://doi.org/10.1016/j.jadohealth.2020.06.015

National Association of School Psychologists, National Association of School Resource Officers (NASRO), & Safe and Sound Schools. (2021). Best practice considerations for schools in active shooter and other armed assailant drills. https://www.nasponline.org/resources-and-publications/resources-and-podcasts/school-safety-and-crisis/systems-level-prevention/best-practice-considerations-for-armed-assailant-drills-in-schools

National Center for Education Statistics and Bureau of Justice Statistics. (2001). *School Crime Supplement to the National Crime Victimization Survey (SCS/NCVS)*. http://www.nces.ed.gov/programs/crime/pdf/student/SCS01.pdf

Nickerson, A. B., & Schildkraut, J. (2024). State anxiety prior to and after participating in lockdown drills among students in a rural high school. *School Psychology Review, 53*(6), 1–13. https://doi.org/10.1080/2372966X.2021.1875790

Rauk, L., Schmidt, C. J., Pelletier, K., Heinze, J. E., Cunningham, R. M., Carter, P. M., & Zimmerman, M. A. (2023). More is not always better: Examining the cumulative effects of school safety policies on perceptions of school safety for youth of color. *Journal of School Violence, 22*(3), 416–428. https://doi.org/10.1080/15388220.2023.2211768

Reynolds, W. M. (2003). *Reynolds bully victimization scales for schools manual.* The Psychological Corporation.

Riggs, A., Bergmann, K. R., & Zagel, A. L. (2023). Self-reported anxiety and perception of safety following school lockdown drills among adolescent youth. *Journal of School Health, 93*(12), 1129–1136. https://doi.org/10.1111/josh.13362

Rostron, A. (2018). The Dickey Amendment on federal funding for research on gun violence: A legal dissection. *American Journal of Public Health, 108*(7), 865–867. https://doi.org/10.2105/AJPH.2018.304450

Schildkraut, J., Greene-Colozzi, E., Nickerson, A. B., & Florczykowski, A. (2023). Can school lockdowns save lives? An assessment of drills and use in real-world events. *Journal of School Violence, 22*(2), 167–182. https://doi.org/10.1080/15388220.2022.2162533

Schildkraut, J., Greene-Colozzi, E. A., & Nickerson, A. B. (2024a). Balancing students' perceptions of safety and emergency preparedness: A quasi-experimental test of protection motivation theory as it relates to lockdown drills. *Victims & Offenders*, 1–22. https://doi.org/10.1080/15564886.2024.2410999

———. (2024b). Emergency preparedness drills for active and mass shootings in schools. *Current Psychiatry Reports, 26*(6), 304–311. https://doi.org/10.1007/s11920-024-01502-7

———. (2024c). Assessing the relationship between exposure to violence and perceptions of school safety and emergency preparedness in the context of lockdown drills. *Journal of School Violence, 23*(3), 319–332. https://doi.org/10.1080/15388220.2023.2291655

Schildkraut, J., & Nickerson, A. B. (2020). Ready to respond: Effects of lockdown drills and training on school emergency preparedness. *Victims & Offenders, 15*(5), 619–638. https://doi.org/10.1080/15564886.2020.1749199

———. (2022). Effects of lockdown drills on students' fear, perceived risk, and use of avoidance behaviors: A quasi-experimental study. *Criminal Justice Policy Review, 33*(8), 787–813. https://doi.org/10.1177/08874034221089867

Schildkraut, J., Nickerson, A. B., & Klingaman, K. R. (2022). Reading, writing, responding: Educators' perceptions of safety, preparedness, and lockdown drills. *Educational Policy, 36*(7), 1876–1900. https://doi.org/10.1177/08959048211015617

Schildkraut, J., Nickerson, A. B., & Ristoff, T. (2020). Locks, lights, out of sight: Assessing students' perceptions of emergency preparedness across multiple lockdown drills. *Journal of School Violence, 19*(1), 93–106. https://doi.org/10.1080/15388220.2019.1703720

Schonfeld, D. J., Melzer-Lange, M., Hashikawa, A. N., Gorski, P. A., & Council on Children and Disasters, Council on Injury, Violence, and Poison Prevention, Council on School Health (2020). Participation of children and adolescents in live crisis drills and exercises. *Pediatrics, 146*(3), e2020015503. https://doi.org/10.1542/peds.2020-015503

Spielberger, C. D. (1973). *Manual for the state-trait anxiety inventory for children*. Consulting Psychologists Press.

Stevens, T., Barnard-Brak, L., Roberts, B., Acosta, R., & Wilburn, S. (2019). Aggression toward teachers, interaction with school shooting media, and secondary trauma: Lockdown drills as moderator. *Psychology in the Schools, 57*(4), 583–605. https://doi.org/10.1002/pits.22329

U.S. Department of Health and Human Services. (2025). Resource: Active shooter drills research: An annotated bibliography [Archived Resource]. https://www.hhs.gov/about/news/2025/01/14/resource-active-shooter-drills-research-annotated-bibliography.html

Van Brocklin, E. (2019, December 18). Lockdown: Living through the era of school shootings, one drill at a time. *The Trace*. https://www.thetrace.org/2019/12/lockdown-podcast-school-shooting-drills/

Walsh, L., Curran, S., & Ernestus, S. M. (2023). What do we know (or NOT know) about school shooter response training? *The Behavior Therapist, 46*(6), 215–222. https://doi.org/10.31219/osf.io/pjr4y

Zhe, E. J., & Nickerson, A. B. (2007). Effects of an intruder crisis drill on children's knowledge, anxiety, and perceptions of school safety. *School Psychology Review, 36*(3), 501–508. https://www.scopus.com/inward/record.uri?eid=2-s2.035248836959&partnerID=40&md5=580a71635f658da9979ffdaaf6dbe285

4
Mental, Emotional, and Behavioral Health Effects of Selected School Security Measures

The committee's charge, as reflected in its statement of task (Box 1-1 in Chapter 1), focuses on the short- and long-term effects of school security measures, particularly those relating to the implementation of active shooter drills. As examples of other security measures of interest, the statement of task mentions metal detectors and police presence; the committee included both security measures in this study. It expanded the category of "police presence" to include school security staff more broadly, including school resource officers (SROs), other sworn law enforcement officers, and non–law enforcement security staff. The committee also included door locks as a security measure of interest because of their widespread use, both generally and specifically in lockdown procedures that are part of some active shooter drills. This chapter focuses on these measures and their potential effects on mental, emotional, and behavioral health.

The relationship between common school security measures and the implementation of active shooter drills is complex, reflecting broader debates about school safety and preparedness. These measures may interact with drills or each other in ways that can either reinforce or complicate the intended objectives of emergency preparedness, school security, and student well-being. Using these measures can influence the outcomes of the drills, as well as the overall school environment and school safety climate (Langhout &

Annear, 2011; Mowen & Freng, 2019; Schildkraut & Nickerson, 2022).

It is important to keep in mind the complexity of assessing the impact of school security measures, recognizing that these interventions are inherently shaped by school climate. In other words, their impact cannot be fully understood in isolation from the relational, social, and cultural dynamics of the school environment.

This chapter provides an overview of the nature, scope, and quality of the empirical evidence bearing on the impact of school security measures—specifically, locked doors, metal detectors, and school-based security personnel—on the mental, emotional, and behavioral health outcomes of K–12 students and staff. The discussion builds on the previous chapters by synthesizing existing research on school security measures currently used in U.S. public schools, with a specific focus on measures that may be implemented as part of school safety strategies or play a role in the implementation of school active shooter drills in particular. The chapter summarizes the available research literature pertaining to each of the above security measures and their relationship to the mental, emotional, and behavioral health outcomes of interest—specifically perceived emergency preparedness or knowledge, perceptions of safety or fear, student trauma and mental health concerns, student perceptions of school connectedness, school violence, and student behavior. The committee specifically includes school connectedness—students' feelings of being cared for, valued, supported, and having a sense of belonging—as an outcome of interest because research indicates that students who feel connected to their school community are less likely to experience poor mental health and are more likely to experience long-term benefits for overall health and well-being (Steiner et al., 2019; U.S. Centers for Disease Control and Prevention, 2023). Moreover, connectedness is a foundational element of a safe and supportive school environment. (Recall that the committee's conceptual framework, presented in Chapter 1, identifies a positive school climate as a critical protective factor shaping the outcomes of interest.)

Studies related to school climate are included, where relevant, to further contextualize the committee's findings. As noted in Chapter 3, this report does not take up the question of security effectiveness; it focuses solely on mental, emotional, and behavioral health outcomes for students and staff. School policymakers will need to weigh the potential harms associated with use of these measures against their possible benefits, taking into account their specific context and circumstances.

ADVANTAGES AND LIMITATIONS OF RESEARCH DESIGNS

Empirical research related to school security measures varies in design, scope, and methodological rigor. Studies span numerous disciplines including education, psychology, public policy, sociology, and criminology. There is a growing body of research on the effectiveness of school security interventions; however, like the evidence bearing the impact of school active shooter drills, the evidence on the effects of school security measures is characterized by several key limitations and gaps in methodological rigor.

The literature reviewed by the committee for this chapter fell into five primary categories: quasi-experimental studies, cross-sectional studies, longitudinal studies, systematic and integrated reviews, and qualitative studies (see Table 4-1). In the context of understanding the effects of school security measures on mental, emotional, and behavioral health outcomes, each of these methodological approaches offers distinct advantages and limitations in assessing both the short- and long-term effects on students and staff. In general, even when a correlation emerged, most studies did not establish causality because of the reliance on observational designs, which made it difficult to isolate the effects of security measures from other factors that could lead to similar outcomes. Variability in the implementation of security measures across schools further complicates comparisons and limits the extent to which effects can be generalized. Unfortunately, very few longitudinal studies are available to help understand and isolate the long-term effects of school security measures. Finally, some school security measures may have unintended negative effects such as increased anxiety, but these effects are not measured consistently across studies.

The following sections further describe the strengths and limitations of the above five research types in assessing the effects of school security measures on the committee's key outcomes of interest—while keeping in mind the complexity of student and staff experiences and the resulting difficulty of isolating specific effects.

Quasi-Experimental Studies

Quasi-experimental studies provide stronger causal evidence than is possible with purely observational studies. They allow for retrospective analysis using existing datasets, which can be more practical than randomized controlled trials for evaluating the effects of school security measures. However, these studies often focus on interventions with limited contexts, which can reduce their generalizability. They may also be vulnerable to unmeasured confounding factors.

Quasi-experimental studies could be used to assess impacts in a variety of ways. For example, pre- and postintervention data could be used to evaluate whether or not increased security presence enhances perceptions of safety or whether it fosters or hinders students' sense of belonging as compared with matched school environments. These studies may also highlight unintended mental, emotional, and behavioral health consequences by tracking anxiety levels and trauma-related symptoms before and after security measures are instituted. Because they often rely on secondary data sources, however, they may not be able to capture impact fully.

Cross-Sectional Studies

Most of the studies reviewed by the committee were cross-sectional in design, highlighting a significant gap in the longitudinal and experimental research necessary for establishing causal relationships. Cross-sectional studies provide a snapshot of the current school security landscape and immediate effects of security measures; they can be both cost-effective and time efficient.

Despite these strengths, they have limited ability to establish causality because they collect data only at one point in time and thus cannot account for some of the changes in outcomes over time that have been observed for some school security measures. Cross-sectional data can highlight variations in outcomes resulting from implementing security measures over time but cannot capture changes in outcomes such as perceived connectedness. These short-term findings may also not reflect long-term outcomes. And while associations between security measures and outcomes can be explored with a cross-sectional design, it is unclear without preintervention data whether these measures contribute to or mitigate mental, emotional, behavioral health effects. Cross-sectional studies are also unable to disentangle whether changes in student behavior result from security interventions or other school climate factors.

Longitudinal Studies

The committee found just two longitudinal studies, and only one related specifically to security measures of interest to the committee (Fisher et al., 2018). The other related to school safety and its effects on participation in school activities (Mowen & Manierre, 2017).

Longitudinal studies could provide valuable insights into how the implementation of various school security measures impacts students and staff over extended periods of time by identifying trends, delayed effects, and developmental consequences. With respect to the committee's outcomes of interest, longitudinal studies could be used to assess whether initial changes in perception of safety after a security intervention persist or change over time, whether there are delayed consequences as a result of prolonged exposure to security measures, whether there are long-term effects on perceptions of belonging and school social cohesion, and whether there are behavioral trends (e.g., in absenteeism, engagement, or disciplinary referrals) that can be linked to school security measures.

Conducting this kind of research on the effects of school security measures present many challenges. For example, outcomes can be affected by changes in school policies and security measures over time, attrition of students and staff, lack of sustained funding, significant time investments, and the need for data to make real-time policy decisions.

Systematic and Integrated Reviews

Given the limited longitudinal data on the effects of school security measures on the mental, emotional, and behavioral health of students and staff, systematic and integrated reviews provide a way to synthesize findings across available studies to assess the overall body of evidence on these measures. The committee identified five such studies. In addition to providing insight into the gaps in the existing evidence base, systematic and integrated reviews can identify patterns in research findings on the effects of security measures (e.g., anxiety or desensitization), clarify whether these measures undermine students' and school staff's sense of safety, provide insights into the relationship between the measures and school climate, and assess which interventions are associated with improvements or declines in mental, emotional, behavioral health across different school contexts.

However, the strength of the findings emerging from such reviews depends on the rigor of the studies they can include. Because of the variability in study designs, outcome measures, interventions, and school and student contexts addressed in the included studies, the comparability of findings may be limited, and the conclusions that can be drawn from those findings may be correspondingly weak.

Qualitative Studies

The committee reviewed five qualitative studies: four focused on school safety and security broadly and one focused on school security staff specifically.

Although few qualitative studies on this topic were found, they have the potential to provide rich, in-depth insights into the experiences of students and school staff and to capture nuances at the school level that could be overlooked in quantitative studies—in particular, unintended consequences and social and contextual dimensions of school safety and security policies. For example, qualitative studies can reveal insights that go beyond statistical outcomes and capture population-specific perspectives—such as why some school security measures may foster reassurance, while others may heighten fear, or how and why a measure may affect relationships between students and staff.

The challenge of qualitative research designs, however, is that their findings can lack generalizability to larger populations, and the studies are not designed to establish causal relationships or quantify the effects of school security measures.

TABLE 4-1 Studies About the Effects of School Security Measures (Other than Active Shooter Drills)

Study	Research Focus					Study Design						Outcome Measures				
	Metal Detectors	Door Locks	School Security Personnel	School Safety and Security	Other (Specify)	Quasi-Experimental	Cross-Sectional	Longitudinal	Systematic/Integrated Review	Qualitative	Other	Sense of Preparedness	Perception of Safety or Fear	Trauma or Mental Health	School Connectedness	Student Behavior
Addington, 2009	X		X			X							X			
Addington, 2018	X		X	X					X			X	X			
Bhatt & Davis, 2018	X					X							X			X
Booren & Handy, 2009		X		X			X						X		X	
Booren et al., 2011	X	X	X	X	School climate		X			X			X		X	
Bosworth et al., 2011				X	School climate								X		X	

Study	C1	C2	C3	C4	Topic	C5	C6	C7	C8	C9	C10	C11
Bracy, 2011			X	X	School climate			X		X	X	X
Brown, 2005	X		X	X		X	X	X		X	X	X
Cecen-Celik & Keith, 2019			X	X	Bullying/victimization		X					X
Chrusciel et al., 2015			X				X		X	X		
Cobbina et al., 2019				X		X		X		X		
Connell, 2018			X	X	Fear of crime		X			X	X	X
Côté-Lussier & Fitzpatrick, 2016				X	Social-emotional functioning		X	X				X
Crawford & Burns, 2015			X				X					X
Cuellar, 2018			X	X	School climate		X			X		X
Cuellar et al., 2017				X		X	X		X	X		
Devlin & Gottfredson, 2018			X	X	School climate			X				X
dit Lapointe, 2016			X							X		
Fisher et al., 2018				X					X	X		

Study						
Fisher et al., 2019						X
Flannery et al., 2021	X				X	X
Gardella et al., 2016		X	Victimization	X	X	X
Gastic, 2011	X			X	X	
Gastic & Johnson, 2015	X			X	X	
Gerlinger & Wo, 2016		X	School discipline	X	X	X
Hankin et al., 2011	X			X	X	X
Hernandez et al., 2010		X		X		X
Jennings et al., 2011		X		X		X
Kitsantas et al., 2004		X		X		X
Kupchik & Farina, 2016		X	Punishment, victimization	X		X
Lacoe, 2016		X	Academic outcomes	X		X
Langhout & Annear, 2011	X	X		X	X	

Study											
Martaindale et al., 2023		X					X	X			
McDevitt & Panniello, 2005			X						X		
Mowen & Freng, 2019			X	X		X			X		
Mowen & Manierre, 2017			X	X	Extracurricular participation	X	X			X	
Nguyen et al., 2020			X	X	Avoidance behaviors	X			X		
Nijs et al., 2014				X	Mental health	X			X	X	
Perumean-Chaney & Sutton, 2013	X			X		X			X		
Randa & Wilcox, 2010				X	School climate/student avoidance	X			X		X
Reingle Gonzalez et al., 2016	X	X	X				X				X

Study				Effects of lockdown drills	Fear of crime		Violence prevention	School climate				
Schildkraut & Nickerson, 2022		X		X						X		X
Schreck & Miller, 2003	X	X	X		X					X			
Seo & Kruis, 2022			X			X							X
Servoss and Finn, 2014	X	X	X			X							X
Skiba et al., 2006			X				X			X			
Tanner-Smith et al., 2018	X	X	X	X				X		X			X
Tanner-Smith & Fisher, 2016	X		X	X									X
Theriot & Orme, 2014		X	X			X					X		
Thibodeaux, 2013			X			X					X		
Wilcox, 2018			X		X						X		

CHARACTERISTICS AND LIMITATIONS OF THE EXISTING EVIDENCE BASE

While existing research provides some insights into the impacts of school security measures, the overall evidence base remains limited in both rigor and generalizability. Each research design contributes valuable insights into the relationship between school security measures and preparedness, perceptions of safety, mental health, school connectedness, and student behavior. However, significant gaps remain, particularly in causal inference and long-term impact assessment. The predominance of cross-sectional studies limits the ability to draw definitive conclusions, while the scarcity of longitudinal and quasi-experimental research constrains understanding of sustained effects. Systematic reviews provide overarching insights, yet their conclusions depend on the quality of the underlying studies. Qualitative research offers depth and context but lacks generalizability. Strengthening research designs will be critical for informing and developing policies aimed at implementing school security measures while mitigating potential harm to the mental, emotional, and behavioral health of students and staff.

Taking account of the nature and quality of the existing evidence, this section examines key patterns of policy and practice in school security bearing on the mental, emotional, and behavioral health of students and staff. Overall, very few studies feature designs rigorous enough to isolate the influence of security measures on student behavioral and emotional outcomes

Three decades of research has explored the use of door locks, metal detectors, and school-based security personnel in schools. Most of this literature relies on analysis of one of four datasets: the School Survey on Crime and Safety (SSOCS); the School Crime Supplement to the National Crime Victimization Survey (SCS); the National Longitudinal Study of Adolescent to Adult Health (Add Health); and the Education Longitudinal Study of 2002. While

SSOCS and the SCS are cross-sectional datasets, the other two are, as their names suggest, longitudinal.

Few studies of metal detectors or school-based security personnel have featured experimental designs, and the committee identified only four quasi-experimental studies related to these security measures and their potential effects on mental, emotional, or behavioral health of students or staff. In addition, research methods used in these studies rarely disentangle the aim of preventing school violence through use of metal detectors from other potential outcomes such as increasing students' sense of safety. The studies reviewed by the committee also lack consistent measures of mental, emotional, and behavioral health outcomes, leading to difficulties in interpreting findings and assessment of causation. For example, Fisher et al. (2019) discussed a number of studies that found that more schools have begun to incorporate formal security measures (e.g., metal detectors, security personnel, surveillance cameras) and examined the effects of these measures on reducing problem behaviors (e.g., bullying, victimization, fighting, drug or alcohol use) among students. However, the literature Fisher et al. (2019) reviewed did not consistently define or measure the same types of behaviors, making it difficult to identify clear patterns of outcomes for specific behavioral issues.

Despite these limitations, the cumulative evidence suggests that school security measures can have different psychological and social consequences that may vary by school contexts. For example, Cobbina et al. (2019) conducted a qualitative study on schools in Flint, Michigan; they interviewed students in grades 7–12 and found that, a large proportion of the students they interviewed reported that the presence of physical security measures made them feel more safe. This contrasts with some studies showing the use of physical security measures to be associated with a decrease in perception of safety. Cobbina et al. (2019) noted that the unique characteristics of both the community, which had high rates of crime, and the school system, which had experienced numerous school closures and a decrease in student population, make it difficult to generalize these findings.

In their qualitative study, Perumean-Chaney & Sutton (2013) found that an increase in the number of security measures was generally associated with a decrease in students' perceptions of safety; however, this was not true for all students in their study. Students who were White, male, had a higher GPA, and felt safe in their neighborhood were more likely to feel safe at school than other groups of students. They also found that school safety was more strongly predicted by individual- and school-level factors than by the presence of security measures (Perumean-Chaney & Sutton, 2013). Taken together, these findings exemplify the need to consider supports and strategies for meeting the needs of individuals and school communities (Cobbina et al., 2019; Perumean-Chaney & Sutton, 2013).

Research has often explored security measures as broad categories, rarely accounting for nuances in how those measures were utilized or for variations in responses to different security measures. For example, most schools rely on one of two types of metal detectors—handheld wands, which are generally used for spot checks or targeted searches, or stationary/walk-through metal detectors, which are generally used at controlled entry points to the school or as part of metal detector checks (Gastic & Johnson, 2015; Schildkraut & Grogan, 2019). However, the committee did not find any studies that specifically discussed the differences in how the potential mental, emotional, and behavioral health effects on students and staff vary by type, frequency of use, or manner of implementation.

Research that accounts for contextual factors such as school demographics, socioeconomic status, and the level of enforcement finds that the same security measures can have divergent effects. For instance, metal detectors implemented in schools with a history of violence, or in communities with higher rates of crime, may be perceived differently from those installed in schools where safety concerns have been minimal, where they may contribute to a sense of excessive surveillance among students (Bhatt & Davis, 2018; Cobbina et al., 2019; Nguyen et al., 2020). This variability suggests that the impact of security measures is not uniform, and that implementation strategies must be carefully considered with attention to school and student contexts to avoid unintended negative mental, emotional, and behavioral health outcomes.

Few studies have explored how one type of security measure may influence how students experience other types of security measures that are in use within a school. One theme that emerged in the committee's review of the research literature is the potential for student outcomes to vary based on the number or combination of visible security measures present within a school (e.g., Tanner-Smith et al., 2018). This is particularly relevant given findings in existing literature that show that the cumulative effect of multiple security measures may be to lower perceptions of safety or amplify student distrust, particularly when those measures are perceived as invasive or disproportionately enforced against certain demographic groups (Kupchik & Farina, 2016; Mowen & Freng, 2019). Thus, security measures need to be evaluated holistically, taking into account the ways in which various measures interact to shape student and staff experiences.

Understanding these contextual influences is critical in evaluating whether security measures achieve their intended goals, as well as the ways in which they may contribute to unintended negative consequences. School climate also plays a crucial role. Bosworth et al. (2011) found that strong relationships between students and teachers, and a sense of school connectedness, play a key role in creating a safe and protective school environment that can foster a sense of safety.

To summarize, while the studies reviewed by the committee provide valuable insights, many rely on student self-reports rather than psychological assessments or analyses of longitudinal data, meaning that the long-term mental, emotional, and behavioral health outcomes, and the ways that outcomes may change over time, remain essentially unexplored. Additionally, individual- and school-level characteristics are often explored without fully disentangling other intersecting factors, such as socioeconomic background and other demographic characteristics, community context, urbanicity, and student developmental needs, which may also play a role in shaping these perceptions.

REVIEW OF EVIDENCE ON PHYSICAL SECURITY INTERVENTIONS

Physical security measures such as door locks have become standard features in many educational institutions. According to the National Center for Education Statistics (Musu et al., 2019), nearly 94% of public K–12 schools in the United States report locking or monitoring their doors during school hours as a security measure. These strategies are designed to reduce or impede potential threats and restrict unauthorized access, particularly in the wake of high-profile school shootings. Locking of school and classroom doors is a practice that is often integrated into school active shooter drill practices. However, the committee did not find any studies that were specifically focused on the effects of door locks—in particular—on mental, emotional, and behavioral outcomes. The committee found only one which focused on door locks as a security measure, which was focused on ease of use. Martaindale et al. (2023) note that while classroom door locks can be a key deterrent to intruders attempting to enter classrooms and no shooter has breached a locked door, the design and ease of use of door locks can affect how quickly and easily they can be used when individuals are under stress. However, the broader impact of door locks remain largely unexamined in the current research literature, representing a significant gap in the evidence base related to their potential mental, emotional, and behavioral health effects on students and staff.

With this important gap in mind, this section examines existing evidence on how door locks may influence students' psychological well-being, emotional security, and behavioral responses, considering these measures' protective benefits as well as potential unintended consequences. Given the limited evidence specific to this security measure, the review includes studies on school security measures that included, but were not limited to, findings related to door locks.

Perceived Emergency Preparedness or Knowledge

The available research reviewed by the committee provides limited but relevant insights into the impact of door locks as a school security measure and their relationship to students' perceptions of preparedness for emergencies.

While several studies have included the presence of door locks as part of broader school security measures, Martaindale et al. (2023) is the only study the committee found that was focused specifically on their use. Their randomized controlled trial evaluated differences in ease of use between two types of classroom door locks used to secure a classroom as part of a lockdown. The study found that push-button locks are easier to use than locks that require a key when individuals are under stress (Martaindale et al., 2023). While evaluating the effectiveness of lockdowns was outside the committee's scope, the inclusion of lockdown procedures in some active shooter drills led the committee to view the ability to implement them as a possible contributor to a sense of preparedness. Further research examining whether students and staff feel more prepared when they are confident in their ability to successfully perform lockdown procedures—or when specific types of locks are used—would provide valuable insights.

The available evidence does not examine whether door locks alone contribute to students feeling more prepared for emergencies. As reviewed in the previous chapter, Schildkraut & Nickerson (2022) found that lockdown drills—which often involve door-locking procedures—were associated with reduced fear and improved perceived preparedness among students. The very act of practicing could be a key aspect of creating this sense of preparedness (rather than the physical presence of the door locks alone), but the available evidence does not disentangle these factors.

In summary, existing research primarily assesses physical security outcomes rather than perceptions of preparedness, leaving a gap in understanding how door locks influence mental, emotional, and behavioral health outcomes for students and staff. As a result, their role in fostering a sense of preparedness remains unclear.

Perception of Safety or Fear

A major impediment in interpreting the studies reviewed by the committee is the difficulty of isolating the effects of door locks from the effects of other security measures such as surveillance cameras, school resource officers or other security staff, and metal detectors. Several studies on school security measures that included discussion of door locks—though not exclusively focused on door locks—provide some indirect insights into perceptions of safety or fear. Mowen & Freng (2019) examined how various security measures (e.g., metal detectors, security guards, security cameras), including locked doors, influence feelings of safety among students and parents. Their findings were mixed, suggesting that multiple security measures did not increase perceptions of safety for either students or parents (Mowen & Freng, 2019). Similarly, in a cross-sectional study of the effects of school security measures on preventing bullying and victimization among students aged 12–18 in U.S. schools, Gerlinger & Wo (2016) reported that that while locked doors and other security measures (e.g., guards, metal detectors) have been shown to increase feelings of physical safety in some cases, evidence has not definitively demonstrated that these measures alleviate students' fear of victimization. By contrast, Cobbina et al. (2019) studied students in grades 7–12 in a school district with high rates of crime; they found that some students felt safer when school and classroom doors could be locked. However, the authors note that the unique school and community contexts of the students in their qualitative study makes it difficult to generalize the findings to broader student populations (Cobbina et al., 2019).

It is important to emphasize that most research on school security evaluates multiple interventions simultaneously, making it challenging to identify the specific impact of door locks on perceptions of safety or fear. Thus, further investigation is needed into the mental, emotional, and behavioral health effects of the use of door locks specifically, rather than school security measures in general.

Student Trauma and Mental Health Concerns

The committee did not identify any research explicitly connecting the use or presence of door locks with outcomes related to trauma or mental health. Studies mentioning these outcomes were focused on school security measures broadly—including door locks—but did not definitively link psychological impact to individual physical security interventions.

Student Perceptions of School Connectedness

The committee found no direct evidence bearing on the effect of door locks on perceptions of school connectedness. Again, most studies evaluated multiple security measures together, making it difficult to determine the individual impact of door locks. Studies pertaining to the effect of high-security environments, which can decrease students' sense of belonging and decrease trust between students and staff, may provide some indirect insight (e.g., Mowen & Freng, 2019; Tanner-Smith et al., 2018). Research focused on door locks is needed to understand what effect they may have on school connectedness.

Student Behavior

No studies appear to have linked the simple presence or use of door locks to changes in student behavior. Discussions of behavior changes have typically been part of broader discussions of security measures, including door locks or lockdown procedures (e.g., Schildkraut & Nickerson, 2022).

REVIEW OF EVIDENCE ON METAL DETECTORS

The use of metal detectors in U.S. schools tends to vary by school level and urbanicity, but they are relatively uncommon—present in roughly 1 in 10 schools—and their prevalence has remained largely unchanged since the mid-1990s; they are more common in urban schools and are used more frequently in secondary than in elementary schools (Addington, 2018; Schildkraut & Grogan, 2019). The intended goal is to deter students from bringing contraband items to school and to create a safe environment where both students and staff feel secure (Brown, 2005; Tanner-Smith et al., 2018).

The literature on school security measures generally does not distinguish between the influence of metal detectors and the influence of security personnel. One study found that, in an analysis of two separate datasets, spanning 2001–2011 and 2004–2010, the use of metal detectors nearly always coincided with schools' use of security cameras and security personnel (Tanner-Smith & Fisher, 2016). Multiple studies examined school security as a composite variable—that is, they used a single measure to capture how many different types of security measures schools had in place—no studies identified by the committee explicitly compared the effects of metal detectors alone with their use in combination with security personnel or other security measures. Thus, there is a notable gap in direct comparative research between singular and combined approaches.

Early analyses focused on the impact of metal detectors on school safety—particularly on carrying weapons and school violence—seeking to determine the extent to which metal detectors have fulfilled their primary objective (Bhatt & Davis, 2018; Hankin et al., 2011; Tanner-Smith et al., 2018). However, much of the research over the past 2 decades has explored the implications of metal detectors for student *perceptions* of safety—generally finding that students may feel *less safe* if they are in schools with metal detectors (Gastic, 2011; Perumean-Chaney & Sutton, 2013). However, there is little research focused on other student outcomes of interest (e.g., perceived emergency preparedness, trauma, or other adverse mental health effects). This section summarizes the available findings on the use of metal detectors as they relate to the committee's interest in mental, emotional, and behavioral outcomes.

Perceived Emergency Preparedness or Knowledge

The committee was unable to identify any studies examining the connection between metal detectors and student perceptions of their preparedness for an emergency or their knowledge of how to respond in an emergency.

Perceptions of Safety or Fear

The committee identified several studies that either focused specifically on metal detectors or included them among the school security measures examined; these studies generally explored associations with perceptions of safety or fear. Studies measure student fear in multiple ways, including fear at school (Bachman et al., 2011a; Tillyer et al., 2011), fear going to and from school (Bachman et al., 2011b), sense of safety at school (Addington, 2018; Cuellar et al., 2017; Gastic, 2011; Mowen & Freng, 2019; Perumean-Chaney & Sutton, 2013), perceived neighborhood safety (Fisher et al., 2018), and school avoidance due to fear (Bhatt & Davis, 2018).

Among the studies examining perceptions of safety or fear, the most useful are two quasi-experimental studies; as mentioned above, both found that students in schools with metal detectors felt less safe than their counterparts in schools without metal detectors (Gastic, 2011; Perumean-Chaney & Sutton, 2013). These findings are largely consistent with the significant body of studies exploring other dimensions of student fear and sense of safety. Gastic's (2011) study using data from Add Health found that use of metal detectors in schools had a negative impact on students' perception of safety; however negative associations between sense of safety and the use of metal detectors were 13% less among students in urban schools relative to students in suburban or rural schools. Gastic (2011) emphasized the need for interventions that not only reduce risk to students but also promote their sense of safety. Perumean-Chaney & Sutton's (2013) study on the impact of school safety measures on students' perceptions of safety also used Add Health data with a nationally representative sample of 13,386 students in grades 7–12 in

130 schools. They found that the use of metal detectors in schools was associated with students having concerns about their safety and that, among the security measures examined, metal detectors may be particularly associated with reduced perceptions of safety (Perumean-Chaney & Sutton, 2013).

A cross-sectional study by Tillyer et al. (2011) examined the effects of crime prevention efforts on students' perception of risk and fear of crime. In their examination of five crime prevention measures (school efficacy, police involvement in the school, presence of metal detectors, locker checks, and bans on book bags/backpacks) they found that only metal detectors were related to lower levels of fear among students, although metal detectors were not found to be associated with lower levels of violence.

The majority of relevant studies reviewed by the committee relied on cross-sectional, self-reported data, making it difficult to determine whether metal detectors cause changes in perceived safety or are simply implemented in response to preexisting concerns (Hankin et al., 2011). Furthermore, the existing evidence base lacks controlled experimental research that isolates the effects of metal detectors from those of other security measures. As a result, while metal detectors are intended to improve school security, their actual impact on perceptions of safety and fear appears to be negative and context dependent.

Student Trauma and Mental Health Concerns

Beyond the research examining the potential impacts on student fear, there have been no studies examining the implications of metal detectors for student trauma and mental health. Given the nature of the evidence, which is based primarily on self-reported perceptions rather than clinical assessments, the committee was unable to draw any conclusions about the effects of metal detectors on student trauma and mental health.

Student Perception of School Connectedness

As noted earlier in this chapter, school connectedness is a key element of a safe and supportive school environment, which can help foster positive mental, emotional, and behavioral health outcomes. A few studies have examined student outcomes related to school connectedness, such as relationships between students and teachers (e.g., Cobbina et al., 2019; Fisher et al., 2019), relationships between students and other school adults (e.g., Cuellar et al., 2017), students' perceptions as to whether school rules are fair or consistent (e.g., Booren et al., 2011; Fisher et al., 2019), and students' perceptions of the school climate (e.g., Addington, 2018). However, the majority of these studies do not focus exclusively on metal detectors but rather on metal detectors used in conjunction with other school security measures.

Using data from the 2011 School Crime Supplement to the National Crime Victimization Survey, Fisher et al. (2019) studied 6,547 students aged 12–18; they found that the presence of metal detectors in schools was associated with weaker student–teacher relationships, but not with student perceptions of the overall fairness or consistency of school rules. Although metal detectors were relatively uncommon across schools, the authors note their disproportionate use in disadvantaged settings. After adjusting for student demographic characteristics, the study found that students in schools with metal detectors were more likely to perceive school rules as fair and consistently enforced. However, the authors cautioned that this finding is likely influenced by confounding between the presence of metal detectors and other student characteristics included in their adjusted model (Fisher et al., 2019).

On the other hand, broader research on school security suggests that school environments with higher security—including, but not limited to, metal detectors—may contribute to or reinforce such factors as lower student trust or perceptions of a punitive school climate, which have the potential to undermine students' sense of connectedness (Gerlinger & Wo, 2016). However, because much of the existing literature examines multiple security measures simultaneously, it remains challenging to isolate the specific impact of metal detectors on school connectedness. Thus, the committee did not identify definitive evidence linking metal detectors to adverse effects across dimensions of school connectedness.

Student Behavior

Research on the impacts of metal detectors on other student behaviors has yielded mixed findings. Some studies explored how the presence of metal detectors (as part of broader security measures) might influence student behaviors such as school avoidance (e.g., Bhatt & Davis, 2018; Tanner-Smith & Fisher, 2016), bullying and victimization (e.g., Schreck & Miller, 2003), or drug or weapon possession (Bhatt & Davis, 2018). However, these studies have not been able to isolate how metal detectors might affect specific behaviors.

A number of studies have explored the relationship between different forms of problematic behavior and the use of visible security measures. However, research on the specific impact of metal detectors on these behaviors is both limited and mixed. For example, Bhatt & Davis's (2018) study on the effectiveness of weapons searches in Broward and Miami-Dade counties, Florida, found that metal detectors may deter students from bringing weapons to school, with findings showing a reduction in reported weapon possession and drug-related incidents in schools that conducted random searches, including those involving metal detectors (Bhatt & Davis, 2018). In their evaluation of School Crime Supplement data, Tanner-Smith & Fisher (2016) found that adolescents in schools that used metal detectors with security personnel reported higher rates of truancy than schools with no security measures; while utilization of security measures are intended to reduce problem behaviors, there may be unintended negative effects. By contrast, a review of literature on the impact of metal detectors was inconclusive about potential benefits of, or correlations between, metal detectors on student and staff behaviors (Hankin et al., 2011).

In summary, the studies reviewed by the committee that examined the relationship between use of metal detectors and effects on student behaviors relied primarily on cross-sectional and self-reported data, making it difficult to determine whether metal detectors are the cause of student behaviors or whether they are used in schools in response to existing student behavior and safety concerns. Overall, the committee found no strong evidence linking the use of metal detectors to changes in student behavior.

EVIDENCE ON THE PRESENCE OF SCHOOL SECURITY PERSONNEL

As noted previously, the committee includes a range of school personnel in the category of "school security personnel," including school resource officers, other sworn law enforcement officers assigned to schools, and non–law enforcement security staff. Depending on the school context, this broad category may also extend to other school staff members with safety-related responsibilities. This section reviews evidence on how the presence of school security personnel may affect the mental, emotional, and behavioral health of students and staff. An aim of this review is to describe the complex interactions between security personnel and the school community, acknowledging both the potential protections and restraints associated with their presence.

Perceived Emergency Preparedness of Knowledge

The duties of school security personnel are generally framed around ensuring protection of students and staff in the event of an emergency and enhancing safety overall. However, the committee did not identify research that correlated the presence of school security personnel with perceptions of emergency preparedness among students and staff.

Perceptions of Safety or Fear

Most research on school security personnel has focused on students' perceptions of fear and safety. As noted earlier, studies have examined multiple aspects of student fear, including fear of being a victim of crime (e.g., Fisher et al., 2018; Schreck & Miller, 2003), fear of going to and from school (e.g., Bachman et al., 2011b), and sense of safety at school (e.g., McDevitt & Panniello, 2005; Perumean-Chaney & Sutton, 2013; Theriot & Orme, 2014). Furthermore, studies have explored both the relationship between students' perceptions of safety and the actual presence of school security personnel (e.g., Bachman et al., 2011a; Fisher et al., 2018; Perumean-Chaney & Sutton, 2013; Schreck & Miller, 2003; Tillyer et al., 2011), as well as the relationship between perceptions of safety and students' attitudes toward these personnel (e.g., Brown, 2005; McDevitt & Panniello, 2005; Theriot, 2016). However, although several studies examine the presence of school security personnel in relation to students' perceptions of safety or fear, these studies generally do not isolate security personnel as the primary factor influencing those perceptions or establish a causal relationship.

Studies have yielded mixed findings regarding the effects of security personnel on perceived safety. Some students and staff report feeling safer with a security presence, especially in schools with high crime rates; however, the school and community contexts limit the extent to which findings are broadly generalizable (Cobbina et al., 2019; Theriot & Orme, 2014). Students in other studies have reported that security guards had little to no influence on their perception of school safety (e.g., Bachman et al., 2011; Booren & Handy, 2009).

Theriot & Orme (2014) analyzed data from 1,956 middle and high school students from a school district in the southeastern United States, examining how school resource officers affected students' feelings of safety. They used latent class analysis to categorize students into two groups: those who felt safe and those who did not. They found mixed outcomes: while interactions with these officers were not associated with increased feelings of safety overall, male students who had reported feelings of school connectedness and had positive attitudes about school resource officers reported feeling safer in their school environment (Theriot & Orme, 2014). While there was no significant relationship between students' number of school resource officer interactions and feelings of safety, having positive attitudes toward these personnel was associated with students being categorized in the group with higher feelings of safety (Theriot & Orme, 2014).

Similarly, in a national evaluation of the school resource officer program in three states, McDevitt & Panniello (2005) found that middle and high school students who had a positive opinion of their school resource officer and felt comfortable reporting crime to them reported more positive perceptions of school safety. And Brown (2005) found that high school students in a majority Hispanic school district in Texas agreed that police officers and security guards did a good job keeping their schools safe.

By contrast, an analysis of National Crime Victimization Survey data by Bachman et al. (2011b) found that White students reported heightened fear of victimization when security guards were present in a school, a pattern not observed among African American students. In a separate study, Brown & Benedict (2005) reported that male students and students with prior victimization experiences were less likely than their peers to view school resource officers as contributing to school safety.

Across studies, the need for additional research—and replication of existing research— using longitudinal data is highlighted as a need to further clarify the real and perceived effects of school security personnel on safety and to identify differences in findings based on the type of personnel that is present in a school. As noted previously, existing research does not always link these feelings of safety or fear to the presence of security personnel directly, which may indicate that there are other elements of the school or community environment that increase the likelihood of security personnel being present and that may be contributing to perceptions of fear.

Student Trauma or Mental Health Concerns

The committee did not identify studies that directly assessed the effects of school security personnel on student trauma or mental health challenges. Although existing studies primarily focused on related but distinct topics, such as students' perceptions of safety or fear, the committee did not find evidence that school resource officers or other law enforcement or security staff contribute to trauma or mental health challenges among students or staff.

Student Perceptions of School Connectedness

The presence of security personnel in schools has been associated with mixed effects on school connectedness. Two studies examined the relationship between the presence of school security personnel and students' perception of school connectedness. Fisher et al. (2019) used survey data from 6,547 students to model associations between school security measures, including security personnel, and student perceptions of social control. They found that the presence of security personnel was associated with students' poorer relationships with teachers—a measure of school connectedness. Presence of school security personnel was not found to affect the relationships between students and other adults in the school. The authors note that future research is needed to replicate their findings with longitudinal data and that the survey data used in their analysis did not allow them to examine intraschool variability at the individual or group level (Fisher et al., 2019).

In an analysis of survey data from 1,956 middle and high school students, Theriot (2016) found differences in feelings of school connectedness related to interactions with school resource officers. The surveyed students were from 12 schools within a single school district and each school had a full-time school resource officer. School resource officers were expected to provide law enforcement, education, and mentoring to students, educators, and other school staff. Analyses showed that while more interactions with school resource officers increased students' positive attitudes about them, those interactions decreased perceptions of school connectedness (Theriot, 2016). The findings suggest that the surveyed students did not generally view the presence of school resource officers negatively. A possible explanation for lower reported school connectedness is that the presence of the school resource officers in these schools may have increased students' perception that their school was less safe, perhaps leading to feelings of discomfort or disconnection at school.

Further research is needed to understand how all types of school security personnel may affect students' feelings of school connectedness and whether those perceptions vary across a wider variety of school contexts and student populations.

Student Behavior

Research on the relationship between school security personnel and student behavior has focused primarily on school discipline as an outcome. However, the use of disciplinary practices as an outcome measure suggests that student behavior has not typically been used as an indicator of students' overall well-being. For this reason, the committee's review of literature also includes findings on specific student behavioral outcomes that may more clearly reflect student experience, such as school avoidance, truancy, and absenteeism. However, findings are mixed and do not establish a strong causal link between the presence of school security personnel and student behaviors.

Tanner-Smith & Fisher (2016) used both the SCS and SSOCS to examine the relationship between visible school security measures, such as school security personnel, and attendance from the perspectives of students and school administrators. Based on student-reported data, adolescents in schools using only security personnel reported significantly higher truancy than those attending schools with no security measures or only cameras. Additionally, administrator-reported data showed lower attendance rates in schools that used security personnel, metal detectors, and cameras compared with those that used no security measures or only security personnel. The authors note that differences in responses between students and administrators may be related to differences in awareness of security measures being utilized in schools (i.e., students may not recognize the presence of all security measures). Tanner-Smith & Fisher (2016) also caution that they were unable to examine the effects of school-level contextual factors.

Other studies have yielded similar findings. Randa & Wilcox (2010) used a national sample of 3,776 students to examine school avoidance behaviors, including avoidance of specific school locations (e.g., hallways, restrooms, parking lots), school extracurricular activities, specific classes, and avoidance of school altogether. While the presence of school security personnel was not the only focus of this study, presence of security guards was included as a security measure in respondents' schools that was potentially related to the reporting of general avoidance behaviors (i.e., avoidance not tied to a specific location within the school). The presence of security personnel was significantly associated with students' reporting of general avoidance (Randa & Wilcox, 2010).

Additionally, Gardella et al. (2016) analyzed survey data from 5,930 adolescents aged 12–18, examining the relationship between school security measures, including security guards, and effects of victimization at school. They found that the presence of school security personnel moderated the relationship between victimization at school and absenteeism, such that their presence was associated with increased student absenteeism. Adolescents who experienced victimizations in schools with security guards were absent nearly twice as often (2.01 days absent per month) compared with students experiencing victimization in schools without a security guard (1.28 absences per month). Gardella et al. (2016) noted that more research is needed to understand how within-school differences affect experiences and how school environments where security measures are used may have a confluence of variables that influence student perceptions and behaviors.

CONCLUSION

Existing research on school security measures, while providing some insight into their effects on mental, emotional, and behavioral health outcomes, remains methodologically thin, particularly in terms of causal inference, long-term impact assessment, and population-level differences in outcomes. While the literature reviewed in this chapter addresses a range of security measures, the committee found that the evidence base is too limited to draw definitive conclusions about variations in outcomes. In particular, the current research does not adequately capture whether positive effects or adverse impacts differ by characteristics such as student age, race, or ethnicity; school urbanicity; or school infrastructure.

The predominance of cross-sectional studies highlights the absence of rigorous empirical evaluations, underscoring the urgent need for more quasi-experimental and experimental designs to establish causal relationships. Additionally, longitudinal studies are essential for understanding the sustained effects of security policies on the well-being of students and staff. Future research that adopts rigorous approaches to examine how security measures differentially affect student populations will be of particular importance, given the wide variation in school contexts and the varying needs of students at different developmental stages and at different levels of vulnerability to adverse outcomes.

Comparative studies evaluating the relative effectiveness of alternative strategies—such as mental health interventions and traditional security measures—are needed to identify more holistic approaches to fostering safe and supportive school environments that can help mitigate potential negative impacts on students and staff.

Strengthening research methodologies across these dimensions will be critical for informing policies that not only enhance security but also promote the well-being of all students and staff. Further research, particularly experimental and longitudinal studies, is needed to provide definitive conclusions on best practices for school safety and the implementation of school security measures.

A positive school environment that fosters positive mental, emotional, and behavioral health, characterized by trust, strong student–teacher relationships, and proactive mental health support, can shape how students and staff experience and respond to school safety and security practices. Schools that focus primarily on security measures without fostering a supportive climate may inadvertently contribute to student distress, making school safety and security practices feel punitive or fear inducing rather than educational and supportive.

The effects of school security measures appear to be influenced by the context in which they are implemented. While measures such as locked doors tend to be perceived as protective, use of metal detectors and routine presence of security personnel may exacerbate feelings of surveillance and criminalization for some students, particularly in marginalized communities. These findings suggest that a one-size-fits-all approach to school security is insufficient and that policymakers need to consider the unique social and environmental contexts of each school.

Overall, schools that balance physical security with a positive school climate may be better positioned to implement other school safety and security practices, including school active shooter drills, in a way that enhances preparedness while minimizing adverse effects on students and staff.

REFERENCES

Addington, L. A. (2009). Cops and cameras: Public school security as a policy response to Columbine. *American Behavioral Scientist, 52*(10), 1426–1446.

_____. (2018). *The use of visible security measures in public schools: A review to summarize current literature and guide future research* (American University School of Public Affairs Research Paper No. 3240204). American University. https://doi.org/10.2139/ssrn.3240204

Bachman, R., Gunter, W. D., & Bakken, N. W. (2011a). Predicting feelings of school safety for lower, middle, and upper school students: A gender specific analysis. *Applied Psychology in Criminal Justice, 7*(2).

Bachman, R., Randolph, A., & Brown, B. L. (2011b). Predicting perceptions of fear at school and going to and from school for African American and White students: The effects of school security measures. *Youth & Society, 43*(2), 705–726.

Bhatt, R., & Davis, T. (2018). The impact of random metal detector searches on contraband possession and feelings of safety at school. *Educational Policy, 32*(4), 569–597. https://doi.org/10.1177/0895904816673735

Booren, L. M., & Handy, D. J. (2009). Students' perceptions of the importance of school safety strategies: An introduction to the IPSS survey. *Journal of School Violence, 8*(3), 233–250. https://doi.org/10.1080/15388220902910672

Booren, L. M., Handy, D. J., & Power, T. G. (2011). Examining perceptions of school safety: Strategies, school climate, and violence. *Youth Violence and Juvenile Justice, 9*(2), 171–187. https://doi.org/10.1177/1541204010374297

Bosworth, K., Ford, L., & Hernandaz, D. (2011). School climate factors contributing to student and faculty perceptions of safety in select Arizona schools. *Journal of School Health, 81*(4), 194–201. https://doi.org/10.1111/j.1746-1561.2010.00579.x

Bracy, N. L. (2011). Student perceptions of high-security school environments. *Youth & Society, 43*(1), 365–395. https://doi.org/10.1177/0044118X10365082

Brown, B. (2005). Controlling crime and delinquency in the schools: An exploratory study of student perceptions of school security measures. *Journal of School Violence, 4*(4), 105–125. https://doi.org/10.1300/J202v04n04_07

Brown, B., & Benedict, W. R. (2005). Classroom cops, what do students think? A case study of student perceptions of school police and security officers conducted in a Hispanic community. *Journal of Police Science and Management, 7*(4), 264–285. https://doi.org/10.1350/ijps.2005.7.4.264

Cecen-Celik, H., & Keith, S. (2019). Analyzing predictors of bullying victimization with routine activity and social bond perspectives. *Journal of Interpersonal Violence, 34*(18), 3807–3832. https://doi.org/10.1177/0886260516672941

Chrusciel, M. M., Wolfe, S., Hansen, J. A., Rojek, J. J., & Kaminski, R. (2015). Law enforcement executive and principal perspectives on school safety measures: School resource officers and armed school employees. *Policing: An International Journal of Police Strategies & Management, 38*(1), 24–39. http://doi.org/10.1108/PIJPSM-11-2014-0115

Cobbina, J. E., Galasso, M., Cunningham, M., Melde, C., & Heinze, J. (2019). A qualitative study of perception of school safety among youth in a high crime city. *Journal of School Violence 19*(3), 277–291. https://doi.org/10.1080/15388220.2019.1677477

Connell, N. M. (2018). Fear of crime at school: Understanding student perceptions of safety as a function of historical context. *Youth Violence & Juvenile Justice, 16*(2), 124–136. https://doi.org/10.1177/1541204016680407

Côté-Lussier, C., & Fitzpatrick, C. (2016). Feelings of safety at school, socioemotional functioning, and classroom engagement. *Journal of Adolescent Health, 58*(5), 543–550. https://doi.org/10.1016/j.jadohealth.2016.01.003

Crawford, C., & Burns, R. (2015). Preventing school violence: Assessing armed guardians, school policy, and context. *Policing: An International Journal of Police Strategies & Management, 38*(4), 631–647.

Cuellar, M. J. (2018). School safety strategies and their effects on the occurrence of school-based violence in U.S. high schools: An exploratory study. *Journal of School Violence, 17,* 28–45. https://doi.org/10.1080/15388220.2016.1193742

Cuellar, M. J., Elswick, S. E., & Theriot, M. T. (2017). School social workers' perceptions of school safety and security in today's schools: A survey of practitioners across the United States. *Journal of School Violence 17*(3), 271–283. https://doi.org/10.1080/15388220.2017.1315308

Devlin, D. N., & Gottfredson, D. C. (2018). The roles of police officers in schools: Effects on the recording and reporting of crime. *Youth Violence and Juvenile Justice, 16*(2), 208–223. https://doi.org/10.1177/1541204016680405

dit Lapointe, D. (2016). Teacher perception of school safety between Mississippi secondary schools with school resource officers and school safety officers. [Doctoral Dissertation, University of Southern Mississippi].

Fisher, B. W., Gardella, J. H., & Tanner-Smith, E. E. (2019). Social control in schools: The Relationships between school security measures and informal social control mechanisms. *Journal of School Violence, 18*(3), 347–361. https://doi.org/10.1080/15388220.2018.1503964

Fisher, B. W., Mowen, T. J., & Boman, J. H. (2018). School security measures and longitudinal trends in adolescents' experiences of victimization. *Journal of Youth and Adolescence, 47*(6), 1221–1237. https://doi.org/10.1007/s10964-018-0818-5

Flannery, D., Fox, J. A., Wallace, L., Mulvey, E., & Modzeleski, W. (2021). Guns, school shooters, and school safety: What we know and directions for change. *School Psychology Review, 50*(2–3), 237–253. https://doi.org/10.1080/2372966X.2020.1846458

Gardella, J. H., Tanner-Smith, E. E., & Fisher, B. W. (2016). Academic consequences of multiple victimization and the role of school security measures. *American Journal of Community Psychology, 58*(1-2), 36–46. https://doi.org/10.1002/ajcp.12075

Gastic, B. (2011). Metal detectors and feeling safe at school. *Education and Urban Society, 43*(4), 486–498. http://doi.org/10.1177/0013124510380717

Gastic, B., & Johnson, D. (2015). Disproportionality in daily metal detector student searches in U.S. public schools. *Journal of School Violence, 14*(3), 299–315. https://doi.org/10.1080/15388220.2014.924074

Gerlinger, J., & Wo, J. C. (2016). Preventing school bullying: Should schools prioritize an authoritative school discipline approach over security measures? *Journal of School Violence, 15*(2), 133–157. https://doi.org/10.1080/15388220.2014.956321

Hankin, A., Hertz, M., & Simon, T. (2011). Impacts of metal detector use in schools: Insights from 15 years of research. *Journal of School Health, 81*(2), 100–106. https://doi.org/10.1111/j.1746-1561.2010.00566.x

Hernandez, D., Floden, L., & Bosworth, K. (2010). How safe is a school? An exploratory study comparing measures and perceptions of safety. *Journal of School Violence, 9*(4), 357–374. https://doi.org/10.1080/15388220.2010.508133

Jennings, W. G., Khey, D. N., Maskaly, J., & Donner, C. M. (2011). Evaluating the relationship between law enforcement and school security measures and violent crime in schools. *Journal of Police Crisis Negotiations, 11*(2), 109–124. http://doi.org/10.1080/15332586.2011.581511

Kitsantas, A., Ware, H. W., & Martinez-Arias, R. (2004). Students' perceptions of school safety: Effects by community, school environment, and substance use variables. *Journal of Early Adolescence, 24,* 412–430. https://doi.org/10.1177/0272431604268712

Kupchik, A., & Farina, K. A. (2016). Imitating authority: Students' perceptions of school punishment and security, and bullying victimization. *Youth Violence and Juvenile Justice, 14*(2), 147–163. https://doi.org/10.1177/1541204014557648

Lacoe, J. (2016). Too scared to learn? The academic consequences of feeling unsafe in the classroom. *Urban Education, 55*(4). http://doi.org/10.1177/0042085916674059

Langhout, R. D., & Annear, L. (2011). Safe and unsafe school spaces: Comparing elementary school student perceptions. *Journal of Community & Applied Social Psychology, 21*(1), 71–86. https://doi.org/10.1002/casp.1062

Martaindale, M. H., Sandel, W. L., & Duron, A. (2023). Successfully securing a classroom door in a lockdown: evaluating two types of door locks. *Journal of Mass Violence Research.* https://doi.org/10.53076/JMVR74565

McDevitt, J., & Panniello, J. (2005). National assessment of school resource officer programs: Survey of students in three large new SRO programs (Document No. 209270).

Mowen, T. J., & Freng, A. (2019). Is more necessarily better? School security and perceptions of safety among students and parents in the United States. *American Journal of Criminal Justice, 44*(3), 376–394.

Mowen, T. J., & Manierre, M. J. (2017). School security measures and extracurricular participation: An exploratory multi-level analysis. *British Journal of Sociology of Education, 38*(3), 344–363. https:///doi.org/10.1080/01425692.2015.1081091

Musu, L., Zhang, A., Wang, K., Zhang, J., & Oudekerk, B. A. (2019). *Indicators of school crime and safety: 2018* (NCES 2019-047/NCJ 252571). National Center for Education Statistics, U.S. Department of Education, and Bureau of Justice Statistics, Office of Justice Programs, U.S. Department of Justice. https://nces.ed.gov/pubs2019/2019047.pdf

Nguyen, K., Yuan, Y., & McNeeley, S. (2020). School security measures, school environment, and avoidance behaviors. *Victims & Offenders, 15*(1), 43–59. https://doi.org/10.1080/15564886.2019.1679307

Nijs, M. M., Bun, C. J., Tempelaar, W. M., de Wit, N. J., Burger, H., Plevier, C. M., & Boks, M. P. (2014). Perceived school safety is strongly associated with adolescent mental health problems. *Community Mental Health Journal, 50*, 127–134.

Perumean-Chaney, S. E., & Sutton, L. M. (2013). Students and perceived school safety: The impact of school security measures. *American Journal of Criminal Justice, 38*(4), 570–588. https://doi.org/10.1007/s12103-012-9182-2

Randa, R., & Wilcox, P. (2010). School disorder, victimization, and general v. place-specific student avoidance. *Journal of Criminal Justice, 38*(5), 854–861. https://doi.org/10.1016/j.jcrimjus.2010.05.009

Reingle Gonzalez, J. M., Jetelina, K. K., & Jennings, W. G. (2016). Structural school safety measures, SROs, and school-related delinquent behavior and perceptions of safety: A state of the art review. *Policing: An International Journal of Police Strategies & Management, 39*, 438–454. http://doi.org/10.1108/PIJPSM-05-2016-0065

Schildkraut, J., & Grogan, K. (2019). *Are metal detectors effective at making schools safer?* WestEd Justice & Prevention Research Center. https://www.wested.org/resource/are-metal-detectors-effective-at-making-schools-safer/

Schildkraut, J., & Nickerson, A. B. (2022). Effects of lockdown drills on students' fear, perceived risk, and use of avoidance behaviors: A quantitative study. *Journal of School Violence, 21*(4), 796–812. https://doi.org/10.1080/15388220.2022.2040602

Schreck, C. J., & Miller, J. M. (2003). Sources of fear of crime at school: What is the relative contribution of disorder, individual characteristics, and school security? *Journal of School Violence, 2*(4), 57–79. http://doi.org/10.1300/J202v02n04_04

Seo, C., & Kruis, N. E. (2022). The impact of school's security and restorative justice measures on school violence. *Children and Youth Services Review, 132*, 106305. https://doi.org/10.1016/j.childyouth.2021.106305

Servoss, T. J., & Finn, J. D. (2014). School security: For whom and with what results? *Leadership and Policy in Schools, 13*(1), 61–92. https://doi.org/10.1080/15700763.2014.890734

Skiba, R., Simmons, A. B., Peterson, R., & Forde, S. (2006). The SRS safe school survey: A broader perspective on school violence prevention. In S. R. Jimerson, & M. Furlong (Eds.), *Handbook of school violence and school safety: From research to practice* (pp. 157–170). Lawrence Erlbaum Associates.

Steiner, R. J., Sheremenko, G., Lesesne, C., Dittus, P. J., Sieving, R. E., & Ethier, K. A. (2019). Adolescent connectedness and adult health outcomes. *Pediatrics, 144*(1). https://doi.org/10.1542/peds.2018-3766

Tanner-Smith, E. E., & Fisher, B. W. (2016). Visible school security measures and student academic performance, attendance, and postsecondary aspirations. *Journal of Youth and Adolescence, 45*, 195–210. https://doi.org/10.1007/s10964-014-0162-1

Tanner-Smith, E. E., Fisher, B. W., Addington, L. A., & Gardella, J. H. (2018). Adding security, but subtracting safety? Exploring schools' use of multiple visible security measures. *American Journal of Criminal Justice, 43*, 102–119. https://doi.org/10.1007/s12103-017-9409-3

Theriot, M. T. (2016). The impact of school resource officer interaction on students' feelings about school and school police. *Crime & Delinquency, 62*(4), 446–469. http://doi.org/10.1177/0011128713503526

Theriot, M. T., & Orme, J. G. (2014). School resource officers and students' feelings of safety at school. *Youth Violence and Juvenile Justice, 14*(2), 130–146. https://doi.org/10.1177/1541204014564472

Thibodeaux, J. (2013). Student perceptions of safety in perceived similar and non-similar race high schools. *Journal of School Violence, 12*, 378–394. https://doi.org/10.1080/15388220.2013.820661

Tillyer, M. S., Fisher, B. S., & Wilcox, P. (2011). The effects of school crime prevention on students' violent victimization, risk perception, and fear of crime: A multilevel opportunity perspective. *Justice Quarterly, 28*(2), 249–277. https://doi.org/10.1080/07418825.2010.493526

U.S. Centers for Disease Control and Prevention. (2023). *School connectedness helps students thrive*. U.S. Department of Health and Human Services. https://www.cdc.gov/youth-behavior/school-connectedness/index.html

Wilcox, N. M. T. (2018). *Building features that impact perceptions of safety* (Doctoral dissertation, Virginia Polytechnic Institute and State University).

5
School Active Shooter Drills and Other School Security Measures: Developmental Contexts

Childhood and adolescence are characterized by significant cognitive, behavioral, and emotional growth as well as sensitivity to social interactions and environments (NASEM, 2019a,b). It is essential to keep these facets of development in mind when considering best practices for school active shooter drills, focusing on practices that have the desired protective effects while minimizing adverse impacts on healthy mental, emotional, and behavioral development. As described in a recent National Academies report, *Fostering Healthy Mental, Emotional, and Behavioral Development in Children and Youth* (NASEM, 2019a), healthy development entails not only preventing mental, emotional, and behavioral disorders but also promoting healthy "cognitive development, psychological and behavioral health, and social and emotional competence" (p. 26). As discussed earlier, this report is guided by an ecological model (see Figure 1-1 in Chapter 1) tailored for considering children within the context of classrooms, schools, families, and communities.

This chapter begins by detailing the developmental and contextual considerations for implementing school active shooter drills and other security measures, such as the presence of school resource officers and the use of metal detectors for pre-K,[21] elementary, middle

---

[21] The committee includes pre-K where applicable, recognizing that some elementary school campuses include pre-K classrooms whose students may participate in school active shooter drills.

school, and high school students. It then briefly outlines unique identities of students, caregivers, teachers, and other school staff that are important to consider when planning for school active shooter drills. Finally, the chapter reviews considerations for caregivers, teachers, and other school staff as they relate to supporting children's mental, emotional, and behavioral development. Although these descriptions are not exhaustive, they highlight individuals who may be at risk for adverse mental, emotional, and behavioral health outcomes from school active shooter drills and other school security measures, as well as groups of interest as identified by the committee's statement of task (see Box 1-1 in Chapter 1). This includes people who have experienced trauma and other adverse life events and individuals with functional or access needs, including multilingual learners who require language supports[22]; people who are deaf or hard of hearing; and those with emotional and behavioral support needs, intellectual disabilities, and physical or other health conditions. Furthermore, the chapter considers challenges specific to transient or new students, as well as those with prior legal system involvement. Throughout the discussion, the emphasis is on supporting the needs of students and school staff while minimizing harmful impacts of school active shooter drills or other security measures on children's mental, emotional and behavioral well-being, as well as promoting positive school climates and a sense of belonging.

CONSIDERATIONS FOR STUDENTS BY DEVELOPMENTAL STAGE

Drawing on reports from developmental science literature as well as current guidance from organizations including—but not limited to—the American Academy of Pediatrics, the National

---

[22] The term *multilingual learners* refers to "students participating in the PreK-12 education system whose home or ancestral language is a language other than English." School systems may use other terms, such as *English learners* or *dual-language learners* to identify these students (Regional Educational Laboratory West, 2024, p. 1; Rose et al., 2024).

Association of School Psychologists (NASP), the National Association of School Resource Officers (NASRO), and Safe and Sound Schools, this section summarizes developmental considerations for school active shooter drills by age group—including pre-K, elementary, middle school, and high school students. These organizations have outlined current best practices for school active shooter drills and offer some of the only written guidance on unique considerations across stages of child development. The discussion also draws on insights from the committee's fall 2024 listening session with students (Box 5-1).

Early Childhood: Pre-K and Kindergarten (Ages 3–5)

Early childhood includes children in pre-K and kindergarten, ages 3–5 years; children in this stage experience tremendous progress in developing physical and social skills, language ability, and numerous aspects of emotional development (Crotty et al., 2023; Institute of Medicine & National Research Council, 2000). However, children in this age group continue to have a limited understanding of abstract concepts and are highly dependent on their caregivers to feel safe. Young children can understand the concepts of danger and emergencies, but only with adult guidance (Schildkraut & Nickerson, 2020).

In the context of a school active shooter drill (preparation for an emergency), children in this age group must rely on adult directions and management. Accordingly, it is important that well-trained staff use simple, clear, and reassuring language and provide students with a sense of calm and confidence.

Elementary School: Grades 1–5 (Ages 6–10)

Children aged 6–10 experience significant advances in concrete operational thought, which enables logical problem-solving (Fang & Fang, 1999; Shapiro & O'Brien, 1970). Compared with early childhood, children in elementary school have an improved understanding of rules and routines and are also developing a sense of independence.

Elementary school students are growing in their awareness of what constitutes danger and in their understanding of why drills are conducted (Hill et al., 2000; Zhe & Nickerson, 2007). However, it should be noted that children at the lower end of this age (i.e., grades 1–2) may be more developmentally similar to students in pre-K and kindergarten in terms of their ability to understand abstract concepts (Byrnes, 2008).

Most children in this age group understand basic concepts of safety and emergency procedures but require clear and simple explanations (Ammirati et al., 2014; Zhe & Nickerson, 2007). They continue to require adult direction during emergencies and are typically able to follow directions and instructions (Ammirati et al., 2014; Waterman et al., 2017; Yang et al., 2020). They also require emotional reassurance and support from adults in the context of school active shooter drills.

Middle School: Grades 6–8 (Ages 10–13)

When children reach middle school (grades 6–8, ages 10–13), their executive functioning skills are continuing to develop (Zelazo et al., 2016). Children in this age group can increasingly differentiate between likely threats and other potential dangers and can understand why active shooter drills occur (Cunningham, 2020; NASP et al., 2021; Schildkraut & Nickerson, 2020). Adult direction is essential for middle school children, but they can also perform practiced actions or roles independently during an emergency.

High School: Grades 9–12 (Ages 14–18)

As children move through their high school years, they experience significant development of their critical thinking and problem-solving skills and assume a greater sense of responsibility (Blakemore & Choudhury, 2006). Relative to younger children, high school students can make sense of complex information (Zhe & Nickerson, 2007). In addition, they are generally capable of abstract reasoning, hypothetical thinking, and strategic decision-making (NASEM, 2019b). These cognitive capacities, along with a growing sense of responsibility and increased executive functioning, may enable them to better navigate challenges that involve complex problem-solving and use creative thinking (NASEM, 2019b). However, these abilities may vary based on individual differences in development, ability to regulate emotions under stress, and previous training.

BOX 5-1
Students' Perspectives on Active Shooter Drills

The committee's information-gathering included listening sessions to understand students' experiences of school active shooter drills. While these listening sessions were not designed to be representative and do not reflect the full range of perspectives or experiences of students, they provided important context for understanding implementation of school active shooter drills from the students' point of view. These discussions served as a backdrop for the committee's review and assessment of the available empirical literature, as well as a reminder of the real-life stories and experiences behind the data. The sessions (along with qualitative data presented in Chapters 3 and 4) served as an important input to the committee's deliberations and provided a context for, though not the basis of, its conclusions and recommendations.

Students shared mixed feelings about active shooter drills, emphasizing the emotional and practical challenges these exercises pose. Their experiences varied significantly depending on age, school context, and personal background. Some students observed that drills often felt more frightening than empowering when they were younger. "When I was younger, it was a lot more scary rather than feeling prepared. But once you get older, emergency preparedness drills are making me feel more safe and more valued," a high school panelist from Maryland explained. Others noted that, as they grew older, they became more

> critical of the drills' realism and effectiveness. "As I grew up, I don't think we ever covered it again. It felt a little dystopian that we would have these school shooting drills, and then right after, be like, 'Okay, let's do math,'" shared a panelist who attended school in New York.
>
> For students with disabilities, active shooter drills reveal gaps in safety protocols. The panelist from New York shared her experiences with the committee as a student with a disability and recounted feeling unsafe during drills, stating, "I can't run. I can't bend. I can't hide in that way. And I definitely can't fight." Another panelist who attended high school in Illinois noted that individualized emergency plans are frequently overlooked, resulting in feelings of exclusion and vulnerability for students with disabilities: "I remember I bought an Apple Watch and programmed into it a text that I could just tap out, which is, 'There's a shooting at school. Come, get me! I love you,' because the protocol really didn't include me."
>
> Students also emphasized the need for greater teacher preparedness and communication during drills, underscoring the critical role of educators in creating a sense of security. "Knowing that the people who are supposed to help and protect you aren't sure what to do either isn't very securing," noted a high school panelist from Connecticut. Overall, students advocated for inclusive, context-specific, and trauma-informed approaches to safety measures that prioritize education, empowerment, and open feedback mechanisms.

CONSIDERATIONS RELATED TO UNIQUE IDENTITIES OF STUDENTS, CAREGIVERS, TEACHERS, AND OTHER STAFF

This section describes several characteristics of subpopulations that represent the diversity within K–12 school communities in the United States—including backgrounds, experiences, identities, access, and functioning—that are relevant to identifying practices for school active shooter drills that minimize harms to mental, emotional, and behavioral health. Although these subpopulations are all members of groups that make up a school community—students, caregivers, teachers, other school staff, and community members—the sections that follow focus primarily on research describing students and their abilities and needs when participating in a school active shooter drill. Similar observations may apply to caregivers, teachers, and other school staff on a school campus—such as a teacher who is pregnant or uses a wheelchair for mobility or a parent who is deaf or has mental health sequelae from experiencing gun violence.

Developmental considerations for mental, emotional, and behavioral well-being need to encompass the disparate and intersecting histories and functionality that everyone, including students, teachers, and other school staff, bring to the classroom and to the broader school campus. It is important to note that although the following sections are organized according to the characteristics of specific subpopulations, it is not uncommon for individuals to have intersecting identities and characteristics that can add multiplicative complexity to the challenge of conducting school active shooter drills that support mental, emotional, and behavioral health.

In a recent nationally representative survey, U.S. teachers reported that school active shooter drills were not generally designed to accommodate subpopulations (Moore et al., 2024). For example, only 26% of teachers reported that their school's active shooter drills were designed to meet the needs of students with physical disabilities, only 23% of teachers reported that drills were designed to meet the needs of students with developmental disabilities, and only 12% of teachers reported that drills were designed to meet the needs of those with past experiences of trauma (Moore et al., 2024). See also Box 5-2 for perspectives from school staff, as shared information-gathering sessions hosted by the committee.

Finally, although the committee here highlights risk factors that can negatively affect mental, emotional, and behavioral health, it is important to emphasize positive childhood experiences that have been shown to promote well-being in children (NASEM, 2019a);

these experiences are associated with "perceived safety, security, and support; and positive and predictable qualities of life" (Narayan et al., 2018, p. 20). These experiences encompass both internal factors (i.e., positive sense of self) and family characteristics (i.e., presence of a trusted and reliable caregiver, financial security), as well as experiences outside of the home, such as positive relationships with peers and teachers, safe and supportive schools, and highly resourced neighborhood contexts. Although definitions of positive childhood experiences vary across the literature, there is robust empirical support (Raghunathan et al., 2024) for a cumulative model, with overlapping positive childhood experiences conferring better outcomes both in childhood and into adulthood. Furthermore, in addition to having a direct benefit for health and well-being outcomes, positive childhood experiences can attenuate the impact of adverse or stressful childhood experiences and thus can play a role in shaping mental, emotional, and behavioral outcomes in multiple ways (Kallapiran et al., 2025; Raghunathan et al., 2024).

BOX 5-2
Perceptions of Active Shooter Drills from School Staff

The committee's information-gathering included listening sessions to understand the perceptions of school staff related to school active shooter drills. While these listening sessions were not designed to be representative and do not reflect the full range of perspectives or experiences of school staff, they provided important context for understanding the implementation of school active shooter drills. These discussions served as a backdrop for the committee's review and assessment of the available empirical literature, as well as a reminder of the real-life stories and experiences behind the data. The sessions (along with qualitative data presented in Chapters 3 and 4) served as an important input to the committee's deliberations and provided a context for, though not the basis of, its conclusions and recommendations.

Much of the lived-experience research on active shooter drills examines school staff's experiences. Generally, school staff recognize the importance and necessity of active shooter drills (Schildkraut & Nickerson, 2020). However, research shows that some K–12 teachers and school counselors feel that these drills could be improved by providing more time for student conversations and offering standardized discussion points (Brossman, 2019).

In recent research, teachers and school health professionals have emphasized the need for trauma-informed approaches; clear communication; and collaboration among all stakeholders, including students and families (Maynard et al., 2019; Schildkraut & Nickerson, 2020). Similar themes emerged during the committee's listening session. For instance, an Indiana teacher observed, "The more the students understand the why, the more we are creating an environment where the students feel safe but understand some of the protocols we have within our building."

School-based health professionals who spoke with the committee reported having observed some negative mental health impacts of drills, especially for students with previous trauma or disabilities, or those from marginalized communities disproportionately impacted by violence. A school nurse from New Jersey noted that: "For students with preexisting anxiety or who have experienced trauma, these drills can be especially triggering." Similarly, a school counselor from Virginia noted: "Depending on how the drills are done, they can be so harmful," emphasizing the potential for retraumatization. A professor of social work from California stressed the importance of including members of the whole school community: "If they're not at the table when the conversation and the planning begins, then we often are missing what is important for that particular population."

Furthermore, school staff reported a desire to shift away from hyper-realistic simulations and to focus instead on calm, routine instructional walkthroughs that include

> supportive post-drill discussions. A school psychologist from Oregon reinforced the importance of age-appropriate instruction and practice. As she described her experience: "We treat the drills more like a fire drill. Students know what to do, but in a way that is calm and routine."

Individuals with Prior Trauma Histories and Adverse Life Experiences

The individual lived experiences of students and staff shape their mental, emotional, and behavioral well-being. In turn, the histories they bring to school can potentially affect their response to school active shooter drills, depending on how they are conducted. Thus, special consideration is needed when an individual has had previous exposure to trauma, adversity, or stress that may affect their response to drills.

The terms *trauma*, *adversity*, and *stress* are often used interchangeably. In general, *trauma* can encompass a range of events including violence, natural disasters, discrimination or racism, life-threatening illness, abuse, or loss of loved ones (Dye, 2018; Kliethermes et al., 2014). While the standard for a "criterion A" traumatic event is typically defined by the *Diagnostic and Statistical Manual of Mental Disorders* (Mol et al., 2005), prior work suggests that other events also produce traumatic stress responses (Davis & Siegel, 2000; Gradus et al., 2022) and thus need to be considered in the context of school active shooter drills. In addition, children may have had experiences that are not specifically categorized as trauma that result in "stress" or other mental and physical reactions to events in the environment, which in turn can affect mental, emotional, and behavioral well-being. These stressors—often referred to as adverse childhood experiences—encompass exposures that may or may not meet the definition of trauma and include being exposed to parental substance abuse, growing up in poverty, or experiencing the divorce of parents or caregivers (Felitti et al., 1998; Hardt & Rutter, 2004).

Similarly, teachers and other school staff come to school with their own histories of stress and trauma. For example, violence directed against teachers, such as threats, harassment, and physical assault has been highlighted as a public health issue that can lead to a decline in teachers' mental health as well as burnout (Reddy et al., 2023).

Childhood traumatic stress is highly prevalent within the United States. Reports estimate that up to 60% of children and adolescents have had at least one direct exposure to violence, crime, or abuse, with 41% having had multiple exposures in the past year (Finkelhor et al., 2015). Among children exposed to trauma, more than 70% experienced more than one trauma (Briggs et al., 2012). Exposure to traumatic events in childhood is associated with an increased likelihood of psychiatric disorders in adulthood (Copeland et al., 2018). Although not everyone experiencing trauma develops trauma-related mental health conditions, both children and adults can develop post-traumatic stress disorder (PTSD) (Breslau et al., 1999), and children may show disruptions in school performance and behavior as a result of trauma (Bell et al., 2013; Perfect et al., 2016). For example, trauma exposure in childhood is associated with impairments in reading ability and executive function (Delaney-Black et al., 2002), increases in externalizing behaviors (Larson et al., 2017), and lower school performance (Goodman et al., 2012). Furthermore, children with trauma histories may show increased reactivity to other emotionally evocative stimuli (Aas et al., 2016; Marusak et al., 2015; van Nierop et al., 2018).

Histories of grief and loss among students also warrant consideration in planning for school active shooter drills. Grief can result in a child's decline in functioning, including regression to younger behaviors, emotional dysregulation, and difficulties concentrating in school (Alvis et al., 2023; Layne et al., 2017; Oosterhoff et al., 2018). When grief involves the traumatic death of a loved one, traumatic grief can develop and result in post-traumatic stress symptoms (Dyregrov et al., 2015). When planning for school active shooter drills, school staff need to be aware of and attuned to students' histories of trauma, grief, and other adverse childhood experiences—

in particular, exposure to gun violence exposure and other traumatic events that a student may recall during a drill. School communities that have experienced mass violence also have a significantly greater presence and persistence of PTSD (Moreland et al., 2024) that may require the availability of additional supports available when a school active shooter drill is conducted.

As noted, other adverse childhood experiences also impact mental, emotional, and behavioral well-being. Exposure to adverse childhood experiences is common in the United States; data from the U.S. Centers for Disease Control and Prevention (CDC) suggest that at least 64% of individuals have had at least one such experience (Swedo et al., 2023). A substantial body of research suggests that these exposures have multifactorial downstream impacts on child development across physical, emotional, and behavioral indices (Bellis et al., 2019). For example, in a global meta-analysis, exposure to adverse childhood experiences was associated with reduced school performance (Qu et al., 2024). These exposures also place individuals at increased risk of developing adverse psychiatric outcomes, including early substance use and PTSD (Khoury et al., 2010; Wu et al., 2010; Yehuda et al., 2002).

An important mechanistic consideration is the presence of heightened discrimination, bullying, and harassment at school—which many public health experts include among adverse childhood experiences—for some subpopulations of children (see, e.g., Cronholm et al., 2015). For example, in the National School Climate Survey—a nationally representative sample of 22,298 LGBTQ+ youth for the 2020–2021 academic year—Kosciw et al. (2022) reported that 81% of respondents felt unsafe at school and 76% reported experiencing verbal harassment. Respondents who experienced higher levels of victimization at school were less likely to report positive feelings of school belonging and connectedness than students who experienced lower levels of victimization (Kosciw et al., 2022). Furthermore, sexual and gender minority youth may experience increased childhood adversity that can contribute to insecurity in housing and social support (Andersen & Blosnich, 2013; DeChants et al., 2022)—protective factors that are relevant when considering school active shooter drills. Additionally, it is necessary to consider the practicalities of students' sexual and gender minority status in the planning of drills. For example, according to news reports, in 2018, a transgender student at a Virginia middle school was allegedly not allowed to move to either the boys' or girls' locker room during a school active shooter drill and instead sat alone in a hallway (Fitzsimons, 2018). Such a scenario—given the mental, emotional, and behavioral health considerations discussed above—may impact student well-being by preventing a sense of safety (e.g., their feeling that plans are in place for them in case of an emergency). It may also contribute to feelings of "othering" that result in adverse mental, emotional, and behavioral health outcomes, particularly if such othering may potentially contribute to bullying or peer victimization directed at the student. Thus, it is necessary to consider how to minimize singling out of these students and meet their unique needs in planning and implementing school active shooter drills.

In addition to their roles as educators, teachers and other school staff often support students undergoing emotional and stressful experiences. Prior research suggests that adults who work with traumatized children, including teachers and school staff, can develop symptoms related to secondary traumatic stress (Essary et al., 2020; Hensel et al., 2015; Hydon et al., 2015; Ireland & Huxley, 2018). They may report high rates of "compassion fatigue" and burnout, which are associated with adverse mental, emotional, and behavioral health outcomes.

Another important consideration for students and staff in the context of active shooter drills is the potential influence of prior "vicarious trauma" or related stress on mental, emotional, and behavioral health and individual responses to active shooter drills. Social media and internet use among youth and adults has risen sharply over the past 2 decades; research from the Pew Research Center indicates that more than 97% of teens use the internet daily, with around 60% using social media sites such as TikTok, Instagram, and Snapchat (Vogels et al., 2022). Frequent reports of mass violence on social media and the internet can result in vicarious trauma and adverse effects on students mental, emotional, and behavioral health. Research on vicarious trauma and social media impacts on children and adolescents is in its nascency, with some meta-analyses suggesting that frequent social media use is associated with worsening mental, emotional, and behavioral health (Jones et al., 2016, 2017; Shannon et al., 2022), while others suggest it has limited impacts (Ferguson et al., 2022), potentially owing to other moderating factors (Ivie et al., 2020).

These impacts may vary among individual students; anecdotal reports from school staff (see Boxes 5-1 and 5-2) show that some individuals experience desensitization related to exposure to violence in their communities while others experience sensitization.

Racially/Ethnically Marginalized Students and Teachers

Students from racially/ethnically marginalized[23] backgrounds may encounter a unique set of challenges in the school environment that present important considerations in the context of school active shooter drills. Polk et al. (2024) described the historical (e.g., segregation, racialized teacher preparation practices) and contemporary factors (e.g., exclusionary discipline policies, differences in teacher expectations of achievement) that have uniquely shaped racial attitudes in the educational system within the United States. These factors are reflected in both individual interactions among peers and students and in the design of systems (e.g., school discipline) (NASEM, 2023; Polk et al., 2024). These factors, and their downstream impacts on the mental, emotional, and behavioral health (e.g., sense of belonging, safety, disproportionate exposure to harsh discipline practices) of children from marginalized populations may be critical to consider when undertaking efforts to shape the broader school climate and environment. Creating safe, supportive, and inclusive learning settings requires attention to how school policies

---

[23] In a scoping review of 50 years of research, Fluit et al. (2024) present an integrated definition of marginalization as "a multifaceted concept referring to a context-dependent social process of 'othering'" where certain individuals or groups are systematically excluded based on societal norms and values, as well as the resulting experiences of disadvantage." The authors note that both the process and outcomes of marginalization can vary significantly across contexts (Fluit et al., 2024).

and practices, including preparedness activities and implementation of security measures, may be experienced by students with diverse backgrounds and needs.

The CDC's Youth Risk Behavior Survey demonstrates that, among high school students, approximately 40%–60% of students from minoritized backgrounds have experienced some form of racial discrimination and—in turn—reported poorer mental health (56.9% among Asian students, 48.8% among multiracial students, 45.9% among Black students, 39.4% among Hispanic students, 38.0% among American Indian/Alaskan Native students, 37.6% among Native Hawaiian and other Pacific Islander students; McKinnon et al., 2024).

Younger children also experience racial/ethnic discrimination; for example, in a survey of 10,354 children aged 10–11, approximately 4.8% of children reported experiencing discrimination because of race, ethnicity, or color. Prevalence was highest among Black children, with 10% reporting having experienced racial discrimination at 9 or 10 years old, including from teachers (8.4%) (Nagata et al., 2021).

Experimental evidence also demonstrates that teachers show biases against racially minoritized boys and characterize more of their behaviors as "problematic" even when those behaviors are the same as those of children from nonminoritized groups (e.g., Owens, 2023). In the context of school active shooter drills, such potential for overattribution of problematic behaviors by staff could contribute to increased disciplinary behavior, which may have downstream mental, emotional, and behavioral consequences for children from racially/ethnically marginalized populations.

With respect to other security measures on campuses, studies have also suggested that students of color—particularly Black students—are referred at higher rates to law enforcement when school resource officers are present on campus (Office for Civil Rights, 2018; Paige & Bushway, 2024). Of note, according to 2017–2018 data from the Office for Civil Rights (2018), American Indian/Alaskan Native (AIAN), Black, and Native Hawaiian and Pacific Islander students are disproportionately arrested at schools.

Meta-analyses further suggest that race-based discrimination is associated with multiple psychological and physical outcomes (Carter et al., 2017). For example, exposure to discrimination experienced during childhood and adolescence is associated with increased depressive symptoms and biological aging measured through DNA methylation (Carter et al., 2019; Lavner et al., 2023).

Children exposed to discrimination may also adopt coping behaviors that impact responses in school. For example, discrimination exposure is associated with ruminative coping (i.e., the process of passive or active focus on negative thoughts or feelings), a behavior associated with more severe depression and anxiety symptoms in adolescents and adults (Bernard et al., 2023; Michl et al., 2013).

The general prevalence of adverse mental, emotional, and behavioral health outcomes is known to vary across racial/ethnic categories. For example, some research suggests that in the United States, Hispanic/Latinx children may be more likely to meet criteria for psychiatric disorders such as PTSD or show heightened baseline levels of anxiety compared with White individuals (Alcántara et al., 2013; McLaughlin et al., 2007). However, it is important to note that prevalence estimates for different racial/ethnic groups can vary, in part because of variability in reporting and in access to receiving a diagnosis (McIntyre et al., 2017). Furthermore, Indigenous and Asian American and Pacific Islander (AAPI) groups—like other racial/ethnic groups in the United States—are highly heterogenous and comprise several cultural groups with unique histories and practices, which can intersect with mental, emotional, and behavioral health outcomes for different individuals and subgroups.

Cultural Influences as Protective Factors

There may also be cultural influences on risk and protective factors that affect mental, emotional, and behavioral states in students and school staff. For example, Hispanic/Latinx youth may be more likely than White non-Latinx youth and African American youth to use certain coping mechanisms (e.g., internalizing distress, describing physical symptoms resulting from emotional distress rather than mental health symptoms to avoid stigma) in response to stress (Varela & Hensley-Maloney, 2009).

Research on AAPI adolescents and young adults suggests that the COVID-19 pandemic may have contributed to a rise in anti-Asian discrimination, leading to adverse outcomes such as depression (Hahm et al., 2021; Huynh et al., 2023). However, other research on AAPI populations highlights the protective benefits of cultural identity and familial engagement with respect to resilience to adverse mental, emotional, and behavioral health outcomes (Stein et al., 2014). Notably, protective or potentiating factors for adverse mental, emotional, and behavioral health outcomes need not be specific to groups (e.g., cultural identity among Hispanic/Latinx individuals may also be protective). The current research landscape thus strongly suggests that multiple intersecting factors affect baseline mental, emotional, and behavioral well-being among students and staff, and may need to be considered in implementing and assessing the practice of school active shooter drills.

The Role of Immigration and Migrant Status

A portion of students and staff may have immigrant or refugee status, which may intersect with issues of trauma history, cultural differences, and other stressors. These can affect performance and other mental, emotional, and behavioral health factors considered in designing and interpreting school active shooter drills. Furthermore, children from immigrant families may experience acculturative stress, which has been associated with reduced academic performance among Hispanic/Latinx middle schoolers (Albeg & Castro-Olivo, 2014).

For example, prior research has observed that children of Asian immigrant families showed physical and mental health disparities, such as increased rates of internalizing disorders, compared with U.S.-born White children (Huynh et al., 2023). Other work suggests that Hispanic/Latinx children may be more likely to experience adverse events related to immigration and acculturation (Barajas-Gonzalez et al., 2021; Crouch et al., 2000; Zvolensky et al., 2019) that may impact mental, emotional, and behavioral well-being. Students and staff with immigrant or migrant status may also experience fear or stress related to the perceived risk of deportation, regardless of their legal status (Eskenazi et al., 2019). Such fear or stress may affect mental, emotional, and behavioral well-being at baseline or in response to school active shooter drills; for example, students or staff may be less likely to attend school during safety drills or interact with personnel associated with drills.

Similarly, research indicates that individuals who are migrants and/or refugees often experience pre- and postmigration stressors that can impact baseline mental, emotional, and behavioral well-being, including more incidences of adversity or traumatic stress (McAuliffe & Triandafyllidou, 2021). For example, premigration stressors may include conflict or war within the country of origin or reduced access to educational opportunities, which may compound postmigration stressors around integration with new communities or resettlement.

In line with such concerns, prior research on Syrian youth resettled into Canada observed that refugee youths' premigratory levels of adversity were positively associated with both internalizing and externalizing difficulties (Speidel et al., 2021). Another report found that in resettled Syrian youth, externalizing behaviors as well as migratory stressors such as amount of time spent in a refugee camp may be negatively associated with English-language learning (Paradis et al., 2022).

Trauma histories are also higher in migrant or immigrant populations, which can impact rates of internalizing disorders such as anxiety or PTSD (Ijadi-Maghsoodi et al., 2024). The confluence of potential stressor exposures experienced by immigrant/refugee children may be important to consider in designing and implementing school active shooter drills to minimize potentially adverse mental, emotional, and behavioral health effects.

Multilingual Learners

More than 350 different languages are spoken in the United States, with nearly 5 million, (10%) K–12 students in the United States designated as multilingual learners (Dietrich & Hernandez, 2022; National Center for Education Statistics [NCES], 2024a). Students whose home language is Spanish (77%) represent the majority of those students designated as multilingual learners, followed by those whose home language is Arabic, Chinese, Vietnamese, or Portuguese. Multilingual learners are a highly heterogenous group not only in terms of spoken languages, but also in terms of life experiences that can impact well-being and school performance, such as immigration and refugee status. Some children may experience emotional distress when navigating language barriers in school, which can put them at increased risk for adverse mental, emotional, and behavioral health outcomes (Han, 2010; Niehaus et al., 2017; Parra at al., 2014). In planning for effective training and communication with students and their parents regarding active shooter drills, available information in the family's primary language is therefore crucial. Box 5-3 discusses supports for multilingual learners during school active shooter drills.

BOX 5-3
Providing Language Supports to Students During School Active Shooter Drills

The committee's public listening session on considerations for students who may need language supports during a school active shooter drill (or similar event) provided important insights for schools to consider as they develop and implement their policies and practices. For students who require language supports, active shooter drills present unique challenges and require tailored approaches to ensure inclusivity and minimize harm. Experts emphasize that clear communication in the languages spoken by students

---

and their families is essential for preventing misunderstandings and reducing anxiety. An expert in multilingual education based in Washington, D.C., underscored the importance of ensuring that "information is communicated to parents and families in a language they can understand." This recommendation reflects the reality that nearly 10% of U.S. K–12 students qualify for language support services across a broad range of languages.

The emotional impact of drills can be particularly heightened for linguistically diverse students, particularly those from immigrant or refugee backgrounds who have experienced prior trauma. As noted by a pediatric psychologist from Virginia, "Immigrant and refugee children are often coming from a trauma background, themselves. Active shooter drills and lockdowns may trigger trauma that they've left their country for or previously experienced." This underscores the importance of trauma-informed practices that consider students' past experiences.

To support understanding, visual aids, culturally relevant materials, resources for parents in their home language, and pre-drill discussions have been identified as promising strategies for helping linguistically diverse students comprehend safety protocols. A licensed clinical counselor with expertise in deaf and hard-of-hearing populations emphasized the value of using "language and maybe graphics to show them what to do, like pictures and other things, to really go around and to help them to understand the process." Moreover, including multilingual and culturally informed feedback loops after drills enables students and their families to effectively ask questions and reflect on the experience.

The experts also emphasize that adult training is critical for conducting drills sensitively and effectively. One panelist—an expert on school safety and a professor of counseling who works with students who are deaf and hard of hearing—noted, "Adults have their own prior trauma experiences. Different words and stages matter," underscoring the importance of guiding educators and administrators in

> addressing the developmental and linguistic needs of students during these exercises.

Individuals Who Use Communication Aids and Supports

Whether on a general school campus or at a school that specializes in meeting the needs of students with special needs, students have a wide variety of communication abilities. Teachers provide tools and strategies for students with specific needs, such as those with partial or full blindness, hearing impairments, and deaf-blindness, as well as students who are nonverbal. Special communication needs can vary in complexity; for example, students with hearing loss can range from having mild hearing impairment to profound hearing loss and deafness. Students with communication needs have also been found to have greater challenges with social-emotional development, which can be influenced, in turn, by cognitive fatigue (increased behavioral issues when having to expend greater energy to communicate), struggles with identity and self-efficacy, bullying by peers, and lack of teacher connectedness (Dalton, 2011; Fellinger et al., 2009).

Clarke et al. (2014) recommended that schools address students' communication needs when planning for safety preparedness as they would for typical educational instruction. As described earlier, students and parents need to receive safety training information in their primary language (including Braille). Alternative communication strategies used in safety drills can include audible prerecorded directions or pairing a student with visual impairments with a sighted peer partner. Students who use alternative communication strategies benefit from having opportunities for additional practice to master emergency procedures.

Individuals with Emotional and Behavioral Support Needs

As discussed earlier in this chapter, individuals with histories of traumatic stress and other adverse life events may benefit from additional supports and special accommodations. Similarly, other students may have significant emotional challenges, including depression and anxiety, while others may require behavioral support to avoid disruptive behavior. In each of these contexts, special considerations may be needed in carrying out school active shooter drills.

Emotional Support Needs

Students who may need additional emotional support during a drill include those with identified or unidentified histories of emotional challenges, including depression or anxiety, and those with a history of grief and loss. Guidelines recommend that schools consider additional previewing of procedures and repeated rehearsal so that the processes become more familiar (Clarke et al., 2014). For students with a history of anxiety, practicing relaxation and other coping strategies in the context of drills may be important tools for educators to use in supporting students.

Behavioral Support Needs

Students who are receiving formal school supports, as well as those who are not, may benefit from behavioral supports during school active shooter drills. For example, students who have a strong preference for routine and sameness, such as those who are neurodivergent, may benefit from having a familiar staff member assigned to them to help them cope with the abrupt change to their routine during a drill. Some researchers suggest that using social stories to assist with this transition to a new environment (e.g., in the form of a picture book illustrating what to expect during this disruption to the usual class schedule) may be helpful (Edmonds, 2017). A social story can also be used to depict the procedures of a school active shooter drill in easy-to-follow pictures in order to assist students who can benefit from previewing a new situation (Clarke et al., 2014). Understanding the additional sensory needs of students with autism is also important, since visual and auditory changes common during an emergency drill may cause some students with autism to become agitated (Peek & Stough, 2010). Individualized modeling, prompting, and reinforcement have been used with young children with autism to teach them how to respond to a fire alarm and exit the classroom by following their teacher (Garcia et al., 2016). Classroom behavior support plans that are effective for neurodivergent students and others can also be applied to school active shooter drills. Students with disruptive behaviors may benefit from strategies such as behavioral contracts and positive reinforcements, which have been found to be effective in helping students follow instructions and remaining quiet, skills required during drills.

Individuals with Intellectual, Developmental, and Learning Disabilities

It is estimated that more than 400,000 students in the United States receive special education services because of an intellectual disability, and about 2.4 million students receive appropriate services to address learning disabilities (NCES, 2024b). For students who have challenges with learning and remembering new knowledge and skills, learning the multistep procedures for a school active shooter drill may require repeated practice, with step-by-step modeling to master the emergency procedures. Research has shown that children with cognitive impairments may not recognize emergency personnel (i.e., personnel wearing badges, uniforms, etc.), so they may benefit from provide opportunities to meet emergency personnel under nonemergent conditions.

Additionally, students with cognitive impairments may fail to recognize or understand a danger or threat (Kailes & Enders, 2007) and so may experience a greater level of confusion and anxiety during a crisis compared with other students (Boon et al., 2012). Emergency planning, including drills, needs to include post-crisis supports for students with special needs, with the understanding that they may be especially affected by the emotional stress of a crisis (Clarke et al., 2014).

Individuals with Physical and Other Health Conditions

Individuals in a school may have a wide variety of health issues, including acute conditions (e.g., a leg fracture requiring a student to use crutches temporarily) and chronic health issues (e.g., diabetes, asthma, seizures, ongoing use of a wheelchair). Students with some health conditions may require more complex supports in the event of an emergency, such as access to needed medications and medical supplies. Planning for accessible routes and adaptive equipment may also be needed.

One concern highlighted in the literature is that schools may not be routinely including students with special health care needs in emergency preparedness planning (Peek & Stough, 2010), potentially leading to greater emotional distress during drills and/or actual school crises for these students. In one study that surveyed 40 state education departments about school crisis plans, 45% reported not including information about working with individuals with mental and physical disabilities (Annandale et al., 2011). Stough et al. (2020) highlighted the continued gap in school emergency management planning due to the failure of many schools to consider children with special needs. Involving special education teachers has been emphasized as a critical foundation for having more inclusive emergency planning (McAdams Ducy & Stough, 2011).

A growing literature recommends that planning for emergency preparedness, such as school active shooter drills, be undertaken by a multidisciplinary team charged with developing inclusive drills for students (Nikolaraizi et al., 2021). Clarke et al. (2014) suggested that for those students receiving special education, special education teachers need to partner with students, parents, and other school and community support staff to create an individualized safety plan. Such a plan outlines specific accommodations that students with special needs may require for accessing the educational and participation components of a school active shooter drill. In considering the individual needs of students, teachers need to first assess the skills required of students during an active shooter drill—skills such as following directions; moving quickly; remaining quiet; and maintaining position in a small, dark and uncomfortable space. Then they can provide guidance for accommodating a student's individual needs, such as providing a designated support person to assist the student or ensuring that students have access to safe spaces that are physically accessible and allow them to remain awa from doors, windows, and lines of sight. Practicing these accommodations during a drill can be important in testing these strategies and revising them as necessary and ensuring that all needed supports are available during the drill.

BOX 5-4
Considerations for Students with Disabilities:
Expert Perspectives

The committee's information-gathering included listening sessions to understand considerations for students with disabilities during school active shooter drills. These listening sessions were not designed to be representative and do not reflect the full range of perspectives or experiences of students with disabilities or the staff who work with these students in schools. However, these discussions served as a backdrop for the committee's review and assessment of the available empirical literature, as well as a reminder of the real-life stories and experiences behind the data. The sessions (along with qualitative data presented in Chapters 3 and 4) served as an important input to the committee's deliberations and provided a context for, though not the basis of, its conclusions and recommendations.

Special education teachers have raised concerns regarding the implementation of active shooter drills in their classrooms. For example, a study by Covarrubias (2023) involving semi-structured interviews with six special education teachers and three campus administrators found that both groups acknowledged that state-based active shooter procedures and emergency management plans often used broad, standardized protocols that fail to account for the specific needs of students with severe disabilities.

The committee's listening sessions provided further insight into these challenges, particularly in mitigating potential adverse mental, emotional, and behavioral outcomes for students with disabilities. Panelists emphasized that students with complex communication needs may rely on augmentative communication devices, and ensuring their continued access during emergencies is essential. Additionally, students with disabilities may experience heightened emotional and behavioral impacts from active shooter drills, including fear, anxiety, and withdrawal. One expert noted that the "chaotic and confusing nature" of these drills can surface past traumas and result in behavioral changes, such as aggression or self-injury.

Beyond the emotional toll, educators have expressed concerns regarding the practical challenges of adapting active shooter procedures for students with disabilities. The Covarrubias (2023) study found that teachers perceived school administrators as lacking a full understanding of the severity of some students' disabilities and the resulting difficulties in implementing state-mandated plans. Furthermore, teachers reported that administrators were often unresponsive or difficult to reach when concerns were raised. As a result, some special education teachers created their own unauthorized emergency plans, frequently in collaboration with paraprofessionals, to provide additional protections for their students.

To address these concerns, experts and educators advocate for greater inclusion of special education teachers in the development of school safety plans and comprehensive professional development for staff. Panelists in the committee's listening sessions with students and experts on students with disabilities further emphasized the importance of universal design principles in school safety planning, ensuring that all students—regardless of ability—can effectively participate in emergency procedures. As one panelist stated, "Universal design benefits all students because it

> ensures accessibility and inclusivity in emergency planning." Establishing inclusive, adaptable safety protocols is essential to safeguarding the well-being and security of students with disabilities during active shooter drills.

Children Involved with Other Formal Social Systems

Children participating in school active shooter drills may also interact with other formal social systems, such as the juvenile justice and foster care systems, both of which are demonstrably associated with long-term adverse mental, emotional, and behavioral health outcomes (Muentner et al., 2022; Snehil & Sagar, 2020; Whitted et al., 2013). Ultimately, that involvement may contribute to difficulties with and necessary considerations for the practice of school active shooter drills to maintain mental, emotional, and behavioral well-being.

Children Involved with the Justice System

When students who are involved in the juvenile justice system may face housing instability or encounter other circumstances that limit their access to school—such as frequent absences or disciplinary removals—they may miss key information about active shooter drill procedures (Almquist & Walker, 2022; Kearney et al., 2023). Furthermore, children having frequent contact with law enforcement may have different perceptions of school-based law enforcement or security personnel that could influence mental, emotional, and behavioral health outcomes such as perceptions of safety or fear and school connectedness.

Children Involved with the Child Welfare System

In the United States, nearly 400,000 children are in foster care at a given time (U.S. Department of Education, 2016), and nearly 70% of children in the foster care system are under 14 years old (U.S. Department of Health and Human Services, n.d.). A recent meta-analysis found that current placement in foster care was moderately associated with mental health problems (Dubois-Comtois et al., 2021). Earlier reports also indicate a higher prevalence of externalizing problems in foster children, with limited training provided to foster parents for dealing with of these behaviors which may emerge during school time (Vanschoonlandt et al., 2013).

At the same time, several protective factors emerged from this research, such as limited number of displacements or a stable long-term stay in the foster home. Children involved in the child welfare system may see frequent moves from school that may prevent them from receiving key information about school active shooter drills such that, when a school active shooter drill is conducted, they experience a threat to their sense of safety (e.g., being unfamiliar with specific practices that are used in a school). Furthermore, children involved in the child welfare system—especially younger children, for whom secure and stable adult relationships are key—may rely on teachers or other school staff for reassurance or extra support during times of heightened stress; yet frequent school changes may impact a child's ability to develop supportive relationships with teachers and peers (Tilbury et al., 2014).

SUPPORTING RESILIENCE IN THE CONTEXT OF SCHOOL ACTIVE SHOOTER DRILLS

School active shooter drills are intended to enhance safety and preparedness, but they also have the potential to contribute to adverse mental, emotional, and behavioral health outcomes for students and staff. Schools have critical opportunities to provide support that can mitigate these outcomes and foster resilience. Ensuring that drills are conducted in a way that prioritizes psychological well-being requires a collaborative effort among teachers; school support staff, including school health care providers; and caregivers and families. This section explores the roles and responsibilities of these key groups in helping students process their experiences with drills;

recover from adverse mental, emotional, and behavioral health effects; and build coping mechanisms that foster resilience.

The Role of Teachers and School Support Staff

Teachers and school support staff often encounter a range of stressors that can impact their mental, emotional, and behavioral health (Greenberg et al., 2016). These challenges may stem from the broader school environment—such as school leadership, resource availability, and collegial relationships—as well as from the specific demands of the job, including instructional pressures and student behavior management. Individual factors, such as stress management and perceived agency, also play a role (Greenberg et al., 2016, NASEM, 2019a). Just as students bring their lived experiences and mental, emotional, and behavioral health needs to school, so too do teachers and school-based health professionals, and they must navigate the complex task of managing their own well-being while supporting the that of their students (NASEM, 2019a). Schools that provide meaningful support and foster the development of educators' social-emotional competencies are better positioned to help staff regulate their emotions and behaviors, which in turn enhances their capacity to cultivate prosocial behavior and social-emotional skills in students (NASEM, 2019a).

Across all stages of development, teachers play a central role in the social-emotional and physical well-being of their students. Teachers are essential in creating a classroom environment that is safe and supportive (Jennings & Greenberg, 2009; NASEM, 2019a). A classroom environment that consistently prioritizes psychological and physical safety and well-being can reduce anxiety during school active shooter drills (Geist, 2019). At the same time, it is important to note that even as they must demonstrate calm during drills to help students regulate their emotions and behaviors, teachers can find drills stressful as well.

While little research has been done on teachers' experiences and needs with respect to school active shooter drills (Schildkraut & Nickerson, 2020), they require clear communications from school leadership on how to teach drill procedures to their students. One small study of preservice teachers (N = 97) found that preservice teachers generally felt underprepared to navigate school active shooter drills and wanted additional training (Laguardia et al., 2024). In addition, an implementation evaluation in Nebraska of the "I Love U Guys" Foundation's Standard Response Protocol also found that surveyed teachers (N = 785) wanted more formal training on how to implement the protocol, as well as guidance on supporting students with functional and access needs and students of different ages (Bulling et al., 2025).

Teachers often depend on collaboration with school-based mental health professionals to work with students who may need additional support or intervention following school active shooter drills. However, in RAND's (2023) American Teacher Panel Survey, which assessed teacher's experience with lockdown drills, 44% of respondents reported that their school does not provide socioemotional support or supplemental resources to students in advance of, during, or after drills (Moore et al., 2024). Furthermore, while this survey found that 48% of teachers reported that drills led them to feel more prepared to respond to an active shooter incident, 50% reported that drills made no difference (i.e., neither more nor less prepared). Only one in five teachers (19.8%) reported that the drills in which they participated made them feel safer at school, whereas 68.5% reported that participating in drills made no difference to their perceptions of safety at school, and 11.7% reported that drills made them feel less safe at school. These results also indicate that a substantial portion of teachers do not receive advance notice of school active shooter drills (14.3%). Box 5-5 provides perspectives from teachers shared with the committee during its fall 2024 listening session series.

BOX 5-5
Teachers' Perspectives on Active Shooter Drills

The committee's held listening sessions to understand teachers' experiences of school active shooter drills. While these were not designed to be representative and do not reflect the full range of perspectives or experiences of teachers, they provided important context for understanding the implementation context of school active shooter drills. The discussions served as a backdrop for the committee's review and assessment of the available empirical literature, as well as a reminder of the real-life stories and experiences behind the data. The sessions (along with qualitative data presented in Chapters 3 and 4) served as an important input to the committee's deliberations and provided a context for, though not the basis of, its conclusions and recommendations.

Teachers reported experiencing significant challenges and conflicting emotions regarding active shooter drills. Their perspectives highlighted both the importance of school safety protocols and the emotional and psychological impact these drills can have. They noted that drills often generate anxiety and stress among both students and staff, particularly for individuals with a history of trauma, who may feel triggered by the simulations. One of the teachers—a Columbine shooting survivor herself—reflected, "What I've noticed in the students since we've made the change to kind of just a more rounded protocol is that I think that they feel safer. We also give them a heads up before it's going to happen, so that they know it's not just a blind drill."

The need for clear communication and preparation emerged as a recurring theme, with teachers advocating for transparency in drill scheduling and the use of age-appropriate explanations. One educator emphasized the critical role teachers play in shaping student responses, stating, "The teacher sets the tone, so if the teacher is not prepared themselves, then their energy will trickle into the students."

> Teachers also expressed concerns about the disproportionate impact of drills on certain student populations, particularly multilingual learners and students with disabilities. A high school teacher working in a school with a large refugee and immigrant population noted that safety protocols were often translated into multiple languages to better support students.
>
> Educators further stressed the importance of incorporating trauma-informed practices into safety drills, ensuring that preparedness efforts minimize harm while maintaining effectiveness. One teacher advocated for teaching students skills to manage anxiety, rather than relying solely on frequent, high-intensity drills, stating, "We can teach our kids skills and have conversations about what to do in these types of situations, especially with our youngest ones." Finally, teachers called for debriefing sessions and mental health support after drills, ensuring that both students and staff have a space to process their emotions, reflect on their experiences, and enhance preparedness without exacerbating trauma.

In addition to teachers, school-based health professionals—including school counselors, school psychologists, school social workers, and school nurses—can play an important role in both informing developmentally appropriate emergency preparedness practices and providing ongoing support for the well-being of students and staff (NASP et al., 2021). As noted previously, when schools have access to these professionals, their expertise in areas such as mental health assessment, crisis intervention, trauma-informed care, and medical support can help shape response strategies while ensuring that students and staff have access to the comprehensive supports needed to foster a safe and healthy school environment year round (NASP et al., 2021).

In the context of school active shooter drills, and emergency preparedness more broadly, school health professionals can provide essential psychological and medical support before, during, and after emergency drills as well as in the event of actual emergencies (Brymer et al., 2012; Gereige et al., 2022). However, as noted earlier in this report, many schools do not have consistent or sufficient access to school-based health professionals (e.g., Willgerodt et al., 2024). School counselors, school psychologists, and school social workers can play a key role in developing trauma-informed approaches to emergency drills, ensuring that preparedness activities do not inadvertently contribute to student anxiety, fear, or retraumatization (Dwyer et al., 2015; Nickerson & Zhe, 2004; Wallengren-Lynch, 2024; Werner, 2015). They can also assist in pre-drill planning as well as education, helping students and staff understand emergency procedures in a way that is developmentally appropriate and emotionally supportive (Gereige et al., 2022). During structured debriefing sessions, they can support students and staff in processing their experiences, identifying emotional reactions, and developing coping strategies (NASP et al., 2021).

School-based health professionals can contribute to emergency preparedness by working with other school staff to ensure that students with medical conditions or disabilities receive the necessary care and accommodations during drills and real emergencies (Dwyer et al., 2015; Gereige et al., 2022). For example, following a drill, school nurses can also be key providers of medical care, addressing physical symptoms of anxiety or distress—such as panic attacks, hyperventilation, or psychosomatic symptoms—and working in coordination with mental health staff to provide holistic care (e.g., Ginsburg et al., 2019).

Beyond emergency preparedness, school mental health professionals and school nurses play an integral role in fostering a safe, healthy, and supportive school environment (Dwyer et al., 2015). They provide direct services to students, including mental health counseling, behavioral interventions, and medical care, to address a broad spectrum of student needs (Gereige et al., 2022). These professionals are instrumental in promoting preventive initiatives, such as social-emotional learning programs, trauma-informed practices, and mental health screenings, all of which can contribute to a more resilient student body (Berardi & Morton, 2018; NASEM, 2019a).

They can also serve as consultants and educators for teachers, staff, and families by providing training on recognizing signs of emotional distress, trauma, and medical emergencies, equipping school personnel with the tools to respond effectively (e.g., Dickson et al., 2025).

Integrating both mental and physical health considerations into school safety and emergency planning may equip schools to support students and staff in managing stress and developing resilience in the face of crises. This approach can ensure that all students and staff, regardless of their medical, mental, emotional, or behavioral needs, receive the support necessary to navigate emergencies and emergency preparedness in a supportive environment.

The Role of Caregivers and Families

Throughout development, children have many relationships that shape their mental, emotional, and behavioral well-being, but perhaps none are more influential than caregivers and family. This report considers *caregivers* to include parents, grandparents, kinship care, foster parents, and others who assume responsibility for children's well-being (Morris et al., 2017). An extensive body of research demonstrates the important role of caregivers in supporting their children's emotion regulation and resilience. A nurturing parent–child relationship that provides a sense of safety and stability has been associated with positive emotional development in children. A caregiver's emotion regulation (i.e., modulating their expression of emotion while caregiving) can influence a child's emotion regulation as the child observes and models the caregiver and responds to their caregiving style (Eisenberg et al., 1998; Hajal & Paley, 2020; Rutherford et al., 2015). Emotion regulation is crucial to overall emotional well-being and is also related to coping with challenging situations, expressing feelings appropriately, and building healthy relationships. For those children who experience adverse life events, studies have shown that strong family relationships promote resiliency (Luthar et al., 2015). As described earlier in the discussion of different student populations, caregivers and families themselves may struggle with challenges (e.g., poverty, trauma, mental illness) as well as caring for children with functional or access needs that require additional support (e.g., intellectual or physical disabilities). School leaders need to consider these needs as they communicate and engage with caregivers in preparation for school active shooter drills.

Given the importance of a caregiver's role in children's mental, emotional, and behavioral development, caregiver involvement in a child's school has been found to have a positive effect on youth development (Epstein & Sanders, 2002; Hill & Tyson, 2009) and overall mental health (Roeser et al., 2000; Wang & Sheikh-Khalil, 2014). Family–school engagement has been shown to predict positive child outcomes across development, with respect to behavior and emotional well-being (Smith et al., 2019). This connection with a child's education can be primarily school based, such as through caregiver–teacher communication, attendance at school events, and volunteering, providing a structure for assisting with homework, monitoring the progress of schoolwork and setting expectations, and encouraging about educational goals.

Strategies for caregiver involvement in schools have been shown to vary by race and ethnicity (Crosnoe, 2001) and socioeconomic status, influenced by structural and historical context (e.g., the legacy of racial exclusion, parental distrust in the educational system), as well as structural economic barriers to participation (Mowen, 2015). What remains constant, however, is the overall value and importance that caregivers place on their child's education (Lareau & Horvat, 1999).

Caregivers' school engagement has also been shown to benefit children with diverse abilities, including those with disruptive behaviors (Sheridan et al., 2017) and autism (Garbacz & McIntyre, 2016). The large body of literature evaluating family–school interventions has demonstrated the positive impact of such interventions on children's social and behavioral competency and mental health, across developmental stages (i.e., pre-K through high school) and across race and ethnicity (e.g., larger effects found for Black students; Sheridan et al., 2019). In identifying the core components of these interventions in a large meta-analysis, Sheridan et al. (2019) highlighted both relational and structural components of effective family–school interventions. They point out that structural tools support parents at home in fostering their child's positive development. The authors found that relational components, such as improving communication and collaboration between caregivers and schools, had the greatest positive effect on children's mental, emotional, and behavioral functioning (Sheridan et al., 2019).

When considering school emergency and disaster preparedness generally, one study found that disseminating emergency preparedness information to schools with limited parent involvement was a major challenge, although parents at these schools voiced interest in learning more about preparedness despite not participating in trainings (Kubicek et al., 2008). These parents instead reported learning from their children about preparedness rather than receiving the information directly, with the researchers concluding that parent leaders needed to be involved in planning of regular preparedness classes for families. In another study, Spanish-speaking Latino parents were more likely to seek disaster mitigation information from friends and family as opposed to government entities (Peguero, 2006), suggesting that culturally salient communication strategies needed to be considered.

Caregivers' Responses and Perceptions

Building on this broader literature of emergency preparedness and applying foundational aspects of how caregivers support positive youth development at home and in collaboration with schools, the discussion that follows turns to what is known about the relationships between caregivers and school active shooter drills and other security measures. There is limited research examining caregivers' responses to and perceptions of school active shooter drills. School counselors in one study reported that caregivers felt worried and protective of their children following school active shooter drills and suggested that more awareness of and training on these drills were needed to mitigate "parents panicking and rushing to the schools" (Goodman-Scott & Eckhoff, 2020).

Guidance from the NASP, the NASRO, and Safe and Sound Schools, as well as the National Child Traumatic Stress Network, provides helpful guidance for supporting caregivers. These practices include involving them in the planning of drills, providing information and resources about the protocols and practices used by the school, notifying parents of the type of drill being used, and offering alternative options for students, such as discussion-based practices, if deemed appropriate (NASP et al., 2021; The National Child Traumatic Stress Network [NCTSN], 2018). These recommendations highlight the importance of a communications strategy that informs families when drills are occurring; provides details about the procedures; and considers the varying backgrounds, languages, experiences, and needs of caregivers.

Given the crucial role of caregivers in their children's emotional development, researchers also suggest that studies be conducted to understand caregivers' perceptions and potential needs during school active shooter drills by using validated tools to measure impact on their emotional well-being, their expressed concerns about drills, and their sense of school safety (Dailey et al., 2024). Box 5-6 provides insights from caregiver and family perspectives on school active shooter drills.

Literature on caregivers' reactions to other security measures at schools is also limited and has been mixed. One study found that the presence of greater security measures (including metal detectors and security guards) was associated with less perceived sense of security at school among parents, controlling for other confounding variables such as neighborhood crime (Mowen & Freng, 2019). In a survey of parents in Pennsylvania, however, parents identified installing metal detectors when asked what schools could do to prepare for an active shooter event (Wallace, 2020). These findings suggest that caregivers' perceptions of school security measures may be influenced by a variety of factors and can differ depending on school context.

> **BOX 5-6**
> **Caregivers, Parents, and Families' Perspectives on Active Shooter Drills**
>
> The committee hosted listening sessions to understand caregivers', parents', and families' experiences of school active shooter drills. While these sessions were not designed to be representative and do not reflect the full range of perspectives or experiences of caregivers, parents, and families, they provided important context for understanding the implementation context of school active shooter drills and areas of potential concern for adverse outcomes. These discussions served as a backdrop for the committee's review and assessment of the available empirical literature, as well as a reminder of the real-life stories and experiences behind the data. The sessions (along with qualitative data presented in Chapters 3 and 4) served as an important input to the committee's deliberations and provided a context for, though not the basis of, its conclusions and recommendations.
>
> Caregivers, parents, and families expressed a range of perspectives on school active shooter drills, often struggling to balance the need to prepare children for potential dangers with concerns about the emotional impact of these exercises. Panelists raised concerns about trauma and desensitization, noting that repeated drills could either heighten children's anxiety or, conversely, lead to desensitization to violence. A father of two elementary-age children—when discussing the use of high-sensorial elements in active shooter drills—reflected on this tension, stating, "Children don't learn under fear; a child will not learn safety if there's a fake rifle parading the school halls of an elementary school."
>
> The need for differentiated approaches was also emphasized. One participant pointed out that traditional, one-size-fits-all drills do not meet the needs of children with disabilities, sensory sensitivities, or trauma histories. He noted

that, for some children, the unpredictability and sensory intensity of drills can lead to heightened stress and anxiety, both at school and at home. Without accommodations, these drills may become distressing rather than instructive, highlighting the importance of individualized safety plans and trauma-informed approaches to emergency preparedness.

Parental involvement was identified as a crucial yet often overlooked component of school safety efforts. Many participants emphasized the importance of advance notice about drills and the need for resources to help children process the experience. One parent noted, "It's very rare that families get engaged in that process to help debrief with their child. Sending out materials about the drill, debriefing strategies for different age groups, and having family conversations could make a world of difference." However, perspectives on involvement can vary. Another parent—who is also a teacher—noted that, "Sometimes parents push back, saying, 'You take care of that at school. Let me know if I need to talk to my kid at home.'"

The speakers collectively advocated for a more nuanced and holistic approach to school safety—one that includes reducing the frequency of drills, reframing them as learning opportunities, and increasing family and community involvement. One participant—a parent whose work focuses on improving school safety—summarized this approach, stating, "We take a life skills approach to ensure kids generalize safety skills everywhere, not just in school. This prevents the mindset that school is the dangerous place requiring such practice." These insights highlight the need for schools to collaborate with families in developing inclusive, trauma-informed safety protocols that support both preparedness and emotional well-being.

CONCLUSION

Although not exhaustive, this chapter provides key developmental considerations and population-level variations that can inform the implementation of active shooter drills and other school security measures in K–12 settings across the United States. Such considerations take into account the strengths, needs, and potential vulnerabilities within school communities.

Recognizing that individuals within a school community often embody multiple intersecting characteristics, the need for person-centered, developmentally appropriate, and trauma-informed approaches to school safety planning are critical. Multiple factors must be considered simultaneously to ensure that all students have access to participation in emergency preparedness efforts. Schools must account for the unique needs of students, caregivers, educators, and support staff in creating safety protocols that are effective and inclusive.

Recent efforts in education practice and policy have emphasized the importance of flexibility in how information is presented, ensuring that learning environments are accessible and responsive to all students. The Universal Design for Learning paradigm offers a model for engaging all learners by incorporating multiple means of engagement, representation, and expression (Basham et al., 2020; Capp, 2017; Levey, 2023). Research suggests that these principles not only enhance learning outcomes but also reduce barriers that may otherwise exclude some students from fully participating in school safety efforts. Applying insights from developmental science and trauma-informed care can help schools assess whether school active shooter drills and other security measures are appropriate for different age groups and student populations.

Furthermore, schools generally have opportunities to engage in collaboration among teachers, administrators, caregivers, school-based health providers, school security personnel, students, and support staff, in order to identify the resources and accommodations needed to promote positive mental, emotional, and behavioral outcomes. However, not all schools have access to these resources, creating disparities in the level of support available for students and staff. It is important to emphasize again that students are not the only individuals who require these supports; school staff also benefit from a school climate that prioritizes their well-being. Research and expert perspectives shared with the committee indicate that adults who are equipped with the skills to remain calm and regulated in an emergency are better able to support students in doing the same.

Ultimately, the well-being of the entire school community depends on an environment that fosters positive mental, emotional, and behavioral health. By integrating developmentally appropriate, trauma-informed, and inclusive strategies into school safety planning, educators and policymakers can ensure that these practices set the stage for the implementation of active shooter drills and other security measures in a positive and supportive school climate to enhance preparedness without compromising the psychological well-being of students and staff.

REFERENCES

Aas, M., Kauppi, K., Brandt, C., Tesli, M., Kaufmann, T., Steen, N., Agartz, I., Westlye, L., Andreassen, O., & Melle, I. (2016). Childhood trauma is associated with increased brain responses to emotionally negative as compared with positive faces in patients with psychotic disorders. *Psychological Medicine, 47*, 669–679. https://doi.org/10.1017/S0033291716002762

Albeg, L. J., & Castro-Olivo, S. M. (2014). The relationship between mental health, acculturative stress, and academic performance in a Latino middle school sample. *Contemporary School Psychology, 18*(3), 178–186. https://doi.org/10.1007/s40688-014-0010-1

Alcántara, C., Casement, M. D., & Lewis-Fernández, R. (2013). Conditional risk for PTSD among Latinos: A systematic review of racial/ethnic differences and sociocultural explanations. *Clinical Psychology Review, 33*(1), 107–119. https://doi.org/10.1016/j.cpr.2012.10.005

Almquist, L., & Walker, S. C. (2022). Reciprocal associations between housing instability and youth criminal legal involvement: A scoping review. *Health & Justice, 10*(1), 15.

Alvis, L., Zhang, N., Sandler, I. N., & Kaplow, J. B. (2023). Developmental manifestations of grief in children and adolescents: Caregivers as key grief facilitators. *Journal of Child & Adolescent Trauma, 16*(2), 447–457.

Ammirati, C., Gagnayre, R., Amsallem, C., Némitz, B., & Gignon, M. (2014). Are schoolteachers able to teach first aid to children younger than 6 years? A comparative study. *BMJ Open, 4.* https://doi.org/10.1136/bmjopen-2014-005848

Andersen, J. P., & Blosnich, J. (2013). Disparities in adverse childhood experiences among sexual minority and heterosexual adults: Results from a multi-state probability-based sample. *PLoS One, 8*(1), e54691.

Annandale, N. O., Heath, M. A., Dean, B., Kemple, A., & Takino, Y. (2011). Assessing cultural competency in school crisis plans. *Journal of School Violence, 10*(1), 16–33. https://doi.org/10.1080/15388220.2010.519263

Barajas-Gonzalez, R. G., Ayón, C., Brabeck, K., Rojas-Flores, L., & Valdez, C. R. (2021). An ecological expansion of the adverse childhood experiences (ACEs) framework to include threat and deprivation associated with US immigration policies and enforcement practices: An examination of the Latinx immigrant experience. *Social Science & Medicine, 282,* 114126. https://doi.org/10.1016/j.socscimed.2021.114126

Basham, J. D., Blackorby, J., & Marino, M. T. (2020). Opportunity in crisis: The role of universal design for learning in educational redesign. *Learning Disabilities: A Contemporary Journal, 18*(1), 71–91.

Bell, H., Limberg, D., & Robinson III, E. M. (2013). Recognizing trauma in the classroom: A practical guide for educators. *Childhood Education, 89*(3), 139–145.

Bellis, M. A., Hughes, K., Ford, K., Rodriguez, G. R., Sethi, D., & Passmore, J. (2019). Life course health consequences and associated annual costs of adverse childhood experiences across Europe and North America: A systematic review and meta-analysis. *The Lancet Public Health, 4*(10), e517-e528. https://doi.org/10.1016/s2468-2667(19)30145-8

Bernard, D. L., López, C. M., Banks, D. E., Hahn, A. M., & Danielson, C. K. (2023). Developmental differences in the impact of racial discrimination on depression and anxiety among Black youth: Examining rumination as a mechanism. *American Journal of Orthopsychiatry, 93*(4), 293. https://doi.org/10.1037/ort0000679

Blakemore, S. J., & Choudhury, S. (2006). Development of the adolescent brain: implications for executive function and social cognition. *Journal of Child Psychology and Psychiatry, 47*(3–4), 296–312. https://doi.org/10.1111/j.1469-7610.2006.01611.x

Boon, H. J., Pagliano, P., Brown, L., & Tsey, K. (2012). An assessment of policies guiding school emergency disaster management for students with disabilities in Australia. *Journal of Policy and Practice in Intellectual Disabilities, 9*(1), 17–26. https://doi.org/10.1111/j.1741-1130.2012.00331.x

Breslau, N., Chilcoat, H. D., Kessler, R. C., & Davis, G. C. (1999). Previous exposure to trauma and PTSD effects of subsequent trauma: Results from the Detroit Area Survey of Trauma. *American Journal of Psychiatry, 156*(6), 902–907. https://doi.org/10.1176/ajp.156.6.902

Briggs, E. C., Greeson, J. K., Layne, C. M., Fairbank, J. A., Knoverek, A. M., & Pynoos, R. S. (2012). Trauma exposure, psychosocial functioning, and treatment needs of youth in residential care: Preliminary findings from the NCTSN Core Data Set. *Journal of Child & Adolescent Trauma, 5*, 1–15. http://doi.org/10.1080/19361521.2012.646413

Brossman, W. S. (2019). *Educator perceptions of the effectiveness of active shooter training in schools*. Immaculata University.

Brymer, M., Taylor, M., Escudero, P., Jacobs, A., Kronenberg, M., Macy, R., Mock, L. A., Payne, L., Pynoos, R., & Vogel, J. (2012). *Psychological first aid for schools: Field operations guide* (2nd ed.). National Child Traumatic Stress Network.

Byrnes, J. P. (2008). Piaget's cognitive-developmental theory. *Encyclopedia of Infant and Early Childhood Development, 87*, 543–552.

Capp, M. J. (2017). The effectiveness of universal design for learning: A meta-analysis of literature between 2013 and 2016. *International Journal of Inclusive Education, 21*(8), 791–807. https://doi.org/10.1080/13603116.2017.1325074

Carter, R. T., Lau, M. Y., Johnson, V., & Kirkinis, K. (2017). Racial discrimination and health outcomes among racial/ethnic minorities: A meta-analytic review. *Journal of Multicultural Counseling and Development, 45*(4), 232–259. https://doi.org/10.1002/jmcd.12076

Carter, S. E., Ong, M. L., Simons, R. L., Gibbons, F. X., Lei, M. K., & Beach, S. R. (2019). The effect of early discrimination on accelerated aging among African Americans. *Health Psychology, 38*(11), 1010. https://doi.org/10.1037/hea0000788

Clarke, L. S., Embury, D. C., Jones, R. E., & Yssel, N. (2014). Supporting students with disabilities during school crises: A teacher's guide. *Teaching Exceptional Children, 46*(6), 169–178. https://doi.org/10.1177/0014402914534616

Copeland, W. E., Shanahan, L., Hinesley, J., Chan, R. F., Aberg, K. A., Fairbank, J. A., Van Den Oord, E. J., & Costello, E. J. (2018). Association of childhood trauma exposure with adult psychiatric disorders and functional outcomes. *JAMA Network Open, 1*(7), e184493–e184493. https://doi.org/10.1001/jamanetworkopen.2018.4493

Covarrubias, J. E. (2023). *A call for protection and planning: A case study of vulnerable populations and school shootings* [Doctoral dissertation, Southeastern University].

Cronholm, P. F., Forke, C. M., Wade, R., Bair-Merritt, M. H., Davis, M., Harkins-Schwarz, M., Pachter, L. M., & Fein, J. A. (2015). Adverse childhood experiences: Expanding the concept of adversity. *American Journal of Preventive Medicine, 49*(3), 354–361. https://doi.org/10.1016/j.amepre.2015.02.001

Crosnoe, R. (2001). Academic orientation and parental involvement in education during high school. *Sociology of Education*, 210–230. https://doi.org/10.2307/2673275

Crotty, J. E., Martin-Herz, S. P., & Scharf, R. J. (2023). Cognitive development. *Pediatrics in Review, 44*(2), 58–67. https://doi.org/10.1542/pir.2021-005069

Crouch, J. L., Hanson, R. F., Saunders, B. E., Kilpatrick, D. G., & Resnick, H. S. (2000). Income, race/ethnicity, and exposure to violence in youth: Results from the national survey of adolescents. *Journal of Community Psychology, 28*(6), 625–641. https://doi.org/10.1002/1520-6629(200011)28:6<625::AID-JCOP6>3.0.CO;2-R

Cunningham, M. (2020). 183 student perceptions of lockdown drills. *Injury Prevention, 26.* https://doi.org/10.1136/injuryprev-2020-savir.129

Dailey, S. F., Campbell, A., & Mjavanadze, E. (2024). Measuring perceptions of school lockdown drills: Development and validation of the lockdown impact scale for caregivers (LIS-C). *Children & Schools, 46*(4), 255–263. https://doi.org/10.1093/cs/cdae021

Dalton, C. J. (2011). Social-emotional challenges experienced by students who function with mild and moderate hearing loss in educational settings. *Exceptionality Education International, 21*(1).

Davis, L., & Siegel, L. (2000). Posttraumatic stress disorder in children and adolescents: A review and analysis. *Clinical Child and Family Psychology Review, 3*, 135–154. https://doi.org/10.1023/A:1009564724720.

DeChants, J. P., Green, A. E., Price, M. N., & Davis, C. K. (2022, February 3). Homelessness and housing instability among LGBTQ youth. *The Trevor Project.* https://www.thetrevorproject.org/research-briefs/homelessness-and-housing-instability-among-lgbtq-youth-feb-2022/

Delaney-Black, V., Covington, C., Ondersma, S. J., Nordstrom-Klee, B., Templin, T., Ager, J., Janisse, J., & Sokol, R. J. (2002). Violence exposure, trauma, and IQ and/or reading deficits among urban children. *Archives of Pediatrics & Adolescent Medicine, 156*(3), 280–285.

Dickson, E., Cogan, R., & Gonzalez-Guarda, R. M. (2025). Role of school nurses in the health and education of children. In *JAMA Health Forum, 6*(1), e250116-e250116. https://doi.org/10.1001/jamahealthforum.2025.0116

Dietrich, S. & Hernandez, E. (2022). *Nearly 68 million people spoke a language other than English at home in 2019.* United States Census Bureau. https://www.census.gov/library/stories/2022/12/languages-we-speak-in-united-states.html

Dubois-Comtois, K., Bussieres, E. L., Cyr, C., St-Onge, J., Baudry, C., Milot, T., & Labbe, A. P. (2021). Are children and adolescents in foster care at greater risk of mental health problems than their counterparts? A meta-analysis. *Children and Youth Services Review*, *127*, 106100. https://doi.org/10.1016/j.childyouth.2021.106100

Dwyer, K. P., Osher, D., Maughan, E. D., Tuck, C., & Patrick, K. (2015). Team crisis: School psychologists and nurses working together. *Psychology in the Schools*, *52*(7), 702–713. https://doi.org/10.1002/pits.21850

Dye, H. (2018). The impact and long-term effects of childhood trauma. *Journal of Human Behavior in the Social Environment*, *28*, 381–392. https://doi.org/10.1080/10911359.2018.1435328.

Dyregrov, A., Salloum, A., Kristensen, P., & Dyregrov, K. (2015). Grief and traumatic grief in children in the context of mass trauma. *Current Psychiatry Reports*, *17*(6), 48. https://doi.org/10.1007/s11920-015-0577-x

Edmonds, C. O. (2017) Designing emergency preparedness resources for children with autism. *International Journal of Disability, Development and Education*, *64*(4), 404–419. https://doi.org/10.1080/1034912X.2016.1264577

Eisenberg, N., Cumberland, A., & Spinrad, T. L. (1998). Parental socialization of emotion. *Psychological Inquiry*, *9*(4), 241–273. https://doi.org/10.1207/s15327965pli0904_1

Epstein, J. L., & Sanders, M. G. (2002). Family, school, and community partnerships. In M. H. Bornstein (Ed.), *Handbook of parenting* (Vol. 5, pp. 407–437). Lawrence Erlbaum Associates.

Eskenazi, B., Fahey, C. A., Kogut, K., Gunier, R., Torres, J., Gonzales, N. A., Holland, N., & Deardorff, J. (2019). Association of perceived immigration policy vulnerability with mental and physical health among US-born Latino adolescents in California. *JAMA Pediatrics*, *173*(8), 744–753. https://doi.org/10.1001/jamapediatrics.2019.1475

Essary, J., Barza, L., & Thurston, R. (2020). Secondary traumatic stress among educators. *Kappa Delta Pi Record*, *56*, 116–121. https://doi.org/10.1080/00228958.2020.1770004

Fang, F., & Fang, G. (19991999). A Longitudinal Study on Concrete Operational Thinking in School Children. *Asia-Pacific Education Researcher*, 8.

Felitti, V. J., Anda, R. F., Nordenberg, D., Williamson, D. F., Spitz, A. M., Edwards, V., & Marks, J. S. (1998). Relationship of childhood abuse and household dysfunction to many of the leading causes of death in adults: The Adverse Childhood Experiences (ACE) Study. *American Journal of Preventive Medicine*, *14*(4), 245–258.

Fellinger, J., Holzinger, D., Beitel, C., Laucht, M., & Goldberg, D. P. (2009). The impact of language skills on mental health in teenagers with hearing impairments. *Acta Psychiatrica Scandinavica*, *120*(2), 153–159. https://doi.org/10.1111/j.1600-0447.2009.01350.x

Ferguson, C. J., Kaye, L. K., Branley-Bell, D., Markey, P., Ivory, J. D., Klisanin, D., Elson, M., Smyth, M., Hogg, J. L., McDonnell, D., Nichols, D., Siddiqui, S., Gregerson, M., & Wilson, J. (2022). Like this meta-analysis: Screen media and mental health. *Professional Psychology: Research and Practice, 53*(2), 205. https://doi/10.1037/pro0000426

Finkelhor, D., Turner, H. A., Shattuck, A., & Hamby, S. L. (2015). Prevalence of childhood exposure to violence, crime, and abuse: Results from the National Survey of Children's Exposure to Violence. *JAMA Pediatrics, 169*(8), 746–754. https://doi.org/10.1001/jamapediatrics.2015.0676

Fitzsimons, T. (2018, October 9). Virginia school allegedly barred trans student from active shooter drill. *NBC News.* https://www.nbcnews.com/feature/nbc-out/virginia-school-allegedly-barred-trans-student-active-shooter-drill-n918216

Fluit, S., Cortés-García, L., & von Soest, T. (2024). Social marginalization: A scoping review of 50 years of research. *Humanities and Social Sciences Communications, 11*(1), 1-9.

Garbacz, S. A., & McIntyre, L. L. (2016). Conjoint behavioral consultation for children with autism spectrum disorder. *School Psychology Quarterly, 31*(4), 450–466. https://doi.org/10.1037/spq0000114

Garcia, D., Dukes, C., Brady, M. P., Scott, J., & Wilson, C. L. (2016). Using modeling and rehearsal to teach fire safety to children with autism. *Journal of Applied Behavior Analysis, 49*(3), 699–704. https://doi.org/10.1002/jaba.331

Geist, E. (2019). Reducing anxiety in children: Creating emotionally safe places for children to learn. *Archives in Neurology & Neuroscience, 5*(2). https://doi.org/10.33552/ann.2019.05.000610.

Gereige, R., Gross, T., & Jastaniah, E. (2022). Individual medical emergencies occurring at school. *Pediatrics, 150*(1). https://doi.org/10.1542/peds.2022-057987

Ginsburg, G., Drake, K., Muggeo, M., Stewart, C., Pikulski, P., Zheng, D., & Harel, O. (2019). A pilot RCT of a school nurse delivered intervention to reduce student anxiety. *Journal of Clinical Child & Adolescent Psychology, 50,* 177–186. https://doi.org/10.1080/15374416.2019.1630833.

Goodman, R. D., Miller, M. D., & West-Olatunji, C. A. (2012). Traumatic stress, socioeconomic status, and academic achievement among primary school students. *Psychological Trauma: Theory, Research, Practice, and Policy, 4*(3), 252. https://doi/10.1037/a0024912

Goodman-Scott, E., & Eckhoff, A. (2020). School counselors' experiences with lockdown drills: A phenomenological investigation. *Journal of Counseling & Development, 98*(4), 435–445. https://doi.org/10.1002/=jcad.12345

Gradus, J. L., Rosellini, A. J., Szentkúti, P., Horváth-Puhó, E., Smith, M. L., Galatzer-Levy, I., Lash, T. L., Galea, S., Schnurr, P. P., & Sørensen, H. T. (2022). Using Danish national registry data to understand psychopathology following potentially traumatic experiences. *Journal of Traumatic Stress, 35*(2), 619–630. https://doi.org/10.1002/jts.22777

Greenberg, M. T., Brown, J. L., & Abenavoli, R. M. (2016). *Teacher stress: Health effects on teachers, students, and schools*. Robert Wood Johnson Foundation. https://www.rwjf.org/en/library/research/2016/07/teacherstress-and-health.html

Hahm, H. C., Ha, Y., Scott, J. C., Wongchai, V., Chen, J. A., & Liu, C. H. (2021). Perceived COVID-19-related anti-Asian discrimination predicts post traumatic stress disorder symptoms among Asian and Asian American young adults. *Psychiatry Research, 303*, 114084. https://doi.org/10.1016/j.psychres.2021.114084

Hajal, N. J., & Paley, B. (2020). Parental emotion and emotion regulation: A critical target of study for research and intervention to promote child emotion socialization. *Developmental Psychology, 56*(3), 403–417.

Han, W.-J. (2010). Bilingualism and socioemotional well-being. *Children and Youth Services Review, 32*(5), 720–731. https://doi.org/10.1016/j.childyouth.2010.01.009

Hardt, J., & Rutter, M. (2004). Validity of adult retrospective reports of adverse childhood experiences: Review of the evidence. *Journal of Child Psychology and Psychiatry, 45*(2), 260–273. https://doi.org/10.1111/j.1469-7610.2004.00218.x

Hensel, J., Ruiz, C., Finney, C., & Dewa, C. (2015). Meta-analysis of risk factors for secondary traumatic stress in therapeutic work with trauma victims. *Journal of Traumatic Stress, 28*(2), 83–91. https://doi.org/10.1002/jts.21998.

Hill, N. E., & Tyson, D. F. (2009). Parental involvement in Middle School: A meta-analytic assessment of the strategies that promote achievement. *Developmental Psychology, 45*, 740–763.

Hill, R., Lewis, V., & Dunbar, G. (2000). Young children's concepts of danger. *British Journal of Development Psychology, 18*, 103–119. https://doi.org/10.1348/026151000165607.

Huynh, J., Chien, J., Nguyen, A. T., Honda, D., Cho, E. E., Xiong, M., Doan, T. T., & Ngo, T. D. (2023). The mental health of Asian American adolescents and young adults amid the rise of anti-Asian racism. *Frontiers in Public Health, 10*, 958517.

Hydon, S., Wong, M., Langley, A. K., Stein, B. D., & Kataoka, S. H. (2015). Preventing secondary traumatic stress in educators. *Child and Adolescent Psychiatric Clinics of North America, 24*(2), 319–333. https://doi.org/10.1016/j.chc.2014.11.003

Ijadi-Maghsoodi, R., Meza, J. I., Bravo, L., Lee, K., & Kataoka, S. (2024). Reimagining social and emotional supports in schools for immigrant students: a contextual and structural approach. *Academic Pediatrics, 24*(5), 32–41. https://doi.org/10.1016/j.acap.2023.11.007

Institute of Medicine & National Research Council. (2000). *From neurons to neighborhoods: The science of early childhood development.* The National Academies Press. https://doi.org/10.17226/9824

Ireland, C., & Huxley, S. (2018). Psychological trauma in professionals working with traumatised children. *The Journal of Forensic Practice, 20*, 141–151. https://doi.org/10.1108/JFP-10-2017-0045

Ivie, E. J., Pettitt, A., Moses, L. J., & Allen, N. B. (2020). A meta-analysis of the association between adolescent social media use and depressive symptoms. *Journal of Affective Disorders, 275*, 165–174. https://doi.org/10.1016/j.jad.2020.06.014

Jennings, P., & Greenberg, M. (2009). The prosocial classroom: Teacher social and emotional competence in relation to student and classroom outcomes. *Review of Educational Research, 79*, 491–525. https://doi.org/10.3102/0034654308325693.

Jones, N. M., Thompson, R. R., Dunkel Schetter, C., & Silver, R. C. (2017). Distress and rumor exposure on social media during a campus lockdown. *Proceedings of the National Academy of Sciences, 114*, 11663–11668. https://doi.org/10.1073/pnas.1708518114

Jones, N. M., Wojcik, S. P., Sweeting, J., & Silver, R. C. (2016). Tweeting negative emotion: An investigation of Twitter data in the aftermath of violence on college campuses. *Psychological Methods, 21*, 526–541. https://doi.org/10.1037/met0000099

Kailes, J. I., & Enders, A. (2007). Moving beyond "special needs" A function-based framework for emergency management and planning. *Journal of Disability Policy Studies, 17*(4), 230–237.

Kallapiran, K., Suetani, S., Cobham, V., Eapen, V., & Scott, J. (2025). Impact of positive childhood experiences (PCEs): A systematic review of longitudinal studies. *Child Psychiatry & Human Development*, 1–16. http://doi.org/10.1007/s10578-024-01807-x

Kearney, C. A., Childs, J., & Burke, S. (2023). Social forces, social justice, and school attendance problems in youth. *Contemporary School Psychology, 27*(1), 136–151. http://doi.org/10.1007/s40688-022-00425-5

Khoury, L., Tang, Y. L., Bradley, B., Cubells, J. F., & Ressler, K. J. (2010). Substance use, childhood traumatic experience, and posttraumatic stress disorder in an urban civilian population. *Depression and Anxiety, 27*(12), 1077–1086.

Kliethermes, M., Schacht, M., & Drewry, K. (2014). Complex trauma. *Child and Adolescent Psychiatric Clinics, 23*(2), 339–361. https://doi.org/10.1016/j.chc.2013.12.009

Kosciw, J. G., Clark, C. M., & Menard, L. (2022). *The 2021 National School Climate Survey: The experiences of LGBTQ+ youth in our nation's schools*. Gay, Lesbian and Straight Education Network (GLSEN). https://www.glsen.org/sites/default/files/2022-10/NSCS-2021-Full-Report.pdf

Kubicek, K., Ramirez, M., Limbos, M. A., & Iverson, E. (2008). Knowledge and behaviors of parents in planning for and dealing with emergencies. *Journal of Community Health, 33*, 158–168. https://doi.org/10.1007/s10900-007-9078-0

Laguardia, E. D., Campbell, L. O., Kelchner, V. P., Hilaire, B., Frawley, C., & Howard, C. (2024). Pre-service teachers" preparedness and perceptions: Active shooter response training. *Educational Research: Theory and Practice, 35*(1), 186–198.

Lareau, A., & Horvat, E. M. (1999). Moments of social inclusion and exclusion race, class, and cultural capital in family-school relationships. *Sociology of Education 72*(1), 37–53. https://doi.org/10.2307/2673185

Larson, S., Chapman, S., Spetz, J., & Brindis, C. D. (2017). Chronic childhood trauma, mental health, academic achievement, and school-based health center mental health services. *Journal of School Health, 87*(9), 675–686. https://doi.org/10.1111/josh.12541

Lavner, J. A., Ong, M. L., Carter, S. E., Hart, A. R., & Beach, S. R. (2023). Racial discrimination predicts depressive symptoms throughout adolescence among Black youth. *Developmental Psychology, 59*(1), 7. https://doi/10.1037/dev0001456

Layne, C. M., Kaplow, J. B., Oosterhoff, B., Hill, R. M., & Pynoos, R. (2017). The interplay between posttraumatic stress and grief reactions in traumatically bereaved adolescents: When trauma, bereavement, and adolescence converge. *Adolescent Psychiatry, 7*(4), 266–285. http://doi.org/10.2174/2210676608666180306162544

Levey, S. (2023). Universal design for learning. *Journal of Education, 203*(2), 479–487. https://doi.org/10.1177/00220574211031954

Luthar, S. S., Crossman, E. J., & Small, P. J. (2015). Resilience and adversity. In R.M. Lerner and M. E. Lamb (Eds.), *Handbook of child psychology and developmental science* (7th ed., Vol. 3, pp. 247–286). Wiley.

Marusak, H. A., Martin, K. R., Etkin, A., & Thomason, M. E. (2015). Childhood trauma exposure disrupts the automatic regulation of emotional processing. *Neuropsychopharmacology, 40*(5), 1250-1258.

Maynard, B., Farina, A., Dell, N., & Kelly, M. (2019). Effects of trauma-informed approaches in schools: A systematic review. *Campbell Systematic Reviews, 15*(1–2). https://doi.org/10.1002/cl2.1018

McAdams Ducy, E., & Stough, L. M. (2011). Exploring the support role of special education teachers after Hurricane Ike: Children with significant disabilities. *Journal of Family Issues, 32*(10), 1325–1345. http://doi.org/10.1177/0192513X11412494

McAuliffe, M., & Triandafyllidou, A. (Eds.) (2021). *World migration report 2022.* International Organization for Migration. Geneva.

McIntyre, C., Harris, M. G., Baxter, A. J., Leske, S., Diminic, S., Gone, J. P., Hunter, E., & Whiteford, H. (2017). Assessing service use for mental health by Indigenous populations in Australia, Canada, New Zealand and the United States of America: A rapid review of population surveys. *Health Research Policy and Systems, 15,* 67. https://doi.org/10.1186/s12961-017-0233-5

McKinnon, I. I., Krause, K. H., Suarez, N. A., Jones, T. M., Verlenden, J. V., Cavalier, Y., Cammack, A. L., Mattson, C. L., Njai, R., Smith-Grant, J., Mbaka, C., & Mpofu, J. J. (2024). Experiences of racism in school and associations with mental health, suicide risk, and substance use among high school students—Youth Risk Behavior Survey, United States, 2023. *Morbidity and Mortality Weekly Report Supplements, 73*(4). https://doi.org/10.15585/mmwr.su7304a4v

McLaughlin, K. A., Hilt, L. M., & Nolen-Hoeksema, S. (2007). Racial/ethnic differences in internalizing and externalizing symptoms in adolescents. *Journal of Abnormal Child Psychology, 35*(5), 801–816. https://doi.org/10.1007/s10802-007-9128-1

Michl, L. C., McLaughlin, K. A., Shepherd, K., & Nolen-Hoeksema, S. (2013). Rumination as a mechanism linking stressful life events to symptoms of depression and anxiety: Longitudinal evidence in early adolescents and adults. *Journal of Abnormal Psychology, 122*(2), 339. https://doi.org/10.1037/a0031994

Mol, S. S., Arntz, A., Metsemakers, J. F., Dinant, G. J., Vilters-Van Montfort, P. A., & Knottnerus, J. A. (2005). Symptoms of post-traumatic stress disorder after non-traumatic events: Evidence from an open population study. *The British Journal of Psychiatry, 186*(6), 494–499. https://doi.org/10.1192/bjp.186.6.494

Moore, P., Diliberti, M. K., & Jackson, B. A. (2024). *Teachers' experiences with school violence and lockdown drills: Findings from a 2023 American Teacher Panel Survey.* RAND Corporation.

Moreland, A. D., Rancher, C., Bottomley, J., Galea, S., Abba-Aji, M., Abdalla, S. M., Schmidt, M. G., Vena, J. E & Kilpatrick, D. G. (2024). Posttraumatic stress disorder among adults in communities with mass violence incidents. *JAMA Network Open, 7*(7), e2423539.

Morris, A. S., Criss, M. M., Silk, J. S., & Houltberg, B. J. (2017). The impact of parenting on emotion regulation during childhood and adolescence. *Child Development Perspectives, 11*(4), 233–238. https://doi/10.1111/cdep.12238

Morton, B. M., & Berardi, A. A. (2018). Trauma-informed school programing: Applications for mental health professionals and educator partnerships. *Journal of Child & Adolescent Trauma, 11*(4), 487-493.

Mowen, T. J. (2015). Parental involvement in school and the role of school security measures. *Education and Urban Society, 47*(7), 830–848. http://doi.org/10.1177/0013124513508581

Mowen, T. J., & Freng, A. (2019). Is more necessarily better? School security and perceptions of safety among students and parents in the United States. *American Journal of Criminal Justice, 44*(3), 376–394. https://doi.org/10.1007/s12103-018-9461-7

Muentner, L., Stone, K., Davis, L., & Shlafer, R. (2022). Youth at the intersection of parental incarceration and foster care: Examining prevalence, disparities, and mental health. *Child Abuse & Neglect, 134*, 105910. https://doi.org/10.1016/j.chiabu.2022.105910

Nagata, J. M., Ganson, K. T., Sajjad, O. M., Benabou, S. E., & Bibbins-Domingo, K. (2021). Prevalence of perceived racism and discrimination among us children aged 10 and 11 years: The Adolescent Brain Cognitive Development (ABCD) study. *JAMA Pediatrics, 175*(8), 861–863. https://doi.org/10.1001/jamapediatrics.2021.1022

Narayan, A. J., Rivera, L. M., Bernstein, R. E., Harris, W. W., & Lieberman, A. F. (2018). Positive childhood experiences predict less psychopathology and stress in pregnant women with childhood adversity: A pilot study of the benevolent childhood experiences (BCEs) scale. *Child Abuse & Neglect, 78*, 19–30. https://doi.org/10.1016/j.chiabu.2017.09.022

National Academies of Sciences, Engineering, and Medicine (NASEM). (2019a). *Fostering healthy mental, emotional, and behavioral development in children and youth: A national agenda.* The National Academies Press. https://doi.org/10.17226/25201

_____. (2019b). *The promise of adolescence: Realizing opportunity for all youth.* The National Academies Press. https://doi.org/10.17226/25388

_____.(2019c). *Vibrant and healthy kids: Aligning science, practice, and policy to advance health equity.* The National Academies Press. https://doi.org/10.17226/25466

_____. (2023). *Closing the opportunity gap for young children.* The National Academies Press. https://doi.org/10.17226/26743

National Association of School Psychologists (NASP), National Association of School Resource Officers (NASRO), & Safe and Sound Schools. (2021). *Best practice considerations for schools in active shooter and other armed assailant drills.* https://www.nasponline.org/resources-and-publications/resources-and-podcasts/school-safety-and-crisis/systems-level-prevention/best-practice-considerations-for-armed-assailant-drills-in-schools

National Center for Education Statistics (NCES). (2024a). *English learners in public schools.* U.S. Department of Education, Institute of Education Sciences. https://nces.ed.gov/programs/coe/indicator/cgf

_____. (2024b). *Students with disabilities*. U.S. Department of Education, Institute of Education Sciences. https://nces.ed.gov/programs/coe/indicator/cgg.

National Child Traumatic Stress Network. (2018). *Creating school active shooter/intruder drills*. https://www.nctsn.org/sites/default/files/resources/fact-sheet/creating_school_active_shooter_intruder_drills.pdf

Nickerson, A. B., & Zhe, E. J. (2004). Crisis prevention and intervention: A survey of school psychologists. *Psychology in the Schools, 41*(7), 777–788. https://doi/10.1002/pits.20017

Niehaus, K., Adelson, J. L., Sejuit, A., & Zheng, J. (2017). Native language background and academic achievement: Is socioemotional wellbeing a mediator? *Applied Developmental Science, 21*(4), 251–265. https://doi.org/10.1080/10888691.2016.1203790

Nikolaraizi, M., Argyropoulos, V., Papazafiri, M., & Kofidou, C. (2021). Promoting accessible and inclusive education on disaster risk reduction: The case of students with sensory disabilities. *International Journal of Inclusive Education*, 1–15. http://doi.org/10.1080/13603116.2020.1862408

Office for Civil Rights. (2018). *2017–18 State and National Tables*. Civil Rights Data Collection, U.S. Department of Education. https://ocrdata.ed.gov/estimations/2017-2018

Oosterhoff, B., Kaplow, J. B., & Layne, C. M. (2018). Links between bereavement due to sudden death and academic functioning: Results from a nationally representative sample of adolescents. *School Psychology Quarterly, 33*(3), 372. https://doi.org/10.1007/s12310-022-09525-2

Owens, J. (2023). Seeing behavior as Black, brown, or white: Teachers' racial/ethnic bias in perceptions of routine classroom misbehavior. *Social Psychology Quarterly, 86*(3), 298–311. https://doi.org/10.1177/01902725231177644

Paige, J. W., & Bushway, S. B. (2024). *The role and impact of school resource officers*. RAND Corporation. https://www.rand.org/research/gun-policy/analysis/essays/school-resource-officers.html

Paradis, J., Soto-Corominas, A., Vitoroulis, I., Al Janaideh, R., Chen, X., Gottardo, A., Jenkins, J., & Georgiades, K. (2022). The role of socioemotional wellbeing difficulties and adversity in the L2 acquisition of first-generation refugee children. *Bilingualism: Language and Cognition, 25*(5), 921–933. https://doi.org/10.1017/S136672892200030X

Parra, E. B., Evans, C. A., Fletcher, T., & Combs, M. C. (2014). The psychological impact of English language immersion on elementary age English language learners. *Journal of Multilingual Education Research, 5*(1), 4. https://research.library.fordham.edu/jmer/vol5/iss1/4

Peek, L., & Stough, L. M. (2010). Children with disabilities in the context of disaster: A social vulnerability perspective. *Child Development, 81*(4), 1260–1270. https://doi.org/10.1111/j.1467-8624.2010.01466.x

Peguero, A. A. (2006). Latino disaster vulnerability: The dissemination of hurricane mitigation information among Florida's homeowners. *Hispanic Journal of Behavioral Sciences, 28,* 5–22. http://doi.org/10.1177/0739986305284012

Perfect, M. M., Turley, M. R., Carlson, J. S., Yohanna, J., & Saint Gilles, M. P. (2016). School-related outcomes of traumatic event exposure and traumatic stress symptoms in students: A systematic review of research from 1990 to 2015. *School Mental Health, 8,* 7–43. https://doi.org/10.1007/s12310-016-9175-2

Polk, W., Hill, N., & Hughes, D. (2024). Sources, conceptualizations, and mechanisms of racism/oppression for academic and mental health outcomes. *AERA Open.* https://doi.org/10.1177/23328584241258464

Qu, G., Shu, L., Liu, H., Ma, S., Han, T., Zhang, H., Huang, C., Wang, J., Yang, L., & Sun, Y. (2024). Association between adverse childhood experiences and academic performance among children and adolescents: A global meta-analysis. *Trauma, Violence, & Abuse, 25*(4), 3332–3345. https://doi.org/10.1177/15248380241246758

Raghunathan, R. S., Sosnowski, D. W., Musci, R. J., & Johnson, S. B. (2024). A scoping review of positive childhood experiences: Measurement and evidence. *Adversity and Resilience Science, 5*(2), 141–158. https://doi/10.1007/s42844-023-00125-w

Reddy, L. A., & Herman, K. C. (2024). School personnel well-being: Advancing measurement, best practices, and policy. Section 2: Role of traumatic experiences in educator well-being. *School Psychology, 39*(5), 445–449. https://doi.org/10.1037/spq0000670

Regional Educational Laboratory West. (2024, May). *An asset-based approach to multilingual learner terminology* [Infographic]. Institute of Education Sciences. https://ies.ed.gov/ncee/rel/regions/west/pdf/2.1.2.2.1_Multilingual Learners_Infographic01_Approved_508c.pdf

Roeser, R. W., Eccles, J. S., & Sameroff, A. J. (2000). School as a context of early adolescents' academic and social-emotional development: A summary of research findings. *The Elementary School Journal, 100*(5), 443–471. http://doi.org/10.1086/499650

Rose, I. D., Lesesne, C. A., Sun, J., Johns, M. M., Zhang, X., & Hertz, M. (2024). The relationship of school connectedness to adolescents' engagement in co-occurring health risks: A meta-analytic review. *The Journal of School Nursing, 40*(1), 58–73. https://doi.org/10.1177/10598405221096802

Rutherford, H. J., Wallace, N. S., Laurent, H. K., & Mayes, L. C. (2015). Emotion regulation in parenthood. *Developmental Review, 36,* 1–14. https://doi.org/10.1016/j.dr.2014.12.008

Schildkraut, J., & Nickerson, A. (2020). Ready to respond: Effects of lockdown drills and training on school emergency preparedness. *Victims & Offenders, 15,* 619–638. https://doi.org/10.1080/15564886.2020.1749199

Shannon, H., Bush, K., Villeneuve, P. J., Hellemans, K. G., & Guimond, S. (2022). Problematic social media use in adolescents and young adults: Systematic review and meta-analysis. *JMIR Mental Health, 9*(4), e33450. https://doi.org/10.2196/33450

Shapiro, B., & O'Brien, T. (1970). Logical thinking in children ages six through thirteen. *Child Development, 41*, 823–829. https://doi.org/10.1111/J.1467-8624.1970.TB01034.X

Sheridan, S. M., Smith, T. E., Moorman Kim, E., Beretvas, S. N., & Park, S. (2019). A meta-analysis of family-school interventions and children's social-emotional functioning: Moderators and components of efficacy. *Review of Educational Research, 89*(2), 296–332. https://doi.org/10.3102/0034654318825437

Sheridan, S. M., Witte, A. L., Holmes, S. R., Wu, C., Bhatia, S. A., & Angell, S. R. (2017). The efficacy of conjoint behavioral consultation in the home setting: Outcomes and mechanisms in rural communities. *Journal of School Psychology, 62*, 81–101. https://doi.org/10.1016/j.jsp.2017.03.005

Smith, T. E., Reinke, W. M., Herman, K. C., & Huang, F. (2019). Understanding family–school engagement across and within elementary- and middle-school contexts. *School Psychology, 34*(4), 363–375. https://doi.org/10.1037/spq0000290

Snehil, G., & Sagar, R. (2020). Juvenile justice system, juvenile mental health, and the role of MHPs: Challenges and opportunities. *Indian Journal of Psychological Medicine, 42*, 304–310. https://doi.org/10.4103/IJPSYM.IJPSYM_82_20

Speidel, R., Galarneau, E., Elsayed, D., Mahhouk, S., Filippelli, J., Colasante, T., & Malti, T. (2021). Refugee children's social–emotional capacities: Links to mental health upon resettlement and buffering effects on pre-migratory adversity. *International Journal of Environmental Research and Public Health, 18*(22), 12180. https://doi.org/10.3390/ijerph182212180

Stein, G. L., Kiang, L., Supple, A. J., & Gonzalez, L. M. (2014). Ethnic identity as a protective factor in the lives of Asian American adolescents. *Asian American Journal of Psychology, 5*(3), 206. https://doi/10.1037/a0034811

Stough, L. M., Ducy, E. M., Kang, D., & Lee, S. (2020). Disasters, schools, and children: Disability at the intersection. *International Journal of Disaster Risk Reduction, 45*, 101447. http://doi.org/10.1016/j.ijdrr.2019.101447

Swedo, E. A., Aslam, M. V., Dahlberg, L. L., Niolon, P. H., Guinn, A. S., Simon, T. R., & Mercy, J. A. (2023). Prevalence of adverse childhood experiences among US adults—Behavioral risk factor surveillance system, 2011–2020. *Morbidity and Mortality Weekly Report, 72*(26). https://doi.org/10.15585/mmwr.mm7226a2

Tilbury, C., Creed, P., Buys, N., Osmond, J., & Crawford, M. (2014). Making a connection: School engagement of young people in care. *Child & Family Social Work, 19*(4), 455–466.

United States Department of Education (ED). (2016). *Students in foster care.* https://www.ed.gov/teaching-and-administration/supporting-students/special-populations/students-foster-care/students-in-foster-care

United States Department of Health and Human Services. (n.d.). *Adoption Foster Care Analysis Reporting System (AFCARS), FY 2013–2022.* Administration for Children and Families, Administration on Children, Youth, and Families, Children's Bureau.

van Nierop, M., Lecei, A., Myin-Germeys, I., Collip, D., Viechtbauer, W., Jacobs, N., Derom, C., Thiery, E., Os, J., & Winkel, R. (2018). Stress reactivity links childhood trauma exposure to an admixture of depressive, anxiety, and psychosis symptoms. *Psychiatry Research, 260*, 451–457. https://doi.org/10.1016/j.psychres.2017.12.012

Vanschoonlandt, F., Vanderfaeillie, J., Van Holen, F., De Maeyer, S., & Robberechts, M. (2013). Externalizing problems in young foster children: Prevalence rates, predictors and service use. *Children and Youth Services Review, 35*(4), 716–724. https://doi/10.1016/j.childyouth.2013.01.015

Varela, R. E., & Hensley-Maloney, L. (2009). The influence of culture on anxiety in Latino youth: A review. *Clinical Child and Family Psychology Review, 12*(3), 217–233. https://doi.org/10.1007/s10567-009-0044-5

Vogels, E. A., Gelles-Watnick, R., & Massarat, N. (2022). *Teens, social media and technology 2022.* Pew Research Center. https://www.pewresearch.org/internet/2022/08/10/teens-social-media-and-technology-2022/

Wallace, L. N. (2020). What will make my child's school safer? Parent perceptions of active shooter preparedness. *Safer Communities, 19*(3), 145–159. https://doi.org/10.1108/SC-03-2020-0010

Wallengren-Lynch, M. (2025). From compassion to action: school social workers at the forefront of emergency response. *Nordic Social Work Research, 15*(2), 253-268.

Wang, M. T., & Sheikh-Khalil, S. (2014). Does parental involvement matter for student achievement and mental health in high school? *Child Development, 85*(2), 610–625. https://doi.org/10.1111/cdev.12153

Waterman, A., Atkinson, A., Aslam, S., Holmes, J., Jaroslawska, A., & Allen, R. (2017). Do actions speak louder than words? Examining children's ability to follow instructions. *Memory & Cognition, 45*, 877–890. https://doi.org/10.3758/s13421-017-0702-7.https://doi.org/10.1186/s12961-017-

Werner, D. (2015). Are school social workers prepared for a major school crisis? Indicators of individual and school environment preparedness. *Children & Schools, 37*(1), 28–35.

Whitted, K., Delavega, E., & Lennon-Dearing, R. (2013). The youngest victims of violence: Examining the mental health needs of young children who are involved in the child welfare and juvenile justice systems. *Child and Adolescent Social Work Journal, 30*, 181–195. https://doi.org/10.1007/S10560-012-0286-9

Willgerodt, M. A., Tanner, A., McCabe, E., Jameson, B., & Brock, D. (2024). Public school nurses in the United States: National school nurse workforce study 2.0. *The Journal of School Nursing, 40*(5), 468–481. https://doi.org/10.1177/10598405241253565

Wu, N. S., Schairer, L. C., Dellor, E., & Grella, C. (2010). Childhood trauma and health outcomes in adults with comorbid substance abuse and mental health disorders. *Addictive Behaviors, 35*(1), 68–71. https://doi.org/10.1016/j.addbeh.2009.09.003

Yang, T., Allen, R., Waterman, A., Zhang, S., Su, X., & Chan, R. (2020). Comparing motor imagery and verbal rehearsal strategies in children's ability to follow spoken instructions. *Journal of Experimental Child Psychology, 203*, 105033. https://doi.org/10.1016/j.jecp.2020.105033

Yehuda, R., Halligan, S. L., & Grossman, R. (2002). Childhood trauma and risk for PTSD: Relationship to intergenerational effects of trauma, parental PTSD, and cortisol excretion. In Steven E. Hyman (Ed.), *Stress and the brain* (1st Ed., pp. 177-197). Routledge.

Zelazo, P. D., Blair, C. B., & Willoughby, M. T. (2016). *Executive function: Implications for education* (NCER 2017-2000). National Center for Education Research. https://ies.ed.gov/ncer/2025/01/executive-function-implications-education

Zhe, E., & Nickerson, A. (2007). Effects of an intruder crisis drill on children's knowledge, anxiety, and perceptions of school safety. *School Psychology Review, 36*(3), 501–508. https://doi.org/10.1080/02796015.2007.12087936

Zvolensky, M. J., Rogers, A. H., Bakhshaie, J., Viana, A. G., Walker, R., Mayorga, N. A., Lopez, K., Garza, M., Lemaire, C., Ruiz, A. C., & Ochoa-Perez, M. (2019). Perceived racial discrimination, anxiety sensitivity, and mental health among Latinos in a federally qualified health center. *Stigma and Health, 4*(4), 473–479. https://doi.org/10.1037/sah0000160

6
Best Practices for Protecting the Mental, Emotional, and Behavioral Health of Students and Staff

As detailed in previous chapters, the research literature on the impact of school active shooter drills on the mental, emotional, and behavioral health of students and staff is thin. Despite the weakness of the existing evidence base, school active shooter drills are routinely implemented in schools across the country. As better research continues to develop, schools, districts, and state departments of education urgently require actionable guidance to inform their decisions on how best to safeguard the mental health and well-being of students and staff while implementing these drills.

The best practices outlined in this chapter are ultimately derived from what is currently known about child and adolescent development and learning, together with qualitative literature and information gathered in listening sessions with students, teachers, and caregivers (see Chapter 5). The guidance also draws on a widespread consensus, promulgated by authoritative professional associations and government agencies, on best practices for implementing school safety and security practices that mitigate the potential harms to mental, emotional, and behavioral health. These authorities include the U.S. Department of Education (ED), the National Association of School Resource Officers (NASRO), the National Association of School Psychologists (NASP), the National Child Traumatic Stress Network (NCTSN), and the American Academy of Pediatrics, among others. With the guidance from these authorities in mind, together with the collective knowledge of its multidisciplinary expert members, the committee recommends a path forward.

It is important for state and local education authorities to monitor and evaluate the implementation of school active shooter drills continuously to minimize the genuine risk of negative impacts of the intervention itself on the mental, emotional, and behavioral health of students and staff. Additionally, the committee urges school officials to take routine steps to adapt and refine practices based on emerging evidence to ensure that current approaches effectively minimize risks and maintain safety while preserving the integrity of the learning environment.

This chapter begins with a discussion of strategies for mitigating mental, emotional, and behavioral health harms when implementing school active shooter drills; in so doing, it outlines best practices for local educational authorities before, during, and after drills are implemented. Recognizing the many factors school administrators and staff must consider when implementing active shooter drills, the chapter highlights the benefits of a multidisciplinary school safety committee charged with identifying necessary planning steps and anticipating potential unintended consequences that may be encountered during implementation. The discussion also examines the broader context in which these drills take place and underscores the need for a comprehensive school safety plan that prioritizes prevention as a fundamental component. The chapter then identifies practices that are likely to cause harm and that professional consensus suggests should be terminated and, if appropriate, prohibited by state legislation. Finally, the chapter outlines implementation considerations, including policy recommendations.

STRATEGIES FOR MITIGATING MENTAL, EMOTIONAL, AND BEHAVIORAL HEALTH HARMS WHEN IMPLEMENTING SCHOOL ACTIVE SHOOTER DRILLS

When planning for and implementing school active shooter drills, it is important to consider the context in which the drills are typically implemented and to assess their potential harms and benefits. In promoting safe learning environments, schools are expected to minimize any potential negative impacts experienced by students and staff. While many schools conduct active shooter drills as part of their emergency preparedness efforts, it is important for the drills to be grounded in the context of the school's comprehensive safety plan. When school active shooter drills are performed in isolation (as they often are), without adequate consideration of the children's emotional and psychological well-being, they can inadvertently and unnecessarily arouse unnecessary anxiety or fear.

When grounded in a positive school climate, these drills—implemented as outlined in this report—can foster a prepared, resilient, and calm school community. Instead of viewing drills as isolated events responding to a hypothesized immediate threat, schools need to connect them to broader discussions about safety, school climate, and well-being. For example, schools can use active shooter drills as opportunities to assess communication channels and ensure that adequate time is allowed to debrief the drills and provide feedback, giving students and staff a voice in the process and facilitating relationship-building between teachers and students. Additionally, schools can use drills to discuss how to handle emergency situations outside of school grounds and to give students an opportunity to undertake other steps to enhance school safety or the overall school climate (Center on Positive Behavioral Interventions and Supports [PBIS], 2022).

While school active shooter drills are important, they represent only one aspect of school safety planning. A comprehensive approach requires a balance between preparedness (and mitigation for immediate threats) and long-term prevention strategies that address the root causes of violence. Schools that focus too narrowly on active shooter drills may miss opportunities to prevent violence before it occurs. A positive school climate, social-emotional learning, and trauma-informed practices can create an environment that not only responds to threats but actively works to prevent them (PBIS, 2022).

This section details strategies for mitigating mental, emotional, and behavioral health harms when implementing school active shooter drills. The discussion includes practices that are least likely to cause mental, emotional, and behavioral health harms (green); practices that need to be implemented with caution as they are more likely to have negative than positive impact (yellow); and those with a high likelihood of causing harm—practices that this committee, in line with broad professional consensus, agrees should be ended (red). These strategies are summarized in Table 6-1 and described in detail in the subsections that follow. The committee's recommendations for addressing the key considerations for decision-makers at all levels—from the national to the school level—entailed in the implementation of school active shooter drills are presented throughout the chapter.

TABLE 6-1 Strategies for Mitigating Mental, Emotional, and Behavioral (MEB) Health Harms When Implementing School Active Shooter Drills

Practices Least Likely to Cause MEB Health Harms

Before:
- Implement robust social-emotional programming to help students develop the skills needed to engage successfully in drills.
- Design drills using discussion-based and standard response practices that foster skill-building, with clearly defined action steps.
- Adapt drills for individuals with functional and access needs.
- Consider the frequency and context of drills to minimize unnecessary stress and disruption.

- Inform, engage, and collaborate with parents to ensure transparency and support.
- Preplan drills with a multidisciplinary team, incorporating student and parent input in both planning and evaluation efforts.

During:
- Use clear communication throughout the drill to ensure understanding and reduce anxiety.
- Ensure that wellness supports are available for students and staff.

After:
- Provide time for students and staff to debrief and process the experience.
- Check in with vulnerable students and staff to assess and address emotional or psychological distress.
- Conduct an after-action assessment to evaluate results, identify gaps, document and demonstrate lessons learned, and highlight successes achieved.

Implement with Caution—More Likely to Have Negative Than Positive MEB Health Impacts:

- Implement options-based practices with caution as they may be more likely to have negative MEB health impacts. Guidance is needed on adapting options-based approaches for different groups and populations, as well as on the appropriateness of these practices for various developmental stages.

> **Do Not Implement—High Likelihood of MEB Health Harms:**
>
> - Do not conduct simulation exercises with students or require all school staff to participate. Simulation exercises often include high-intensity, hyper-realistic, or highly sensory components that can cause MEB health harms to both students and staff.
> - Do not include high-intensity, hyper-realistic, or high-sensorial components in any school active shooter drill.
> - Do not use deception or mislead students and staff to believe a real active shooter event is occurring.

PRACTICES LEAST LIKELY TO CAUSE MENTAL, EMOTIONAL, AND BEHAVIORAL HEALTH HARMS

Recommendation 1: Schools should adopt trauma-informed, developmentally appropriate approaches to school active shooter drills that balance preparedness with emotional and psychological safety. It is essential for the design and implementation of drills to prioritize student and staff well-being in order to prevent unnecessary mental, emotional, and behavioral health harms and ensure that drills foster environments conducive to the learning and skill-building they are intended to impart. State-level legislation mandating drills should require the implementation of trauma-informed, developmentally appropriate drills designed with input from experts in mental health and child development.

In addition to drill design, the committee was asked to consider the supports, school programs, and staff expertise necessary to implement, monitor, and evaluate best practices effectively. Given the varying needs of students and staff, school districts and school safety teams need to carefully determine the appropriate level of practice for active shooter drills, taking into account the community's familiarity with the school's emergency operations plan, the overall purpose of emergency drills, and the developmental needs of students. It is also essential to consider whether specific practices are appropriate for the school setting, as well as the broader school environment and community context in which the drills are conducted. Finally, assessing the readiness of individuals within the school community is critical before introducing more complex emergency response procedures. By carefully evaluating these considerations, schools can implement drills that create opportunities for skill-building and enhance a sense of preparedness while minimizing potential negative impacts.

Best Practices When Planning for School Active Shooter Drills

Best practices for implementing drills include setting clear educational goals; teaching emergency response skills using standard response practices, incorporating student and family input, and establishing a consistent communication plan with families and community partners. These practices prioritize the health and well-being of students and staff while minimizing potential harm. Schools with strong social-emotional programming and a positive climate create an environment that supports resilience and skill-building and can help mitigate the negative mental, emotional, and behavioral health impacts of school active shooter drills (CDC, 2009; Durlak et al., 2011; National Conference of State Legislatures, 2025; Osher & Berg, 2017; Thapa et al., 2013). Establishing a multidisciplinary team to support the planning for drills may also play a critical role in ensuring that drills are developmentally appropriate, trauma-informed, and tailored to the specific needs of the school community. Planning may need to include evaluating the frequency and context of drills to balance instructional time with efforts to ensure student well-being.

Having clear procedures in place for emergency events is a critical component of overall preparedness. Establishing communication strategies, accessibility accommodations, and plans for ensuring emotional well-being can foster a sense of security for students and staff. Communicating a well-structured plan can also help reassure students, staff, and families that comprehensive measures are in place to address a range of needs during an emergency. By proactively identifying the needs of the school community and addressing support systems, schools ensure that emergency drills focus on practicing essential response actions and preparedness for real-world scenarios. Box 6-1 outlines common considerations for school administrators when addressing needs for preparedness planning and staff training.

BOX 6-1
General Emergency Preparedness Planning and Staff Training

Build Staff Awareness
Ensure that all staff are familiar with the school's emergency operations plan (EOP) and understand how active shooter drills align with it.

- Conduct a site assessment at the beginning of the school year to identify potential safety concerns.
- Provide staff with clear instructions on how to access the EOP.
- Educate staff about the various hazards and emergencies that may impact the school and familiarize them with the types of drills planned for the school year.
- Identify and communicate with the members of the school safety committee.
- Inform staff of any updates to the EOP in a timely manner.
- Ensure that all staff are aware of safety features and programs available at the school, such as tip lines, emergency alert mobile apps, and intercom activation systems. Provide opportunities to practice using these tools.

- Adapt drill and emergency procedures for students and staff with accessibility limitations to ensure all students and staff have access to safe locations.

Staff Emergency Preparedness Training
Consider the different types of learning required to ensure staff understand emergency preparedness procedures effectively.

- Educate staff about the various hazards and emergencies that may impact the school and familiarize them with the types of drills planned for the school year.
- Offer proper training on the EOP and school safety procedures to ensure preparedness.
- Allocate time during staff meetings or professional development sessions to review the emergency management plan and address any questions.
- Orient staff to the school campus, including designated reunification sites.
- Ensure that new staff and substitute teachers receive this orientation and training before assuming their duties.
- At the beginning of the school year, consider conducting tabletop activities or walkthroughs to allow staff to practice initiating an emergency response, introducing drills to students, and addressing frequently asked questions.

Best practices for preparing to lead a drill include thoughtful planning, proactive communication, and comprehensive support structures. These practices proactively consider the mental, emotional, and behavioral health impacts of drills. Without this groundwork, drills may be experienced as isolated, anxiety-inducing events rather than as part of a coordinated strategy that fosters preparedness, confidence, and emotional well-being. Beyond reducing harm, good planning—transparent communication, trauma-informed strategies, and inclusive planning efforts—can build supports that ensure that students, staff, and families feel informed, reassured, and empowered before they participate in a drill, creating an environment conducive to learning essential safety and preparedness skills. In this way, preparedness efforts extend beyond drills, creating a school safety culture that prioritizes both security and well-being.

Implement Robust Social-Emotional Programming Within the School in Order to Prime Students to Take on the Skills Needed for Drills

Chapter 3 reviewed studies on how active shooter drills impact perceptions of school safety. Most showed either negative or no changes in how students and staff perceived safety, even if they felt more prepared (Huskey & Connell, 2021; Moore-Petinak et al., 2020; Schildkraut et al., 2024a,b). These findings suggest that preparedness alone is not enough to foster a sense of safety and that additional approaches are needed to support social-emotional well-being alongside preparedness efforts. Consistent with the science of learning, both students and school staff will be in a better position to learn how to proceed with the drill activities and respond in emergencies if they are calm and anxiety is minimized. A key goal for drills, then, is to avoid using elements that can induce stress and trauma, which can lead to negative outcomes such as reduced concentration and school avoidance, which can, over time, impact educational achievement (Balfanze & Byrnes, 2012; Barrett et al., 2012; Boulton et al., 2008). Additionally, as highlighted in Chapter 5, previous exposure to trauma may trigger unpredictable behaviors during high-stress events such as active shooter drills. Schools can anticipate the possibility of these behaviors and take steps to mitigate their frequency and intensity to ensure the safety not only of the individual student with previous trauma exposure but also of other students and staff.

The importance of a calm and well-organized approach to school active shooter drills, with a focus on imparting skills that promote a sense of safety and security among students and staff, is consistent with guidelines from ED (2025), NASP, NASRO, and Safe and Sound Schools (NASP et al., 2021); NCTSN (NCTSN, 2018); and the Maryland Center for School Safety (2024). By equipping students and staff with the skills needed to manage their responses and support one another, these practices provide a critical foundation for maintaining a sense of safety and security in drills and emergency situations.

Design Drills Using Discussion-Based and Standard Response Practices That Foster Skill-Building with Clearly Defined Action Steps

Discussion-based practices can apply to overall emergency operations, and they may be particularly beneficial for school active shooter drills. Discussion-based practices focus on building foundational knowledge through activities such as staff-led discussions, social stories or storybook readings, and student–teacher tabletop exercises that use games or child-friendly activities to teach emergency procedures. They do not require students to physically practice emergency actions (see Chapter 1).

Discussion-based practices provide an opportunity for staff and students to understand the purpose of school active shooter drills, helping them to be better able to grasp the context for learning standard response practices.[24,25] They may also allow time for reflection and processing and foster a sense of connectedness among students and staff, promoting resilience for both groups. These discussions also provide an opportunity for staff to highlight additional safety measures that are already in place to protect the school community. New students who are unfamiliar with these procedures, as well as

---

[24] During this committee's listening sessions, multiple speakers stressed the importance of familiarizing staff with drill procedures before practicing them with students.

[25] For the purposes of this report, the committee uses the term *standard response practices* to refer to individual, predefined actions or procedures designed to guide students and staff in responding to different types of emergency situations, including school active shooter events.

students with functional and access needs, may require additional time and support to fully engage with discussion-based practices. Ensuring that all individuals have a strong foundational understanding can enhance a sense of preparedness.

Schools may also choose to use standard response practices—with students and staff physically rehearsing the actions needed to respond to an emergency, such as a school active shooter event—when implementing active shooter drills. For each response practice, staff and students are taught specific steps to take to complete the response. For example, for "lockdown," the actions include locking the doors, turning off the lights, moving out of sight, and remaining silent. These practices emphasize procedural repetition to reinforce emergency responses. Such action-focused approaches emphasize practical safety skills, which highlight and teach specific skills (e.g., "hold" or "lockdown"), rather than highlighting or reinforcing fear of specific threats. In doing so, schools may be able to promote essential emergency preparedness without reinforcing the potential for violence. However, it is important to note that research evaluating the mental, emotional, and behavioral health effects of this approach is needed.

A standardized, action-based framework may also help streamline preparedness efforts and thereby reduce the overall number of drills required throughout the school year. For younger students and those new to emergency drills, it may be necessary to spend additional time on discussion-based practices before transitioning to standard response practices.

Universal design principles can be incorporated into standard response practices to ensure that terms and actions are clear and accessible to create a more supportive environment for all students during drills. For example, information on each standard response practice and its associated actions can be made available to parents, allowing them to understand the procedures and reinforce key safety steps with their children before a drill takes place and helping them bolster their children's resilience—a protective factor against mental, emotional, and behavioral health harms. Additionally, materials can be translated into multiple languages, ensuring broader accessibility, and specific instructions are provided for announcing each type of drill. However, although research has been conducted on drills practicing the standard response to the directive "lockdown," the committee is unaware of any specific causal evaluation of the mental, emotional, and behavioral health impacts of standard response practices overall and more research is needed to fully understand their effects.

A 2025 implementation evaluation of the "I Love U Guys" Foundation's (2021) Standard Response Protocol (SRP) and Standard Reunification Method (SRM) in Nebraska offers some initial insights into possible training needs for staff. As part of this evaluation, 1,530 participants in 14 SRP/SRM training sessions—with some attending multiple times—were surveyed. The participants noted concise language and standardized terminology for emergency response protocols as strengths of the SRP (Bulling et al., 2025). However, they also identified areas for improvement: more guidance on accommodating students with functional and access needs; strategies for very young children (pre-K) during drills; and clarification on student cellphone use during emergency drills. Additionally, participants emphasized the need for formal training for both regular staff and substitute teachers. They also recommended that training opportunities be offered in both asynchronous (self-paced) and face-to-face formats to accommodate different learning needs (Bulling et al., 2025).

Consistency of approaches across districts and schools offers additional benefits. Standard response practices can help reduce confusion among students and staff by providing clear, actionable steps for each emergency scenario. In eliminating the need to learn multiple, varying emergency protocols for different sites, this consistency may be particularly beneficial for substitute teachers, educators working across multiple schools, staff who have recently transitioned into new roles, and students who may make frequent school transitions such as those involved in the foster care system. Parents with children in multiple schools could also benefit from learning a single, uniform protocol, which enhances overall community preparedness. Having structured, well-defined action steps could also be an asset for research on emergency preparedness and school safety.

Designing drills to emphasize clarity and consistency and build foundational knowledge in a developmentally appropriate manner is likely to foster a sense of preparedness among students and staff, and limit exposure to activities that may create fear and anxiety.

Guidance and recommendations from NASP, NASRO, and Safe and Sound Schools (NASP et al., 2021) as well as the American Academy of Pediatrics (Schonfeld et al., 2020) similarly emphasize the importance of teaching emergency response skills rather than simulating distressing crisis events, with the goal of promoting competence and preparedness rather than overwhelming participants.

Tailor Drill Design to Meet the Developmental Needs of the School Community

Chapter 5 provides an in-depth discussion of age and developmental considerations for implementing school active shooter drills. Table 6-2 highlights selected developmentally appropriate practices.

TABLE 6-2 Selected Practices for Developmentally Appropriate Implementation of School Active Shooter Drills That Mitigate Adverse Mental, Emotional, and Behavioral Health Harms

Population	Practices
Early Childhood	• Use clear, concrete, and reassuring language with the understanding that this age group does best with structured routines. Staff should be well-trained in maintaining calm.
Elementary School	• Give simple explanations, reinforce safety procedures, and ensure that adults provide emotional reassurance.

Middle School	• Provide simple explanations, reinforce safety procedures, and ensure emotional reassurance from adults. • Introduce emergency roles, discuss school safety, and provide adult guidance to reinforce preparedness. • Address potential distress from deeper threat understanding.
High School	• Give simple explanations, reinforce safety procedures, and ensure that adults provide emotional reassurance. • Discuss school safety and the rationale for drills and provide adult guidance to reinforce preparedness. • Address potential distress from deeper threat understanding.

Adapt Drills for Individuals with Functional and Access Needs

Chapter 5 outlines key considerations for planning school active shooter drills, including the functional and accessibility needs of students and staff; the roles of essential school personnel in emergency preparedness; and characteristics of individuals who may be particularly vulnerable to negative mental, emotional, and behavioral effects from these drills. Some students may require additional considerations or support based on their experiences, communication needs, or health conditions. These students include those who have experienced trauma or adverse life events; individuals with disabilities affecting mobility, cognition, communication, or sensory processing; and those who rely on behavioral health services or assistive technologies. To ensure that all students can participate in drills, schools and school safety teams can assess the functional and accessibility needs present within the school community. These needs often fall into broad categories, including sensory; physical/mobility; cognitive/developmental; speech/language; and social, emotional, and behavioral considerations. While disabilities are often documented and known to staff, individuals who have experienced trauma may not be identified as easily. Given the goal of minimizing potential negative mental, emotional, and behavioral health impacts, a universal design approach can help create a more supportive environment for all students during drills. Providing emotional support and allowing for additional accommodations or practice when needed can further support students who face barriers to participation.

Safe and Sound Schools' (2021) *Especially Safe* curriculum introduced the TEAMS framework, which categorizes the functional and access needs within a school community. Table 6-3 provides an overview of these categories as an example and highlights potential strategies for addressing individual safety accommodations and supports that may be needed during school active shooter drills or in the event of an actual emergency.

TABLE 6-3 TEAMS Framework of School Safety and Emergency Planning Considerations for Individuals with Functional and Accessibility Needs

Population	Example Strategies
T = *Transportation & Mobility* Individuals who need accommodations to move to safety, an alternative location, or a protective position (e.g., people who are in wheelchairs, on crutches, or pregnant)	• Develop a plan for individuals using wheelchairs or crutches in cases where physical barriers limit entry or exit. • Ensure that assigned staff are trained in the proper use of adaptive equipment. • Equip assigned staff with knowledge of the safest methods for assisting individuals with mobility challenges in reaching a protective position.

E = *Emotional, Mental, & Behavioral Health*
Individuals who need accommodations, personnel, procedures, or specialized preparedness to support mental, emotional, and behavioral health (e.g., people with attention deficit hyperactivity disorder, sensory disorders, trauma histories, or anxiety; people who have recently migrated to the United States; people who have had a negative experience with police/first responders)

- Provide comfort items such as earplugs, headphones, and fidget tools.
- Practice calming and self-regulation strategies before initiating drills.
- Assign a staff member as a buddy to guide individual students through drill elements.
- Provide additional time with discussion-based practices for students who are unfamiliar with drills or emergency protocols.

A = *Auxiliary Communication*
Individuals who need extra support to receive, understand, and relay information during a drill (e.g., people who are deaf or hard of hearing, have blindness or visual impairments, speak a language other than the primary language taught, or have cognitive impairments)

- Incorporate visual aids to reinforce communication.
- Use clear and simple language to ensure accessibility.
- Provide materials in multiple primary languages reflective of the school community, including braille and American Sign Language.
- Use augmentative communication devices and technologies to support diverse communication needs.

M = *Medical Health*
Individuals who have chronic health conditions and need specific medication, supplies,

- Develop a plan to account for medical needs, including identifying students who require services, medical equipment (e.g., people who have medical conditions such as asthma, medical fragility, seizure disorders, or severe allergies)

S = *Security & Supervision*
Individuals who need additional support to maintain accountability and security (e.g., people for whom traditional lockdown presents a physical, sensory, or emotional challenge; people who cannot remain quiet or stationary; people who are known to run away)

access to medical devices or medications and medical equipment that may not be stored in their classroom.
- Establish procedures for timely access to essential medical devices and medications and medical equipment during an emergency, in alignment with school policies and regulations.
- Train assigned staff in the proper use of medical devices and procedures.
- Train staff in distraction techniques, calming strategies, and de-escalation methods.
- Assign a staff member to assist individuals with required actions during drills.
- Provide additional practice opportunities between individuals and their assigned staff member to reinforce preparedness.

SOURCE: Adapted from Safe and Sound Schools, 2021.

As discussed in Chapter 3, no published studies have specifically examined the mental, emotional, and behavioral impacts of school active shooter drills on students and staff with functional and accessibility needs. Addressing this gap is essential to ensure that schools can minimize mental, emotional, and behavioral health risks and adapt practices to better support all individuals. During the committee's listening sessions, both students and school staff emphasized the need for greater attention to accessibility considerations in planning for active shooter drills. Some expressed concerns that current drill practices and emergency preparedness planning lack sufficient detail to ensure their needs are met. One student who required mobility assistance noted that her school did not have an emergency evacuation plan for her, prompting her to develop her own strategy for contacting family members for assistance during an emergency. A 2024 RAND survey of a randomly selected sample of 1,020 K–12 teachers asking about the 2022–2023 school year reached similar conclusions, reinforcing the need for more inclusive emergency preparedness efforts. These concerns inform the committee's guidance on the importance of school safety teams planning drills that accommodate students and staff with functional and accessibility needs.

Both the National Child Traumatic Stress Network (2018) and Safe and Sound Schools (2021) recommend developing individualized safety plans to ensure that students receive the accommodations necessary to participate in drills. These plans outline the specific supports needed, assign staff to assist students in completing drill actions, and identify additional intervention strategies that can help during emergency preparedness activities. When applicable, individualized safety plans may be integrated into students' Individualized Education Programs (IEPs) or 504 plans to align with their broader educational and support needs[26] (see Recommendation 8). By developing these plans, school safety teams, special education staff, nursing staff, and mental health professionals can collaborate to address the specific needs of their school community. These considerations can then be incorporated into drill design. For instance,

---

[26] According to ED (2000), "To create an effective IEP, parents, teachers, other school staff—and often the student—must come together to look closely at the student's unique needs. These individuals pool knowledge, experience, and commitment to design an educational program that will help the student be involved in, and progress in, the general curriculum" (p. 1). Similarly, developing an individualized safety plan can help ensure that school staff know their responsibilities for helping a student with safety limitations related to such areas as transportation/mobility; emotional, behavioral, mental, and medical health; auxiliary communication; and security and supervision (ED, 2000).

staff who are not assigned to a classroom can be positioned strategically in areas where additional personnel may be needed to facilitate the drill effectively (PBIS, 2025b).

Individualized safety plans also help identify training needs before a drill. Staff supporting students who rely on adaptive equipment or medical devices benefit from training in their proper use, ensuring readiness before an emergency occurs. Additionally, for students who require a buddy system during a drill, ensuring that the assigned support person understands their role in advance is essential. For students who require access to medication during emergencies, plans can outline how staff will coordinate retrieval or access in alignment with school policies and regulations, even if medication access is not a component of the drill itself.

Drills can also help identify unforeseen barriers, allowing schools to address these challenges and adapt practices accordingly. After-action reviews provide an opportunity to evaluate the effectiveness of individualized safety plans, ensuring that special education staff and other key personnel contribute to the review process. Where appropriate, student and parent input can also be incorporated to refine strategies.

Consider the Frequency and Context of Drills

The frequency of emergency drills, including school active shooter drills, varies significantly across the country, often influenced by state law requirements. As described in Chapter 3, however, research to date has not identified an optimal frequency for active shooter drills. ED (2025) reached a similar conclusion, noting the lack of definitive evidence on how often these drills should be conducted.

A study by Schildkraut et al. (2023) provides some insight into drill frequency through an evaluation of lockdown drills in a school district in New York. Their findings suggest that four to seven drill implementations were necessary to achieve approximately 80% fidelity—a threshold for adequate, though not perfect, compliance. Beyond this point, additional drills did not lead to further improvements, indicating a plateau effect. The study also found that some lockdown procedures were more difficult than others to implement consistently, making perfect fidelity even more challenging to achieve across classrooms. While these findings offer preliminary guidance, they have not been widely replicated across different school contexts or environments and do not specifically measure the relationship between the number and frequency of drills and mental, emotional, and behavioral health outcomes. As a result, it remains unclear whether similar patterns would emerge in other schools or among different student populations. More research is needed to determine how drill frequency, school characteristics, and training methods interact to optimize preparedness while minimizing potential negative mental, emotional, and behavioral health effects.

The committee acknowledges the multiple demands placed on schools and the importance of preserving instructional time while optimizing emergency preparedness and minimizing potential negative mental, emotional, and behavioral health effects. Drills need to be scheduled with sufficient frequency for students and staff to retain familiarity with the necessary actions. However, the optimal number of drills remains unclear, as more research is needed to determine how frequency, school context, and individual needs interact in establishing and maintaining preparedness while minimizing potential negative effects. Participants in the committee's listening sessions noted that overly frequent drills could lead to fatigue, increased stress, and emotional overload, potentially diminishing their effectiveness. Moreover, a study by Schildkraut (2023) found that skills learned through drills were retained over several years.

Given the limited evidence on drill frequency, however, schools may need to evaluate their own data to determine the most appropriate frequency for their community. Additionally, some students—particularly new students unfamiliar with emergency procedures and those with functional and accessibility needs—may require additional practice. Schools can consider targeted strategies for ensuring that these students receive the necessary support without increasing the overall drill burden for the broader school population.

When determining the frequency of drills, school safety teams can assess which standard response practices are appropriate for their campus and then establish a schedule for practicing each response practice throughout the school year. States and localities with drill mandates can also consider whether the activation of an emergency response protocol may count as a drill practice if responding to the emergency required the use of the same standard response practice used in a drill. In the absence of legal mandates, schools may choose to conduct an after-action review following an emergency activation, gathering input from staff, parents, and students rather than conducting an additional drill.

When reviewing schedules, schools can also consider timing active shooter drills to avoid unnecessary distress—for example, scheduling drills outside of high-stress academic periods, such as exam periods and standardized testing days. To support psychological safety, school communities where incidents of school violence have occurred may wish to avoid conducting drills on the anniversary of events that may hold significance for the local community. Adjustments may also be necessary following recent mass violence or school shooting incidents, as these events can heighten safety concerns and anxiety within the school community. In such cases, postponing the drill or replacing it with a discussion-based lesson plan that reviews the necessary response actions may be more appropriate. Regardless of the approach taken, it is beneficial during these periods of increased vulnerability to have additional mental health support available to assist students and staff.

While discussing the timing of drills during the committee's listening sessions, participants in the student panel suggested that school active shooter drills be practiced at different times of the day, including both structured periods (e.g., class time) and unstructured periods (e.g., recess, lunch, class transitions), taking account of the fact that active shooter events may not always take place when students are in a classroom. Practicing drills at varying times allows students and staff to hear activation communications in different situations and apply safety actions in multiple locations throughout the school building or campus.

These considerations highlight the need to broaden discussions about drill frequency beyond the number of drills conducted to include when and where drills take place. The committee aligns with the ED (2025) recommendation that schools consider limiting the duration of drills to what is necessary and varying the timing of drills throughout the day. These approaches can help ensure that school communities understand how to respond effectively across a range of situations, time periods, and locations on school grounds.

Inform, Engage, and Collaborate with Parents

As noted in Chapter 5, schools can partner with parents to help reduce the negative mental, emotional, and behavioral health impacts of active shooter drills. One key area of collaboration is parent representation on school safety committees, ensuring that family perspectives are included in emergency preparedness planning. Additionally, professional organizations consistently recommend that parents receive clear and timely communication regarding drills, including details on the type of drill being practiced, an overview of procedures and objectives, information on the general frequency of drills, contact information for school staff available to answer questions, and notice when drills occur (ED, 2025; NASP et al., 2021; NCTSN, 2018). The committee acknowledges that schools may have safety and security concerns about sharing specific details in advance regarding the timing and location of drills. However, just as clear communication before drills begin can support students' well-being, schools can also use existing communication channels to inform parents, helping them better prepare to support their children.

Schools can also support parents by offering resources that help explain drills in a developmentally appropriate manner, enabling families to discuss emergency preparedness at home. Given the variation in active shooter drill procedures, providing parents with specific details about the drill format can help alleviate anxiety and reinforce a consistent message of preparedness and safety (NCTSN, 2018).

Clear communication and open discussions with parents can help minimize the emotional impact of active shooter drills on students. Many adults are not familiar with what is involved in a school active shooter drill. Providing resources in parents' primary languages promotes accessibility, and offering informational meetings—particularly at the beginning of the school year—can help build trust and transparency between schools and families. These meetings offer an opportunity to:

review comprehensive school safety efforts, emphasizing that active shooter drills are just one component of a broader safety strategy;

- provide information about the types of drills students will practice throughout the year;
- demonstrate a drill for parents of younger students or families new to the district, allowing them to understand what their children will experience; and
- clarify how drill notifications and real emergency alerts will be communicated to parents, reducing uncertainty and anxiety.

When introducing new active shooter drill programs, schools can offer additional opportunities for parents to ask questions, collaborate on implementation strategies, and contribute to evaluation efforts. For students with functional or accessibility needs, parents play a key role in developing individualized safety plans and identifying effective adaptations to ensure that their children can participate meaningfully (ED, 2025; NCTSN, 2018; PBIS, 2025a).[27]

Preplan Drills with a Multidisciplinary Team

As previously discussed, emergency response drills require careful planning and oversight by a multidisciplinary team that includes

---

[27] School staff may also have functional or accessibility needs, and there may be opportunities to identify effective adaptations to ensure that these staff can participate meaningfully in school active shooter drills.

members of the school staff such as administrators, teachers, custodians, school nurses and school-based mental health professionals; school resource officers or security personnel; special education specialists; and parents. When appropriate, students may also be involved (ED, 2025; NASP et al., 2021). Each team member plays a specific role in the planning, execution, and evaluation of these drills. Expertise in child development, special education, and health conditions is important to ensure that drills account for the developmental and accessibility needs of all students (NASP et al., 2021). District personnel, including the school board, superintendent, assistant superintendents, and police and sheriff's departments (when applicable), also can play a crucial role in providing support, resources, and oversight. The *Maryland Best Practices Guide* (Maryland Center for School Safety, 2024) notes that school safety committees/teams need to be large enough to include key representatives from various disciplines but small enough to facilitate effective collaboration and decision-making. Additionally, state legislative requirements may influence the composition and responsibilities of school safety teams.

Many school safety teams also collaborate with local law enforcement; emergency management agencies; and first responders, such as fire departments and emergency medical personnel. These partnerships help ensure that school active shooter drills align with broader community emergency plans while also allowing for adaptations based on a school's unique needs. For example, first responders can be informed about:

- the location of special education classrooms and the specific medical or accessibility needs of some students, ensuring a more effective emergency response; and
- crisis management or school safety expertise offered by nonprofit organizations, which may assist in planning and executing drills.

When planning active shooter drills, school safety teams need to first consider the goals of each drill, as those goals will determine the level of participation required:

- Drills using discussion-based practices, especially for new students, may focus on familiarization with school emergency protocols and will not require the involvement of community partners.
- School active shooter drills can be planned with a developmentally appropriate, trauma-informed approach, ensuring accessibility adaptations for students with functional and access needs while addressing the needs of both students and staff (Box 6-3).

Additionally, planning needs to account for logistical factors, such as:

- ensuring that sufficient wellness supports (e.g., access to school-based mental health staff) are available for students and staff;
- implementing evaluation strategies to assess the drill's effectiveness and impacts on mental, emotional, and behavioral health (NASP et al., 2021; PBIS, 2025b); and
- verifying that drills comply with state regulations and align with best practices, addressing any potential legal implications (PBIS, 2025b).

Training all staff in self-regulation techniques before drills take place can also enhance their ability to support students in distress while maintaining their own emotional stability. When adults remain regulated, students are more likely to feel secure and calm during the drill (Braun et al., 2020). For example, an increasing number of states, including Texas, Nebraska, and New Mexico, are also pre-training school staff in Psychological First Aid for Schools (PFA-S) (Brymer et al., 2012), an evidence-informed intervention recognized as a best practice in ED's (2013) *Guide for Developing High-Quality School Emergency Operations Plans*. PFA-S can be used during and after drills to provide immediate support to students and staff in distress (NCTSN, 2017). Any school staff or community partners can be trained in PFA-S, making it a valuable tool for schools with limited mental health personnel. Staff without direct student supervision duties can be strategically positioned in areas where additional support may be needed during drills, ensuring that students and staff have access to emotional support and reassurance (PBIS, 2025b). When adults remain regulated, students are more likely to feel secure and calm during the drill (Braun et al., 2020).

Conducting School Active Shooter Drills

Once a drill is under way, the focus shifts to activating the essential components of the established plan and ensuring that key procedures are practiced in a structured and purposeful manner. As noted in Chapter 3, while the committee found little empirical research directly linking active shooter drills to specific mental, emotional, and behavioral health outcomes, best practices can still be identified by drawing on expert consensus and well-established principles from research on child and adolescent development. These insights can help ensure that drills are conducted in ways that reinforce safety, minimize distress, and foster a sense of control and confidence among participants. By ensuring that drills are conducted thoughtfully and supportively, schools can help students and staff engage in these preparedness activities in a way that is both effective for learning and skill development and psychologically safe. This section presents guidance on how schools can use careful planning, clear communication, and well-structured support systems in place to approach active shooter drills as part of a broader safety strategy that prioritizes both preparedness and well-being.

As the time for the drill approaches, preparations may be necessary for students with functional and accessibility needs to help them feel more secure and prepared; if necessary, they can be provided with an alternative learning opportunity, such as discussion-based drill activities. Preparations may include reminders about the drill, specific actions the students will take, and coping strategies. For instance, a teacher might reference techniques from a social-emotional learning or wellness program, such as slow breathing exercises, to help students regulate their emotions during the drill. All accommodations need to be in place for students with individualized safety plans before the drill begins—for example, ensuring that headphones are available for students with sound sensitivity or that a designated buddy is positioned nearby to assist students who require additional support (NCTSN, 2018; PBIS, 2025b).

Finally, school staff can be reminded of the purpose of the drill, the specific action steps, and the availability of mental health supports throughout the drill. In listening sessions, the committee heard that when staff were well-prepared, understood their roles, and took the drills seriously, students reported feeling less anxious. Ensuring that all participants—both students and staff—feel informed and supported helps ensure a more structured, predictable, and psychologically safe experience.

Use Clear Communications During Drills

When a drill begins, school officials can clearly announce to all students and staff that a drill is occurring, possibly using the school's emergency communication system. Additionally, a communication mechanism can be in place to notify parents, emergency responders, and other relevant external partners to prevent unnecessary alarm. This may involve automated messaging systems, text alerts, or emails that mirror the in-school announcement, reinforcing the message that the event is a drill rather than an actual emergency (NCTSN, 2018; PBIS, 2025a).

Such communications need to be accessible to all members of the school community, including multilingual learners and those who require communication supports (e.g., students who are deaf or hard of hearing). For example, drills may be designed to avoid relying solely on verbal commands, which may exclude students with special communications needs from fully understanding the instructions. To promote this practice, schools can:
- pair verbal commands with standard symbols that indicate required actions;
- ensure that emergency messages are repeated in common languages spoken by students;

- use both verbal and visual cues in drills so students become familiar with multiple ways of receiving emergency instructions;
- explore technological solutions for providing alerts that accommodate students who are multilingual learners, deaf, or hearing impaired; and
- use standardized follow-up communication for the standard response practice being rehearsed—along with visual icons—to further improve comprehension and response accuracy.

ED (2025) and NASP, NASRO, and Safe and Sound Schools (2021) also recommend clear and effective communication throughout the drill, including letting students and staff know when the drill has concluded to ensure that all participants are aware that normal activities may resume (ED, 2025; NASP et al., 2021). By prioritizing accessible and well-structured communication, schools can enhance preparedness, reduce confusion, and create a better safety experience for all students and staff.

Ensure That Wellness Supports Are Available

Professional organizations consistently recommend that wellness supports—such as access to school-based mental health staff and opportunities to debrief—be available both during and after active shooter drills to help mitigate stress and anxiety (ED, 2025; NASP et al., 2021; NCTSN, 2018; PBIS, 2025b). Additionally, as noted earlier in this chapter, pretraining staff in common trauma reactions can equip them to recognize when a student is struggling and may need to step away from the drill that is in progress to seek support (NASP et al., 2021; NCTSN, 2017).

After School Active Shooter Drills Occur

The period after a school active shooter drill is a critical time for ensuring that students and staff are emotionally supported. Having structured post-drill procedures allows schools to check in with students and staff, particularly those who may be vulnerable to distress, while also gathering valuable feedback with which to refine safety practices. This section outlines best practices for post-drill support, including facilitating debriefing opportunities, conducting targeted check-ins with vulnerable students and staff, and compiling an after-action assessment. These steps not only help schools identify any immediate adverse outcomes but also create an opportunity to strengthen future preparedness efforts. By prioritizing communication, evaluation, and emotional well-being, schools can ensure that drills are not only informative and effective at imparting the knowledge and skills necessary to respond to an emergency but also supportive and responsive to the needs of the entire school community.

Provide Time for Students and Staff to Debrief

Regular debriefing and evaluation of drills are essential for identifying areas for improvement and ensuring that practices remain developmentally appropriate and trauma informed. Taking time to discuss the experience immediately after a drill, before resuming academic instruction, reinforces the purpose of the drill, allows for reviewing the action steps taken, and provides an opportunity to address any concerns or questions from students (PBIS, 2025a). It also allows teachers and school mental health staff to remind students of available mental health resources and how to access them (ED, 2025; NCTSN, 2018; PBIS, 2025a). Box 6-4 summarizes insights from the committee's listening session with school social workers related to their role in supporting students before, during, and after drills—including during debriefings.

> **BOX 6-2**
> **Perspectives from School Social Workers, School Psychologists, and School Nurses**
>
> The committee hosted listening sessions to understand how school social workers support students before, during, and after school active shooter drills. While these listening sessions were not designed to be representative of all school social workers' perspectives or practices, they provided valuable context for understanding the real-world implementation of drills and identifying areas of potential concern regarding adverse outcomes. These discussions served as a backdrop for the committee's review and assessment of the available empirical literature, as well as a reminder of the real-life stories and experiences behind the data. The sessions (along with qualitative data presented in Chapters 3 and 4) served as an important input to the committee's deliberations and provided a context for, though not the basis of, its conclusions and recommendations.
>
> Participants in the committee's listening sessions described how drills often heighten stress and fear, with some students experiencing panic during the exercises or in anticipation of the exercises. One participant, a school nurse in New Jersey, described how some students experience physical symptoms, such as stomachaches and headaches, on drill days, and that some students, particularly those with preexisting mental health conditions or disabilities, may be particularly vulnerable to heightened anxiety and fear. Another panelist reinforced this point, saying, "People with preexisting mental health conditions may be more adversely affected by these drills than those without."
>
> Another participant noted, "Being able to show up to school and just have to do school is great. Being able to show up to school and having to be concerned about someone coming in your building—it's a terrible feeling." Panel participants recognized that active shooter drills may have

a disproportionate impact on some students of color, particularly those who may have heightened concerns about safety because of exposure to racism or violence, which can be exacerbated by active shooter drills.

Panelists emphasized the need for collaborative planning that includes mental health professionals, educators, families, and other key school community members. One participant highlighted the risks of excluding critical perspectives, explaining, "If they're not at the table when the conversation and planning begin, then we often are missing what is important for that particular population." School social workers advocated for modifications to drills that account for students with trauma histories, disabilities, and language barriers, ensuring that preparedness efforts do not inadvertently cause harm. A lack of debriefing after drills was frequently cited as a concern as it leaves students without a proper outlet to process their emotions, potentially compounding distress.

Clear communication also emerged as a critical factor in reducing anxiety and fear surrounding active shooter drills. A school psychologist from Maryland emphasized the importance of using visual tools and clear language to support students' understanding of active shooter drills. She recommended incorporating graphics, pictures, and other visual aids to help students comprehend emergency procedures in a way that is accessible and developmentally appropriate. Multilingual learners may also face additional challenges in understanding instructions during emergencies without appropriate language supports. One panelist emphasized the need for language accommodations when working with multilingual populations to ensure that families and students who have a home language other than English receive clear and supportive communication.

Another participant—a professor and school psychologist from California—highlighted the potential unintended consequences of school emergency preparedness measures. They reinforced the importance of engaging parents and community groups as essential in creating an approach that reflects the backgrounds, experiences, and needs of the entire school community and creates an environment where everyone feels informed, supported, and prepared.

Concerns about retraumatization and unnecessary fear were also central to the discussion. Another participant stressed the importance of weighing risks, stating, "Statistically, an active shooter event probably won't happen to students while they're in school, so we need to weigh the importance of preparedness against the possibility of retraumatizing certain groups of students." One panelist warned about the risks of unnecessarily intense drills, stating, "You have the potential of traumatizing individuals—both the students and the staff—with that. Those pieces aren't necessary when conducting the drills and helping to understand what are the steps that are needed to be safe in an active assailant situation."

To address these challenges, participants recommended trauma-informed practices, structured debriefing sessions, and preventive measures that help foster a sense of safety and resilience while minimizing harm. For example, a pediatric nurse practitioner who participated in the session advocated for the integration of mental health and emotional support in schools to address chronic stress and prevent compounded trauma. Another panelist similarly stressed the value of individualized planning, explaining, "School nurses are always making individualized plans for students who may have special needs." These suggested adaptations included such practices as offering tailored debriefings for students who may struggle with processing the drill experience.

Another school nursed described how, "after the drill, we offer that safe space for students who may have had an emotional response . . . to help them process emotions." Participants emphasized the need to move from reactive to responsive safety measures. They noted that this shift

> underscores the importance of proactive, trauma-informed planning that ensures students are not only prepared for emergencies but also supported in managing their emotional responses.

To help students regain focus and transition back to learning, teachers may guide them through grounding exercises or emotion-regulation strategies, ensuring that they feel calm and prepared for the remainder of the school day. Additionally, recognizing students' efforts and participation—such as acknowledging how they followed safety protocols or supported one another—can help reinforce positive engagement with the drills (NCTSN, 2018, PBIS, 2025a).

ED (2025) recommends creating a systematic process for documenting feedback gathered during debriefing sessions an incorporating findings as part of the school safety committee's planning. This feedback can help in refining protocols to minimize negative mental, emotional, and behavioral health impacts and to improve future drill experiences (ED, 2025; NCTSN, 2018). ED (2025) recommends that debriefing discussions include

- reinforcing the importance of practicing emergency procedures in case of a real emergency;
- soliciting student feedback on what went well and what could be improved;
- addressing concerns and answering questions that arose during the drill;
- assessing whether students need additional time or support before returning to academic activities; and
- ensuring that all students know how to access additional mental health or wellness supports. (p. 10)

By prioritizing post-drill discussions and evaluation, schools can strengthen both safety preparedness and emotional well-being, ensuring that drills serve their intended purpose without causing unnecessary distress for students and staff.

Check in with Vulnerable Students and Staff

As previously discussed, some students may be particularly vulnerable to adverse mental, emotional, and behavioral effects of school active shooter drills. Students with a history of trauma or loss, as well as those who experience anxiety, may benefit from meeting with a school counselor, school psychologist, school social worker, or school nurse to develop a personalized plan for active shooter drills; they also may need reminders and reassurance about their plan to help them navigate the experience and the time period afterward. These students as well may be positioned to offer their perspective and feedback on how to make the drills more trauma informed, and schools may benefit from using student leadership or focus groups to guide these practices.

Staff can provide additional support by reaching out proactively to students who have previously expressed concerns or been identified as needing extra assistance, ensuring that they feel prepared and supported. During the committee's listening session with school nurses, panelists described the varied reactions they observed among students and emphasized the importance of checking in with those who may be at especially high risk for adverse mental, emotional, and behavioral health outcomes. These check-ins with vulnerable students allow staff to discuss the students' experiences during a drill in a supportive and nonjudgmental way, provide guidance on coping strategies and assist in applying previously taught self-regulation techniques, and reinforce a sense of safety and control by addressing lingering concerns or distress (NCTSN, 2018; PBIS, 2025a).

Parents also can be engaged, if necessary, to keep them informed about the outcome of these check-ins and to provide suggestions for reinforcing coping skills at home. This collaborative approach can ensure that students receive consistent support across both school and home environments, helping to strengthen their emotional resilience both in future drills and in emergency situations.

School staff may also need extra support after a drill and can be encouraged to access available mental health resources. Having access to wellness supports and debriefing opportunities helps ensure that staff have the resources they need to process their experiences, manage stress, and continue to provide reassurance and guidance to students (NCTSN, 2018).

Conduct an After-Action Assessment That Evaluates Results, Identifies Gaps, and Documents Lessons Learned and Successes Achieved

After completing a drill, schools can use a quality improvement process to evaluate the drill's effectiveness at imparting preparedness skills and its impacts on mental, emotional, and behavioral health, and to identify areas for refinement. Seeking input from students, staff, school safety team members, and parents allows for a comprehensive review of the drill experience, enabling an assessment of how well protocols were followed, how participants experienced the drill, and where adjustments may be necessary. Engaging parents in this evaluation can also offer an opportunity to update them on the drill's implementation, share available resources for students who may need additional support, and gather information on any concerns or suggestions they have for future planning (ED, 2025). This feedback can be compiled into an after-action report that documents lessons learned, successes achieved, and adverse outcomes of concern while also outlining opportunities for improvement (ED, 2025; NCTSN, 2018). Documenting action steps for improvement after each drill and keeping all relevant members of the school community informed of any changes can ensure that lessons learned translate to meaningful updates to safety procedures that reflect feedback from participants on how they experienced the drill, as well as promote positive mental, emotional, and behavioral health outcomes.

Through this ongoing review process, school safety teams may uncover unintended negative mental, emotional, and behavioral health impacts not previously recognized. During the committee's listening sessions, for example, some participants described compliance checks conducted as part of school active shooter drills. One practice involved checking that doors were properly locked by jiggling door handles during lockdown drills. While this practice was intended to evaluate procedural fidelity, it was noted that this activity elicited emotional distress for some students, even when they were informed in advance that it would occur. Although these accounts are anecdotal, this type of information highlights the types of insights that might be shared after a drill and areas in which adjustments might be considered to maintain the effectiveness of drills while minimizing unnecessary stress.

Consistently collecting feedback over time provides schools with valuable insights into the real-world impact of their emergency preparedness efforts. By adapting practices based on direct input from students, staff, and parents, schools can refine their approach in ways that balance safety, procedural integrity, and foster practices that mitigate potential adverse mental, emotional, and behavioral health outcomes.

Practices with High Likelihood of Mental, Emotional, and Behavioral Health Harm

This section describes practices likely to cause significant and unnecessary mental, emotional, and behavioral health harms when implemented in the context of school active shooter drills. These practices include simulation exercises involving student participation; high-intensity, hyper-realistic, or high-sensorial components; and deception.

The committee recognizes the importance of simulation exercises for training emergency responders, but it is important to conduct these exercises outside regular school hours and without the presence of students and most school staff. Although mandatory participation is to be avoided, selected staff members from the school safety team may choose to participate or observe to help ensure that the school's emergency response plans align with established emergency responder protocols.

Simulation exercises tend to mimic a school shooting or other school violence and typically include emergency responders practicing how they will respond to an active shooter event in a school, which heightens the intensity of these exercises for those who participate in them. They may also include high-sensorial, high-intensity, and hyper-realistic components (e.g., using realistic actors firing blanks, having emergency personnel act like an intruder, using fake blood). In some cases, drills may simulate a real emergency by incorporating deceptive strategies, such as falsely announcing a real emergency or having a law enforcement officer enter the school as if they were an active shooter (Schonfeld et al., 2020).

As described in Chapter 3, there has been a paucity of research assessing how different elements of drills and simulation exercises affect participants' reactions. As yet, no head-to-head studies have compared participants' reactions to different types of school active shooter drills. While no direct research has been done on how high-intensity, hyper-realistic, or high-sensorial elements affect the mental, emotional, and behavioral health outcomes of students and staff, there is a growing professional consensus on the likely adverse impact of these practices. In some cases, legal complaints have been filed when the implementation of such drills has led to harm (Frosch, 2014; Safe Havens International, n.d.; Sawchuk, 2020; Trump, 2014). A recent RAND Corporation study (Moore et al., 2024) reports the finding from a 2023 American Teacher Panel Survey of 1,020 teachers that most schools do not incorporate these elements in their drills. However, 57% of teachers in rural schools reported that their drills included at least one realistic element, compared with 32% in urban schools and 46% of those in suburban schools (Moore et al., 2024).

The use of realistic elements in drills is grounded in the erroneous assumption that high-intensity, hyper-realistic, or high-sensorial elements that replicate the distress experienced in actual shooting events will better prepare students to perform the desired behaviors during a real incident. Examples in the media have suggested that such practices are effective in accomplishing the goal of evoking distress, but with no indication that these practices increase preparedness (Schonfeld et al., 2017). Despite the lack of direct evidence, it is clear from the developmental sciences that effective learning—for both adults and students—does not typically take place under conditions in which individuals are experiencing excessive stress or anxiety (see Chapter 5). The purpose of school active shooter drills is for students and staff to learn the appropriate response when an emergency occurs at school, and the growing body of anecdotal evidence (including accounts from educators and other school staff during the committee's listening sessions) suggests that simulation exercises are highly likely to impede rather than facilitate the learning of appropriate skills. There is no evidence that simulation elements, including deceptive tactics, improve students' and staff's perceptions of preparedness. Rather, these practices may dramatically heighten negative mental, emotional, and behavioral health impacts; result in injuries; and hinder the ability of teachers and students to resume academic learning (Frosch, 2014; Moore-Petinak et al., 2020; Sawchuk, 2020; Schonfeld et al., 2020).

In sum, there is wide consensus across professional associations that the use of simulation exercises with simulated violence and high-sensorial elements should be avoided, and that drills need to be developmentally and age appropriate, as well as trauma informed (Donovan, 2023; ED, 2025; Miotto & Cogan, 2023; Schonfeld et al., 2020). In presentations to the committee during its public information-gathering session, experts from NASRO, National School Safety and Security Services, Safe Havens International, and Safe and Sound Schools all concurred that students should not participate in school active shooter simulations or exercises or in any drill with high-sensorial and hyper-realistic components. In addition, an American Academy of Pediatrics (AAP) policy statement recommends that children not routinely participate in high-intensity exercises during regular school time (Schonfeld et al., 2020). The statement suggests that children should not ordinarily participate in live crisis drills or exercises, and that they should do so only if their participation advances their personal preparedness or resiliency and/or meets the unique needs of children as a group that cannot otherwise be advanced. In one incident described by Simonetti (2020), for example, a training drill included "students posing as injured individuals while others were chained to chairs as hostages and fastened to mock explosives" (Simonetti, 2020, p. 1021). These findings raise the question of what educational benefit or skill acquisition is gained by students in playing these roles as helpless victims.

Donovan (2023) affirms the AAP policy statement: "Drills that involve students should not realistically simulate active shooter situations" (p. 442). Miotto & Cogan (2023) agree that "children should not be routinely involved in high-intensity drills or exercises" and conclude that "live-action, hyper-realistic drills unsupported by research have no place in a student-centered, trauma-responsive learning environment" (p. 8). The Council for Exceptional Children's Division of Emotional and Behavioral Health (CEC-DEBH) has observed that there appears to be "no evidence of any benefit or rationale for including a sensorial experience in these drills" and that "live simulations of assailants attacking a school are unnecessary" (p. 120).

In addition, several states have drawn a firm distinction between drills and simulation exercises. They ban mandatory student participation in simulation exercises (e.g., Minnesota Students Safe at School Act); or they encourage schools to conduct such exercises only when school is not in session; or they permit participation only after specific parental notification or consent[28]; or they restrict drills from mimicking a shooting, violence, or any emergency.[29] The committee agrees with these alternative legislative approaches. Moreover, it is worth noting that some school simulation exercises have resulted in legal complaints that have led to state legislative action prohibiting students from being required to participate in these types of exercises (Frosch, 2014; Ind. Code § 20-34-3-27, 2024; Safe Havens International, n.d.; Sawchuk, 2020; Trump, 2014).

Although a strong consensus has now emerged that students should not be required to participate in simulation exercises,

---

[28] Tex. Educ. Code § 37.1411, 2025.
[29] N.Y. Comp. Codes R. & Regs., tit. 8, § 155.17, 2025; Md. H.B. 416, 2024.

practices regarding staff participation vary. The Cybersecurity and Infrastructure Security Agency (CISA) Active Shooter Drills and Program Assessment (2025) acknowledges that simulations and full-scale exercises need to be limited to staff and local first responders, but it does not provide additional guidance on whether staff should be required to participate. School staff and administrators who participated in the committee's listening sessions expressed many of the same concerns about simulations and reported their own negative experiences. Additionally, insurance companies have reported an increase in medical bills due to staff physical injuries as a result of drills, some of which led to lawsuits (O'Regan, 2019), mirroring similar concerns raised about drills conducted in nonschool settings. The American Federation of Teachers and the National Education Association, along with the Everytown for Gun Safety Support Fund, concluded in a recent report, "While there is almost no research affirming the value of these drills, stories abound in the media of incidents where students, educators, and staff have experienced distress and sometimes lasting trauma as a result of active shooter drills" (Everytown for Gun Safety Support Fund et al., 2020).

As noted in Chapter 2, first responders receive specialized tactical training as recruits (e.g., Civilian Response to Active Shooter Events, which is offered by the ALERRT Center at Texas State University); many states (e.g., Indiana, Tennessee, South Carolina) require additional active shooter training for their law enforcement officers and agencies. These types of courses are geared to first responders and civilians in the community, but not to educators in their official job capacities (Martaindale & Blair, 2019). Given that simulation and full-scale exercises are complex trainings designed to replicate real emergencies and test first responders under highly stressful conditions, the committee does not recommend mandating that administrators or staff participate in these exercises, although some educators or school staff may wish to observe these simulations or volunteer to take part.

In summary, the committee recommends that, to minimize harm to students and staff, active shooter drills in schools exclude high-intensity, high-sensorial elements. It also recommends that deception, including false claims of an actual shooter or staged injuries or deaths, be forbidden. Such practices can cause significant psychological distress. Instead, preparedness efforts need to prioritize safety while safeguarding the mental, emotional, and behavioral well-being of participating students and staff. This approach aligns with professional consensus, as other experts in the field have explicitly stated that drills should not include deceptive practices (CEC-DEBH, 2024; Schonfeld et al., 2017).

Recommendation 2: State legislatures and education agencies should enact policies prohibiting the use of high-intensity or high-sensorial simulations and exercises, as well as deception, as part of active shooter drills in K–12 schools. If statewide action is not taken, local school districts should prohibit the use of these practices as part of active shooter drills and should require that all drills be announced to students, staff, and parents before they begin.

One appropriate measure of progress toward this recommendation would be the number of states banning high-intensity and deceptive drills. Success at the local level could be measured by tracking the percentage of schools eliminating use of high-intensity, high-sensorial elements and deception in drills; the number of schools allowing opt-out policies; and the number of students and staff reporting distress related to drills.

Moreover, consistent with its recommendation, the committee suggests that law enforcement personnel and emergency responders conducting high-intensity school active shooter response training do so outside of school hours and without student participants. The AAP recommends that, if adolescent students wish to volunteer to participate in such training activities, explicit parental consent be required, and the respective schools should establish safeguards to ensure that student participation is truly voluntary (Schonfeld et al.,

2020). The effectiveness of these policies could be measured by tracking reductions in the number of schools used as training sites during school hours, by increasing the adoption of alternative training models that exclude student involvement, and by tracking compliance with ethical standards for emergency preparedness exercises.

Practices More Likely to Have Negative Than Positive Mental, Emotional, and Behavioral Health Impact

Options-Based Practices

Options-based practices emphasize critical thinking and in-the-moment decision-making when standard response practices cannot be implemented (Donovan, 2023; Miotto & Cogan, 2023; Schonfeld et al., 2020; Simonetti, 2020). By contrast, standard response practices provide structured, predefined actions that students and staff should take during emergencies instead of situational decision-making. While options-based strategies may be necessary in specific instances during real active shooter events (e.g., if a shooter enters a classroom), these skills may not be appropriate for the entire school community (NASP et al., 2021). Their application in a school setting requires caution. The limited evidence on their potential mental, emotional, and behavioral health impacts and on whether they are more effective than, or even equivalent to, alternative practices dictates caution in applying them in a school setting. Furthermore, the landscape of practices used during school active shooter drills caution remains regarding the appropriateness of options-based practices for all students and staff, revealed some indications that these practices may not be suitable for certain age groups for individuals with severe functional and access needs, or for those with trauma histories (NASP et al., 2021). Yet none of these programs specify with clarity who should not participate in these practices.

Although standard response practices address most emergency situations in schools, they do not cover every scenario involving an active shooter. As a result, some schools may consider incorporating options-based practices into their drills to prepare for rare but high-risk situations. However, given the potential for adverse mental, emotional, and behavioral health effects and the limited research available, schools need to weigh the costs and benefits of introducing these practices carefully. This includes considering how they align with the specific context and needs of the particular school community, understanding whether they are developmentally appropriate, evaluating the overall time and resources required for implementation, and considering factors such as training requirements and costs. Additionally, the school needs to address staff and parental concerns and to evaluate any drills using these practices for potential negative mental, emotional, and behavioral health impacts.

While options-based practices may offer certain benefits, including flexibility, the committee does not advise mandating these programs through state legislation for the entire school community. Given the significant level of readiness required for successful implementation, options-based practices may not be suitable for all schools or all individuals within a school setting. Additionally, the existing evidence is unclear regarding the age groups for which various practices are appropriate, and how students and staff with severe functional and access needs, special educational needs, and those with experiences of trauma can effectively engage in these activities. Given these considerations and the very limited evidence currently available, the committee cautions against the use of options-based practices.

Timing and Manner of Prior Announcement of Drills

Unannounced school active shooter drills can create confusion and uncertainty about whether there is or is not an active threat—a state of uncertainty that can generate extreme emotional distress for students, staff, and parents. Moreover, unannounced active shooter training exercises that included high-sensorial, high-intensity, and deceptive components conducted outside of the school setting have resulted in legal complaints and at least one settlement related to claims about the significant adverse mental, emotional, and behavioral health impacts on the participants (Frosch, 2014; Kalmbacher, 2024; Sawchuk, 2020; Trump, 2014). Additionally, at least one lawsuit that occurred after an unannounced school active shooter drill in which an educator claimed she developed post-traumatic stress disorder (PTSD) (O'Regan, 2019). Announcing these drills before they begin can allow students to prepare for the experience, reinforce previously taught social-emotional skills, and address any questions students may have beforehand. The committee aligns with the ED (2025) recommendation that schools consider announcing when a drill is beginning and integrating them into existing lesson plans.

Although there is consensus that active shooter drills should be announced in advance, there is less agreement on the timing and manner of these announcements. For example, guidance from NASP, NASRO, and Safe and Sound Schools recommends that all participants be informed when a drill is about to begin and understand what it will entail, and that notifications be sent to parents, caregivers, and key community partners (if necessary) when drills are taking place (NASP et al., 2021). By contrast, ED (2025) has indicated that "unplanned" drills, meaning the exact time of the drill is not known to all participants may occur, but still notes that students and staff should be given prior notice that there will be an upcoming drill even if precise details of timing are not given. Given the potential for negative mental, emotional, and behavioral health impacts, the committee does not favor conducting "unplanned" and unannounced drills, and if such drills take place, it is important that they not include deceptive components; in particular, the organizers need to state explicitly that the event is a drill, not a real emergency to avoid deceiving participants. This announcement needs to be made before all drills begin to ensure that both students and staff are aware and can adequately prepare to participate.

Providing advance notice about the nature of practices that will be used allows schools to implement necessary accommodations for students who may be at particular risk of distress, such as those with anxiety, past trauma, or disabilities. This approach ensures that flexible support measures—such as alternative participation options—are in place to protect student well-being. To support these students, schools can incorporate discussion-based practices such as standardized lesson plans that outline the steps for practices that will be used as part of the drill. These lesson plans can include visual aids and social stories to explain the purpose of the drills in an accessible and reassuring way. Providing alternative learning opportunities aligns with civil rights laws and other legal requirements, ensuring that all students can participate meaningfully in school programs and activities. This can be achieved through clear communication with students and parents, provision of accessible materials in a format they understand, and proactive efforts to remove barriers to participation (ED, 2025; Safe and Sound Schools, 2021; see also Recommendations 8 and 9).

IMPLEMENTATION CONSIDERATIONS

School active shooter drills and other security measures do not operate in isolation, as most schools implement multiple strategies to prevent school violence. However, substantial autonomy exists at district and even school levels in selecting programs and approaches that align with their specific needs. Decision-makers must weigh a range of factors, including federal, state, district, and school policies; feedback from key constituencies; appropriateness and fit for their specific context; a strategy's perceived effectiveness; capacity for implementation; and cost considerations.

This section presents recommendations and actionable strategies tailored to each level of potential influence, ranging from national policy initiatives to school-based implementation efforts. Additionally, it explores opportunities for philanthropic organizations and interested researchers to support schools in identifying, refining, and evaluating best practices. By fostering multilevel collaboration, schools can strengthen their emergency preparedness strategies while ensuring that student and staff well-being remain at the center of these efforts.

Guidance to Prioritize Health and Safety Across All School Settings

As discussed previously in this report, despite the prevalence of mandates requiring schools to conduct active shooter drills, no standardized guidance exists on their implementation, which has led to significant variations in approaches. This inconsistency has created an urgent need for minimally acceptable standards that prioritize student health and safety across all school settings. At the same time, universal, one-size-fits-all safety plans are not practical, as individual schools need to meet the needs of their specific school populations and face unique safety challenges. The broad range of school security strategies across disciplines further complicates efforts to establish a single, standardized model. Instead, best practices must balance consistency in core safety principles with flexibility to meet local needs.

The responsibility for developing guidance on active shooter drills has been spread across multiple entities, including professional associations, researchers, state and federal agencies, foundations, and advocacy organizations. While these groups have offered valuable recommendations, including best practices and policies, a cohesive, coordinated approach is necessary to ensure that schools have the resources, training, and support needed to implement safe strategies for all students.

Recommendation 3: Federal agencies, including the Department of Education, the Department of Health and Human Services, the Federal Emergency Management Agency, and the Centers for Disease Control and Prevention, should issue national best-practice guidelines aligned with the committee's guidance to follow trauma-informed and developmentally appropriate principles.

The committee recognizes the role of school active shooter drills in emergency preparedness, but their implementation needs to prioritize student and staff well-being to prevent unnecessary harm and ensure that the drills foster environments conducive to the learning and skill-building they are intended to impart. As noted throughout this report, the use of high-intensity or high-sensorial simulations and exercises, as well as outright deception, has been shown to increase distress for both students and school staff. Use of these approaches with students and in school settings is not supported by research evidence. The essential path forward is to adopt trauma-informed, developmentally appropriate approaches that balance preparedness with emotional and psychological safety. Success in this area could be measured by the number of states adopting national best-practice guidelines and the publication of high-quality, methodologically rigorous research on effectiveness and best practices for school active shooter drills. (See also Chapter 7 for a discussion of priorities for future research.) To continue refining national-level guidance on best practices, federal funding can support research on the long-term psychological impact of drills on students and staff.

Recommendation 4: Research funders, including philanthropic organizations and research institutions, should fund independent studies on the effects of school active shooter drills on mental, emotional, and behavioral health, and support the adoption of trauma-informed safety practices to ensure that school safety practices are evidence based and centered on the health of students and school staff.

Additionally, these organizations can support initiatives that promote trauma-informed, developmentally appropriate school safety practices at the state and national levels. Success in this area could be measured by the number of high-quality, methodologically rigorous studies funded that examine the effectiveness and psychological impact of drills, increased public awareness of trauma-informed school safety practices, and the adoption of evidence-based policy recommendations by education agencies.

Universities and research institutions can collaborate with education agencies to assess and identify best practices in school safety that minimize negative mental, emotional, and behavioral health impacts. By conducting rigorous evaluations of existing programs and practices, these institutions can provide data-driven recommendations to inform future policy decisions. The effectiveness of these efforts could be measured by the number of research studies conducted, the implementation of evidence-based policies, and documented improvements in outcomes related to school safety and mental health and well-being. (See also Chapter 7 for a detailed description of priorities for future research.)

Few school security measures require accreditation or formal oversight, leaving schools to navigate a rapidly expanding market of safety solutions with limited guidance. Without accepted standards, decision-makers must assess programs and strategies on their own, often without access to clear, evidence-based information on effectiveness. A common vocabulary for discussing safety and preparedness practices—along with transparent reporting from providers about the rationale for preferred practices, implementation data, and empirical evaluation—could help schools and districts make well-informed decisions about which practices best align with their needs and goals.

Training on School Safety Practices to Support Mental, Emotional, and Behavioral Health

The responsibility for training, implementation, monitoring, and sustainability for school active shooter drills and other security measures often falls on school leaders and staff, many of whom receive little to no formal training on school safety practices. While some districts have created designated safety roles such as "safety liaison" or "safety specialist," most school personnel—including teachers, school-based health care professionals, and administrators—are expected to carry out these responsibilities with limited professional development or structured support. Prioritizing training for school community members can help ensure that best practices are implemented with fidelity while also reducing strain on staff members involved in school security planning and response.

Additionally, pretraining staff in common trauma reactions can equip them to recognize when a student is struggling and may need to step away from a drill (NASP et al., 2021; NCTSN, 2017). Training all staff in self-regulation techniques can also enhance their ability to support students in distress while maintaining their own emotional stability. As noted previously, when adults remain regulated, students are more likely to feel secure and calm during a drill (Braun et al., 2020).

Recommendation 5: School districts should ensure that school nurses, school counselors, school psychologists, school social workers, and other school-based health professionals are engaged in proactively monitoring students for signs of anxiety or distress during and following school active shooter drills. School districts should provide educators and school staff with training that equips them to recognize and monitor signs of psychological distress in students when school active shooter drills are implemented. School districts, informed by mental health professionals, should ensure that appropriate mental, emotional, and behavioral health support services for students are available when drills are conducted.

School-based health professionals and child development specialists can also play a key role by reviewing school district policies and providing guidance on how drills may impact students and staff. The effectiveness of this practice could be measured by surveying changes in the involvement of health experts in drill planning, the expansion of school-based mental health interventions for students affected by drills, and the percentage of schools incorporating trauma-informed practices into their drill protocols. Teachers can also advocate within their districts for trauma-informed safety policies that prioritize student well-being. The effectiveness of these efforts could be assessed by monitoring student distress levels after drills, tracking the adoption of appropriate training models that incorporate best practices for teachers, and surveying teachers on their ability to recognize and respond to student distress during and after school active shooter drills.

As a necessary part of a comprehensive school safety plan, active shooter drills are designed to prepare students, staff, and emergency responders for potential threats of violence. Law enforcement can play an important role not only in the implementation of these drills but also as part of a broader culture of school safety. In particular, school resource officers receive specialized training that can equip them with skills beyond traditional law enforcement duties, including crisis response, de-escalation techniques, and youth-engagement strategies. Their presence in schools can support both emergency preparedness efforts and the ongoing well-being of students and staff. The following recommendation outlines best practices for supporting the integration of law enforcement into school safety efforts in a way that is supportive, strategic, and trauma informed.

Recommendation 6: Any sworn law enforcement officer assigned to work in elementary or secondary schools should be properly trained to work with students in an educational environment and properly prepared to respond in a developmentally appropriate manner to the mental, emotional, and behavioral health needs of school-aged children and adolescents.

- **State legislatures should require that all law enforcement officers assigned to schools—including full-time school resource officers and other sworn law enforcement officers stationed temporarily in schools—complete specialized training in supporting student well-being and contributing to safe, developmentally appropriate emergency responses that mitigate adverse**

mental, emotional, and behavioral health outcomes for students and school staff.
- Law enforcement officers assigned to work in elementary or secondary schools should be trained in the specific drills and security measures used in the schools they serve to ensure coordinated and effective responses.
- School districts and law enforcement agencies should verify that all officers working in schools have completed the required training prior to any school assignment.
- Researchers, education policy organizations, law enforcement training institutes, and law enforcement professional organizations should conduct research on the effectiveness of school resource officer training for all law enforcement officers assigned to schools, with a particular focus on their role in school active shooter drills and develop standardized training curricula for use nationwide.

Required training for law enforcement officers assigned to schools can include child and adolescent development, trauma-informed care, developmentally appropriate practices, ways of supporting students with disabilities, and approaches that can serve students across different school environments and community settings. To minimize harm during active shooter drills, training can emphasize the exclusion of high-intensity, high-sensorial elements and prohibit the use of deceptive tactics such as false alarms or staged injuries.

To ensure that officers are adequately prepared for their role in school active shooter drills, training curricula could also cover coordinated emergency response protocols, strategies for minimizing student trauma during drills, and best practices in communication for guiding school staff and students in high-stress situations. State law enforcement training academies could adopt curricula aligned with the committee's best-practice guidance. The impact of this policy could be measured by the number of officers completing certified training programs aligned with the best practices identified by the committee, by law enforcement participation in school emergency drills, and by student and staff perceptions of officer preparedness and responsiveness.

Districts can also explore opportunities to include school resource officers in ongoing professional development related to mental, emotional, and behavioral health, in alignment with the training received by school staff. The success of these efforts could be measured by school climate assessments; evaluations of officer involvement in emergency preparedness; and student feedback on how drills—and the role of law enforcement officers specifically—impact mental, emotional, and behavioral health outcomes.

To understand the effectiveness of training efforts, studies can evaluate how well law enforcement officers apply their training in emergency scenarios, the psychological impact of drills on students, and best practices for ensuring that drills are both effective and developmentally appropriate. NASRO could collaborate with researchers, emergency management experts, and education agencies to develop and refine training curricula and standards aligned with evidence-based guidance. Findings could inform continuous improvement of training for law enforcement officers and related policy decisions at the state and local levels. Measurable outcomes include the generation of an evidence-based standardized curriculum for school resource officer training; adoption of evidence-based improvements to training and drill protocols; documented changes in policies and practices; and documented changes in mental, emotional, and behavioral health outcomes reported by students and staff.

Funding and Resources Needed to Implement Best Practices

Beyond the challenge of navigating an unregulated school safety landscape, many schools lack the funding and resources needed to implement best practices effectively. School safety strategies vary widely in startup costs, implementation demands, and long-term sustainability, and not all schools have access to the financial and personnel resources required for success. Additionally, the true costs of school safety decisions extend beyond direct financial investments. Schools must also account for the time, training, and capacity required to implement these strategies, as well as their potential unintended consequences. For instance, while fear and stress resulting from exposure to school active shooter drills or other security measures is difficult to measure, available research suggests that effects may extend beyond the drill itself.

The committee recognizes that school leaders often must make difficult trade-offs when allocating safety resources, balancing available funding, personnel, and time with the need to adopt effective, evidence-based strategies. To ensure that all schools can implement best practices, addressing funding gaps and resource disparities needs to be a priority. The following recommendation outlines policy aims and funding strategies that can help schools adopt and sustain high-quality safety practices, regardless of the financial constraints they face.

Recommendation 7: To ensure that all schools have sufficient resources to implement best practices in school safety, federal, state, and local governments should ensure that adequate funding is provided and sustained to promote a positive school climate; to foster safe and healthy learning environments; and to design, monitor, and evaluate school safety measures and policies, especially as they relate to reducing potential negative mental, emotional, and behavioral health impacts.

- **Congress should fund the provisions of the Bipartisan Safer Communities Act pertaining to school safety initiatives, violence prevention efforts, and programs that promote a positive school climate.**
- **In the absence of federal action, state legislatures and education agencies should establish school safety**

grant programs to provide targeted funding for safety initiatives, student mental health, and program evaluation.
- **Local school boards and municipal governments should allocate discretionary education funds to support school safety programs if federal or state funding is unavailable or inadequate.**
- **Foundations, corporate sponsors, and community organizations should be engaged to provide supplemental funding for developmentally appropriate school safety initiatives, particularly in underfunded districts.**

Federal funding pertaining to school safety initiatives, violence prevention, and programs to improve school climate can ensure that schools have access to an adequate number of school-based health and well-being staff, including school counselors, school psychologists, school nurses, and school social workers, to support students in general, and specifically to assist with planning and implementing school active shooter drills and broader school violence prevention strategies. The funding should also support program evaluation to ensure that (1) resources are allocated to the most effective interventions; (2) they do not negatively impact mental, emotional, and behavioral health; (3) they promote positive mental, emotional, and behavioral health; and (4) schools have sufficient access to qualified professionals to support student mental health and overall well-being. Measurable outcomes for this action include increasing the number of schools receiving funding; collecting comprehensive data on program impact that include assessment of mental, emotional, and behavioral health impacts; documenting favorable student reports of school safety and school climate; and providing increased access to school-based mental health professionals.

State-level safety grant programs could be modeled after legislation such as the Bipartisan Safer Communities Act to provide targeted funding for safety initiatives, student mental health, and program evaluation. These programs could prioritize schools in under-resourced areas and ensure that best practices are implemented statewide. The success of these efforts could be measured by tracking the number of schools funded at the state level, reductions in disciplinary incidents, increased availability of school-based health professionals, and improvements in student and staff perceptions of school safety.

At the local level, school boards and municipal governments can allocate discretionary education funds to support school safety programs. By integrating safety initiatives into existing budget allocations, school districts can ensure that critical programs continue without disruption. The impact of these actions could be measured by monitoring the number of schools implementing developmentally appropriate safety measures, improvements in school climate as reported by students, and positive trends in school discipline.

Partnerships with foundations, corporate sponsors, and community organizations may also fill critical resource gaps and ensure that schools have access to necessary resources even in the absence of government support. The success of this approach could be measured by the total amount of private funding secured, the number of schools benefiting from these funds, and the assessments of the effectiveness of safety programs.

Accommodations for Students and Staff with Disabilities and Functional and Access Needs

The committee's review found significant variation in how school active shooter drills are implemented across districts and schools, and very little information addressing accommodations for students and staff with disabilities and functional and access needs. At the committee's public information-gathering sessions and during its series of listening sessions, multiple speakers highlighted planning; accessibility compliance; and the availability of supports for students with mobility, sensory, and other functional needs.

In some cases, inadequate planning or inadequate staffing results in drills that fail to account fully for the needs of all students.

Beyond logistical challenges, the lack of consistency in implementation also affects how safe and supported students feel during these drills. Ensuring that all students—including those with disabilities—are considered, accommodated, and included in planning efforts is critical for fostering a school environment in which every student feels secure. The following recommendation is aimed at supporting the effective implementation of school active shooter drills.

Recommendation 8: Students with disabilities should have equal access to emergency preparedness activities—including school active shooter drills—to ensure their safety during emergencies. Policies at the federal, state, and local levels should ensure that emergency preparedness measures address the individual needs of students, and schools should provide accommodations that allow students with disabilities to participate effectively in active shooter drills without compromising their well-being.

- **Federal agencies, including the U.S. Department of Education, the Department of Justice, and the Federal Emergency Management Agency, should issue formal guidance clarifying how schools should apply the Americans with Disabilities Act, the Individuals with Disabilities Education Act, and Section 504 of the Rehabilitation Act of 1973 to school active shooter drills.**
- **If federal action is delayed, state education agencies, legislatures, and emergency management agencies should take the lead in ensuring that students with disabilities are fully included in emergency drills with necessary accommodations. State laws and policies should mandate that schools plan proactively for accessibility in preparedness efforts.**
- **School districts, local education agencies, and municipal governments should take immediate steps to ensure that active shooter drills are accessible to**

students with disabilities by integrating clear accessibility measures into their planning and implementation.
- Disability advocacy organizations, educational foundations, and private- sector partners should collaborate to develop training materials and best-practice toolkits that support schools in implementing accessible active shooter drills.
- Researchers, universities, and disability advocacy organizations should collaborate to study the effectiveness of accessible active shooter drills, particularly their impact on students with disabilities.

Federal guidance clarifying how schools should the Americans with Disabilities Act (ADA), the Individuals with Disabilities Education Act (IDEA), and Section 504 of the Rehabilitation Act of 1973 to school active shooter drills could articulate the need for accessible emergency preparedness activities, including testing and evaluation of accommodations for students and staff with disabilities during school active shooter drills. Schools need guidance on integrating drill-related accommodations into IEPs and Section 504 plans, ensuring meaningful inclusion without causing undue distress or safety risks. Additionally, federal guidance can outline best practices for students with disabilities, their families, and service providers in drill planning to ensure that functional and access needs are considered at every stage. To monitor compliance with federal law, agencies can recommend regular reviews of emergency drill policies, data collection on accessibility challenges, and reporting on barriers and solutions. The effectiveness of these measures could be tracked by monitoring the number of schools incorporating individualized emergency plans for students with disabilities and feedback from students, parents, and educators on the implementation of these accommodations. Additionally, federal agencies could publish periodic reports summarizing accessibility improvements and ongoing challenges to support the refinement of future guidance and best practices.

State laws and policies can mandate that schools plan proactively for accessibility in preparedness efforts by requiring that IEPs and 504 plans address emergency drills and response strategies. Additionally, states can establish clear accessibility requirements for all school emergency drills, ensuring the inclusion of students with disabilities in preparedness planning. States can also consider accountability measures, such as periodic audits of school compliance and the collection of feedback from students, families, and disability advocates.

At the district and local levels, school districts can ensure that active shooter drills are accessible to students with disabilities by integrating clear accessibility measures into their planning and implementation. This includes providing instructions in accessible formats; ensuring that necessary supports are available before, during, and after drills; and guaranteeing reasonable accommodations tailored to individual student needs. Schools can collaborate with disability service providers and advocacy groups to offer staff training in supporting students with disabilities during drills. Municipal governments can establish local policies and internal protocols that incorporate universal design principles and require accessibility audits. The effectiveness of these efforts could be measured by tracking school and municipal compliance with accessibility protocols, monitoring the number of institutions adopting inclusive drill policies, and conducting post-drill evaluations that gather feedback from students with disabilities on both the adequacy of accommodations and the impact of these drills on their mental, emotional, and behavioral health.

Training materials and best-practice toolkits that support schools in implementing accessible active shooter drills can provide clear guidance on accommodations and incorporate universal design principles and strategies to ensure that students with disabilities can participate safely. Philanthropic funding can be leveraged to support pilot programs that test and refine accessibility strategies in schools, particularly where government funding is unavailable. Success could be measured by the number of schools receiving training and support, the distribution and utilization of accessibility resources (e.g., visual aids, sensory accommodations, text-based alerts), and the integration of best practices into school policies. Additionally, tracking the adoption of emergency preparedness strategies that include practices for improving accessibility in K–12 schools could help in assessing the long-term impact of these efforts.

Studies of the effectiveness of accessible active shooter drills, particularly their impact on students with disabilities, can assess how different accommodation strategies influence student safety, preparedness, and overall well-being, while also identifying best practices for implementation. Research can focus on evaluating real-world emergency outcomes, ensuring that accommodations meaningfully enhance both participation and safety. Findings can be used to inform school policies at all levels, driving improvements in emergency preparedness for students with disabilities. The impact of this research could be measured by the number of high-quality, methodologically rigorous studies conducted; by the extent to which research-based recommendations are adopted in school emergency plans; and by documented improvements in students' experiences with drills, including both the effectiveness of accommodations and their overall well-being.

While federal laws such as the ADA, IDEA, and Section 504 of the Rehabilitation Act have historically established protections for students with disabilities, some students with functional and access needs may not be covered under these statutes. For example, students experiencing temporary impairments, heightened anxiety, sensory sensitivities, or other acute challenges may require additional considerations during school active shooter drills.

Schools can take proactive steps to support these students by identifying individual needs, incorporating flexible accommodations, and ensuring that all students are able to participate safely in emergency preparedness efforts. Creating a schoolwide culture of accessibility not only benefits students with legally recognized disabilities but also provides critical support to those who may otherwise fall outside existing legal protections.

Recommendation 9: Schools should establish clear standards to ensure that active shooter drills are accessible to all students and staff and accommodate functional and access needs to ensure full participation and safety during emergencies. To address this obligation, specific requirements should be established to guide the planning and implementation of school active shooter drills that prioritize safety for all students and staff.

- **The U.S. Department of Education, the Federal Emergency Management Agency, and the Department of Justice should issue guidance for ensuring that functional and access needs are addressed in school emergency preparedness efforts.**
- **State legislatures and education agencies should implement policies requiring schools to proactively identify and support students and staff with functional and access needs in emergency preparedness activities.**
- **School districts should develop clear protocols for meeting functional and access needs during school active shooter drills.**
- **Philanthropic organizations and private-sector partners should support the development of training materials and guidance for school staff and safety teams, as well as pilot programs that help schools implement inclusive emergency preparedness practices.**
- **Universities, research institutions, and advocacy groups should collaborate to study the effectiveness of accessible emergency preparedness measures, particularly their impact on students with functional and access needs.**

Federal guidance for ensuring that functional and access needs are addressed in school emergency preparedness efforts can include best practices for identifying and accommodating students and staff with needs related to mobility, sensory capacity, cognitive capacity, communication, and mental health issues during active shooter drills. Federal agencies can also fund research and pilot programs to evaluate accessibility strategies that promote inclusive participation without compromising safety. Compliance with these best practices can be encouraged through federal school safety grants. The effectiveness of these efforts could be measured by the number of states incorporating federal guidance into their emergency preparedness policies, by the extent to which federally funded programs improve accessibility in school drills, and by feedback from schools on the implementation of these strategies.

State-level policies can require schools to conduct accessibility audits of their active shooter drills to ensure that emergency plans account for those with mobility impairments, sensory processing differences, and communication barriers, as well as the needs of individuals with heightened vulnerabilities such as anxiety or PTSD. States can also establish training programs for school personnel on how to recognize and address functional and access needs in emergency drills. To assess impact, states could track the number of districts conducting accessibility audits and adopting inclusive drill policies, and seek feedback from students, staff, and families on the effectiveness of these accommodations.

Clear protocols for supporting functional and access needs during school active shooter drills can encompass offering instructions in accessible formats (e.g., visual, auditory, simplified language, multiple languages); ensuring that necessary supports are available before, during, and after drills; and providing alternative participation options for those who are likely to experience distress. For districts developing protocols, collaboration with disability service providers, families, and students can ensure that drills are designed to be inclusive and minimally disruptive. Success at the school level could be measured by the percentage of schools implementing accessibility protocols in active shooter drills; by student and staff feedback on the adequacy of accommodations; by documented improvements in student preparedness; and by documented improvements in mental, emotional, and behavioral health outcomes resulting from the implementation of these supports.

To support the development of training materials and guidance for school staff and safety teams, and pilot programs that help schools implement inclusive emergency preparedness practices. Philanthropic organizations and private-sector partners could fund demonstration projects that test and refine accessibility strategies, particularly in under-resourced schools where government funding may be unavailable. Additionally, philanthropic organizations can play a role in raising awareness about the importance of meeting functional and access needs in emergency preparedness. Success could be measured by the number of schools receiving training and resources, the expansion of pilot programs that test inclusive preparedness strategies, and the integration of best practices into school policies.

Finally, universities, research institutions, and advocacy groups collaborating to study the effectiveness of accessible emergency preparedness measures, particularly their impact on students with functional and access needs, can focus research on evaluating different accommodation strategies; assessing real-world emergency outcomes; identifying any effects on mental, emotional, and behavioral health outcomes; and identifying best practices for ensuring full participation in drills. These findings can inform school policies and state-level guidance. The impact of these efforts could be tracked by the number of high-quality, methodologically rigorous studies conducted to examine these topics; by the extent to which research-based recommendations are adopted in school emergency plans; and by documented improvements in the inclusivity of school preparedness activities.

CONCLUSION

School active shooter drills can be conducted in a way that mitigates the potential to harm mental, emotional, and behavioral health. Success depends on their being integrated within a comprehensive school safety strategy that prioritizes prevention, preparedness, and well-being. Schools are responsible not only for responding to emergencies but also for creating an environment that minimizes risks, fosters resilience, and supports student and staff well-being. A strong foundation of violence prevention, mental health support, and a positive school climate ensures that emergency preparedness efforts, including active shooter drills, can enhance safety without causing unnecessary distress. Without these foundational supports, drills risk being isolated events that heighten anxiety instead of reinforcing confidence in emergency response procedures.

A major challenge in implementing active shooter drills is the lack of a strong evidence base accompanied by standardized guidance and oversight. As a result of this widespread deficiency, active shooter drills differ widely across schools and districts. Responsibility for school safety has been dispersed among professional associations, state and federal agencies, and advocacy groups. Addressing this underlying deficiency is a high priority for school systems throughout the country. Responding to this challenge is also a high priority for the nation.

To begin, the nation needs a much stronger evidence base that can inform cohesive, informed approach to safety protocols. Unfortunately, the absence of a clear, research-based set of best practices has left the field open to the use of harmful or ineffective strategies, including high-intensity, hyper-realistic drills; the use of deception; and other elements that can cause distress.

To ensure that drills are conducted in a developmentally appropriate, trauma-informed, and effective manner, schools require strong social-emotional programming, transparent communication, and a well-structured multidisciplinary approach to planning and evaluation. Best practices include planning to tailor drills to the various needs of the school community, ensuring clear communication throughout the exercise, and making wellness supports available during and after the drill. Following a drill, a structured operational debriefing, targeted check-ins with vulnerable students, and an after-action review can help schools assess effectiveness, identify unintended consequences, and continuously improve their emergency preparedness efforts.

The implementation of active shooter drills also needs to be understood within the broader context of school safety. Drills are not a stand-alone solution, but one component of a larger system that includes planning, training, social-emotional learning, trauma-informed approaches, and comprehensive mental health support. When integrated thoughtfully, these elements work together to create an environment where students and staff feel secure, prepared, and supported rather than fearful or overwhelmed. However, achieving this balance requires adequate resources, staff training, and ongoing evaluation—elements not equally accessible across all schools in the nation. School leaders often face difficult trade-offs in resource allocation, weighing available funding, personnel, and time against the need to adopt evidence-based safety strategies that align with their school's unique needs. Ensuring that all schools have the capacity to implement best practices requires attention to funding disparities, professional training, and policy guidance that support schools in making informed decisions.

By embedding school active shooter drills within a holistic framework that balances security and well-being, schools can enhance safety without instilling fear, and nurture a learning environment in which students and staff feel confident, prepared, and supported.

REFERENCES

American Journal of Nursing (2020). *Preparedness or pandemonium? American Journal of Nursing, 120*(5), 14–15. https://doi.org/10.1097/01.NAJ.0000662736.03404.cd

Balfanz, R.W., & Byrnes, V. (2012). The importance of being in school: A report on absenteeism in the nation's public schools. *Education Digest: Essential Readings Condensed for Quick Review, 78*(2), 4–9.

Barrett, K. L., Jennings, W. G., & Lynch, M. J. (2012). The relation between youth fear and avoidance of crime in school and academic experiences. *Journal of School Violence, 11*(1), 1–20. https://doi.org/10.1080/15388220.2011.630309

Boulton, M. J., Trueman, M., & Murray, L. (2008). Associations between peer victimization, fear of future victimization and disrupted concentration on class work among junior school pupils. *The British Journal of Educational Psychology, 78*(3), 473–489. https://doi.org/10.1348/000709908X320471

Braun, S., Schonert-Reichl, K., & Roeser, R. (2020). Effects of teachers' emotion regulation, burnout, and life satisfaction on student wellbeing. *Journal of Applied Developmental Psychology, 69*, 101151. https://doi.org/10.1016/j.appdev.2020.101151

Brymer, M., Taylor, M., Escudero, P., Jacobs, A., Kronenberg, M., Macy, R., Mock, L., Payne, L., Pynoos, R., & Vogel, J. (2012). *Psychological first aid for schools: Field operations guide* (2nd ed). National Child Traumatic Stress Network.

Bulling, D., Farley, J. M., Mantonya, K., Quinn, A., Hanson, B., & Shonerd, J. (2025). *Evaluation of standard response protocol trainings and standard reunification method exercises in Nebraska.*

Center on Positive Behavioral Interventions and Supports (PBIS). (2022). *Supporting schools during and after crisis: A guide to supporting states, districts, schools, educators, and students through a multi-tiered systems of support framework.* https://cdn.prod.website-files.com/5d3725188825e071f1670246/6352e138e38d380284699c57_Supporting%20Schools%20During%20and%20After%20Crisis.pdf

_____. (2025a). *Communicating with families about school safety drills.* https://cdn.prod.website-files.com/5d3725188825e071f1670246/6788818a0e365869b2aa6c17_Communicating%20with%20Families%20about%20School%20Safety%20Drill.pdf

_____. (2025b). *Supporting students who need additional assistance during safety drills.* https://cdn.prod.website-files.com/5d3725188825e071f1670246/67888218d544094a2286718d_Supporting%20Students%20Who%20Need%20Additional%20Assistance%20During%20Safety%20Drills.pdf

Centers for Disease Control and Prevention. (2009). *School connectedness: Strategies for increasing protective factors among youth.*
Cybersecurity and Infrastructure Security Agency. (2025, January 14). *K-12 active shooter drills and programs landscape assessment (in response to DHS Executive Order on Combating Emerging Firearms Threats).* U.S. Department of Homeland Security. https://www.cisa.gov/sites/default/files/202501/DHS%20SchoolBased%20Active%20Shooter%20Drill%20EO_Drills%20Landscape%20Assessment_01-14-25-508.pdf
Division for Emotional and Behavioral Health–CEC. (2024). School shootings: Current status and recommendations for research and practice. *Behavioral Disorders, 49*(2), 116–127. https://doi.org/10.1177/01987429231214801
Donovan, D. J. (2023). Active shooter drills in schools: Are we helping or hurting our kids? *Clinical Pediatrics, 63*(4), 441–443. https://doi.org/10.1177/00099228231180707
Durlak, J., Weissberg, R., Dymnicki, A., Taylor, R., & Schellinger, K. (2011). The impact of enhancing students' social and emotional learning: a meta-analysis of school-based universal interventions. *Child Development, 82* 1, 405–432. https://doi.org/10.1111/j.14678624.2010.01564.x
Everytown for Gun Safety Support Fund, American Federation of Teachers, & National Education Association. (2020). The impact of active shooter drills in schools. Everytown Research. https://everytownresearch.org
Frosch, D. (2014, September 4). Active-shooter drills spark raft of legal complaints. *The Wall Street Journal.* https://www.wsj.com/articles/active-shooter-drills-spark-raft-of-legal-complaints-1409760255
Huskey, M. G., & Connell, N. M. (2021). Preparation or provocation? Student perceptions of active shooter drills. *Criminal Justice Policy Review, 32*(1), 3–26. https://doi.org/10.1177/0887403419900316
The "I Love U Guys" Foundation. (2021). K-12 standard response protocol toolkit. Texas School Safety Center. https://txssc.txstate.edu/tools/srp-toolkit
Kalmbacher, C. (2024, February 1). Michigan agrees to pay $13 million over active shooter drill that left staff and patients at children's psychiatric hospital traumatized because they thought they were going to die. *Law and Crime.* https://lawandcrime.com/lawsuit/michigan-agrees-to-pay-13-million-over-active-shooter-drill-that-left-staff-and-patients-at-childrens-psychiatric-hospital-traumatized-because-they-thought-they-were-going-to-die/
Martaindale, M., & Blair, J. (2019). The evolution of active shooter response training protocols since Columbine: Lessons from the Advanced Law Enforcement Rapid Response Training Center. *Journal of Contemporary Criminal Justice, 35,* 342–356. https://doi.org/10.1177/1043986219840237

Maryland Center for School Safety. (2024). Guidelines for active assailant emergency preparedness: Best practice guidelines for active assailant drills and exercises (MCSS-AA-Drill-Guidelines-2024). Maryland Center for School Safety. https://schoolsafety.maryland.gov/Documents/Reports-Docs/Guidelines/MCSS-AA-Drill-Guidelines-2024.pdf

Miotto, M. B., & Cogan, R. (2023). Empowered or traumatized? A call for evidence-informed armed-assailant drills in U.S. schools. *The New England Journal of Medicine, 389*(1), 6–8. https://doi.org/10.1056/NEJMp2301804

Moore, P., Diliberti, M. K., & Jackson, B. A. (2024). *Teachers' experiences with school violence and lockdown drills: Findings from a 2023 American Teacher Panel Survey*. RAND Corporation.

Moore-Petinak, N., Waselewski, M., Patterson, B. A., & Chang, T. (2020). Active shooter drills in the United States: A national study of youth experiences and perceptions. *Journal of Adolescent Health, 67*(4), 509–513. https://doi.org/10.1016/j.jadohealth.2020.06.015

National Association of School Psychologists (NASP), National Association of School Resource Officers (NASRO), & Safe and Sound Schools. (2021). Best practice considerations for schools in active shooter and other armed assailant drills. https://www.nasponline.org/resources-and-publications/resources-and-podcasts/school-safety-and-crisis/systems-level-prevention/best-practice-considerations-for-armed-assailant-drills-in-schools

National Child Traumatic Stress Network (NCTSN). (2017). *Creating, supporting, and sustaining trauma-informed schools: A system framework*. https://www.nctsn.org/resources/creating-supporting-and-sustaining-trauma-informed-schools-system-framework

_____. (2018). *Creating school active shooter/intruder drills*. https://www.nctsn.org/sites/default/files/resources/fact-sheet/creating_school_active_shooter_intruder_drills.pdf

National Conference of State Legislatures. (2025, April). Supporting safe schools: A report focused on prevention, response, and positive climate. https://www.ncsl.org/education/supporting-safe-schools-a-report-focused-on-prevention-response-and-positive-climate

O'Regan, S. V. (2019, December 13). The company behind America's scariest school shooter drills. *The Trace*. https://www.thetrace.org/2019/12/alice-active-shooter-training-school-safety/

Osher, D., & Berg, J. (2017). *School climate and social and emotional learning: The integration of two approaches*. Edna Bennet Pierce Prevention Research Center, Pennsylvania State University.

Safe and Sound Schools. (2021). *Especially safe: An inclusive approach to safety preparedness in educational settings*. Teaching and training guide. https://safeandsoundschools.org/wp-content/uploads/2021/10/Especially-Safe-Teaching-and-Training-Guide.pdf

Safe Havens International. (n.d.). Lawsuit filed—School employee injured during ALICE training. http://safehavensinternational.org/lawsuit-filed-school-employee-injured-alice-training/

Sawchuk, S. (2020). Indiana teachers sue law enforcement over 'active shooter' simulation. https://www.edweek.org/leadership/indiana-teachers-sue-law-enforcement-over-active-shooter-simulation/2020/08?cmp=SOC-SHR-FB

Schildkraut, J., Greene-Colozzi, E., Nickerson, A. B., & Florczykowski, A. (2023). Can school lockdowns save lives? An assessment of drills and use in real-world events. *Journal of School Violence, 22*(2), 167–182. https://doi.org/10.1080/15388220.2022.2162533

Schildkraut, J., Greene-Colozzi, E. A., & Nickerson, A. B. (2024a). Balancing students' perceptions of safety and emergency preparedness: A quasi-experimental test of protection motivation theory as it relates to lockdown drills. *Victims & Offenders*, 1–22. https://doi.org/10.1080/15564886.2024.2410999

Schildkraut, J., Nickerson, A. B., Vogel, M., & Finnerty, A. (2024b). Assessing the relationship between exposure to violence and perceptions of school safety and emergency preparedness in the context of lockdown drills. *Journal of School Violence, 23* (3), 319–332. https://doi.org/10.1080/15388220.2023.2291655

Schonfeld, D. J., Melzer-Lange, M., Hashikawa, A. N., Gorski, P. A., & Council on Children and Disasters, Council on Injury, Violence, and Poison Prevention, Council on School Health (2020). Participation of children and adolescents in live crisis drills and exercises. *Pediatrics, 146*(3), e2020015503. https://doi.org/10.1542/peds.2020-015503

Schonfeld, D. J., Rossen, E., & Woodard, D. (2017). Deception in schools—When crisis preparedness efforts go too far. *JAMA Pediatrics, 171*(11), 1033–1034. https://doi.org/10.1001/jamapediatrics.2017.2565

Simonetti, J. A. (2020). Active shooter safety drills and US students—Should we take a step back? *JAMA Pediatrics, 174*(11), 1021–1022. https://doi.org/10.1001/jamapediatrics.2020.2592

Trump, K. S. (2014). School active shooter drills trigger lawsuit, injury claims. http://www.schoolsecurity.org/2014/09/school-active-shooter-drills-trigger-lawsuit-injury-claims

U.S. Department of Education (ED). (2000). *A guide to the Individualized Education Program (IEP)*. U.S. Department of Education. https://www.ed.gov/sites/ed/files/parents/needs/speced/iepguide/iepguide.pdf

_____. (2013). *Guide for developing high-quality school emergency operations plans*. https://rems.ed.gov/docs/School_Guide_508C.pdf

_____. (2025). *Considerations for education leaders in preparing for active shooter drills in schools*. https://www.ed.gov/media/document/considerations-education-leaders-preparing-active-shooter-drills-schools

7
Future Research and Evaluation Needs

As often pointed out in this report, the limited body of research bearing on school active shooter drills leaves many important gaps in our knowledge and a corresponding—and compelling—need for new research on the mental, emotional, and behavioral health effects of these active shooter drills. Expanding the research base related to school active shooter drills and other school security measures—and ascertaining their effects on mental, emotional, and behavioral health outcomes—is imperative. The aim of this chapter is to review and summarize the limitations of current knowledge and to sketch a comprehensive plan for future research. This chapter begins with a discussion of limitations of existing research. The chapter then identifies research priorities and key questions for future research to address. It concludes with guidance for improving the data infrastructure available to support this research and opportunities to leverage existing data sources.

CURRENT RESEARCH LIMITATIONS

The committee's review of the available research literature identified key limitations of the existing research on the impact of school active shooter drills and other school security measures on the mental, emotional, and behavioral health of students and staff. This section summarizes those limitations of existing research, as well as the methodological and practical challenges that account for the weak evidence base in this domain.

Challenges with Research Design and Funding

The section "Research Designs" in Chapter 3 identifies key gaps in existing research on school active shooter drills, particularly in the drills' ability to prepare students to respond appropriately during a shooting event and to mitigate harm should such an event occur. The committee identified only one study (Zhe & Nickerson, 2007) that used a control group design with random assignment—the gold standard for determining the causal effect of an intervention such as an active shooter drill. The other studies reviewed relied primarily on weaker research designs, limiting the researchers' ability to determine whether these drills effectively improve students' ability to respond appropriately during a drill or if an actual event occurs. Additionally, the lack of rigorous studies has made it difficult to assess whether active shooter drills have unintended psychological effects that could undermine their intended benefits. As a result, the committee could not draw strong causal conclusions about the extent to which active shooter drills enhance preparedness; reduce harm; or otherwise impact children's mental, emotional, and behavioral health.

Conducting research in K–12 schools can present a unique set of challenges. Methodologically, the lack of standardization of practices for active shooter drills across schools makes it difficult to compare outcomes and effectiveness. Longitudinal studies of mental, emotional, and behavioral health outcomes are complicated by the need to track students, educators, and other school staff over time. In addition, constraints on access to schools, competing priorities for use of instructional time, student and parent consent requirements, and privacy laws can each complicate data collection efforts. Research in educational settings also presents ethical challenges, such as navigating the potential for unintended harm to students and staff, as well as the ethical dilemma posed by research that uses control group designs, with the result that some students may be excluded from potentially beneficial interventions.

Further complicating these challenges—especially with respect to building an evidence base for better understanding the impact of school active shooter drills—are the long-standing impediments to funding research related to firearm violence in the United States. As previously noted, the lack of federal funding for research on prevention of firearm violence is primarily grounded in legislative restrictions such as the Dickey Amendment (1996), which prevented the Centers for Disease Control and Prevention (CDC) from using federal funds to advocate for gun control (Institute of Medicine, 1999). While this law did not explicitly ban research on firearm violence, it led to a significant decrease in funding for such. In 2018, however, Congress clarified that the Dickey Amendment was not intended to prevent CDC from conducting research on firearm violence, and in 2019, allocated $25 million to CDC and the National Institutes of Health to study firearm violence as a public health issue, marking the first federal funding for such research in more than 2 decades (Van Sant, 2019).

The legislative and funding landscape surrounding the Dickey Amendment predated the widespread implementation of active shooter drills in K–12 schools. By 2018, when the law was clarified, approximately 95% of schools were conducting such drills. This figure rose to 98% in the 2019–2020 school year (Rockefeller Institute of Government, 2023). Thus, as many states and school districts began mandating active shooter drills, while rigorous research on their effectiveness, best practices, or the potential psychological impact on students and staff was largely lacking. This delay in pertinent research and assessment has also made it difficult for researchers to evaluate the impact of security measures in schools, such as the presence of armed law enforcement or security personnel and emergency preparedness training. Although some organizations undertook studies during this time to provide guidance, the scope of that research remained limited by the lack of funding needed to build the evidence base.

Data Needs

While the committee sought to examine both short- and long-term impacts of school active shooter drills, almost all the studies reviewed assessed only immediate mental, emotional, and behavioral health outcomes, or used retrospective procedures for which the duration of any changes could not be established. This gap in current knowledge highlights a compelling need for research that prospectively assesses mental, emotional, and behavioral health outcomes over a longer duration (at least several months) after a drill.

Based on its review of the evidence, the committee identified six key areas for future research: (1) best practices for implementing school active shooter drills; (2) the development of standardized measures for assessing the effectiveness of drills; (3) short- and long-term effects on the mental, emotional, and behavioral health of students and staff; (4) ethical considerations for research on, and implementation of, school active shooter drills; (5) funding and the cost of implementation; and (6) community and population contexts. These research needs are discussed in greater detail later in this chapter.

An additional challenge is that existing research lacks uniformity in terminology used to describe school active shooter drills and associated policies and security measures. Greater clarity and specificity of terminology would improve the ability to compare study findings in general, and specifically to identify trends and patterns; aggregate findings across multiple studies; improve the reliability of measurement tools; translate research into consistent, actionable practices in schools; and ensure that researchers, practitioners, policymakers, and other decision-makers are communicating about the same concepts in the same way.

Limited Outcome Measures

Many studies reviewed by the committee used brief, ad hoc outcome measures rather than more comprehensive validated instruments. Use of those measures limits the range of potential outcomes assessed, as well as the committee's confidence that the results of this research are meaningful. For example, it would be important to know whether students become desensitized to drills over time, but this question has yet to be studied. Studies have routinely measured changes in emotions or perceptions post-drill instead of measuring changes in observable behaviors, such as disruptive classroom behaviors, absenteeism, academic achievement, or utilization of mental health support services. For example, many qualitative responders in literature reviewed by the committee in Chapter 3 described how drills disrupt the school day and impede learning, but no studies have assessed learning outcomes (e.g., Bonanno et al., 2021; Jackson & Golini, 2024).

School active shooter drills can affect the school climate, as well as the mental, emotional and behavioral health of individuals in a school. Understanding both short- and long-term outcomes is necessary to identify opportunities for early intervention as well as prevention of adverse effects (CDC, 2024, n.d.; National Institute of Justice, 2022). Short-term outcomes—such as anxiety and depression, social withdrawal, changes in sleep, decreased academic engagement, and burnout and stress among educators and staff—can signal that students or school staff may need support, allowing schools to intervene before negative effects escalate. In addition, an assessment of potential long-term effects is crucial given the risk that unaddressed adverse effects will lead to chronic mental health issues (e.g., long-term anxiety and depression, chronic posttraumatic stress disorder [PTSD], persistent emotional dysregulation) (NASEM, 2019). For educators and other school staff, prolonged stress may also increase burnout and staff turnover. At the same time, while addressing potential risks is critical, it is equally important to identify positive outcomes so as to identify effective and beneficial practices (NASEM, 2019). Building an evidence base to understand these outcomes would give schools, school districts, and policymakers the evidence needed to inform resource allocation for support services, as well as selection of appropriate practices.

Current evidence does not sufficiently capture the full spectrum of potential effects of practices implemented during school active shooter drills on students and staff. Further research employing comprehensive measures is needed to develop a more complete understanding of the ways in which these practices may affect mental, emotional, and behavioral health, as well as how drills may foster the development of prosocial behaviors and competency in self-regulation. It would also be useful to design studies that can identify unanticipated and unintended consequences related to the implementation of school active shooter drills and other security measures. For example, some active shooter drills include training to engage an armed assailant. While such training may decrease the perceived risk in some students or staff, it is unknown whether receiving that training will result in guilt if an individual fails to subdue an assailant in an actual event, or if it may increase the risk of injury in the process.

A comprehensive understanding of both potential positive and negative outcomes of drills will require a research design that incorporates a methodology that goes beyond an examination of anticipated outcomes.

Lack of Subgroup Analysis

Empirical information on how active shooter drills might affect subgroups of students is virtually nonexistent. The committee identified only a few studies assessing different age groups or considering student race, gender, or self-reported trauma exposure as moderators, and even this evidence was limited. Furthermore, aside from a single qualitative study of educators of students with autism spectrum disorder (Jackson & Golini, 2024), the committee found no research investigating how active shooter drills might differentially affect students with functional or access needs (e.g., students with physical or learning disabilities, multilingual learners).

Examination of variations in outcomes by population subgroup is crucial for a number of reasons. Mental, emotional, and behavioral health outcomes can be influenced by a wide array of factors (e.g., age, trauma exposure, community contexts, population-specific stressors, barriers to care, access to social support). Analysis of subgroup variations in outcomes can provide a means of identifying the causes of specific outcomes, which in turn can allow researchers to develop targeted interventions to address adverse impacts on health and well-being and to prevent more severe negative outcomes. These data could also help policymakers make more informed decisions about how to allocate funding, services, and resources to schools to address identified needs.

Insufficient Focus on Individual Drill Components

Very few studies on the impact of school active shooter drills have directly investigated how different types or elements of drills or simulations might affect students and staff (e.g., announced vs. unannounced drills; high-intensity vs. low-intensity), and the committee identified no studies that explored the impact of high-intensity simulations or those involving deception. Most studies featured a group of participants who were all exposed to the same type of drill(s) that happened to be implemented in their school district (e.g., Schildkraut et al., 2022, 2023, 2024). Other studies measured drill components in some way but neglected to assess links between those components and health outcomes. Some studies combined didactic trainings with drills, even though these are different kinds of interventions with different risks (e.g., Dickson & Vargo, 2017). The committee found no "dismantling studies"[30] assessing how different elements of drills affected participants' reactions, nor were there any head-to-head studies comparing participants' reactions to different types of drills. Thus, despite concerns and even lawsuits objecting to high-intensity drills (e.g., Frosch, 2014) those involving realistic actors firing blanks or other simulation elements), the committee found no direct research on how these elements affect students and staff. Likewise, there was no information on how drill type or frequency may contribute to health outcomes of interest—a key question, since some states mandate multiple drills, and all schools must choose how often to implement them.

Some studies on the use of lockdowns in schools using standard response practices examined the committee's outcomes of interest

---

[30] A *dismantling study* isolates and tests individual components of multicomponent treatments to identify which components are responsible for changes and the degree to which individual components are essential or nonessential, and which may be ineffective or harmful.

(e.g., perceptions of emergency preparedness in Schildkraut et al., 2020), but more research is needed to evaluate specific practices, identify supports necessary to ensure proper implementation, and identify effects on mental, emotional, and behavioral health outcomes. As noted in Chapter 2, several states have already adopted the "I Love U Guys" Foundation's Standard Response Protocol. As implementation continues and potentially expands to other states, there is a critical opportunity to evaluate both the specific components of these protocols and their impact on mental, emotional, and behavioral health outcomes across a range of school contexts and student populations.

In this report, the committee recommends that options-based practices be approached with caution because of the existing gaps in the evidence base and increased potential for harms to mental, emotional, and behavioral health. Some options-based practices do not have developmentally appropriate adaptations or alignment with current guidance on appropriate training for students (e.g., NASP et al., 2021). Although some options-based practices provide adaptations for school settings and various age groups, important questions remain about the safeguards necessary to protect the mental, emotional, and behavioral health of students and staff. Additional research is needed to better understand potential risks and determine which components are developmentally appropriate for students at different developmental stages.

Impacts on School Staff and Caregivers

The available research base on the impacts of school active shooter drills focuses primarily on students rather than school staff and says little about how school active shooter drills affect teachers, administrators, school health care providers, security staff, or other key personnel—even though staff reactions to drills, and the overall school climate around drills, could be major influences on student responses (Berk, 2022; Dickson & Vargo, 2017; Kingston et al., 2018; Sprague & Walker, 2021). There is also very little research on caregivers' reactions and preferences around drills, even though parents play an important role in the school's ecosystem while serving as a primary source of support for their children (Eisenberg et al., 1998; Hajal & Paley, 2020; Rutherford et al., 2015).

Within a school ecosystem, the well-being of students and school staff are interconnected. Stress and poor mental health experienced by the adults within the school can negatively impact students and staff's ability to serve as a source of emotional support for students. By contrast, adults who experience their own positive mental health can help to create a school environment where students are more resilient and have better emotion regulation (NASEM, 2019). Moreover, the success of programs, practices, and activities intended to foster positive mental, emotional, and behavioral health depends on the buy-in of school staff and their positive mental health as an essential foundation for implementing those practices effectively. Improving understanding of the impacts of these practices on adults within the school can provide both an opportunity to understand how to mitigate adverse effects on adults and to provide an additional level of support for students.

Evidence on Impacts of School Security Measures on Mental, Emotional, and Behavioral Health Outcomes

Research investigating the potential impacts of school security measures other than school active shooter drills on mental, emotional, and behavioral health outcomes remains thin. A significant constraint in the existing studies is the lack of focus on individual security measures as isolated variables. The majority of studies reviewed by the committee assessed school environments where multiple security interventions—such as the presence of school resource officers, metal detectors, and door locks—were implemented in combination. As a result, it is difficult to disentangle the specific effects of each measure, making it challenging to determine whether particular interventions contribute to or mitigate adverse mental, emotional, and behavioral health outcomes. This research gap underscores the need for more targeted investigations into the independent and combined effects of school security measures on student well-being.

Physical Security Interventions (Door Locks)

The committee found little empirical research focused on door locks. Only one study focused specifically on ease of use of door locks (Martaindale et al., 2023) and the potential for stress to impact the ability to operate certain locking mechanisms. Given the increasing emphasis on school security, this gap represents a significant limitation in understanding how both the presence and functionality of door locks influence perceptions of school safety and the well-being of students and staff. Most research on school security assesses overall safety outcomes instead of isolating the specific role of door locks in shaping experiences of security, fear, or anxiety.

While locks are often assumed to enhance safety, they may also introduce unintended challenges. In older school buildings, for example, infrastructure limitations can prevent the installation of modern, easy-to-use locks. In some cases, if teachers may need to step outside their classrooms to engage a lock, they face the potential for heightened risk exposure during an emergency, which in turn could cause additional stress for both students and staff. Furthermore, research has yet to examine whether variation in the design of door locks influences perceptions of preparedness, or whether students and staff in schools with outdated or malfunctioning locks experience increased anxiety among students and teachers compared with those in schools with more secure locking mechanisms.

Beyond their use in active security incidents, more research is needed to understand how door locks may contribute to the broader psychosocial climate of schools. Because this topic has received very little attention in the empirical literature, variations in experiences and perceptions remain largely unexplored. Research needs to move beyond general evaluations of door locks as a security measure to investigate how the design, accessibility, and usability of locks affect both safety outcomes and mental, emotional, and behavioral health outcomes. Perceptions of staff members would be of particular interest given that they may be responsible for operating door locks or other controlled entry mechanisms.

By focusing on security measures individually, researchers could provide more nuanced guidance for policymakers and school administrators, helping them assess not only the effectiveness of different security measures in preventing harm but also their influence on daily school experiences, anxiety levels, and perceptions of preparedness.

Surveillance Interventions (Metal Detectors)

Metal detectors are one of the most visible school security measures in use, yet their effectiveness both in preventing violence and in their broader impact on student well-being remains underexplored. Evidence reviewed by the committee suggests that metal detectors may be both a deterrent and a potential source of stress. For some individuals, they may contribute to perceptions of security and control over potential threats. For others, however, they may heighten feelings of surveillance or fear (e.g., Cobbina et al., 2019; Gastic, 2011; Perumean-Chaney & Sutton, 2012). In both cases, the extent to which metal detectors contribute to these psychological effects—independent of other security measures—remains unclear.

Research is needed to explore the impact of metal detectors and other surveillance interventions on student and staff perceptions of safety, assessing whether they foster a sense of security or contribute to heightened stress and a punitive atmosphere. Additionally, studies could examine the relationship between metal detectors and mental, emotional, and behavioral health outcomes, particularly whether frequent screenings are associated with increased anxiety or school avoidance behaviors. The role of school infrastructure and implementation also warrants investigation because factors such as building design, multiple entry points, and staffing limitations may affect the effectiveness and perceived fairness of security screenings. Moreover, research is needed to assess how metal detectors interact with other security measures—for example, by determining whether their effectiveness is enhanced when combined with other interventions, including access to mental health supports. A more comprehensive approach to studying metal detectors would provide a clearer understanding of their broader implications for school safety and student well-being beyond their immediate role in preventing violence.

School Security Personnel Interventions

The role of school resource officers and other school law enforcement or security personnel—as part of emergency planning as well as within the broader school context—is complex. As discussed in Chapter 4, there is limited evidence on whether school security personnel influence students' perceptions of safety in a consistent way. For some students, positive interactions with school resource officers may lead them to feel safer in school, while for others, the presence of school resource officers and other school security personnel may signal that the school environment is more dangerous and may therefore decrease perceptions of safety or school connectedness (e.g., McDevitt & Panniello, 2005; Theriot & Orme, 2014). Despite the widespread implementation of these programs, there is little research on the long-term effects of school resource officers on school climate and student well-being. Short-term impacts that have been studied are related primarily to school security and discipline rather than the direct effect of school security personnel on mental, emotional, and behavioral health outcomes. Research on the preventive role of school resources officers and other school security personnel on preventing school violence is also limited and remains inconclusive. Additional research on the direct role of school resource officers and other school security personnel in violence prevention and emergency preparedness activities in schools, and any related effects on mental, emotional, and behavioral health outcomes, is needed.

RESEARCH PRIORITIES AND KEY QUESTIONS

Best Practices for Drill Implementation

Extensive variation in the components of active shooter drills described throughout this report underscores the need for attention to both implementation and outcome. Implementation studies are needed to determine whether schools and training providers conduct the procedures as intended, whereas outcome studies aim determine whether school active shooter drills adequately prepare students and staff for an actual emergency. As discussed in Chapter 4, many school security measures now being implemented lack a robust evidence base, with inconsistent or underdeveloped support of their efficacy. However, given the ethical and practical challenges of using randomized controlled trials and other experimental designs to study school active shooter drills and other security measures, alternative research methodologies—including quasi-experimental, observational, and mixed-methods approaches—are needed to establish best practices for drill implementation.

A key goal of strengthening the research base on drill implementation is to develop guidelines for evidence-based practices that can help in ensuring that drills are both effective and psychologically safe. The needed research includes examining different models of drill implementation, including components that may not be directly enacted during drills themselves, such as the "run, hide, fight" framework. Understanding how different models impact preparedness and well-being can help schools refine their approaches to safety training.

The committee emphasizes that research in this area must also adhere to ethical guidelines that prioritize student and staff well-being. The committee strongly discourages conducting research with students that involves practices already identified as harmful, such as using high-intensity, highly sensorial elements or deception. Randomization is appropriate only when the risks and potential benefits of different options are believed to be equivalent, and there is sufficient consensus that the risks of high-intensity drills outweigh any potential benefits. Research can still be conducted through natural experiments, retrospective studies, and controlled comparisons that do not introduce additional harm.

While some widely used approaches, such as options-based drills, have been promoted as best practices, their effectiveness has not been thoroughly studied. Options-based drills entail training staff and, in some cases, students to assess a situation and decide whether to flee, hide from, or engage an armed assailant. Furthermore, there is concern that these drills—when they are not adapted to be developmentally appropriate for use in schools— may encourage students or staff to put themselves in unnecessary danger. For example, practices that encourage individuals to subdue attackers as heroes may inadvertently reinforce risky behavior or create pressure to act in ways that unduly increase personal risk. Existing best practice guidance emphasizes that confronting an assailant should never be encouraged as part of training students (NASP et al., 2021).

Even well-intentioned interventions may have significant unintended and unanticipated negative consequences. While some students and school personnel report feeling more prepared after participating in drills, self-reports alone are insufficient for guiding policy. Individuals who feel empowered by these drills may underestimate the distress experienced by others with different coping styles, trauma histories, or vulnerabilities. Additionally, the perceived benefits of active participation in training may be misleading; feeling prepared prior to an event does not necessarily translate to effective decision-making or emotional resilience in an actual crisis.

Practices that encourage active participation in emergency response need to be evaluated not only for their immediate effects but also for their long-term psychological impact and potential for unintended harm. Research therefore needs to go beyond measuring short-term confidence to assess outcomes over longer periods, using case studies to explore unintended effects that may not be captured easily with traditional research methods.

In addition to studying active shooter drills, research needs to examine the effects of different standard response practices being used in response to perceived threats, rather than as planned drills.

These unplanned security measures may have different psychological and behavioral impacts on students and staff, particularly in schools where lockdowns are frequent. Data are needed on how often these events occur, how they are experienced by different student subgroups, and what interventions, if any, help mitigate their negative effects.

Some approaches have been proposed for helping students and staff cope with the stress of drills. These include implementing preventive social and emotional learning approaches, ensuring access to school-based mental health professionals, and utilizing psychological first aid techniques. Research is needed to examine the impact of these practices on students' and staff's mental, emotional, and behavioral health outcomes.

While active shooter drills themselves are now widespread, new school safety practices continue to emerge, often with little empirical evidence to support them. It is essential to establish standards for evaluating the effectiveness of new interventions before they are widely adopted. Schools and policymakers should not assume that an intervention is beneficial simply because it is well intended or widely used. Without sufficient evaluation, children and staff effectively become involuntary participants in research on untested safety measures. Research needs to focus on developing clear criteria for evaluating new interventions before they are implemented at scale, ensuring that schools make informed decisions based on strong empirical evidence.

Finally, while much attention has been paid to school active shooter drills, research is also needed on other school security measures, such as armed teachers, metal detectors, and the presence of school resource officers and other school security personnel. Given that schools may use school resource officers or other school security personnel in a variety of ways, differences in training—or lack thereof—among different types of personnel is an area for future research. For example, whether outcomes differ based on trained officers compared with untrained security personnel. If schools are implementing drills in contexts where teachers or other school staff are armed, it is critical to assess the mental, emotional, and behavioral health effects of these policies. Research should examine whether armed personnel impact students' perceptions of safety, increase or reduce fear, and influence student–teacher relationships. Similarly, the psychological effects of security infrastructure, such as metal detectors and surveillance, need to be studied to determine whether these measures contribute to a climate of security or one of fear and distrust.

Ensuring that school safety practices are both effective and psychologically safe requires a strong research foundation. By examining different models of drill implementation, addressing ethical considerations, and evaluating unintended consequences, research can provide critical guidance for schools and policymakers. Ultimately, improving the evidence base for school safety interventions will allow schools to make informed, responsible decisions that balance preparedness with well-being.

Standardized Measures for Assessing the Effectiveness of Drills and Other Security Measures

Assessing the effectiveness of school active shooter drills and other security measures requires a standardized approach to measurement that ensures consistency, reliability, and applicability across varying school contexts. Without clear, validated measures, it is difficult to determine whether these interventions achieve their intended outcomes or inadvertently cause harm. Currently standardized criteria for evaluating the effectiveness of school active shooter drills are lacking, making it challenging to compare results across schools, districts, and student populations. Recent guidance on achieving procedural integrity during the lockdown component of some drills offers a specific and helpful example of the types of effectiveness measures that could be considered (Schildkraut, 2022). However, existing research on the effectiveness of school security measures such as metal detectors, the presence of law enforcement personnel, and the use of door locks has not yet been sufficiently explored across varying school contexts, either individually or when used in combination with one another.

The development and use of standardized outcome measures for assessing active shooter drills and other security measures would provide several key benefits. First, establishing clear, uniform criteria ensures consistency in evaluation across different schools, student populations, and geographic regions. Without standardized measures, assessments may rely on subjective interpretations, making it difficult to compare outcomes meaningfully. Reliable and valid measures also increase confidence in the accuracy of assessments by ensuring that results are consistent over time and truly capture the intended outcomes. This strengthens the ability of schools and researchers to make informed decisions based on sound data.

Standardized measures also allow for comparability across contexts and over time. By using consistent assessment tools, researchers and policymakers can identify patterns, strengths, and areas for improvement across school settings. This comparability enhances understanding of how different approaches to drills impact students and staff, helping in turn to refine best practices. Additionally, having a structured evaluation framework promotes accountability and transparency by providing clear evidence of the impacts on mental, emotional, and behavioral health. Schools can use these data to demonstrate the effectiveness of their practices or to justify adjustments to policies and procedures.

Finally, standardized measures support evidence-based decision-making by helping schools allocate resources effectively and identify areas for improvement. By providing clear, actionable data, such measures allow schools to balance safety preparedness with the psychological and emotional well-being of students and staff. With a better understanding of the effectiveness of active shooter drills, schools can ensure that their safety practices are not only well-intentioned but also truly beneficial.

To develop and validate standardized measures for assessing the effectiveness of active shooter drills, research will need to address several critical questions:
- What outcome measures are needed to assess the effectiveness of drills? Research needs to determine what specific aspects of drills should be measured—such as preparedness,

knowledge retention, or behavioral responses—to provide a comprehensive picture of the effects of drills on students and staff.
- What outcome measures are needed to assess the effectiveness of other school security measures?
- What factors need to be considered in creating and evaluating standardized measures? The committee proposes six factors to consider.
    - *Reliability*: Do the measures produce consistent results over time, ensuring that findings are not influenced by random variations or inconsistencies?
    - *Validity*: Do the measures accurately assess the intended outcomes? Are they truly capturing preparedness and other key constructs related to school safety?
    - *Fairness*: Do the measures work equitably across different school contexts and student populations, including students with disabilities; multilingual learners; and students from differing racial, ethnic, and socioeconomic backgrounds? Are there biases in administration or interpretation that could affect certain groups disproportionately?
    - *Practicality*: Are the measures easy for schools and researchers to use, score, and interpret? Are they cost-effective and feasible for broad implementation?
    - *Impact*: Can the measures detect meaningful changes over time? How do they inform decision-making? Are the results clear and actionable for school leaders, educators, and policymakers?

By addressing these questions, research can help establish robust, ethical, and scientifically sound measures for evaluating school active shooter drills and other school security measures. This research, in turn, can provide schools with the necessary tools needed to make informed, evidence-based decisions that prioritize student and staff well-being while maintaining effective emergency preparedness strategies.

Mental, Emotional, and Behavioral Health Effects on Students and Staff

To advance understanding of the impacts of school active shooter drills and other school security measures on students and staff from a developmental perspective, research is needed to address key questions that can inform evidence-based practices and policies. It is essential to study the immediate, short-, and long-term mental, emotional, and behavioral health outcomes for children and staff in relation to both participation in school active shooter drills and exposure to other school security measures.

To begin, research is needed explore the immediate and short-term mental, emotional, and behavioral health effects of these interventions. For example, studies could assess emotional responses such as anxiety, fear, and stress, and examine how these responses influence classroom behaviors, learning environments, and staff experiences in the workplace. Understanding these short-term reactions is critical to determining whether drills and other security measures create a sense of preparedness or—to the contrary—inadvertently heighten distress.

Beyond these immediate effects, it is essential to investigate the longer-term impacts of both school active shooter drills and other security measures, including whether these practices are associated with shifts in students' school engagement, perceptions of safety, and overall mental well-being over time. Similarly, for staff, research is needed to assess whether repeated exposure to drills and security protocols contributes to changes in job satisfaction, stress levels, or burnout. Ideally, studies would measure mental, emotional, and behavioral health outcomes across multiple time points, including assessments before and immediately after exposure, and at extended intervals postexposure.

In addressing these short- and long-term effects, research will need to consider individual differences that may influence how students and staff experience these interventions. Factors such as age, prior trauma exposure, and disability status are likely to shape responses, with some groups experiencing heightened distress or unique challenges. Additionally, research is needed to examine the differential impacts on subgroups of students, such as multilingual learners or students from communities with high levels of violence, where exposure to safety threats outside of school may interact with the effects of drills. Identifying these differences would facilitate the development of tailored approaches that can minimize harm and better support the needs of all students and staff. To capture these variations, future research will require large sample sizes that support subgroup analyses for populations of interest. Future research also would benefit from including high-quality assessments of mental, emotional, and behavioral health outcomes that are age appropriate and reflect dimensions of both distress and resilience.

To build a comprehensive understanding of how school active shooter drills and security measures impact mental, emotional, and behavioral health outcomes, future research will need to address the following critical questions:

- What are the short-term effects of school active shooter drills and other security measures on mental, emotional, and behavioral health outcomes?
  - How do students experience and react to active shooter drills or the presence of other security measures?
  - How do outcomes vary by age?
  - What are the mental, emotional and behavioral health effects on school staff?
- What are the long-term effects of school active shooter drills and exposure to school security measures?
  - How do active shooter drills and other security measures shape students' perceptions of safety, school engagement, and mental health over time?
  - What are the cumulative effects of repeated exposure to these interventions on staff well-being and workplace satisfaction among staff?
- What measures should be prioritized in research, and what time frames are most appropriate for research?

- What validated measures should be used to assess mental, emotional, and behavioral health outcomes related to drills and security interventions?
- How can research ensure the inclusion of multiple outcome measures to provide a comprehensive understanding of mental, emotional, and behavioral health effects?
- What time frames are most appropriate for assessing both short- and long-term outcomes, and how can data collection be standardized across studies?

By addressing these research questions, future studies could help clarify the full scope of the effects of school active shooter drills and other school security measures, thereby informing policies that support student and staff well-being while balancing safety preparedness with psychological health considerations.

Addressing Ethical Considerations

Research on school active shooter drills presents a complex ethical challenge. These drills, along with other school security measures, are intended to prepare students and staff for potentially life-threatening situations and to protect them from harm. While active shooter events are rare, the consequences of failing to prepare for them can be devastating. At the same time, there is a real concern that some practices that have been implemented in school active shooter drills—particularly the use of high-intensity elements or deception—may cause psychological harm to students and staff. This tension creates a dilemma: How can researchers study the effects of these interventions without either exposing students and staff to unnecessary trauma or withholding preparation that could potentially save lives?

This fundamental ethical tension is not unique to school safety research. Many areas of clinical research, such as medical trials for new drugs or treatments, face similar questions about balancing potential benefits and harms. Ethical research frameworks developed in those fields can inform the design of studies of school active shooter drills and other security measures. For example, one guiding principle from clinical research relevant to this context is "clinical equipoise"—the idea that researchers should conduct trials only when there is genuine uncertainty about which treatment option is best. In the case of school safety interventions, there is little genuine uncertainty about the harms of high-intensity, unannounced, or highly realistic active shooter drills and simulations. Basic science and child development research already indicate that such drills are likely to cause harm, and there is insufficient evidence to suggest that their benefits outweigh these harms. Therefore, it would be unethical to deliberately expose students to high-intensity drills as part of a study just to confirm that they are harmful. However, there are several ethical research strategies that *can* be used to study school active shooter drills without introducing new risks to students and staff.

Instead of traditional randomized controlled trials, researchers could use alternative designs that leverage existing school safety practices while minimizing harm:

- *Waitlist control designs*: Common in PTSD and anxiety treatment studies, this design allows researchers to compare outcomes for students who experience an intervention immediately versus those who experience it later. Schools planning to introduce a new type of drill or policy could stagger implementation, allowing researchers to assess the effects without denying schools access to preparation.
- *Staggered enrollment*: Used in some vaccine trials, this method involves phasing in an intervention over time, allowing for comparisons between early adopters and later participants. In school safety research, this approach could be applied if a district were rolling out a new drill policy across multiple schools, enabling researchers to study the effects over time while ensuring that all schools eventually receive the intervention.
- *Natural experiments*: Since active shooter drills and other school security measures are already in place across the

country with substantial variation among states, districts, and schools, researchers could analyze differences that already exist instead of introducing new interventions. For example, comparing schools that already conduct drills at different frequencies could help in assessing the impact on student and staff wellbeing using statistical controls to adjust for non-random assignment.
- *Embedded adaptive trials*: Common in drug trials, these studies actively monitor for negative effects and adjust protocols accordingly. Schools implementing new safety practices could partner with researchers to track mental, emotional, and behavioral health outcomes in real time, adjusting drill intensity or format if signs of harm were to emerge.
- *Longitudinal pre–post studies*: Many existing studies on active shooter drills rely on cross-sectional designs instead of tracking the same students over time. High-quality longitudinal studies that followed students before and after drills could provide stronger evidence on the long-term psychological effects of these interventions without requiring new, potentially harmful drill scenarios.

Regardless of the specific research design used, nearly all ethically sound studies on the mental, emotional, and behavioral health effects of school safety measures require close collaboration with schools, districts, or even multiple jurisdictions. Partnerships between researchers and educational institutions can facilitate access to data, ensure that studies align with school needs, and help implement findings in a way that benefits students and staff. Without these partnerships, conducting rigorous and ethical research in this space will be significantly more difficult.

Given the ethical complexities of studying school active shooter drills and other security measures, research is needed to explore both the ethical considerations involved in conducting such studies and the responsible implementation of these interventions in schools. On the one hand, researchers have to determine how to study the effects of school active shooter drills and other security measures without introducing unnecessary harm to students and staff. On the other hand, schools need guidance on how to design and implement drills in ways that minimize potential adverse outcomes while still achieving the intended safety and preparedness goals. The following questions highlight key areas for further research:

- Ethical considerations in research
  - How can researchers study the effects of school safety measures without exposing students and staff to unnecessary harm?
  - What research designs provide the most ethical and methodologically sound way to assess mental, emotional, and behavioral health outcomes resulting from participation in school active shooter drills or the use of other security measures?
  - How can researchers and school leaders collaborate to conduct high-quality studies while prioritizing student and staff well-being?
- Research on ethical implementation of school active shooter drills
  - How can active shooter drills be conducted in a trauma-informed manner?
  - How should decision-makers balance the need for safety with the potential for harm?
  - What are the ethical considerations for implementing drills across varying student populations and community contexts, including students with disabilities, multilingual learners, and students from communities with high exposure to violence?

By addressing these ethical and practical questions, future research could help schools refine their safety practices in ways that would both protect students from external threats and support their long-term mental, emotional, and behavioral well-being.

Funding and Cost of Implementation

Schools and districts are tasked with making critical safety decisions within the constraints of limited budgets. While the committee has proposed practices for mitigating the negative impacts of school active shooter drills and other security measures on mental, emotional, and behavioral health outcomes, the financial feasibility of implementing these practices remains a key challenge. Understanding the costs associated with various interventions and identifying sustainable funding sources are essential to ensuring that schools can adopt effective, evidence-based approaches without compromising other essential services.

However, funding decisions cannot be made in isolation—they must be informed by a broader understanding of intervention effectiveness, student and staff outcomes, and community and population needs. Without this context, limited resources may be directed toward interventions that are ineffective, exacerbate harm, or fail to meet the needs of schools across a variety of contexts. Research into the costs associated with the implementation of school safety and emergency preparedness measures needs to be integrated with research on the effectiveness of interventions, the specific outcomes associated with policies and practices, and community and population contexts. When schools must make decisions about how to allocate resources, understanding which interventions yield the best outcomes for students and staff would enable them to prioritize strategies that can promote safety without negatively impacting mental, emotional, and behavioral health outcomes when deciding how to allocate resources. Research that goes beyond cost assessments to examine the real-world impacts of interventions could help to ensure that financial investments lead to meaningful improvements in the well-being of students and staff rather than unintended harm. Moreover, research on community and population contexts can help schools and districts better understand their local needs and constraints, enabling them to prioritize investments in interventions that are both effective and contextually appropriate.

By examining these financial considerations, research could help ensure that school safety policies are not only evidence based but also economically viable, available for all schools, and aligned with the best interests of students and staff. It will be important for research to assess the financial burden of various school safety and emergency preparedness measures, including school active shooter drills, the presence of school resource officers, surveillance technologies, and alternative trauma-informed approaches, while also examining their effectiveness in promoting student well-being. However, understanding cost alone is not enough; policymakers and administrators must also consider how financial constraints influence the implementation of these measures and weigh their potential benefits and harms. They therefore need research into cost-effectiveness; resource distribution; and the trade-offs between these interventions and other essential student support services, such as mental health services and other prevention-based interventions.

At the same time, funding decisions are shaped by the broader landscape of available financial resources. Historically, federal, state, and local funding streams have dictated which policies and practices are adopted. However, these funding mechanisms come with limitations, including restrictions on how funds can be used and disparities in how resources are allocated across districts. A clearer understanding of these financial constraints can help policymakers and school leaders identify opportunities to invest in evidence-based practices that better align with student and staff needs. Key research questions include the following:

- What is the cost of existing interventions and policies?
- What are key considerations for schools, districts, and states as they make funding decisions, and how do these considerations vary in relation to community and population contexts?
- What are the funding streams available to implement policies and practices?
- What are the long-term costs—both financial and social—of failing to implement effective interventions?

- Do ineffective or underfunded interventions result in greater long-term economic or social costs?

Embedding financial considerations within the broader research agenda would help to ensure that schools are equipped to make informed and sustainable decisions that meet their needs and implement practices that meet the needs of all students and staff.

Community and Population Context

Schools exist within broader community ecosystems that can influence the implementation of school security and preparedness interventions. Understanding the potential impacts of school active shooter drills or the use of other security measures across community and population contexts is essential for ensuring that policies are effective for all students and do not exacerbate potential adverse outcomes. Research needs in this area include exploring how student and staff experiences vary based on such factors as demography, geography, resource availability, community safety levels, and prior traumatic experiences. Examining these variations can aid in better assessing the extent to which school safety and preparedness practices support or hinder well-being and identify strategies for mitigating potential harms.

Mental, emotional, and behavioral health outcomes related to school security measures vary across student populations. Factors such as age, disability status, home language, and prior trauma exposure can shape how students experience and respond to school active shooter drills and other school security measures. Key research questions include the following:

- How do different age groups perceive and respond to school active shooter drills?
- Are younger children more likely than older students to experience fear and anxiety?
- How do perceptions of school safety differ across urban, suburban, and rural communities?

- Do students in areas with higher levels of community violence perceive school security measures differently compared with those in lower-crime areas?
- How do students with disabilities or functional and access needs, including those with sensory sensitivities or cognitive differences, experience school active shooter drills or such practices as the use of metal detectors and surveillance measures? What accommodations can be made to minimize their distress?
- Do linguistic barriers impact students' understanding of and response to school safety protocols?
- How can schools ensure that emergency preparedness measures are accessible to students and families who speak a home language other than the primary language of instruction?
- How do community attitudes toward law enforcement and institutional trust shape students' responses to school safety measures?
- How do active shooter drills and other security measures affect students and staff with prior trauma exposure, including those from communities disproportionately impacted by violence? Are there evidence-based strategies for reducing the potential to retraumatize students and staff?
- What are the differential impacts of school safety and preparedness practices on students from different backgrounds or community contexts?
- In what ways do local policy decisions and state-level mandates influence the frequency, intensity, and psychological impact of school safety and emergency preparedness interventions?

Centering research on the realities of students and staff across a variety of contexts offers an opportunity to move beyond a singular approach to school safety. A more nuanced understanding of how security measures affect different populations can help to inform policies that protect students and staff without causing undue harm to their mental, emotional, and behavioral health and well-being.

IMPROVING DATA INFRASTRUCTURE

As described in the previous chapters, a great deal of variation is seen across schools, districts, states, and regions with respect to the types, features, and frequency of school active shooter drills and other school security measures and safety practices. What is known about these variations is often cobbled together and piecemeal; no comprehensive data infrastructure exists with which to track school security and safety measures at the national or state levels.

Improved data infrastructure will be essential if research is to formulate a clear account of the impact, including both benefits and costs, of school active shooter drills and other school security measures. While some data exist on school crime and safety, there are significant gaps in understanding how drills and other security practices affect students' mental health and overall well-being, as well as school climate. Strengthening data collection efforts and ensuring more comprehensive tracking of security policies and practices across schools can therefore help inform evidence-based decision-making. Existing surveys, databases, and collections of guidance documents do provide resources for use by schools, administrators, policymakers, and other decision-makers in navigating these complex issues (see Box 7-1). These resources can serve as a starting point for enhancing data collection—whether by adding questions to existing surveys, incorporating supplementary guidance documents, or developing new indicators—to track the effects of school active shooter drills and other security measures on students and staff.

BOX 7-1
Schools Safety Resources

SchoolSafety.gov
SchoolSafety.gov is a collaborative, interagency website created by the federal government to provide schools and

---

districts with actionable recommendations for creating safe and supportive learning environments for students and educators. The site serves as a one-stop access point for information, resources, guidance, and evidence-based practices on a range of school safety topics. Through the site, members of the K–12 academic community can also use tools to prioritize school safety actions, find applicable resources and funding opportunities, connect with state and local school safety officials, and develop school safety plans. SchoolSafety.gov is the public website of the Federal Clearinghouse on School Safety Evidence-Based Practices, an interagency effort among the departments of Education, Health and Human Services, Homeland Security, and Justice. The Clearinghouse serves as an ongoing and coordinated effort that includes regular interagency review of evidence-based content and recommended best practices for keeping schools safe, as well as the curation and distribution of resources, guidance, and tools for school communities across the country.

Center for Homeland Defense and Security (CHDS) School Shooting Safety Compendium

This compendium provides links to relevant data on and analyses of gun violence in American primary and secondary schools from reputable sources including the CHDS. While no amount of scientific study can fully explain the tragedy of school shooting incidents, singly or as a phenomenon, it is hoped that this compilation of knowledge can contribute to solutions and ultimately to the security of these vital institutions.

Readiness and Emergency Management for Schools (REMS)[a]

The U.S. Department of Education's Office of Safe and Supportive Schools has administered the REMS Technical Assistance Center to serve two critical functions aimed at helping education agencies, along with their community partners, manage safety, security, and emergency management programs. The Center helps build the preparedness capacity (including prevention, protection, mitigation, response, and recovery efforts) of schools, school districts, higher education institutions, and their community partners at the local, state, and federal levels. Through its website it also serves as their primary source of information on emergency management.

National Conference of State Legislatures: School Safety Archived Database[b]

This searchable database tracks school safety legislation introduced by state legislatures from 2018 to 2022. Issues tracked include firearms in K–12 schools, use of school resource officers, training requirements, and building security.

K–12 School Shooting Database (SSDB)[c]

This database, started as a school project in 2018 after the Parkland High School shooting, includes school shootings dating back to 1966 (expanded from 1970). It includes detailed information about every school shooting, a reliability score that quantifies the dependability of the information, and the verified primary source citation(s) (e.g., newspaper articles, court records, interviews, police reports) to allow for further academic research. Its scope is widely inclusive to allow for a comprehensive analysis of school shooting data.

Averted School Violence Database[d]

An averted incident of school violence is a shooting or other planned violent attack that was prevented before any injury or loss of life occurred at the targeted educational institution. Since 2015, school personnel, law enforcement officers, mental health professionals, and others involved in school safety have had the opportunity to share their averted school violence stories and lessons learned, with the aim of improving school safety and helping to prevent future tragedies. Cases are included in the database on the basis of means, opportunity, motive, and intent to carry out

> a targeted school attack. Incidents of violence on school grounds not related to the school (e.g., gang-related violence) and social media threats not deemed credible by law enforcement are excluded from the database.
>
> a https://rems.ed.gov
> b https://www.ncsl.org/education/school-safety-overview-and-legislative-tracking
> c https://k12ssdb.org
> d https://www.avertedschoolviolence.org

Fortunately, there are opportunities to leverage existing data collection and reporting efforts to better understand the landscape of school active shooter drills and other school security measures at the state and national levels, as well as their impacts on the mental, emotional, and behavioral health of students and staff.

The National Center for Education Statistics (NCES) administers a number of surveys and collects data through direct student assessments, longitudinal studies, and adult surveys, among others. NCES data collections could incorporate information about, for example, participation in school active shooter drills, utilization of mental health professionals, lost learning time, or absenteeism after drills. NCES's National Teacher and Principal Survey[31] may be a particularly useful vehicle for examining impacts on staff, and the Early Childhood Longitudinal Studies[32] could provide opportunities to gain insights into the potential cumulative effects of experiencing drills year after year.

Similarly, the Youth Risk Behavior Surveillance System,[33] administered by CDC, monitors adolescent health behavior and experiences of injury and violence, school connectedness, and exposure to community violence. Questions related to active shooter drills and other school security measures could be added to this instrument to

---

[31] See http://nces.ed.gov/surveys/ntps
[32] https://nces.ed.gov/ecls
[33] https://www.cdc.gov/yrbs/index.html

assess youth perceptions and mental, emotional, and behavioral health outcomes.

Specific to school crime and safety, the *Report on Indicators of School Crime and Safety* reports on school crime and safety data in the United States. Produced by NCES with contributions from the U.S. Department of Justice's Bureau of Justice Statistics, it provides indicators on elementary and secondary student and teacher victimization; school environment; fights and weapons; safety, security, and mental health practices; and postsecondary campus safety and security. To better understand the mental, emotional, and behavioral health effects of other school security measures, questions designed to assess changes in perceptions of safety resulting from the use of multiple and individual security measures, effects on school attendance and avoidance, and effects on school climate could be added to this data collection.

Similarly, the School Survey on Crime and Safety (SSOCS),[34] administered to school principals, is a nationally representative cross-sectional survey of about 4,800 public elementary and secondary schools. This survey offers the ability to explore the impacts of other school security measures on student and staff mental, emotional, and behavioral health, providing estimates of school crime, discipline, disorder, and programs and policies. The SSOCS questionnaire asks principals to report on a variety of topics related to crime and safety, including frequency and types of crimes at schools (e.g., homicide, rape, sexual assault, attacks with or without weapons, robbery, theft, vandalism), perceptions of other disciplinary problems (e.g., bullying, verbal abuse, disorder in the classroom), description of school policies and programs concerning crime and safety, description of the pervasiveness of student and teacher involvement in efforts that are intended to prevent or reduce school violence, mental health services available to students at school, responsibilities of sworn law enforcement officers and school resource officers, and general school characteristics. In order to better understand the mental, emotional, and behavioral health effects of other

---

[34] https://nces.ed.gov/surveys/ssocs

school security measures, questions assessing student perceptions of safety and anxiety related to the use of physical safety measures, trust in school resource officers, impact on school climate and feelings of belonging, changes in school avoidance and engagement, and staff perceptions of the impact of security measures on their ability to build positive relationships with students could be added to this data collection.

As detailed in previous chapters, school active shooter drills and other school security measures need to be part of comprehensive school safety planning, and school climate is a critical component of safety planning in supporting students' development, safety, and well-being. Yet, school climate is not regularly assessed, and many districts lack the baseline infrastructure needed to support improvements in or examination of district-level conditions that might enable or facilitate better school environments. California offers one such state-level model for encouraging local educational agencies to administer school climate surveys and integrate the results into reporting and continuous improvement systems. In 2024, California began requiring local educational agencies to administer school climate surveys annually and to report the results as part of their local control and accountability plans and the state-level public data dashboards (Klevan et al., 2024).

Growing public concern about the safety of students in schools over the past 25 years has led to increasing interest in research on the frequency of school violence occurring within the United States, especially since the shooting at Columbine High School. However, there is no federal reporting requirement for school shooting events. Here, too, data are collected in a piecemeal fashion through a number of public information sites and databases. While these resources offer accessible opportunities to investigate the trends and patterns in school violence, they are not comprehensive. A federal reporting requirement for school shooting events is needed, to include a standard definition and prospective and ongoing data collection, including when active shooter protocols or related practices (e.g., lockdowns) are implemented in schools.

CONCLUSION

Ensuring school safety while minimizing harm to students and staff during active shooter drills is a complex but essential task. It is an unfortunate reality that youth and adults armed with firearms pose a genuine threat to the nation's schools. School active shooter drills and other school security measures are widely implemented despite a notably thin evidence base bearing on their effectiveness and safety of these preventive interventions. As a result, this committee was charged with assessing current school practices and recommending an evidence-based path forward. Specifically, the committee was charged with addressing growing concerns about the potential mental, emotional, and behavioral health effects of school active shooter drills on students and staff. While emergency preparedness is necessary, current practices need to be reshaped. Better understanding of the adverse effects of those practices is crucial—especially given the widespread implementation of school active shooter drills across the United States, which affects millions of students and staff (and their families) annually. Advancing the research needed to gain this understanding would enable decision-makers to minimize harm, develop interventions that are responsive to participants' needs, identify and evaluate best practices, allocate resources effectively, and create safe and supportive learning environments.

One of the central findings of this report is the wide variation in how schools conduct active shooter drills and implement other security measures. Without standardized criteria for evaluation, it is difficult to determine which approaches, if any, effectively enhance safety and preparedness without causing psychological harm. Developing standardized measures for monitoring and assessing the outcomes of drills and other security measures would improve data reliability, enable meaningful comparisons across contexts, and strengthen the ability of schools to implement evidence-based practices.

Future research needs to investigate the cumulative impact of repeated drills, as these are not isolated experiences for most students but a recurring feature of their school lives. Given that these drills often occur multiple times each year, understanding how repeated exposure influences long-term mental, emotional, and behavioral health outcomes is critical. Additionally, more attention is needed on the effects of drills on adults, both to avoid harm to their own well-being and to better understand how their responses influence students' experiences. Similarly, it will be important for future research to shift toward investigating demonstrable behavioral changes post-drill instead of relying solely on self-reported perceptions, which may not always align with actual preparedness or decision-making in high-stress situations.

Equally important is the need for research that accounts for community and population contexts. The lack of empirical data on how school active shooter drills affect different subgroups of students and staff highlights a clear gap in the existing evidence base. Individual characteristics—such as age, disability status, prior trauma exposure, or need for additional supports—may significantly influence how individuals participate and are affected by drills. Future studies will need to incorporate a more inclusive approach to ensure that school safety practices do not disproportionately harm the most vulnerable populations.

It will be critical for ethical considerations to remain at the forefront of future research efforts. Many traditional experimental methods, such as randomized controlled trials, are impractical or unethical in this context. However, thoughtful and creative research designs—such as modified waitlist–control protocols, natural experiments, and longitudinal studies—can help researchers overcome these ethical challenges while maintaining methodological rigor. It is essential that research focus on developing best practices for drill implementation that balance safety preparedness with trauma-informed approaches to minimize distress and maximize effectiveness.

Additionally, research needs to extend beyond active shooter drills to examine the broader landscape of school security measures. Policies such as arming teachers, employing school resource officers, and using surveillance technologies, carry their own risks and possible benefits. Unfortunately, they often lack strong empirical support. Future studies are needed to explore the mental, emotional, and behavioral health effects of these practices, ensuring that all school safety policies are rooted in a robust evidence base.

Finally, while many school safety policies and practices have already been implemented without thorough prior evaluation, it is imperative—going forward—that new interventions undergo rigorous assessment before widespread adoption. Establishing minimum standards for evaluating school safety interventions can prevent harmful or ineffective practices from becoming entrenched and help schools make informed, responsible decisions. Without careful prior evaluation, students and staff may accurately be characterized as research subjects who are being subjected to untested safety measures, a situation that is both ethically and practically unacceptable.

Moving forward, a coordinated research agenda that prioritizes collaboration among researchers, schools, and policymakers is a necessary condition for improving school safety policies and practices. Strengthening the evidence base, developing ethical and effective methodologies, and promoting transparency in decision-making, can help ensure that school safety interventions not only prepare students and staff for emergencies but also protect their long-term mental, emotional, and behavioral well-being.

REFERENCES

Berk, L. E. (2022). *Development through the lifespan.* Sage Publications.

Bonanno, R., McConnaughey, S., & Mincin, J. (2021). Children's experiences with school lockdown drills: A pilot study. *Children and Schools, 43*(3), 175–185. https://doi.org/10.1093/cs/cdab012

Centers for Disease Control and Prevention (CDC). (2024). *Whole School, Whole Community, Whole Child (WSCC): A collaborative approach to learning and health.* U.S. Department of Health and Human Services. https://www.cdc.gov/whole-school-community-child/about/index.html

_____. (n.d.). Youth Risk Behavior Surveillance System (YRBSS). https://www.cdc.gov/yrbs/index.html

Cobbina, J. E., Galasso, M., Cunningham, M., Melde, C., & Heinze, J. (2019). A qualitative study of perception of school safety among youth in a high crime city. *Journal of School Violence*, *19*(3), 277–291. https://doi.org/10.1080/15388220.2019.1677477

Dickson, M. J., & Vargo, K. K. (2017). Training kindergarten students lockdown drill procedures using behavioral skills training. *Journal of Applied Behavior Analysis*, *50*(2), 407–412. https://doi.org/10.1002/jaba.369

Eisenberg, N., Cumberland, A., & Spinrad, T. L. (1998). Parental socialization of emotion. *Psychological Inquiry*, *9*(4), 241–273. https://doi.org/10.1207/s15327965pli0904_1

Frosch, D. (2014, September 4). Active-shooter drills spark raft of legal complaints. *The Wall Street Journal*. https://www.wsj.com/articles/active-shooter-drills-spark-raft-of-legal-complaints-1409760255

Gastic, B. (2011). Metal detectors and feeling safe at school. *Education and Urban Society*, *43*(4), 486–498. http://doi.org/10.1177/0013124510380717

Hajal, N. J., & Paley, B. (2020). Parental emotion and emotion regulation: A critical target of study for research and intervention to promote child emotion socialization. *Developmental Psychology*, *56*(3), 403–417.

Institute of Medicine. (1999). *Reducing the burden of injury: Advancing prevention and treatment.* The National Academies Press. https://doi.org/10.17226/6321

Jackson, M. A., & Golini, E. J. (2024). Lockdown drills and young children with autism spectrum disorder: Practitioner confidence, experiences, and perceptions. *Journal of Autism and Developmental Disorders*, *55*. https://doi.org/10.1007/s10803-023-06201-5

Kingston, B., Mattson, S. A., Dymnicki, A., Spier, E., Fitzgerald, M., Shipman, K., Goodrum, S., Woodward, W., Witt, J., Hill, K. G., & Elliott, D. (2018). Building schools' readiness to implement a comprehensive approach to school safety. *Clinical Child and Family Psychology Review*, *21*(4), 433–449. https://doi.org/10.1007/s10567-018-0264-7

Klevan, S., Leung-Gagné, M., & Nakajima, T. M. (2024). *Using data to improve school climate: Insights from three California schools.* https://learningpolicyinstitute.org/media/4475/download?inline&file=Data_School_ClimateREPORT.pdf

Martaindale, M. H., Sandel, W. L., & Duron, A. Successfully securing a classroom door in a lockdown: Evaluating two types of door locks. *Journal of Mass Violence Research.* https://doi.org/10.53076/JMVR74565

McDevitt, J., & Panniello, J. (2005). *National assessment of school resource officer programs: Survey of students in three large new SRO programs* (Document No. 209270).

National Academies of Sciences, Engineering, and Medicine (NASEM). (2019). *Fostering healthy mental, emotional, and behavioral development in children and youth: A national agenda*. The National Academies Press. https://doi.org/10.17226/25201

National Association of School Psychologists (NASP), National Association of School Resource Officers (NASRO), & Safe and Sound Schools. (2021). Best practice considerations for schools in active shooter and other armed assailant drills. https://www.nasponline.org/resources-and-publications/resources-and-podcasts/school-safety-and-crisis/systems-level-prevetion/best-practice-considerations-for-armed-assailant-drills-in-schools

National Institute of Justice. (2022, February 23). *Creation of school shooting open-source database fuels understanding*. U.S. Department of Justice. https://nij.ojp.gov/topics/articles/creation-school-shooting-open-source-database-fuels-understanding

Perumean-Chaney, S. E., & Sutton, L. M. (2013). Students and perceived school safety: The impact of school security measures. *American Journal of Criminal Justice, 38*(4), 570–588. https://doi.org/10.1007/s12103-012-9182-2

Rockefeller Institute of Government. (2023). School lockdown drill dashboard. https://rockinst.org/gun-violence/school-lockdown-drill-dashboard/

Rutherford, H. J., Wallace, N. S., Laurent, H. K., & Mayes, L. C. (2015). Emotion regulation in parenthood. *Developmental Review, 36*, 1–14. https://doi.org/10.1016/j.dr.2014.12.008

Schildkraut, J. (2022, August). Lockdown drills: A widely used yet often misunderstood practice [Policy brief]. Rockefeller Institute of Government, Regional Gun Violence Research Consortium. https://rockinst.org/wp-content/uploads/2022/08/Lockdown-Drills.pdf

Schildkraut, J., Greene-Colozzi, E., Nickerson, A. B., & Florczykowski, A. (2023). Can school lockdowns save lives? An assessment of drills and use in real-world events. *Journal of School Violence, 22*(2), 167–182. https://doi.org/10.1080/15388220.2022.2162533

Schildkraut, J., Nickerson, A. B., & Klingaman, K. R. (2022). Reading, writing, responding: Educators' perceptions of safety, preparedness, and lockdown drills. *Educational Policy, 36*(7), 1876–1900. https://doi.org/10.1177/08959048211015617

Schildkraut, J., Nickerson, A. B., & Ristoff, T. (2020). Locks, lights, out of sight: Assessing students' perceptions of emergency preparedness across multiple lockdown drills. *Journal of School Violence, 19*(1), 93–106. https://doi.org/10.1080/15388220.2019.1703720

Schildkraut, J., Nickerson, A. B., Vogel, M., & Finnerty, A. (2024). Assessing the relationship between exposure to violence and perceptions of school safety and emergency preparedness in the context of lockdown drills. *Journal of School Violence, 23*(3), 319–332. https://doi.org/10.1080/15388220.2023.2291655

Sprague, J. R., & Walker, H. M. (2021). *Safe and healthy schools: Practical prevention strategies*. Guilford Publications.

Theriot, M. T., & Orme, J. G. (2014). School resource officers and students' feelings of safety at school. *Youth Violence and Juvenile Justice, 14*(2), 130–146. https://doi.org/10.1177/1541204014564472

Van Sant, W. (2019, December 16). Congress reaches agreement to fund gun violence research for the first time in decades. *The Trace*. https://www.thetrace.org/2019/12/congress-gun-violence-research-budget-agreement-cdc-nih/

Zhe, E., & Nickerson, A. (2007). Effects of an intruder crisis drill on children's knowledge, anxiety, and perceptions of school safety. *School Psychology Review, 36*, 501–508. https://doi.org/10.1080/02796015.2007.12087936

Appendix
Committee and Staff Biosketches

COMMITTEE BIOSKETCHES

RICHARD J. BONNIE (*Chair*) is Harrison Foundation professor of medicine and law emeritus and director emeritus of the Institute of Law, Psychiatry, and Public Policy at the University of Virginia. He specializes in criminal law, mental health law, and public health law and has authored leading texts in these subjects. Dr. Bonnie also has research and policy interests in law relating to adolescence and aging. He has been involved in public service throughout his career, including appointments as secretary for the National Advisory Council on Drug Abuse from 1976 to 1980 and chair of Virginia's Commission on Mental Health Law Reform (2005–2011). Dr. Bonnie has served as an advisor to the American Psychiatric Association since 1979, receiving the Isaac Ray Award in 1998 and presidential commendations for service to American psychiatry in 2003 and 2016. He has also served on three MacArthur Foundation research networks, including Law and Neuroscience most recently. Dr. Bonnie was elected to the National Academy of Medicine in 1991 and has chaired more than a dozen studies for the National Academies, including "Pain Management and the Opioid Epidemic" (2017) and "The Promise of Adolescence" (2019). He received the University of Virginia's highest honor, the Thomas Jefferson Award, in 2007.

MELISSA J. BRYMER is director of the Terrorism and Disaster Program of the University of California, Los Angeles (UCLA)/Duke

University National Center for Child Traumatic Stress and its National Child Traumatic Stress Network. In this capacity, Dr. Brymer has been involved with the development of acute interventions, assessment, and educational materials in the areas of terrorism, disasters, mass violence, public health emergencies, and school crises. She is also a researcher at the David Geffen School of Medicine at UCLA. Dr. Brymer was a presenter and reviewer for the National Academies of Sciences, Engineering, and Medicine report "Addressing the Long-Term Impact of COVID-19 on Children and Families." She has served as a consultant for many federal, state, and local agencies across the country and internationally after disasters, terrorism, school shootings, and other mass emergencies and in school safety preparedness and prevention measures. Dr. Brymer was the lead advisor to the Newtown Public Schools Recovery Program; principal investigator for a National Institute of Justice project examining the short- and long-term impact of mass violence on communities; and a key partner to the National Mass Violence Resource Center, which includes preparedness, response, and recovery efforts. Dr. Brymer earned both her doctorates from Nova Southeastern University.

NATHANIEL G. HARNETT is an assistant professor of psychiatry at Harvard Medical School and director of the Neurobiology of Affective and Traumatic Experiences Laboratory at McLean Hospital. His laboratory and research program investigates the neurobiological basis of susceptibility to trauma and stress-related disorders. Dr. Harnett further investigates how inequities in socioenvironmental contexts affect neural signatures of posttraumatic stress disorder. He has been funded by a Ford Foundation Fellowship and has received a National Alliance for Research on Schizophrenia & Depression young investigator award and competitive grants from the National Institute of Neurological Disorders and Stroke and the National Institute of Mental Health. He earned by Ph.D. in psychology and behavioral neuroscience from the University of Alabama at Birmingham in 2018 and completed postdoctoral training at McLean Hospital in 2021.

KRISTEN HARPER is vice president for public policy and engagement at Child Trends, a nonprofit research institute devoted to improving outcomes for children and families. In this role, she oversees the communications functions for Child Trends and serves as a strategic advisor working to improve the policy relevance of Child Trends' portfolio and to connect researchers with public officials. Prior to working at Child Trends, Harper served for seven years in the U.S. Department of Education as a policy advisor, crafting regulations and supporting interagency partnerships to improve conditions for learning. She is a nationally recognized expert on education policy, racial and ethnic disparities in education, school discipline policy, and school health and climate, and she has been cited and quoted by *The Wall Street Journal*, the Associated Press, *Politico*, *Education Week*, *U.S. News & World Report*, and *The 74*, among other publications. Harper has provided expert testimony before Congress and the U.S. Commission on Civil Rights on these issues. She is a proud member of the 2019–2021 class of the Annie E. Casey Foundation's Child and Family Fellowship. Harper has an Ed.M. in education policy and management from the Harvard Graduate School of Education and a B.A. in political science from Loyola College in Maryland.

JUSTIN HEINZE is currently an associate professor in the Department of Health Behavior and Health Education in the School of Public Health at University of Michigan and holds an appointment with the Combined Program in Education and Psychology. Dr. Heinze's research investigates how schools influence disparities in violence and other risk outcomes from an ecological perspective that includes individual, interpersonal, and contextual influences on development. He is particularly interested in how structural features of school context and policy perpetuate inequity in violence and firearm outcomes but also how these institutions can serve as a setting for intervention. Dr. Heinze is the director of the National Center for School Safety, the faculty lead for Public Health IDEAS for Preventing Firearm Injury, and principal investigator of the Healthy Minds Study. He completed his

Ph.D. in education psychology from the University of Illinois Chicago in 2011.

SHERYL KATAOKA is professor emeritus in the Division of Population Behavioral Health, Department of Psychiatry at the University of California, Los Angeles (UCLA), Semel Institute for Neuroscience and Human Behavior. As a national leader in school mental health, she has directed the Schools Committee for the American Academy of Child and Adolescent Psychiatry and the National Child Traumatic Stress Network. Dr. Kataoka has spent more than two decades conducting research examining ways to promote the mental and emotional health of children in schools. Her research has led to a greater understanding of the effects of traumatic stress on children and how school-based mental health services can improve students' wellbeing and ability to learn. Dr. Kataoka served as a scientific advisor for the Federal Commission on School Safety for the U.S. Department of Health and Human Services in 2018 and served as a committee member for the National Academies of Sciences, Engineering, and Medicine's consensus study "Fostering Healthy Mental, Emotional, and Behavioral Development among Children and Youth." She received her Bachelor of Science degree at UCLA and her medical degree at the George Washington University School of Medicine in Washington, D.C.

CELESTE MALONE is an associate professor of school psychology at Howard University and immediate past president of the National Association of School Psychologists. Her primary research interest relates to multicultural and diversity issues embedded in the training and practice of school psychology. Specifically, Dr. Malone's work addresses the development of multicultural competence through education and training, diversification of the profession of school psychology, and the relationship between culturally responsive practice and pre-K–12 student outcomes. A national expert in multicultural school psychology, she focuses her research on culturally responsive practices in school mental health and diversifying the school psychology workforce. Dr. Malone has received several awards for her ongoing leadership and commitment to social justice including from the American Psychological Association, the Black School Psychologists Network, and the Maryland School Psychologists' Association. She received her master's degree in school counseling from Johns Hopkins University and her doctorate in school psychology from Temple University. Dr. Malone completed a postdoctoral fellowship in child clinical and pediatric psychology at the Johns Hopkins University School of Medicine.

ANTHONY PEGUERO is a foundation professor of T. Denny Sanford School of Social and Family Dynamics & School of Criminology and Criminal Justice at Arizona State University. His research interests involve youth inequality and justice, socialization and marginalization, schools, and the adaptation of the children immigrants. Dr. Peguero is the director of the Laboratory for the Study of Youth Inequality and Justice. He is also a research affiliate at the Center on Crime, Race, and Justice at Northeastern University. Dr. Peguero is a member of the Racial Democracy, Crime, and Justice Network and Latina/o/x Criminology, which hold the dual goals of advancing research on the intersection of race, crime, and justice and of promoting racial democracy within the study of these issues by supporting junior scholars from underrepresented groups. He currently serves as president of the Academy of Criminal Justice Sciences, vice president of the Society for the Study of Social Problems, vice president-elect of the Southern Sociological Society, and executive counselor of the American Society of Criminology. Dr. Peguero is also currently the deputy editor of *Sociology of Education*, associate editor of *Race and Justice*, and on the editorial board of *Youth & Society, Journal of Crime and Justice, Deviant Behavior, Social Currents, Social Problems*, and *Journal of Ethnicity in Criminal Justice*.

ANDREA PULSKAMP serves as the Health and Safety Implementation Consultant for the Colorado Department of Education and is focused on building alignment across school climate, safety, and mental health supports. In her current role, Pulskamp coordinates across multiple state, local, and national agencies to coordinate and integrate health and safety efforts in schools. She also supports local education agencies in identifying needs and recognizing disparities in data, policies, and practices to inform systematic improvements in how students, staff, and families experience school. Pulskamp serves on numerous statewide and national committees focused on school safety and mental health, and led the development and implementation of the *Landscape of Wellbeing and Belonging* website to provide guidance to schools and districts on the interconnected best practices to support students, staff, and families. She holds a bachelor's degree from the University of Colorado Boulder and a master's degree in public administration from the University of Colorado Denver.

SONALI RAJAN is a professor in the Department of Health Studies & Applied Educational Psychology at Teachers College, Columbia University. She also holds a secondary faculty appointment in the Department of Epidemiology at the Mailman School of Public Health. From 2022 to 2024, Dr. Rajan served as the inaugural/founding president of the Research Society for Firearm-Related Harms, and she was appointed as the senior director of research at Everytown Research in June 2025. Dr. Rajan is a school violence prevention researcher, studying gun violence, school safety, and adverse childhood experiences. She has co-led research in these areas funded by the National Institutes of Health (NIH) and the Centers for Disease Control and Prevention. Dr. Rajan's work prioritizes the needs for schools and communities to collectively attend to the wellbeing of children while keeping them safe, reducing their exposure to violence, and ensuring opportunities for them to thrive. She earned her bachelor's degree from Cornell University, completed her graduate training at Columbia University, and completed her NIH-funded postdoctoral training at the National Development and Research Institutes.

DAVID J. SCHONFELD is a developmental–behavioral pediatrician (president of the Society for Developmental and Behavioral Pediatrics, 2006–2007) and founder/director of the National Center for School Crisis and Bereavement at Children's Hospital Los Angeles and professor of clinical pediatrics at Keck School of Medicine. He was faculty in pediatrics at Yale University School of Medicine; Head of the Section of Developmental and Behavioral Pediatrics at Cincinnati Children's Hospital Medical Center; and pediatrician-in-chief at St. Christopher's Hospital for Children and pediatric chair at Drexel University School of Medicine. For 35 years, Dr. Schonfeld has provided consultation and training on supporting students and staff at times of crisis and loss in the aftermath of numerous school and community crisis events and disasters within the United States and abroad. He has conducted school-based research (e.g., funded by National Institute of Child Health and Human Development, National Institute of Mental Health, National Institute on Drug Abuse, Maternal and Child Health Bureau, and the Willam T. Grant Foundation) involving children's understanding of and adjustment to serious illness/death and school-based interventions to promote adjustment and risk prevention. Dr. Schonfeld is chair of the National Advisory Committee on Children and Disasters and member of the executive committee of the American Academy of Pediatrics Council on Children and Disasters. In addition, he served on the National Biodefense Science Board and as a commissioner for both the National Commission on Children and Disasters and the Sandy Hook Advisory Commission.

NATALIE SLOPEN is an assistant professor in the Department of Social and Behavioral Sciences at Harvard T.H. Chan School of Public Health. Her primary areas of expertise are social epidemiology and life course theory, with a focus on examining how social and environmental factors and traumatic experiences influence health and wellbeing in childhood and across the lifespan. Dr. Slopen has conducted extensive research on the biological embedding of early childhood experiences and health across the life course, as well as on structural inequities and their role in shaping children's health. She has received awards from National Institutes of Health and other organizations to support her research. In 2019, Dr. Slopen served on the National Academies of Sciences, Engineering, and Medicine's committee that produced *Vibrant and Healthy Kids: Aligning Science, Practice, and Policy to Advance Health Equity*. She received her doctoral degree from Harvard T.H. Chan School of Public Health and completed postdoctoral training at the Center on the Developing Child at Harvard University.

JEFF R. TEMPLE is a professor, licensed psychologist, and the Associate Dean for Clinical Research at the School of Behavioral Health Sciences at the University of Texas Health in Houston, where he also holds the Betty and Rose Pfefferbaum Chair in Child Mass Trauma and Resilience. As the founding director of the Center for Violence Prevention, his research focuses on the prevention of interpersonal and community violence, including firearm violence. Dr. Temple has been funded through the National Institute of Justice, National Institutes of Health, and Centers for Disease Control and Prevention. He has over 275 scholarly publications in a variety of high-impact journals including *JAMA*, *JAMA Pediatrics*, *The Lancet Child and Adolescent Health*, *Pediatrics*, and the *Journal of Adolescent Health*. He recently coedited a book on adolescent dating violence, cochaired the Texas Task Force on Domestic Violence, served on the Board of Directors of the Texas Psychological Association, and currently serves on the Board of Directors for the Society for Prevention Research. Locally, Dr. Temple served for seven years as the vice president of the Galveston Independent School District Board of Trustees. His work has been featured on *Forbes*, *CNN*, *New York Times*, *TIME*, *Washington Post*, and even the satirical website, *The Onion*.

APPENDIX

CONSULTANT BIOSKETCH

LUCY GUARNERA is a licensed clinical psychologist and assistant professor of psychiatry and neurobehavioral sciences at the Institute of Law Psychiatry & Public Policy (ILPPP). Her research seeks to improve the fairness and accuracy of the justice system, both by studying biased decision making among forensic experts and by investigating the legal experiences of vulnerable individuals. Dr. Guarnera's original research on the legal experiences of women who become pregnant from rape was honored with the Best Dissertation Award and multiple grants from the American Psychology-Law Society. She specializes in forensic evaluations involving traumatic stress. As a clinician, Dr. Guarnera completed a predoctoral internship focused on traumatic stress in Charleston, South Carolina, and a postdoctoral fellowship in forensic psychology at the ILPPP.

STAFF BIOSKETCHES

NATACHA BLAIN serves as the senior board director of the Board on Children, Youth, and Families and the Committee on Law and Justice at the National Academies of Sciences, Engineering, and Medicine. She has more than 20 years of experience working with policymakers and senior legislative officials on a variety of social justice issues and campaigns including serving as a Supreme Court Fellow, chief counsel to Senator Dick Durbin on the Senate Judiciary Committee and lead strategic advisor for the Children's Defense Fund's Cradle to Prison Pipeline Campaign. Prior to joining the National Academies, Dr. Blain served as associate director/acting executive director of Grantmakers for Children, Youth and Families. There she played a critical role in helping convene and engage diverse constituencies, fostering leadership, collaboration and innovation-sharing through a network of funders committed to the enduring wellbeing of children, youth, and families. Dr. Blain earned her Master of Science and Doctorate in clinical psychology from Allegheny University of Health Sciences and Medical College of Pennsylvania–Hahnemann University (now Drexel University) respectively, and her Doctor of Jurisprudence degree from Villanova School of Law.

EMILY BACKES is deputy board director of the Committee on Law and Justice and the Board on Children, Youth, and Families in the Division of Behavioral and Social Sciences and Education at the National Academies of Sciences, Engineering, and Medicine. During her time at the National Academies, she has served as study director for the reports *Decarcerating Correctional Facilities during COVID-19: Advancing Health, Equity, and Safety*; *The Promise of Adolescence: Realizing Opportunity for All Youth*; *Birth Settings in America: Outcomes, Quality, Access, and Choice*; and *Transforming the Financing of Early Care and Education*. Backes has also provided analytical and editorial assistance to National Academies projects on juvenile justice reform, policing, forensic science, illicit markets, science literacy, science communication, and science and human rights. She received an M.A. and B.A. in history from the University of Missouri, specializing in U.S. human rights policy and international law, and a J.D. from the University of the District of Columbia, where she represented clients as a student attorney with the Low Income Taxpayer Clinic and the Juvenile and Special Education Law Clinic.

REBEKAH HUTTON (*Study director*) is senior program officer with the National Academies of Sciences, Engineering, and Medicine. She is served as study director of the Committee on the Impact of Active Shooter Drills on Student Health and Wellbeing. Previously, she was study director of the Committee on a New Vision for High-Quality Pre-K Curriculum; Committee on Summertime Experiences and Child and Adolescent Education, Health, and Safety; and Committee on Exploring the Opportunity Gap for Young Children from Birth to Age Eight. Prior to working at the National Academies, Hutton was an education management and information technology consultant working on projects in the

United States, as well as in Haiti, Equatorial Guinea, and Djibouti. She has also worked as a program manager and researcher at the National Center on Performance Incentives at Vanderbilt University and as an English-language lecturer in Tourcoing, France. During her time with the Board on Children, Youth, and Families, Hutton worked on projects focused on fostering the educational success of children and youth learning English, reducing child poverty, and promoting the mental, emotional, and behavioral health of children and youths. She received her M.Ed. from Vanderbilt University in international education policy and management.

TARA NAZARI is a senior program assistant with the Board on Children, Youth, and Families. Currently, she supports the Committee on the Impact of Active Shooter Drills on Student Health and Wellbeing, and the Committee on Understanding Breastfeeding Promotion, Initiation, and Support Across the United States. Before joining the National Academies of Sciences, Engineering, and Medicine, Nazari previously worked as a research assistant at the University of Maryland, assisting development of family and community-based interventions. She is a recent graduate from the University of Maryland, College Park and holds a Bachelor of Science in family science. She plans to pursue a Master of Public Health in the near future.

SUNIA YOUNG is a research associate with the National Academies of Sciences, Engineering, and Medicine's Board on Children, Youth, and Families. She previously worked as a case manager at a Washington, DC-based behavioral health organization and as a contact tracer during the COVID-19 pandemic for the State of Utah. Young also interned at the Carter Center's Mental Health Program and with a DC-based organization that supports Asian women who have experienced domestic violence and sexual assault. Additionally, she has studied the Persian language extensively and spent the summer of 2018 in Tajikistan studying the Iranian and Tajik dialects of Persian through the United States Department of State. Young graduated from Davidson College with a B.S. in psychology and a minor in Arab studies. She is currently pursuing her Master's in Public Health at Johns Hopkins Bloomberg School of Public Health.